The Polity Reader
in
Gender Studies

Polity Press

First published in 1994 by Polity Press in association with Blackwell Publishers.

Editorial office:
Polity Press
65 Bridge Street
Cambridge CB2 1UR, UK

Marketing and production:
Blackwell Publishers
108 Cowley Road
Oxford OX4 1JF, UK

ISBN 0 7456 1209 1
ISBN 0 7456 1210 5 (pbk)

British Library Cataloguing-in-Publication Data
A CIP catalogue record for this book is available from the British Library.

Typeset in 10 on 12 pt Times
by Graphicraft Typesetters (HK) Limited
Printed in Great Britain by Hartnolls Ltd, Bodmin, Cornwall

This book is printed on acid-free paper.

Contents

The extracts in this volume are taken from the following Polity Press books:

Carol J. Adams, *The Sexual Politics of Meat* (1990)

Seyla Benhabib, *Situating the Self* (1992)

Robert Bocock and Kenneth Thompson, *Social and Cultural Forms of Modernity* (1992)

Harriet Bradley, *Men's Work, Women's Work* (1989)

Rosi Braidotti, *Patterns of Dissonance* (1991)

Deborah Cameron and Elizabeth Frazer, *The Lust to Kill* (1987)

Pat Carlen et al., *Criminal Women* (1985)

Nancy J. Chodorow, *Feminism and Psychoanalytic Theory* (1989)

Peter Collier and Helga Geyer-Ryan, *Literary Theory Today* (1990)

R.W. Connell, *Gender and Power* (1987)

Rosemary Crompton and Michael Mann, *Gender and Stratification* (1986)

Christine Delphy and Diana Leonard, *Familiar Exploitation* (1992)

Moira Gatens, *Feminism and Philosophy* (1991)

Anthony Giddens, *The Transformation of Intimacy* (1992)

Catherine Hall, *White, Male and Middle Class* (1992)

Lesley A. Hall, *Hidden Anxieties* (1991)

Christina Hardyment, *From Mangle to Microwave* (1988)

Susan J. Hekman, *Gender and Knowledge* (1990)

Susanne Kappeler, *The Pornography of Representation* (1986)

Henrietta Moore, *Feminism and Anthropology* (1988)

Philip Pacey, *Family Art* (1989)

Carole Pateman, *The Disorder of Women* (1989)

Anne Phillips, *Engendering Democracy* (1991)

June Purvis, *Hard Lessons* (1989)

Barbara Sichtermann, *Femininity* (1986)

Michelle Stanworth, *Reproductive Technologies* (1987)

Klaus Theweleit, *Male Fantasies*, Volume 2 (1989)

Judy Wajcman, *Feminism Confronts Technology* (1991)

Sylvia Walby, *Patriarchy at Work* (1986)

Natalie Zemon Davis, *Society and Culture in Early Modern France* (1987)

Acknowledgements

All the selections in this book are taken from works published by Polity Press. The choice of articles, Introduction, and descriptive material at the opening of the sections were the result of a collaborative editorial enterprise. The following individuals were involved: Anthony Giddens, David Held, Dan Hillman, Don Hubert, Debbie Seymour, Michelle Stanworth and John Thompson. We would like to thank the authors and, for sources that originally appeared in other languages, the publishers, for permission to reprint extracts as follows: 1, Henrietta Moore; 2, Sylvia Walby; 3, R.W. Connell; 4, Nancy Chodorow; 5, Susan Hekman; 6, Rosi Braidotti; 7, Editions Denoël; 8, Seyla Benhabib; 9, Moira Gatens; 10, Carole Pateman; 11, Stanford University Press; 12, June Purvis; 13, Philip Pacey; 14, Harriet Bradley; 15, Christine Delphy and Diana Leonard; 16, Christina Hardyment; 17, Michael Mann; 18, Anne Phillips; 19, Judy Wajcman; 20, Michelle Stanworth; 21, Jeffrey Weeks; 22, Anthony Giddens; 23, Lesley Hall; 24, Susanne Kappeler; 25, Deborah Cameron and Elizabeth Frazer; 26, Verlag Klaus Wagenbach; 27, Catherine Hall; 28, Crossroad/Continuum; 29, Josie O'Dwyer and Pat Carlen; 30, Verlag Roter Stern.

Every effort has been made to trace all copyright holders, but if any has been inadvertently overlooked, the publishers will be pleased to make the necessary arrangement at the first opportunity.

Introduction

The feminist movement and feminist thought have made an extraordinary impact in the social sciences and humanities over the past twenty or thirty years. Feminism, of course, has a long history and for something like two centuries women authors have produced works attacking male-dominated society and suggesting avenues of women's emancipation. Over the period since the 1960s, however, there has occurred an upsurge in feminist writing unlike anything that happened before. The scope of feminist thought has become much wider and its impact much more profound; there are few aspects of intellectual life or academic study today which remain untouched by it.

Women were for many years, as Sheila Rowbotham has put it, 'hidden from history'. Recent feminist scholarship, therefore, sought first of all to render women's experience visible. In so many areas of social thought, either history was assumed to be male, with women confined to the 'unchanging' domestic milieu, or gender differences were simply taken to be irrelevant to whatever issues were being discussed. One of the most fundamental contributions of this phase of feminist work was to demonstrate that 'adding in' gender is not just a matter of making social or cultural analysis 'more comprehensive'. Such interpretation tends instead to revolutionize it, posing many new questions, as well as rendering suspect pre-existing 'knowledge' deriving from established views.

Feminism is of course a political movement, asserting and seeking to overcome the oppression of women. Hence a great deal of research over the past few decades has been devoted to documenting, and seeking to identify, the sources of gender inequalities – as well as trying to combat them. There appear to be no societies in which women are not subservient to men, even if there are many differences in the degree and nature of that subservience. The concept of *patriarchy*, referring to the structures through which male domination over women is established, has had its vicissitudes; some hold that the notion is so general that it conceals more than it illuminates – and that it obscures politically and socially significant differences between women. Yet it makes sense to say that the investigation and explication of patriarchal systems is the core focus of feminist writing and thinking.

Patriarchy is deeply embedded in the sexual division of labour (although affected by other influences too); women find themselves more or less universally charged with responsibility for childcare and domestic work. How far this is changing and the likely prospects for further transformation constitute important issues of current social research. In all the industrialized countries, women are in the paid labour force in large numbers. But childcare and domestic duties still remain a core task for most women. Women have lower average incomes than men, even when working in very similar paid jobs; and they tend to be clustered in occupations characterized by routine work, poor job security and few promotion chances.

As a result of the struggles of the feminist movement, these and many other issues affecting women's lives have become important aspects of debate and academic study. 'Women's studies' is today an accepted part of the curriculum in many universities. Some feminists do not see this wholly as a positive step. For 'women's studies' is a bland term that tends to mute the challenge and excitement of feminism; it also tends to present the discussion of women's experience as just one academic speciality among many others.

Yet the institutionalizing of the study of women's voices and experiences has produced some important developments in intellectual work. The earlier wave of feminist intervention tended to see women's involvement in the domestic domain as an expression of their exclusion from the male world. In the newer phase, however, many authors have come to emphasize the special and distinct nature of women's attitudes to, and outlooks upon, social life. Problems to do with the private sphere, such as family relations and sexuality, have come to be studied more in their own right. Work in these domains is today often more prepared to engage directly with malestream thinking. For example, although many feminists feel hostile to Freud as the promoter of a misogynist theory, others have drawn upon Freud, Lacan and other male interpreters of psychoanalysis to develop their own ideas. The works of Michel Foucault have also influenced many feminist authors.

Feminism has become a highly diverse body of thought. There exist major differences of judgement and opinion about how feminist theory should best be understood, about what sorts of empirical work should best be undertaken and about the political orientations of feminist practice. This diversity should not be taken to signal simply the break-up of all fixed views as to what should constitute feminism; rather, it should be taken to indicate the intensity and excitement that feminist work has generated.

As a political movement, feminism seems to have declined in its impact in the 1980s and early 1990s. Some influential writers, in fact, have spoken of a male 'backlash' against feminism, a digging-in of the heels to hold back advances beyond those women have already made. Yet feminist issues remain important in political and cultural agendas everywhere and have become more and more firmly established in colleges and universities.

We see today in the academy a third transition occurring, away from 'women's studies' and towards 'gender studies'. It is the feminist movement which has made gender so central to theoretical thinking and research; yet plainly gender studies means focusing upon men as well as women, masculinity as well as femininity. Some have interpreted the increasing prominence of gender studies as itself part of the 'backlash'. Thus we see the emergence of 'men's groups', devoted to the pursuit of specifically masculine concerns and interests. From a situation in which the topic was hardly ever discussed, books on masculinity have suddenly become ten-a-penny. However, it would be a mistake to see most such literature as merely a takeover bid, a renewal of hegemony in areas to which women had laid claim. Rather, the problematizing of masculinity is an important step forward in a political as well as an intellectual sense. For men have not previously confronted themselves as 'masculine'; masculinity, and male sexuality, remained largely unproblematized, while it was women who were the 'dark continent'. The move towards gender studies hence seems in general to be a progressive and fruitful one.

There are dangers in this development, however. Feminists in colleges and universities have won quite small resources to fund their work compared with those existing for more traditional academic pursuits. The analysis of women-centred problems and questions could suffer if the agenda shifts exclusively to concentrate upon issues shared with men.

This book is intended to be a comprehensive but integrated introduction to work on gender. We have arranged the various contributions in such a way that they develop a sequence of arguments, even when the views of one author are pitted against those of another. We hope, however, that the volume offers a reasonable balance of empirical and theoretical writing. The material is grouped into three parts. Part I is slanted mainly towards theoretical issues to do with gender and the representation of women. Part II is a more empirical section, concentrating primarily upon women's work and patterns of gender exploitation. Part III is more focused upon masculinity and its relation to patriarchy.

An ellipsis has been used whenever material from the original has been omitted. Where more than a paragraph has been excluded, a line space appears above and below [...].

PART I

Theorizing Gender and Sexual Difference

ALL CULTURES RECOGNIZE a differentiation between 'men' and 'women', but how variable are these categories between different cultures? In Reading 1 Henrietta Moore addresses this question by analysing gender symbolism cross-culturally. Her beginning point is the work of Sherry Ortner. Ortner poses the question: How can it be that all cultures place a lower value upon women than men? Since, according to Ortner, this imbalance does not have any biological origin, it must derive from cultural factors. Such cultural factors must be connected with something that is devalued in every culture. 'Nature' fits this bill, since human beings everywhere rank their own cultural products above the realm of the physical world. Women, Ortner hypothesizes, tend to be identified with nature, men with culture. Women are closer to nature because of their specialized role in reproduction and because of their involvement with the bringing up of children. She is careful to specify that the association of women with nature is not itself 'natural', but is a symbolic component of patriarchy.

Moore points out that the inferior symbolic position of women is frequently reinforced by concepts of pollution. Women in certain categories are commonly held to be polluting – for example, after childbirth and during menstruation. The study of beliefs about pollution reinforces Ortner's argument, since notions of pollution so frequently centre upon natural bodily processes. Moore provides a concrete example of concepts of pollution among the Kaulong. The Kaulong believe that women who are polluted offer specific dangers to adult men and as a consequence must be kept in isolation from them. Men in Kaulong society are relatively passive compared, for example, with Western males; nevertheless the association between women, nature and pollution keeps a patriarchal order firmly in place. Moore concludes by pointing out certain reasons, however, why the association of women with nature and men with culture is, at best, problematic and complex.

Sylvia Walby (Reading 2) takes up the concept of patriarchy in a direct way. Patriarchy, she says, is not just a matter of the differential distribution of power; it is built into the very mechanics of production. We can speak in fact of the existence of a 'patriarchal mode of production'. Because he derives resources from his participation in the public sphere, the male in the household is able to control his input into the household economy. His wife, by contrast, lacks such control; and she does not receive an adequate return for the labour she puts into the domestic arena.

Why doesn't the wife simply refuse to put up with such exploitation and establish a separate home of her own? Most women are prevented from doing so by the intersection of patriarchy in the household and patriarchy in the domain of paid work. Patriarchy in the economic order operates through the exclusion of women from certain types of occupation, lack of promotion opportunities on a par with men and the existence of barriers to promotion beyond certain levels. Patriarchal threads also run through the spheres of state and government. Women are denied access to equal political representation with men; even the welfare state tends to support existing gender inequalities rather than act to rectify them. Men's violence towards women in the form of sexual attacks, rape and battering is important in the maintenance of patriarchy; the state, Walby suggests, in effect accepts much of such violence as legitimate.

What Walby analyses as patriarchy R.W. Connell (Reading 3) discusses under the heading of 'gender regimes'. Writings such as those of Walby focus on the connections between institutions – like the family, work and the state – as if these did not involve direct relations between people. Connell agrees with Walby that inequalities of gender are sustained through a complex of institutions, but argues that we have to show how gender is actually reproduced within such institutions through the active strategies and interactions of those involved.

Connell's concept of a 'gender regime' is intended to integrate the cultural symbols of gender mentioned by Moore with the more institutional factors referred to by Walby. A gender regime is a cluster of practices, ideological and material, which, in a given social context, acts to construct various images of masculinity and femininity and thereby to consolidate forms of gender inequality.

Connell gives schooling as an example. In a school the curriculum and the various extra-curricular activities engaged in – like the discipline of the classroom, the timetable of subjects or sports activities – incorporate notions of what it is appropriate for boys and girls to 'be like'. Sometimes gender regimes include openly sexist attitudes, but more often they express more diffuse ideologies of gender and sexual behaviour.

If gender is a key element of the symbolic order (as Moore emphasizes) and the institutional order (as Walby and Connell demonstrate) it is also a paramount dimension of individual identity. In Reading 4 Nancy Chodorow takes up the disputed issue of the relationship between feminism and psychoanalysis. Gender inequalities, and divisions between masculinity and femininity, are so all-pervasive that they surely have very general psychological sources. Whatever its shortcomings, Chodorow argues, Freud's theory – when appropriately revised – provides the most sophisticated source of psychological theorizing about gender relationships.

Most children, girls and boys, are cared for in the early years of their lives by their mothers. Contact with the mother is the dominant feature of the infant's early experience and central to her or his sense of self. Gender identity is not a given, but develops as part of the very process of self-formation. The dynamics of maleness differ substantially from those of femaleness. Here Chodorow effectively reverses Freud. It is masculinity that is more tensionful and ambiguous. For the boy must be defined as 'not female'; he must break his association with the mother in a more dramatic way than is the case for girls.

According to Chodorow, men tend (for the most part unconsciously) to reject feminine feelings within themselves: they have less access to their emotions, reject dependence, take an instrumental relation to the world and find intimate relations difficult. Girls, on the other hand, are able to maintain a closer identification with the mother and are therefore much more comfortable with their own feelings and with emotional identification with others. Because they do not undergo such a clear-cut break with the mother, nevertheless, women may experience difficulties with the boundaries of self – with separating their own ideas and emotions from those of other people.

Chodorow's ideas have been criticized by some feminists, who think that she comes dangerously close to identifying women with irrationality – seeing women as just the flighty, whimsical creatures men so often portray them as. Yet, as others have pointed out, this argument can be turned on its head: 'rationality' could be seen as an expression of male dominance of Western intellectual culture – as 'male reason'. Feminist thinkers have explored this issue in great detail, drawing upon a variety of theoretical and empirical resources in order to do so. Many have been influenced by particular philosophical positions associated with 'postmodernism' and it is to this that we turn in the first instance.

Postmodernism, as Susan Hekman points out (Reading 5) has strongly influenced some branches of feminist thinking over the past two decades or so. The terms 'postmodernism' and 'postmodernity' (which are often used synonymously, although some authors draw distinctions between them) are not easy to define. They include so many different traits that many have concluded that the concepts have no coherent meaning. Yet there probably is a thematic core to them. A postmodern world is one where, in the words of Jean-François Lyotard, there are no longer any 'grand narratives'. The universalizing claims associated with Western philosophy, and perhaps particularly with Marxism, become dissolved. There are no absolute truths to be striven for; knowledge is contextual and pluralistic. In the context of feminist theory, postmodernism has been associated with the critique of 'essentialism' – the sort of view, in fact, represented by Walby, Chodorow and others, according to which there are general characteristics which separate 'women' from 'men'.

Postmodernism in philosophy rejects some core ideas of the Enlightenment, the main origin of contemporary philosophical discourse. Feminists have put their own slant upon this critique, claiming that universalizing, instrumental reason is an expression of male attitudes towards the world. The feminist attack upon rationality, Hekman says, is actually more radical than postmodernism as such, for it specifies its origins – in gender differences – rather than only dealing with its surface characteristics. The division between the rational and irrational has its source in the definition of women as 'all that rationality is not'.

Hekman discusses the view of various feminist thinkers on these issues, including Luce Irigaray. Some versions of feminism, in trying to make a way for women in the world of men, have accepted an inadequate – because masculine – definition of what the world is. According to these accounts, women should not renounce the domains of the home and childcare in order to enter the 'rational' public sphere; rather they should engage in a much more full-blown questioning of the male realm of abstract reason. If the tenets of postmodernism are accepted, we cannot say that the arena of emotions, care and communication forms women's 'true nature', because this would obviously be a kind of essentialism. Rather, we should recognize that femininity is a 'mode of being' that breaks down the oppressiveness of universalist claims to rationality.

Luce Irigaray has sought to specify in some detail the 'absence' that is femininity. According to her what is feminine is what is 'not said', a realm of the unconscious and of desire excluded from representation in the male language-centred universe of action. The key question Irigaray poses, according to Braidotti (Reading 6), is how to give voice to the innovative and subversive character of women's thought, while avoiding the language of male rationality. How can women think about their own condition yet avoid the 'femino-phobic' character of Western conceptual thought? Irigaray seeks to answer this question by the style in which she writes, the imagery she creates and the movement she institutes between denunciation and creation. 'Women's writing' generates a relation to meaning other than that intrinsic to male-centred discourse. Such meaning, as Irigaray puts it, is 'always in the process of weaving itself, of embracing itself with words, but also of getting rid of words in order not to become fixed, congealed in them'. Women are specifically a 'mystery' to men because they stand outside male speech and action; that 'mystery' is only an obscurity when it is forced into male classifications. Striving to achieve economic and political equality with men, Irigaray says, is obviously important; yet it is also essential that the privileged emotional and conceptual space occupied by women be fully acknowledged. In common with postmodernism Irigaray sees women's movements as a multiplicity of groups and tendencies. To reduce these to a single set of aims would be to succumb to the universalizing claims of male discourse.

Julia Kristeva (Reading 7) pursues similar themes, this time in relation to the literature of James Joyce. Joyce was perhaps already postmodern, for he emphasized multiple interpretations, ambiguity and ambivalence. Joyce's Catholicism was central to his life and writing. In this respect he drew upon religious ideas whose only place for woman is the divinity of Mary; yet he made of this heritage an emotional diversity in which women's experience is basic. Molly's monologue at the conclusion of *Ulysses* turns out to be the dominant thread of the work. Literary creation and amorous experience, where the religious meanings have lost much of their hold, are means whereby creative humanity can continue to adapt and change. Carl Jung spotted Joyce's affinity with the feminine; Joyce, he remarked, 'knows the female soul as if he were the Devil's grandmother'. Kristeva points out that this sympathy with femininity co-existed uneasily with some quite traditional masculinist assumptions. The achievement of Joyce was to show that these assumptions are actually more of 'mystery' than is the feminine.

Seyla Benhabib (Reading 8) offers a critical overview of the alleged convergence between feminism and postmodernism. Many feminists, she says, have accepted three main theses associated with postmodernism. One is that of the 'death of man', the end of humanism. The death of man is the dissolution of philosophies that begin with 'the subject' – subjectivity, human consciousness. For feminists the phrase obviously has a double meaning: it is also a rejection of the masculinity of rationalist thought. A second theme, the 'death of history', refers to an idea introduced above: the disappearance of 'grand narratives'. 'History' has no unity or teleology. The third element, the 'death of metaphysics' means the end of the attempt to discover absolute truth or the essences of things.

These themes, Benhabib accepts, are valuable in the context of feminist thought. But if they are embraced too uncritically they threaten not only to eliminate feminist theory as distinct enterprise but to dissolve its emancipatory goals as well. There are two ways, she points out, in which each of these theses can be expressed. In their less radical versions they are defensible; but put too strongly they are either self-contradictory or counterproductive for feminist thought and action.

A weaker version of the 'death of man' thesis would situate the subject in context; and it is indeed valuable to stress the variability of male and female attributes. The more radical version of the thesis, however, reduces 'man' to an endless flux of meanings with no centre. Such a view, Benhabib argues, should be rejected; it provides no means of understanding how women could become more autonomous and alter the circumstances of their lives. Much the same holds of the 'death of history'. It is right to say that there are no guarantees of progress in historical change; but if we reject all forms of theorizing about patterns of change there is no way of promoting successful emancipatory struggles. For how would 'success' be defined?

The 'death of metaphysics' thesis, Benhabib says, has largely been directed at positions that never existed. Philosophers such as Kant or Hegel held much more sophisticated views than the critics of metaphysics attribute to them. To do away with metaphysical philosophy altogether would in any case be as arbitrary and sweeping as the metaphysical views objected to.

Moira Gatens (Reading 9) warns against the pitfalls of what she calls a 'woman-centred philosophy'. She has in mind authors such as Irigaray and others. According to their view the very activity of theorizing, or constructing conceptual categories, is an intrinsically male endeavour. Such writers, according to Gatens, effectively exclude women from the domain of intellectual discourse. For unless we assume that women should simply abandon intellectual culture altogether they must take on, and utilize, some philosophical or theoretical categories in order to reject others.

Gatens's objections to a woman-centred philosophy are severalfold. Criticizing past forms of philosophy need not imply that philosophical thought will continue in the same vein in the future. Philosophy, like the social sciences and humanities, reflects the values and power relations of the larger society in which it is produced. Change in that society, which can be informed by intellectual critique, can serve to produce transformations in styles of thought.

Feminist theorists who attack all grand categories fail to diagnose tensions or contradictions in the texts produced by male philosophers. Thus Rousseau's political writings contain many openly sexist ideas and are clearly a 'patriarchal discourse'. An appropriate response to this, however, is not to withdraw from engagement with his texts, but to demonstrate that his theory of the social contract implies a possible radical improvement in the social and political situation in which women find themselves at the moment.

Gatens takes as an example Genevieve Lloyd's *The Man of Reason*.

Lloyd develops the theme that reason in Western intellectual culture has been defined in opposition to femininity, arguing that femininity is in some part created by this very exclusion. Lloyd shows that this position can be used to demonstrate that the supposed close association of women with nature (examined by Moore above) is in some part a result of the ways in which dichotomies between nature–culture, public–private and rational–irrational have been conceived. In Rousseau's discussion the social contract is entered into only by men; this very formulation treats women as existing in a 'state of nature'. This 'natural' association is thus defined through discourse, and has to be discursively as well as practically contested.

Rousseau also forms the starting point of the selection from Carole Pateman (Reading 10). Rousseau, she notes, sees women as dragging men away from the rational business of politics. The 'disorder of women', in Rousseau's eyes, is a vice worse than drunkenness, which it resembles; here again we see a thinly veiled version of woman as polluting. There is a parallel, Pateman argues, between Rousseau and Freud. Freud speaks of women as standing 'in opposition to' civilization and as a source of disorder.

What is the sense of 'disorder' here? Disorder can have two meanings. It can refer to a breakdown of civil order, as in a riot or rebellion. It can also refer to an illness of the body, as when we speak of a stomach disorder. In the political theory which formed the origin of modern liberalism women are a source of disorder in this second sense. Their very being corrupts public life. For both Rousseau and Freud women are unable to develop a proper sense of justice. They are swayed by emotion and by sentiments deriving from their 'natural' condition.

Since women remain in a state of nature it follows that civil society or civilization is exclusively the achievement of men. Civilization, Freud wrote, depends upon 'instinctual suppressions of which women are little capable'. Men's capacity to repress their emotional whims is the condition of a stable and democratic political order.

Of course, following Chodorow, whatever validity there is in such observations would be seen in an entirely different light. Since women tend to have greater compassion and communicative understanding with others, feminine values might promote forms of justice and democracy superior to those created by males.

1

The Cultural Constitution of Gender

Henrietta Moore

One of the most outstanding contributions of the anthropology of women has been its sustained analysis of gender symbols and sexual stereotypes. The main problem facing researchers in this area is how to explain both the enormous observable variation in cultural understandings of what the categories 'man' and 'woman' mean, and the fact that certain notions about gender appear in a wide range of different societies. This is how Sherry Ortner expressed the problem at the beginning of her essay 'Is female to male as nature is to culture?':

> Much of the creativity of anthropology derives from the tension between two sets of demands: that we explain human universals, and that we explain cultural particulars. By this canon, woman provides us with one of the more challenging problems to be dealt with. The secondary status of woman in society is one of the true universals, a pan-cultural fact. Yet within that universal fact, the specific cultural conceptions and symbolizations of woman are extraordinarily diverse and even mutually contradictory. Further, the actual treatment of women and their relative power and contribution vary enormously from culture to culture, and over different periods in the history of particular cultural traditions. Both of these points – the universal fact and the cultural variation – constitute problems to be explained.[1]

Ortner's essay, together with Edwin Ardener's article 'Belief and the problem of women', initiated an influential and powerful framework for studying the problem of women's subordination through an analysis of gender symbolism. Ortner began with the proposition that female subordination is universal, and, since this condition is not inherent in the biological differences between the sexes, an alternative explanation must be found. Starting from the idea that biological differences between men and women take on significance only within culturally defined value systems, she located the problem of sexual asymmetry at the level of cultural ideologies and symbols. The question she then posed was: what could be common to every culture such that all cultures place a lower value on women? Her answer was that women everywhere must be associated with something which every culture devalues. In Ortner's view there is only 'one thing that would fit that description, and that is "nature", in the most generalized sense'.[2] All cultures recognize and make a distinction between human society and the natural world. Culture attempts to control and transcend nature, to use it for its own purposes. Culture is therefore superior to the natural world and seeks to mark out or 'socialize' nature, in order to regulate and maintain relations between society and the forces and conditions of the environment. Ortner suggests that women are identified, or symbolically associated, with nature, while men are associated with culture. Since culture seeks to control and transcend nature, then it is 'natural' that women, by virtue of their close association with 'nature', should also be controlled and contained.

It is worth setting out some of Ortner's argument in detail, because the grounds she asserts for associating women with nature – or for women being seen as closer to nature than men – raise a whole series of issues which form the foundations of the feminist critique, but which also threaten, at moments, to overwhelm it. The universality of Ortner's proposition forces her to provide equally generalized arguments to support her thesis. Her two main arguments may be summarized in the following way:

1   Woman's physiology and her specialized reproductive functions make her appear closer to nature. Men, unlike women, have to seek cultural means of creation – technology, symbols – while women's creativity is naturally fulfilled through the process of giving birth. Men, therefore, are associated more directly with culture and with the creative power of culture, as opposed to nature. 'Woman creates naturally from within her own being, whereas man is free to, or forced to, create artificially, that is through cultural means, and in such a way as to sustain culture.'[3]

2   Women's social roles are seen as closer to nature because their involvement in reproduction has tended to limit them to certain social functions which are also seen as closer to nature. Here, Ortner is referring to women's confinement within the domestic domain. In the context of the domestic family, women are primarily associated with the rearing

of children, and thus with the pre-social or not yet culturally created person. Ortner points out than an implicit association between children and nature is a feature of a number of societies.[4] The 'natural' association of women with children and the family provides an additional level of categorization. Since women are confined to the domestic context, their main sphere of activity becomes intra- and inter-familial relations, as opposed to men, who operate in the political and public domain of social life. Men thus become identified with society and the 'public interest', while women remain associated with family and therefore with particularistic or socially fragmenting concerns.

Ortner is careful in her presentation to emphasize that 'in reality' women are not any closer to, or further from, nature than men. Her aim is, rather, to identify and locate the cultural valuations which make women appear 'closer to nature'.

The formulation that 'nature is to culture as female is to male' provided social anthropology with a powerful analytical framework which had a wide impact on the discipline in the late 1970s and early 1980s. It was powerful because it offered a way of linking sexual ideologies and stereotypes both to the wider system of cultural symbols and to social roles and experience. Sexual ideologies and stereotypes vary greatly, but certain symbolic associations between gender and many other aspects of cultural life occur across a wide range of societies. The differences between men and women can be conceptualized as a set of opposed pairs which resonate with other sets of oppositions. Thus men may be associated with 'up', 'right', 'high', 'culture' and 'strength', while women are associated with their opposites, 'down', 'left', 'low', 'nature' and 'weakness'. These associations are not inherent in the biological or social nature of the sexes, but are cultural constructs, which are powerfully reinforced by the social activities which both define and are defined by them. The value of analysing 'man' and 'woman' as symbolic categories or constructs lies in the identification of the expectations and values which individual cultures associate with being male or female. Such analysis provides some indication of the ideal behaviour of men and women in their different social roles, which can then be compared with the actual behaviour and responsibilities of the two sexes. It is in understanding how men and women are socially constructed, and how those constructions define and redefine social activities, that the value of a symbolic analysis of gender becomes apparent. There have, of course, been criticisms of the nature/culture–female/male opposition, but it provides a useful starting point for discussing the cultural construction of gender, and for examining how the symbolic associations given to the categories 'man' and 'woman' can be understood as the result of cultural ideologies, rather than of inherent qualities or physiology.

One of the features of gender symbolism which has attracted a great deal of attention from scholars who wish to explain women's 'inferior status' is the concept of pollution. Behavioural taboos and restrictions, like those which many women experience after childbirth and during menstruation, provide clues as to how people categorize one another and thus structure their social world. An analysis of pollution beliefs and their relationship to sexual ideologies is revealing, because such beliefs are frequently associated with the natural functions of the human body. Examples of societies which view women as polluting, either in general or at particular times, can be found all over the world. However, for the purposes of illustration, I concentrate here on the Kaulong Melanesian society because of the richness of ethnographic material on pollution beliefs and sexual antagonism within the society.

Among the Kaulong of New Britain, women are considered polluting from before puberty to after menopause, but they become particularly 'dangerous' during menstruation and childbirth. During these periods women must stay away from gardens, dwellings and water sources, and a woman must also be careful not to touch anything with which a man might come into contact.[5] Female pollution is dangerous only to adult men, who may become ill by ingesting anything polluted or by placing themselves directly underneath a contaminated object or polluting woman. Normally, pollution is transmitted in a downward vertical direction which does not necessitate the lateral separation of the sexes.[6] However, during menstruation and childbirth, pollution spreads outwards from the woman and this necessitates her physical separation from all locations and objects used by both sexes. As a result, women are isolated during childbirth and menstruation, away from the main residential and gardening areas.

The fear of pollution among the Kaulong is important because it both characterizes the nature of gender relations and defines the qualities of men and women. According to Goodale, the Kaulong equate sexual intercourse with marriage, and 'men are quite literally scared to death of marriage (and sex)'.[7] Sexual intercourse is considered polluting for men, and because it is also thought to be 'animal-like' it must take place in the forest, away from dwellings and gardens. Men and women marry to reproduce themselves, and this is the central meaning and purpose of a sexual relationship. This particular view of marriage is powerfully reinforced by the fact that suicide used to be an accepted way of ending an 'unproductive relationship'.

Since Kaulong men are afraid and reluctant to enter into a marriage partnership, it is therefore not surprising that it is the women who take the dominant role in courtship.[8] Girls may offer food or tobacco to the man of their choice, or they may physically attack him. The man must either flee or stand his ground without retaliating until an agreement is reached concerning what items and valuables the girl may expect to receive from him. Goodale points out that from infancy girls are encouraged to behave aggressively towards males, and that men must either submit without retaliation or run away. If a man were to initiate an approach towards a woman it would be considered rape. Women have almost complete freedom in their choice of husband, although they do consult their close kin. A woman may deceive or lure a reluctant groom to his 'fate', often with the help of her brothers, while women themselves are only very rarely forced into undesired marriages.[9]

From a consideration of these few facts concerning male–female relations among the Kaulong, a number of points can be raised concerning the cultural variability of definitions of gender, and the validity of seeing women as 'closer to nature' than men. First, it is clear that, if Kaulong ideas of the appropriate behaviour of men and women, and the nature of marriage, were to be compared with contemporary European or North American attitudes, a series of contrasts would appear. Women are not highly valued as 'initiators' in Western society, and this is especially true with regard to sexual relations. Furthermore, Western society encourages men to be active and 'stand up for themselves', while the Kaulong view apparently reverses the Western idea of the passive woman and the active man. The desire to have children is a potent reason for marriage in Western society, but marriage itself is conceived of as a partnership, with companionship and family life as key attributes. Kaulong marriage would seem to be a very different sort of institution. These points illustrate the kinds of cross-cultural variability which can exist not only in men's and women's behaviour but also in the kinds of individuals men and women are meant to be. It also raises the issue of the cross-cultural variability of institutions like marriage. However, variability is not the only issue at stake. The idea of the woman as 'seducer', the 'ensnarer of men', and the corresponding picture of the 'reluctant groom' are all images which find resonances in Western culture. The issue which the symbolic analysis of gender raises is how we use this complex and shifting imagery to arrive at an understanding of women's position. Kaulong women apparently have a considerable degree of economic independence, including control over resources and the products of their labour.[10] Yet the same women are considered dangerous and polluting to men. It is not necessarily clear how such contradictions are to be understood and balanced in any analysis.

Ortner's suggestion that women are seen as 'closer to nature' because of their physiology and reproductive roles could be applied to the Kaulong data. A chain of associations linking women–marriage–sexual intercourse–animal-like behaviour–the forest would seem to connect the physiology and reproductive roles of women, which are polluting, to the domain of the non-human, 'natural' forest. It is a short step from this to suggest that women are inferior because they are polluting, and they are polluting because of the 'natural' functions of their bodies, which in turn makes them seem bound to the natural world in some sense. This chain of associations is powerfully reinforced by the physical isolation of women in the forest during childbirth and menstruation. However, as Goodale points out in her article (on the Kaulong), there are certain deficiencies in this simple equation of women with nature, and men with culture. First, it is clear that both men and women are associated with the forest and the 'natural world' through their involvement in sexual relations. The central dwellings in each residential clearing are occupied by unmarried men and women, and it is the married couples who live in huts on the margins of the cultivated areas – the margins, in fact, of the cultural and natural worlds. Goodale depicts the Kaulong model thus:

Culture   : Nature
Clearing   : Forest
Unmarried : Married[11]

In other words, both men and women become associated with nature through their involvement in reproduction, rather than just women. Furthermore, the Kaulong system of representation seems to provide no strong evidence for the singular association of culture with men. It is a notable feature of a number of analyses utilizing the nature/culture–female/male model that an association between women and nature is often taken to imply a similar association between men and culture. This assumption is not always valid.

Second, the formulation that women are seen as 'closer to nature' because of their reproductive functions raises a number of difficulties. If women are 'seen' as 'closer to nature', who sees them in this way? Do women see themselves as closer to nature, as polluting, or even as defined by their reproductive functions? It seems that Kaulong women might respond negatively to all these queries. The nature/culture–female/male model assumes a cultural unity which is unjustified, and leaves no room for the possibility that different groups in society might see and experience things in different ways. Goodale points out that Kaulong women are unconcerned, for the most part, about their potentially polluting effects on men – with the exception, however, of the fact that mothers may express concern about the harmful effects of pollution on their sons.[12] This confirms a further difficulty in postulating a simple opposition between 'woman' and 'man' as symbolic categories, and that is that there is an undue focus on a single set of gendered relations. Opposition between the sexes is usually constructed, by implication, on the basis of opposition between spouses, and little mention is made, if any, of the other sets of gendered relations, brother/sister, mother/son, father/daughter, which are an equally important part of being a woman or a man. The fact that relations between spouses may not be appropriate as a model for other gendered relations is highlighted among the Kaulong by the fact that a brother may side with his sister to help her secure a marriage partner. This suggests that the potential anxiety which characterizes relations between spouses may not be a feature of relations between siblings.

The third point to be raised *vis-à-vis* the nature/culture–female/male opposition is one concerning the culturally specific nature of analytical categories. 'Nature' and 'culture' are not value-free, unmediated categories; they are cultural constructs in exactly the same way as the categories 'woman' and 'man'. The notions of nature and culture, as they are used in anthropological analysis, derive from Western society, and, as such, they are the products of a particular intellectual tradition and of a specific historical trajectory. Just as we cannot assume that the categories 'woman' and 'man' everywhere mean the same, so we must also be aware that other societies might not even perceive nature and culture as distinct and opposed categories in the way that Western culture does. Furthermore, even where such a distinction exists we must not assume that the Western terms 'nature'/'culture' are adequate or reasonable translations of the categories other cultures perceive.

Notes and References

1   S. Ortner, 'Is female to male as nature is to culture?', in *Women, Culture and Society*, ed. M. Rosaldo and L. Lamphere (Stanford University Press, Stanford, Calif., 1974), p. 67.

2   Ibid., p. 72.
3   Ibid., p. 77.
4   Ibid., p. 78.
5   J. Goodale, 'Gender, sexuality and marriage', in *Nature, Culture and Gender*, ed. C. MacCormack and M. Strathern (Cambridge University Press, Cambridge, 1980), p. 129.
6   Ibid., pp. 130–1.
7   Ibid., p. 133.
8   Ibid., p. 135.
9   Ibid.
10 Ibid., pp. 128, 139.
11 Ibid., p. 121.
12 Ibid., pp. 130–1.

2

Towards a Theory of Patriarchy

Sylvia Walby

The patriarchal mode of production necessarily exists in articulation with another mode of production. The husband uses his labour power which has been produced by the domestic labourer within this other mode. Because he has control over his labour power he has possession of the proceeds from putting it into action. Within the patriarchal mode of production, the husband does not use the proceeds of his labour power to compensate the domestic labourer fully for the work she puts into producing it.

It is crucial to be able to explain why the woman does not set up on her own to produce lower power and why she remains in the home to produce the labour power of her husband. I would argue that the reason for this varies according to the mode of production with which the patriarchal mode is in articulation. When the patriarchal mode articulates with the capitalist mode, the primary mechanism which ensures that women will serve their husbands is their exclusion from paid work on the same terms as men. Patriarchal relations within waged work are crucial in preventing women from entering that work as freely as men, and are reinforced by patriarchal state policies. However, other sets of patriarchal relations are also important. When the patriarchal mode of production articulates with other modes, other levels of the social formation become critical for the continuation of the patriarchal one. Under feudalism, for instance, fertility and reproduction are of critical significance. This dynamic articulation with capitalism will be further explored later.

I do not wish to suggest that the patriarchal mode of production has any autonomous laws of development. On the contrary, I would suggest that the other mode of production with which the patriarchal mode is in articulation is particularly important in governing the nature of change.

This does not discredit the concept of patriarchal mode of production since the central element in this is not its laws of motion, but rather that of the extraction of surplus. It is the highly distinctive method of extraction of surplus within patriarchy (which plays a key role in the determination of other gender relations) which is the basis of the claim that there is a patriarchal mode of production.

The patriarchal division of labour in the household does not completely determine the form of patriarchal relations in a particular society; other sets of patriarchal relations also have significance. A most important set of patriarchal relations when the patriarchal mode of production is in articulation with capitalism is that in paid work. Patriarchal relations in paid work are necessary, if not sufficient, to the retention of women as unpaid labourers in the household. The control of women's access to paid work is maintained primarily by patriarchal relations in the workplace and in the state, as well as by those in the household.

The form of this control has varied with time and place to a significant extent. The forms of control include non-admittance of women to forms of training, such as apprenticeships and university degrees which are a condition of practising a particular trade; the non-admittance of women to certain occupations; the restriction of the percentage of women in certain occupations (e.g. the quota on women which has historically been imposed by medical schools); discrimination in hiring practices which reduces or eliminates the number of women in a particular occupation; the ejection of women from an occupation, or the reduction in their rights to remain in it on marriage; the sacking of women, and in particular married women, before men in situations of redundancy; the sacking of part-timers, who are almost exclusively married women, before full-timers in situations of redundancy; practices such as 'last-in, first-out', the indirect consequence of which is that women go before men; the ejection of women from certain occupations by legislative action; the restriction on the amount of certain kinds of paid work that women can do, with implications for their entry to those occupations at all, such as the reduction in women's hours in the Factory Acts of the nineteenth century. These exclusionary practices fall into two types: restriction of entry to particular occupations; and ways of ejecting women, rather than men, from certain occupations. They exist in varying forms of directness, from rigid rules which are consistently enforced, such as the ban on women taking degrees at universities in the UK before the late nineteenth century, to more indirect forms which may not always produce the same effect, such as the 'last-in, first-out' practice in redundancy situations.

The agents carrying out these exclusionary practices include male-dominated trade unions; other male-dominated organizations; prejudiced employers; and the state. The immediate social and historical context in which these practices have existed is also immensely varied.

Most existing analyses of patriarchy have taken patriarchal relations in the workplace insufficiently into account. Yet an adequate analysis of patriarchy must incorporate this as a highly significant element. These forms of exclusionary practice may be seen as a form of social closure. They are both a product of, and themselves create, highly significant divisions among paid workers. They are to a considerable extent a result of patriarchal divisions elsewhere in society, especially in the household, but cannot be reduced to these. There is an extent to which the struggles around these practices have their own autonomy. However, the resources which are brought to these struggles are related to the resources available to the competing groups in different areas of social life.

Patriarchal relations in the workplace and the state as well as the family are central to the determination of the position of women in paid work. Capital and patriarchy have rival interests in women's labour, and the position that women hold in paid work cannot be understood without an analysis of the tension between the two. There are theoretical reasons for the importance of paid work for contemporary gender relations: paid work is a crucial site in capitalist relations and this is transmitted to the relations between patriarchal structures when the system of patriarchy is in articulation with capitalism.

The state is a site of patriarchal relations which is necessary to patriarchy as a whole. The state represents patriarchal as well as capitalist interests and furthers them in its actions. This conception of the state as patriarchal as well as capitalist runs counter to most other analyses of it; most accounts do not consider gender relations at all, focusing instead on class relations within capitalism and the relations between these and the state. Such accounts of the state are inadequate in that they fail to take into account either the impact of gender inequality and women's political struggles on the state, or the significance of state actions on gender relations. The omissions are serious both because these are significant dimensions of state action, and because they lead to a flawed analysis of the issues that these writers purport to address. For instance, an analysis of the development of the welfare state which does not take into account the role of women's political struggles as women would be seriously in error as to the political forces which were operating in that situation. Yet this has been a common practice in much writing on the development of the welfare state.

However, there have been important, if rare, attempts to analyse the relationship between the state and the position of women seriously. McIntosh suggests that the state upholds the oppression of women by supporting a form of household in which women provide unpaid domestic services for a male.[1] She argues that the state should be viewed as capitalist, since it is acting to maintain the capitalist mode of production. Capitalism benefits from a particular form of family which ensures the cheap reproduction of labour power and the availability of women as a reserve army of labour. She suggests, however, that the family is not the ideal form for the reproduction of labour power for two reasons. First, the ratio of earner to dependent is widely variable in actual families and thus some families cannot survive on earned income. The state steps in to shore up the family structure in those instances when it would otherwise fail. Second, families by themselves do not necessarily produce the right number of children to meet capitalist requirements for population size, so sometimes explicit population policies are introduced to ensure the maintenance of its members. Thus, for McIntosh, the state's support for the oppression of women is indirect, not direct, since it is through the maintenance of this family form that the state acts to the detriment of women.

While McIntosh does point to various contradictions in capitalism and in state policy her argument nonetheless hinges on the notion that the family is maintained because it is functional for capitalism. This position is problematic in that it does not take sufficient account of the benefits that men derive from the contemporary family structure, and of the divergence between patriarchal and capitalist interests, such as whether women should stay at home or take paid work. Further, the analysis pays insufficient attention to the struggles that take place on the political level which need to be accorded greater autonomy in the analysis.

I would argue that, when patriarchy is in articulation with capitalism, the state should be seen as both patriarchal and capitalist. Such a dualist conception of the state is only a problem if the state is incorrectly considered to act in a monolithic manner. Much of the recent literature on the capitalist state sees state actions as the result of the political struggle of competing classes and class fractions, so one more set of competing interests is not an insuperable conceptual problem. The state should be considered equally an arena for political struggle and an actor intervening in particular situations. Its actions should be seen as the result of the struggles between different interests. It should not be seen as the instrument of a dominant class or class fraction.

In a theory like this, it is possible to conceive of the state as both patriarchal and capitalist. Its specific actions in any instance are the outcome of the struggle on the political level of the competing interests involved in both patriarchal and capitalist relations. The state should not be reduced to, or derived from, the economic level, but rather the political level should be seen to have considerable autonomy. Any theory of a patriarchal and capitalist state must analyse the struggles of patriarchal and capitalist interests as they are represented on the political level, while also tracing the links to other levels, especially the economic.

The intervention of the state has been, at certain times, of crucial significance in the shaping of patriarchal relations in society. Yet at the same time it is not the basis of patriarchal power. Rather its actions should be seen as the outcome of the representation of patriarchal interests which are mediated in the political process. While the actions of the state are linked to the economic level of patriarchy, they have a level of autonomy in which the actual outcome of conflicting interests is mediated by conflicts and negotiation at the political level.

Women, who are subordinated within the productive process, have little access to forms of political representation. This is partly because of their lack of power in the sphere of production, and partly because the particular forms of the state and its mode of functioning act to suppress the effective representation of women's interests. In terms of the recent state in a society in which patriarchy articulates with capitalism, these problems of representation have been exacerbated by the late granting of the franchise to women and the formation of the major political parties along lines of division representing the interests of the classes of the capitalist rather than the patriarchal system. Thus there is a limited historic tradition of women's participation in parliamentary politics compounded by the absence of political parties organized around issues of gender relations.

The state acts to support patriarchal relations in a variety of ways. These include the limiting of women's access to paid work (e.g. the Dilution Acts); the criminalization of forms of fertility control (e.g. at certain times and places abortion, contraception); support for the institution of marriage through, for example, the cohabitation rule, discriminatory income maintenance and by regulating marriage and divorce; actions against some sexual relations through, for instance, criminalizing male homosexual relations in some periods and denying custody of children to lesbian mothers; actions against radical dissent, for instance, in the coercive response to the suffrage movement.

One example of the patriarchal actions of the state is that which enabled male workers in the First World War to ensure their re-entry into the relatively highly paid and skilled engineering jobs that they ceded to women for the duration of the hostilities. The economic pressures in this situation would have led the employers to continue to employ the cheaper women workers, if they had been able. However, male workers such as the engineers had sufficient power in conjunction with the government to prevent this from occurring. These men had power in the labour process in that only they could effectively train new workers, and this enabled them to have the power to refuse to train new female employees. The men also had political power in that their interests were represented in the state to a greater extent that that of women, and they were organized in a powerful and effective body in the Amalgamated Society of Engineers. Women, by contrast, had little economic or political power, not even having the right to vote, at this time.

Here we see both the limits and the significance of patriarchal state power. There were limits in that it required other bases of patriarchal power to mobilize the state's resources on behalf of patriarchal interests; and significance in that it prevented the erosion of that form of patriarchal power which was based in the exclusion of women from the skilled engineering trades.

Another example of the patriarchal nature of the state is its response (or rather lack of response) to male violence against women in contemporary Britain. Here women's lack of access to state power ensures that men who rape, batter and otherwise molest women will rarely be punished by the criminal justice system. Women's interests are not sufficiently represented in the state to force any consistency between the rhetoric – that the state attempts to protect everyone against illegal violence – and the reality of widespread male violence against women.

Minor modifications to the state's practices on this issue of men's violence to women have taken place in times of feminist agitation. For instance, in 1976 the Sexual Offences Amendment Act was passed with the express purpose of giving a raped woman anonymity and of preventing her sexual history being discussed in court. A further example is the introduction, at the end of the nineteenth century, of violence as a sufficient reason for judicial separation. Both these reforms occurred in periods of feminist activity, which led to an increase in the representation of women's interests at the level of the state on the issue of male violence. This is an example of the relative autonomy of the state from the economy and of the significance of events at the political level affecting state actions. But again, there are limits to the significance of the state, in that no serious possibility of effective state action against violent men is possible while the material basis of patriarchy exists.

This lack of prosecution of men who are violent towards women raises important questions as to the traditional definition of the state as a body which has the monopoly of legitimate violence in a given territory. I would argue that the state *de facto* accepts male violence against women as legitimate, despite its being carried out by agents who are not usually considered as part of the state apparatus. According to the traditional definition, these violent men must then be seen as agents of the state in carrying out this violence. I would suggest that an alternative approach might be to modify the definition of the state so that it is no longer defined as having the monopoly on legitimate violence. The first position is problematic in that it involves a movement away from the notion of the state as a centralized cohesive body. I would suggest that this is central to the notion of the state. Instead the notion of having the monopoly on legitimate violence should be modified in recognition of men's unpunished violence against women.

Reference

1   M. McIntosh, 'The state and the oppression of women', in *Feminism and Materialism*, ed. Annette Kuhn and Ann Marie Wolpe (Routledge and Kegan Paul, London, 1978).

3

Gender Regimes and the Gender Order

R.W. Connell

Theories of gender, with hardly an exception, focus either on one-to-one relationships between people or on the society as a whole. Apart from discussions of the family, the intermediate level of social organization is skipped. Yet in some ways this is the most important level to understand. We live most of our daily lives in settings like the household, the workplace and the bus queue, rather than stretched out in a relation to society at large or bundled up in a one-to-one. The practice of sexual politics bears mostly on institutions: discriminatory hiring in companies, non-sexist curricula in schools and so on. Much of the research that is changing current views of gender is about institutions like workplaces, markets and media.

When the social sciences have made the connection, it has usually been by picking out a particular institution as the bearer of gender and sexuality. The family and kinship have usually been elected to this honour. Accordingly the structure of the family is the centre-piece of the sociological analysis of sex roles. The flip-side of this election was that it allowed other institutions to be analysed as if gender were of no account at all. In text after text on the classic themes of social science – the state, economic policy, urbanism, migration, modernization – sex and gender fail to get a mention or are marginalized.

One of the most important effects of the new feminism on the social sciences has been a comprehensive proof that this approach is untenable. Murray Goot and Elizabeth Reid's classic demonstration of the mixture of gender-blindness and patriarchal prejudice in mainstream political science is one example of a series of critiques.[1] They range from electoral sociology through the welfare state to class analysis, showing not just that gender relations are present in major institutions but also that they are systematically important to them.

I will not repeat the details of this research, simply taking the general conclusion now firmly established. We cannot understand the place of gender in social process by drawing a line around a set of 'gender institutions'. Gender relations are present in *all* types of institutions. They may not be the most important structure in a particular case, but they are certainly a major structure of most.

The state of play in gender relations in a given institution is its 'gender regime'. An example may help to clarify the idea. In a research project on education we found an active though not always articulate politics of gender in every school. Among both students and staff there are practices that construct various kinds of femininity and masculinity: sport, dancing, choice of subject, class-room discipline, administration and others. Especially clearly among the students, some gender patterns are hegemonic – an aggressively heterosexual masculinity most commonly – and others are subordinated. There is a distinct, though not absolute, sexual division of labour among the staff, and sex differences in tastes and leisure activities among the students. There is an ideology, often more than one, about sexual behaviour and sexual character. There are sometimes conflicts going on over sexism in the curriculum or over promotion among the staff, over prestige and leadership among the kids. The pattern formed by all this varies from school to school, though within limits that reflect the balances of sexual politics in Australian society generally. No school, for instance, permits open homosexual relationships.

Compact formal organizations like schools perhaps have particularly clear gender regimes, but others have them too. Diffuse institutions like markets, large and sprawling ones like the state, and informal milieux like street-corner peer-group life, also are structured in terms of gender and can be characterized by their gender regimes. In this analysis I will take up three cases. The discussions are very condensed, and represent no more than a start with each case. I hope they will still be enough to get some bearings on the institutionalization of gender.

As the first case I look at the family. Conservative ideology speaks of the family as the 'foundation of society' and traditional sociology has often seen it as the simplest of institutions, the building-block of more elaborate structures. Far from being the basis of society, the family is one of its most complex products. There is nothing simple about it. The interior of the family is a scene of multilayered relationships folded over on each other like geological strata. In no other institution are relationships so extended in time, so intensive in contact, so dense in their interweaving of economics, emotion, power and resistance.

This is often missed in theorizing because of a concentration on the normative standard case. Enough has been said elsewhere about how little we can rely on that concept; but it is worth noting that even families which match it to a reasonable degree are internally complex. Lillian Rubin's *Worlds of Pain* documents the ambivalences and complexities of conventional working-class families in the United States. Laing and Esterson's *Sanity, Madness and the Family*, dealing with the more combustible materials of schizophrenia, shows the extraordinary tangles that can be produced in British families by the pursuit of respectable normality.

To understand gender and the family, then, it is necessary to unpack the family. Three structures provide a framework for the attempt.

The sexual division of labour within families and households has a specific literature and is well recognized. Both broad types of work and very fine details are subject to this division. In the English village studied by Pauline Hunt, for instance, wives clean the insides of window panes and husbands clean the outsides. The division of tasks is not absolute, and does change with time. There are now fewer wives than in the 1920s of whom it could be said: 'Her husband was a steady man, but the same as other men – went out and left her to it [i.e. to bring up the children and run the home] to do as she liked.'[2]

Yet not all the changes reduce sexual divisions. The autobiography of a shepherd's son notes that as the eldest surviving child he had 'to be mother's help, to nurse the baby, clean the house, and do sewing like a girl'.[3] That was in England in the 1830s. There are few households now that depend on children's labour to such an extent and hence give boys experience in mothering. Studies of the changing sexual division of labour over more recent periods, like Michael Gilding's research on the family in Sydney up to 1940, suggest that the main effects have been redistribution of housework among women rather than from women to men.

It is equally well recognized that the contemporary urban family/household is constituted by a division of labour that defines certain kinds of work as domestic, unpaid and usually women's, and other kinds as public, paid and usually men's. The interplay of the structure of production inside and outside the family changes character in different class settings. In Mirra Komarovsky's American working-class families this revolves around the husband's *wage*. In a study of American bourgeois 'lives in progress' done at much the same time by Robert White, the connection revolves around the husband's *career*. The latter case is an important qualification to the picture of domestic labour as a form of appropriation by the husband. A professional's or businessman's wife may well maximize her own lifetime income by integration into a successful husband's career.

Most households include children for a considerable part of their history, and this affects the division of labour in two ways. Childrearing is itself work, and bulks large in the sexual division of labour as a whole. Since in rich capitalist countries most care of young children is done unpaid and in the home by their mothers, this has particular prominence in the domestic division of labour. So it is not surprising that R.E. Pahl's recent study in southern England finds the most clearcut and conservative sexual division of labour in those households which currently have children under 5 to care for. The second point is made by the shepherd's son already quoted: children themselves work, both in the home and at school. This work too is structured on gender lines. Given the points already made, it is not surprising that the study of Sydney adolescents by W.F. Connell and others found housework to be done by girls about twice as often as by boys.

The sexual division of labour reflects ideas about 'a woman's place'; but who defines that? As Colin Bell and Howard Newby observe, the way families work is partly a consequence of the husbands' power to define their wives' situation. The underlying interest appears to be consistent and strong. The patriarchal pattern, with young people subordinated to old and women subordinated to men, reappears in a long series of sociological researches on families in different countries, together with the ideologies of masculine authority that support it.

Research into family power structure, by and large, has taken a conventional approach to the definition of 'power' as influence in decision-making. Other kinds of evidence suggest this is not enough. The work on domestic violence shows that force is important in many families. On the other hand the research on 'schizophrenia' by Gregory Bateson, R. D. Laing and others indicates the fierce emotional pressures that can be brought to bear on family members without any open command or display of power. These cases often concern the power of mothers over their children; but the prohibition on escape in Bateson's double-bind theory of schizophrenia is also reminiscent of the 'factors preventing women leaving violent relationships' in domestic violence research. In more ways than one the family can be a trap. Finally the marital sexual relationship can itself embody power. The topic is not very thoroughly studied but it seems likely, from evidence such as Lillian Rubin's, that in most cases it is the husbands who hold the initiative in defining sexual practice.

Given some awareness of this, it is understandable that critics of marriage like Emma Goldman should declare the husbands' 'protection' of their wives a farce. It is also understandable that one way of handling a strong power imbalance is to build a praxis of compliance. Marabel Morgan's stunning *The Total Woman*, a Florida dream of being totally subordinate and loving it, is at the same time a shrewd how-to-do-it manual for this kind of practice. It is notable that her rightwing religion and social outlook are strongly flavoured with eroticism. In getting the husband to stay home, it is the wife's business to titillate:

> 'For an experiment I put on pink baby-doll pyjamas and white boots after my bubble bath. . . . When I opened the door that night to greet Charlie, I was unprepared for his reaction. My quiet, reserved, nonexcitable husband took one look, dropped his briefcase on the doorstep, and chased me around the dining-room table.'[4]

The power of husbands shows in the family, but it is certainly not based in the family alone. Studies of the erosion of patriarchal authority by migration, such as Gillian Bottomley's research on Greek families in Australia, show that domestic patriarchy is dependent on support from its environment. Even without the drastic upheaval of migration, this support has not always been consistent or sufficient. The family sociologies, even in the 1950s, found some power-sharing between husbands and wives. Some families show a pattern of eroded patriarchy, where a claim to authority is made by the husband but is not successful – where wives control the household in reality. Under the impact of the New Left and feminism in the 1970s, conscious attempts have been made in some families and households to dismantle power relations altogether. This has not been easy, but a certain amount of experience about egalitarian households has now accumulated.

[. . .]

At several points already the interplay between structures within the family has been evident. Wage and career affect domestic power; domestic power affects the definition of the division of labour; Marabel Morgan eroticizes powerlessness. The very ideas of 'the housewife' and 'the husband' are fusions of emotional relations, power and the division of labour. The gender regime of a particular family represents a continuing synthesis of relations governed by the three structures.

This synthesis is not trouble-free: the components of a family gender regime may contradict each other. In the traditional patriarchal household, a marked sexual division of labour actually places some limits on the patriarch's ability to exercise power, since women monopolize certain kinds of skill and knowledge. Vanessa Mahler describes a considerable degree of psychological independence for women in Moroccan culture, where patriarchal domination is massive and the division of labour strong. A very sharp division of labour may produce a degree of segregation of daily life that makes it difficult to sustain patriarchal power as a routine. This is suggested, for instance, by Annette Hamilton about Australian Aboriginal societies.

Such contradictions mean potential for change within the family as an institution, most likely to be realized when its context changes markedly. The case of migration has been mentioned. Another powerful pressure is the arrival of capitalist market relations in a non-capitalist setting. The pressure is not all in the one direction. A study of peasant households in Mexico by Kate Young shows a splitting of family patterns as class stratification develops, with gender regimes moving in different directions.

Secondly I look at the state as a gender regime. Theoretical literature on the state is at the other pole from the family: almost no one has seen it as an institutionalization of gender. Even in feminist thought the state is only just coming into focus as a theoretical question.

Yet reasons to address it are easy to find. The personnel of the state are divided by sex in quite visible, even spectacular, ways. State elites are the preserve of men, with a very few exceptions. The state arms men and disarms women. President Carter, though supporting the Equal Rights Amendment, still announced that he would not give women a combat role in the military. The diplomatic, colonial and military policy of major states is formed in the context of ideologies of masculinity that put a premium on toughness and force. The South Pacific is at present having a textbook demonstration of this from the French, with atomic testing at Muroroa Atoll, the bombing of the *Rainbow Warrior* in New Zealand in 1985, and anti-independence violence by French settlers in Kanaky (New Caledonia).

The state engages in considerable ideological activity on issues of sex and gender; this very diverse activity ranges from birth control in India and China, through the re-imposition of the *chador* on women in Iran, to the Soviet efforts to increase the number of women in paid work. States attempt to control sexuality: criminalizing homosexuality, legislating on age of consent, venereal disease, AIDS and so on. The state intervenes in the sexual division of labour in ways ranging from subsidized immigration to equal opportunity policies. It regulates workplaces and families, provides schools, builds houses.

Given all this, control of the state is a major stake in sexual politics.

Accordingly the state has been a major object of strategy. From the Seneca Falls convention of 1848 to the Equal Rights Amendment (ERA) campaign of the 1970s, American feminism has placed demands on the state and tried to guarantee women's access to it. Australian feminism has put considerable energy into gaining a presence inside the state bureaucracy, through welfare funding and the 'femocrats'. The main focus of groups like the Campaign for Homosexual Equality in Britain has been legal reform through lobbying of parliamentarians and bureaucrats. The American New Right in its turn has attempted to roll back feminism through control of courts and legislatures.

[...]

But – especially in its repressive capacity – the state both institutionalizes hegemonic masculinity and expends great energy in controlling it. The objects of repression, e.g. 'criminals', are generally younger men themselves involved in the practice of violence, with a social profile quite like that of the immediate agents of repression, the police or the soldiers. However, the state is not all of a piece. The military and coercive apparatus has to be understood in terms of relationships between masculinities: the physical aggression of front-line troops or police, the authoritative masculinity of commanders, the calculative rationality of technicians, planners and scientists.

The internal complexity of the state is now well recognized in class theory and is equally important in relation to gender. Actual states are by no means consistent in their processing of gender issues. The political leadership in New South Wales has introduced a broad equal opportunity programme mainly directed at women; much of the bureaucracy, which is of course run by men, has quietly resisted it. Recent policy in a number of Western countries has been to hand more welfare functions from the state to 'the community', i.e. to the unpaid work of women; but at the same time the training of girls for paid work has been expanded, with rising retention rates in school and new occupational preparation programmes. Equal employment opportunity programmes have been expanding in Australia at the same time that funds for childcare, which would make them effective, have been cut. The gradual extension of the civil rights of homosexual men via decriminalization and antidiscrimination laws is contradicted by continued exclusion from state employment and now by official scaremongering over AIDS.... The patriarchal state even finds itself funding feminism, across a considerable spectrum from rape crisis centres through women's units in the bureaucracy to grants for feminist academic research. Some of this is mere incoherence, to be expected from the sheer complexity of the state as a set of instrumentalities. But some is real contradiction.

How can these points be built into a gender analysis of the state? They suggest that the state is not inherently patriarchal, but is historically constructed as patriarchal in a political process whose outcome is open. The process of bureaucratization is central here, as conventional bureaucracy is a tight fusion of the structure of power and the division of labour. Together with selective recruitment and promotion, these structures form an integrated mechanism of gender relations that results in the exclusion of women from positions of authority and the subordination of the areas of work in which most women are concentrated. But conventional bureaucracy is itself under pressure, as the huge contemporary output of management-theory repair manuals testifies. Demands for more efficiency, for decentralization, even for more democracy, can unhinge parts of this mechanism. It is largely in the spaces where gender politics and organizational reform intersect that feminists in the state have gained ground.

[. . .]

A further instance of a gender regime is to be found in the life of the street. The street is not often thought of as an institution. It is something we walk and drive along, or that chickens cross. Yet a famous sociological text is called, with only mild irony, *Street Corner Society*, and we speak of 'street-wise' kids. It is at least a definite social milieu, with particular social relations.

A good deal of work goes on in the street. Jobs that concern children, like pushing them around in strollers, are almost all done by women. So is most shopping and most prostitution. Selling of newspapers, food and other small objects is mixed. Driving cars, trucks and buses, petty crime and policing, repairing vehicles and the street itself are mainly done by men. Though women have been working as bus drivers more often, heavy trucks are still a masculine speciality.

The street is the setting for much intimidation of women, from low-level harassment like wolf-whistling to physical manhandling and rape. Since it is not always predictable when the escalation will stop, in many parts of the city women rarely walk, especially after dark. The street then is a zone of occupation by men. Concentrations of young adult men are the most intimidating and dangerous.

Such concentrations are commonest in areas where there is high unemployment and ethnic exclusion to go with it, like Brixton in London, Redfern in Sydney, the South Side in Chicago. Contests of daring, talk about sport and cars, drugs (mainly alcohol) and sexism provide entertainment in a bleak environment. Women generally avoid this; but since there are no women's streets and few welcoming public buildings, the effective alternative is the home: 'A woman's place . . .'. In outer suburbs this effect is not as strong, but threat still occurs.

The young men who offer this threat are also subject to it. The street is a scene of intermittent but routine conflict between different groups, which the media call 'gangs', and between them and the police. It is in fact young men who are the main victims of street violence, not elderly people, though the elderly are kept in a chronic state of fear about it. The police are the Great Power in street life, though in a few cases like the Watts insurrection of August 1965 in Los Angeles they may vanish as an authority. The reserve power of the state is still great enough to 'restore order' by military means if the political leadership is willing to pay the price, as in Belfast.

In some ways the street is a battleground; in others it is a theatre. In an urban shopping centre the street is full of advertising displays: shop windows, billboards, posters. Their content is heavily sex-typed and has become more heavily eroticized over recent decades. Some particularly crude appeals to masculine violence, like the London poster in 1984 showing a car fired from a pistol and captioned 'The trigger is under your right foot', have been forced off the street. But the cigarette and beer ads continue in the same merry way.

The pavement is equally full of displays, though more varied. People convey messages about themselves by dress, jewellery, posture, movement, speech. The street is one of the great theatres of sexuality and styles of masculinity and femininity. A bus queue or shopping crowd will show a wide range of styles and manners, some extroverted and attention-seeking, some dowdy or uncaring. During the cycle of a day or week the dominant styles turn over as the population changes: shift-workers, commuting business men, shopping mothers, after-school teenagers, late-night lads hanging out.

The street as a milieu thus shows the same structures of gender relations as the family and state. It has a division of labour, a structure of power and a structure of cathexis. Similarly the local patterning of these relationships is linked to the structure of gender relations outside. As Emma Goldman observed, women working the street as prostitutes are not in it for the fun; they are there because women's wages are low. 'Opportunist submission' (the phrase is Jan Morris's) to patriarchy may be obligatory given the different resources that people bring to it. Gay relationships are rarely displayed on the street outside tightly defined areas; it could be very dangerous to do so.

At the same time there is something specific to a loosely structured milieu like a street that distinguishes it from deeply sedimented institutions like family and state. It gives room not only to diversity but also to quick turnover of styles. The theatre of the street may be experimental theatre. A recent example is young women appropriating and making-over an aggressive style of sexuality, in punk fashions with a good deal of black and leather about them. Something of a negotiation goes on about new forms in gender. There are even attempts to turn this into a conscious political practice, through feminist street theatre or events like the gay Mardi Gras in Sydney. I suspect the dominance of the car now prevents any full-blown new development of the street as festival. But it is still an extremely interesting register of sexual politics.

At several points in this analysis of institutions the importance of context has become obvious, especially the context provided by other institutions. To compile a complete structural inventory it is therefore necessary to go beyond a collation of gender regimes to the relationships between them.

In some cases this relationship is additive or complementary. The patterns surrounding women's part-time employment are a familiar example. The conventional division of labour in working-class families in Western cities assigns most childcare and housework to the wife-and-mother; and femininity is constructed in a way that defines the work of caring for other family members as womanly. The labour market constructed by capitalist industry and the state offers some low-paid, low-status part-time jobs; and curiously enough most of the people recruited to these part-time jobs are married women. This pattern of recruitment is justified by employers on the grounds that married women only want part-time work because of their domestic responsibilities and only need low pay because theirs is a 'second wage'. At home the much heavier domestic work of women is justified by husbands because their wives can only get part-time jobs.

The dovetailing is neat, and it is anything but accidental. The pattern has developed particularly in the 1970s and 1980s, and in the context of the recession represents a practical accommodation between the institutions involved. The dovetailing of structures is produced by a meeting of strategies: the profit-maximizing strategies of employers in a slack labour market and the household work strategies (as Pahl calls them) of the employees.

If this kind of fit were the normal case, we would indeed have the tightly integrated system presupposed by categoricalism. But the gender regimes of interacting institutions are rarely so harmonious. I know of no starker example than 'The Blood Vote', a famous poem and poster used in the First World War campaign against conscription in Australia. Two stanzas run:

> Why is your face so white, Mother?
>   Why do you choke for breath?
> O I have dreamt in the night, my son,
>   That I doomed a man to death.
>
> I hear his widow cry in the night,
>   I hear his children weep;
> And always within my sight, O God!
>   The dead man's blood doth leap.[5]

The conflict dramatized here, between the emotional relationships of the family and the demands of a state at war, is a common theme in pacifist campaigns, including the current campaign against nuclear weapons. A well-known poster reads: 'What to do in the event of nuclear war: Kiss your children goodbye.'

A more complicated pattern of institutional abrasion surrounds the reversals of state policy about welfare. There has long been a conflict between the goal of redistribution implicit in welfare policy and the goal of stabilization implicit in the machinery of repression and ideological control. Once internal to the state, a classic 'steering problem' in the language of Jürgen Habermas, this has been externalized by the recession as a conflict over the terms of the relationship among state, family and labour market. The welfare conservatism of the post-war boom, predicated on full employment, managed class and gender tensions with a gradual extension of welfare measures. But the state was never accepted as wholly benign. A constituency developed for the New Right swing towards welfare cuts, labour market discipline and selective direct repression.

Given the feminization of poverty the welfare cuts have deepened the economic disadvantages of women, while, as we have seen, the military and police are the preserves of men. The changing balance of advantage in gender relations is perhaps reflected in opinion-poll data showing a much heavier support for Reagan among men than women in the United States presidential election of 1980.[6] But there is no simple translation of sexual politics into votes. One of the first governments to use the New Right rhetoric, the Fraser government in Australia, was elected in 1975 with heavier support from women than men; and even in the 1983 election that ousted it, women stayed with the conservative parties more than men did.

A third pattern of connection between institutions sets them in parallel, so to speak, as the domain of a common strategy or movement. For instance the equal employment opportunity campaigns have moved from one organization to another, attempting to bring them into line with the policy, using experience gained in one to move things along in the next. At another level, 'coming out' as gay has to be done in a whole series of settings: workplace, family, friendship networks, etc. As Wendy Clark observes, the emotional patterns to be dealt with vary: coming out to your parents is different. But the logic of the process still links the institutions.

What is common to the three patterns is the fact of politics, the social struggle around the terms of relationship between institutions.

Notes and References

1   M. Goot and E. Reid, *Women and Voting Studies* (Sage, London, 1975).
2   M.L. Davies (ed.), *Life As We Have Known It* (Virago, London, 1977), p. 62.
3   J. Burnett (ed.), *Destiny Obscure* (Allen Lane, London, 1982), p. 72.
4   M. Morgan, *The Total Woman* (Hodder and Stoughton, London, 1975), p. 94.
5   J. Harris, *The Bitter Fight* (University of Queensland Press, St Lucia, 1970), p. 259.
6   B. Friedan, *The Second Stage* (Michael Joseph, London, 1982), p. 210.

4

Gender, Relation and Difference in Psychoanalytic Perspective

Nancy Chodorow

Along with the earliest development of its sense of separateness, the infant constructs an internal set of unconscious, affectively loaded representations of others in relation to its self, and an internal sense of self in relationship emerges. Images of felt good and bad aspects of the mother or primary caretaker, caretaking experiences, and the mothering relationship become part of the self, of a relational ego structure, through unconscious mental processes that appropriate and incorporate these images. With maturation, these early images and fragments of perceived experience become put together into a self. As externality and internality are established, therefore, what comes to be internal includes what originally were aspects of the other and the relation to the other. (Similarly, what is experienced as external may include what was originally part of the developing self's experience.) Externality and internality, then, do not follow easily observable physiological boundaries but are constituted by psychological and emotional processes as well.

These unconscious early internalizations that affect and constitute the internal quality of selfhood may remain more or less fragmented, or they may develop a quality of wholeness. A sense of continuity of experience and the opportunity to integrate a complex of (at least somewhat) complementary and consistent images enables the "I" to emerge as a continuous being with an identity. This more internal sense of self, or of "I," is not dependent on separateness or difference from an other. A "true self," or "central self," emerges through the experience of continuity that the mother or caretaker helps to provide, by protecting the infant from having continually to react to and ward off environmental intrusions and from being continually in need.

The integration of a "true self" that feels alive and whole involves a particular set of internalized feelings about others in relation to the self. These include developing a sense that one is able to affect others and one's environment (a sense that one has not been inhibited by over-anticipation of all one's needs), a sense that one has been accorded one's own feelings and a spontaneity about these feelings (a sense that one's feelings or needs have not been projected onto one), and a sense that there is a fit between one's feelings and needs and those of the mother or caretaker. These feelings all give the self a sense of agency and authenticity.

This sense of agency, then, is fostered by caretakers who do not project experiences or feelings onto the child and who do not let the environment impinge indiscriminately. It is evoked by empathic caretakers who understand and validate the infant as a self in its own right, and the infant's experience as real. Thus, the sense of agency, which is one basis of the inner sense of continuity and wholeness, grows out of the nature of the parent–infant relationship.

Another important aspect of internalized feelings about others in relation to the self concerns a certain wholeness that develops through an internal sense of relationship with another. The "thereness" of the primary parenting person grows into an internal sense of the presence of another who is caring and affirming. The self comes into being here first through feeling confidently alone in the presence of its mother, and then through this presence's becoming internalized. Part of its self becomes a good internal mother. This suggests that the central core of self is, internally, a relational ego, a sense of self-in-good-relationship. The presence or absence of others, their sameness or difference, does not then become an issue touching the infant's very existence. A "capacity to be alone," a relational rather than a reactive autonomy, develops because of a sense of the ongoing presence of another.

These several senses of agency, of a true self that does not develop reactively, of a relational self or ego core, and of an internal continuity of being, are fundamental to an unproblematic sense of self, and provide the basis of both autonomy and spontaneity. The strength, or wholeness, of the self, in this view, does not depend only or even centrally on its degree of separateness, although the extent of confident distinctness certainly affects and is part of the sense of self. The more secure the central self, or ego core, the less one has to define one's self through separateness from others. Separateness becomes, then, a more rigid, defensive, rather fragile, secondary criterion of the strength of the self and of the "success" of individuation.

This view suggests that no one has a separateness consisting only of "me"–"not-me" distinctions. Part of myself is always that which I have taken in; we are all to some degree incorporations and extensions of others. Separateness from the mother, defining oneself as apart from her (and from other women), is not the only or final goal for women's ego strength and autonomy, even if many women must also attain some sense of reliable separateness. In the process of differentiation, leading to a genuine autonomy, people maintain contact with those with whom they had their earliest relationships: indeed this contact is part of who we are. "I am" is not definition through negation, is not "who I am not." Developing a sense of confident separateness must be a part of all children's development. But once this confident separateness is established, one's relational self can become more central to one's life. Differentiation is not distinctness and separateness, but a particular way of being connected to others. This connection to others, based on early incorporations, in turn enables us to feel that empathy and confidence that are basic to the recognition of the other as a self.

How does all this relate to male–female difference and male dominance? Before turning to the question of gender difference, I want to explain what we as feminists learn from the general inquiry into "differentiation." First, we learn that we can only think of differentiation and the emergence of the self relationally. Differentiation occurs, and separation emerges, in relationship; they are not givens. Second, we learn that to single out separation as the core of a notion of self and of the process of differentiation may well be inadequate; it is certainly not the only way to discuss the emergence of self or what constitutes a strong self. Differentiation includes the internalization of aspects of the primary caretaker and of the caretaking relationship.

Finally, we learn that essential, important attitudes toward mothers and expectations of mothers – attitudes and expectations that enter into experiences of women more generally – emerge in the earliest differentiation of self. These attitudes and expectations arise during the emergence of separateness. Given that differentiation and separation are developmentally problematic, and given that women are primary caretakers, the mother, who is a woman, becomes and remains for children of both genders the other, or object. She is not accorded autonomy or selfness on her side. Such attitudes arise also from the gender-specific character of the early, emotionally charged self and object images that affect the development of self and the sense of autonomy and spontaneity. They are internalizations of feelings about the self in relation to the mother, who is then often experienced as either overwhelming or over-denying. These attitudes are often unconscious and always have a basis in unconscious, emotionally charged feelings and conflicts. A precipitate of the early relationship to the mother and of an unconscious sense of self, they may be more fundamental and determining of psychic life than more conscious and explicit attitudes to "sex differences" or "gender differences" themselves.

This inquiry suggests a psychoanalytic grounding for goals of emotional psychic life other than autonomy and separateness. It suggests, instead, an individuality that emphasizes our connectedness with, rather than our separation from, one another. Feelings of inadequate separateness, the fear of merger, are indeed issues for women, because of the ongoing sense of oneness and primary identification with our mothers (and children). A transformed organization of parenting would help women to resolve these issues. However, autonomy, spontaneity, and a sense of agency need not be based on self–other distinctions, on the individual as individual. They can be based on the fundamental interconnectedness, not synonymous with merger, that grows out of our earliest unconscious developmental experience, and that enables the creation of a non-reactive separateness.

I turn now to the question of gender differences. We are not born with perceptions of gender differences; these emerge developmentally. In the traditional psychoanalytic view, however, when sexual difference is first seen it has self-evident value. A girl perceives her lack of a penis, knows instantly that she wants one, and subsequently defines herself and her mother as lacking, inadequate, castrated; a boy instantly knows having a penis is better, and fears the loss of his own.[1] This traditional account violates a fundamental rule of psychoanalytic interpretation. When the analyst finds trauma, shock, strong fears, or conflict, it is a signal to look for the roots of such feelings.[2] Because of his inability to focus on the pre-Oedipal years and the relationship of mother to child, Freud could not follow his own rule here.

Clinical and theoretical writings since Freud suggest another interpretation of the emergence of perceptions of gender difference. This view reverses the perception of which gender experiences greater trauma, and retains only the claim that gender identity and the sense of masculinity and femininity develop differently for men and women.[3] These accounts suggest that core gender identity and masculinity are conflictual for men, and are bound up with the masculine sense of self in a way that core gender identity and femininity are not for women. "Core gender identity" here refers to a cognitive sense of gendered self, the sense that one is male or female. It is established in the first two years concomitantly with the development of the sense of self. Later evaluations of the desirability of one's gender and of the activities and modes of behavior associated with it, or of one's own sense of adequacy at fulfilling gender role expectations, are built upon this fundamental gender identity. They do not create or change it.

Most people develop an unambiguous core gender identity, a sense that they are female or male. But because women mother, the sense of maleness in men differs from the sense of femaleness in women. Maleness is more conflictual and more problematic. Underlying, or built into, core male gender identity is an early, non-verbal, unconscious, almost somatic sense of primary oneness with the mother, an underlying sense of femaleness that continually, usually unnoticeably, but sometimes insistently, challenges and undermines the sense of maleness. Thus, because of a primary oneness and identification with his mother, a primary femaleness, a boy's and a man's core gender identity itself – the seemingly unproblematic cognitive sense of being male – is an issue. A boy must learn his gender identity as being not-female, or not-mother. Subsequently, again because of the primacy of the mother in early life and because of the absence of concrete, real, available male figures of identification and love who are as salient for him as female figures, learning what it is to be masculine comes to mean learning to be not-feminine, or not-womanly.

Because of early developed, conflictual core gender identity problems, and later problems of adequate masculinity, it becomes important to men to have a clear sense of gender difference, of what is masculine and what is feminine, and to maintain rigid boundaries between these. Researchers find, for example, that fathers sex-type children more than mothers. They treat sons and daughters more differently and enforce gender role expectations more vigorously than mothers do.[4] Boys and men come to deny the feminine identification within themselves and those feelings they experience as feminine: feelings of dependence, relational needs, emotions generally. They come to emphasize differences, not commonalities or continuities, between themselves and women, especially in situations that evoke anxiety, because these commonalities and continuities threaten to challenge gender difference or to remind boys and men consciously of their potentially feminine attributes.

These conflicts concerning core gender identity interact with and build upon particular ways that boys experience the processes of differentiation and the formation of the self. Both sexes establish separateness in relation to their mother, and internalizations in the development of self take in aspects of the mother as well. But because the mother is a woman, these experiences differ by gender. Though children of both sexes are originally part of herself, a mother unconsciously and often consciously experiences her son as more of an "other" than her daughter. Reciprocally, a son's male core gender identity develops away from his mother. The male's self, as a result, becomes based on a more fixed "me"–"not-me" distinction. Separateness and difference as a component of differentiation become more salient. By contrast, the female's self is less separate and involves a less fixed "me"–"not-me" distinction, creating the difficulties with a sense of separateness and autonomy that I mentioned above.

At the same time, core gender identity for a girl is not problematic in the sense that it is for boys. It is built upon, and does not contradict, her primary sense of oneness and identification with her mother and is assumed easily along with her developing sense of self. Girls grow up with a sense of continuity and similarity to their mother, a relational connection to the world. For them, difference is not originally problematic or fundamental to their psychological being or identity. They do not define themselves as "not-men," or "not-male," but as "I, who am female." Girls and women may have problems with their sense of continuity and similarity, if it is too strong and they have no sense of a separate self. However, these problems are not the inevitable products of having a sense of continuity and similarity, since, as I argue here, selfhood does not depend only on the strength and impermeability of ego boundaries. Nor are these problems bound up with questions of gender; rather, they are bound up with questions of self.

In the development of gender identification for girls it is not the existence of core gender identity, the unquestioned knowledge that one is female, that is problematic. Rather, it is the later-developed conflicts concerning this identity, and the identifications, learning, and cognitive choices that it implies. The difficulties that girls have in establishing a "feminine" identity do not stem from the inaccessibility and negative definition of this identity, or its assumption by denial (as in the case of boys). They arise from identification with a negatively valued gender category, and an ambivalently experienced maternal figure, whose mothering and femininity, often conflictual for the mother herself, are accessible, but devalued. Conflicts here arise from questions of relative power, and social and cultural value. I would argue that these conflicts come later in development, and are less pervasively determining of psychological life for women than are masculine conflicts around core gender identity and gender difference.

Men's and women's understanding of difference, and gender difference, must thus be understood in the relational context in which these are created. They stem from the respective relation of boys and girls to their mother, who is their primary caretaker, love-object, and object of identification, and who is a woman in a sexually and gender-organized world. This relational context contrasts profoundly for girls and boys in a way that makes difference, and gender difference, central for males – one of the earliest, most basic male developmental issues – and not central for females. It gives men a psychological investment in difference that women do not have.

According to psychoanalytic accounts since Freud, it is very clear that males are "not females" in earliest development. Core gender identity and the sense of masculinity are defined more negatively, in terms of that which is not female or not-mother, than positively. By contrast, females do not develop as "not-males." Female core gender identity and the sense of femininity are defined positively, as that which is female, or like mother. Difference from males is not so salient. An alternative way to put this is to suggest that, developmentally, the maternal identification represents and is experienced as generically human for children of both genders.

But, because men have power and cultural hegemony in our society, a notable thing happens. Men use and have used this hegemony to appropriate and transform these experiences. Both in everyday life and in theoretical and intellectual formulations, men have come to define maleness as that which is basically human, and to define women as not-men. This transformation is first learned in, and helps to constitute, the Oedipal transition – the cultural, affective, and sexual learnings of the meaning and valuation of sex differences. Because Freud was not attentive to pre-Oedipal development (and because of his sexism), he took this meaning and valuation as a self-evident given, rather than a developmental and cultural product.

We must remember that this transformed interpretation of difference, an interpretation learned in the Oedipal transition, is produced by means of male cultural hegemony and power. Men have the means to institutionalize their unconscious defenses against repressed yet strongly experienced developmental conflicts. This interpretation of difference is imposed on earlier developmental processes; it is not the deepest, unconscious root of either the female or the male sense of gendered self. In fact, the primary sense of gendered self that emerges in earliest development constantly challenges and threatens men, and gives a certain potential psychological security, even liberation, to women. The transformed interpretation of difference is not inevitable, given other parenting arrangements and other arrangements of power between the sexes. It is especially insofar as women's lives and self-definition become oriented to men that difference becomes more salient for us, as does differential evaluation of the sexes. Insofar as women's lives and self-definition become more oriented toward themselves, differences from men become less salient.

What are the implications of this inquiry into psychoanalytic understandings of differentiation and gender difference for our understanding of difference, and for our evaluation of the view that difference is central to feminist theory? My investigation suggests that our own sense of differentiation, of separateness from others, as well as our psychological and cultural experience and interpretation of gender or sexual difference, are created through psychological, social, and cultural processes, and through relational experiences. We can only understand gender difference, and human distinctness and separation, relationally and situationally. They are part of a system of asymmetrical social relationships embedded in inequalities of power, in which we grow up as selves, and as women and men. Our experience and perception of gender are processual; they are produced developmentally and in our daily social and cultural lives.

Difference is psychologically salient for men in a way that it is not for women, because of gender differences in early formative developmental processes and the particular unconscious conflicts and defenses these produce. This salience, in turn, has been transmuted into a conscious cultural preoccupation with gender difference. It has also become intertwined with and has helped to produce more general cultural notions, particularly that individualism, separateness, and distance from others are desirable and requisite to autonomy and human fulfillment. Throughout these processes, it is women, as mothers, who become the objects apart from which separateness, difference, and autonomy are defined.

It is crucial for us as feminists to recognize that the ideologies of difference which define us as women and as men, as well as inequality itself, are produced, socially, psychologically, and culturally, by people living in and creating their social, psychological, and cultural worlds. Women participate in the creation of these worlds and ideologies, even if our ultimate power and access to cultural hegemony are less than those of men. To speak of difference as a final, irreducible concept and to focus on gender differences as central is to reify them and to deny the reality of those processes which create the meaning and significance of gender. To see men and women as qualitatively different kinds of people, rather than seeing gender as processual, reflexive, and constructed, is to reify and deny relations of gender, to see gender differences as permanent rather than as created and situated.

We certainly need to understand how difference comes to be important, how it is produced as salient, and how it reproduces sexual inequality. But we should not appropriate differentiation and separation, or difference, for ourselves and take it as a given. Feminist theories and feminist inquiry based on the notion of essential difference, or focused on demonstrating difference, are doing feminism a disservice. They ultimately rely on the defensively constructed masculine models of gender that are presented to us as our cultural heritage, rather than creating feminist understandings of gender and difference that grow from our own politics, theorizing, and experience.

Notes and References

1   N. Brown, *Life Against Death* (Vintage, New York, 1959), p. 153.
2   Ibid., p. 57.
3   H. Marasse, *Eros and Civilization* (Vintage, New York, 1962), p. 17.
4   Brown, *Life Against Death*, p. xii.

5

The Feminist Critique of Rationality

Susan Hekman

The feminist critique of rationality is a wide-ranging and by no means monolithic exposition of the "maleness" of reason in Western thought. Linguists, anthropologists, rhetoricians as well as philosophers have contributed to this critique. Many of the themes that dominate the critique are similar to those of postmodernism. Some, particularly those of the radical feminists, are contradictory. It is possible, however, to define one theme that unites all of these critiques: an emphasis on language and discourse. This emphasis on language represents a significant connection between postmodernism and feminism. The attack on rationality by both feminists and postmoderns is an attack on a particular discourse and the power deployed by that discourse. The contemporary crisis in modernity that has fostered the postmodern critique is an epistemological crisis rooted in an attack on Enlightenment rationalism. Feminists have contributed to this critique by pointing out that it is a crisis in a set of discourses created by men. Even though some feminists reject the postmodern diagnosis of this crisis and many postmoderns ignore its gendered connotations, they are linked by a common opponent – rationalism – and a common emphasis – language/discourse.

Postmodern reflections on language and discourse led to Foucault's connection between language and power, Derrida's attack on dualism, and even his insight that logocentrism is phallocentrism. The postmodern critique attacks the hierarchical nature of Enlightenment thought and its privileging of an abstract rationality. Feminists concur in many of these arguments. But their attack on rationality is more radical than the postmodern critique: it defines causes whereas the postmoderns are only dealing with symptoms. The fact that women are identified with the irrational and men with the rational is a symptom of the underlying problem that all the dualisms of Enlightenment thought are defined by the basic masculine/feminine dualism. Even more significantly, feminists have pointed out that this dualism is not symmetrical. Woman is always defined as that which is *not* man; she is a "minus male"[1] who is identified by the qualities that she lacks. Language establishes and maintains the basic gender identity that creates female inferiority. It effectively erases the distinction between female and feminine that is central to an understanding of the nature of the oppression of women. The language that we speak creates a situation in which the qualities that women possess as a result of their biological sex become indistinguishable from those that they are told they *should* possess in order to be "feminine"; sex and gender, in other words, become intertwined. Much of the work of contemporary feminists has been aimed at separating biological sex from imposed gender roles in linguistic practice.

Many feminist analyses of language focus on the way in which linguistic practice forges a connection between personal identity and gender identity. In an insightful article on language, sex and gender, Barbara Fried argues that language and gender identity appear at the same time in children's lives, a fact that is far from coincidental: "Language does not simply communicate the link between one's sex and one's gender identity; it constitutes that link."[2] Children who grow up hearing English spoken, furthermore, never learn a sense of "personhood,"[3] only female personhood and male personhood. It is not the case, however, that personhood is merely tied to biological sex. It is linked, rather, to a specific gender identity, an identity which embodies the society's understanding of what is "feminine." This feminine gender identity covers a broad range of qualities, but central to that identity is irrationality. One feminist linguist has demonstrated that by age 5, both boys and girls have learned separate languages that relegate women to the sphere of irrationality. Men, who are identified as the "natural" occupants of the sphere of rationality, are contrasted to women whose sphere is that of emotion and feeling, the irrational. This dichotomy leaves women two unacceptable options: either they can talk like women and be "feminine" but irrational or they can talk like men and be rational but "unfeminine."[4]

The fact that, through their control of language, men have dominated not only women but every aspect of the world in which we live is obvious. The consequences of linguistic domination have been extensively documented in the feminist literature. Two aspects of that literature are particularly relevant here because they structure the way in which knowledge has been produced and deployed in academic institutions. The first is a discussion of how linguistic practices in the knowledge-creating institutions have been structured along gendered lines since their inception with the Greeks. Walter Ong has been the pioneer in these studies.[5] Ong argues that the roots of Western academicism are both oral and agonistic. The Socratic emphasis on speech and Plato's reservations about writing established an oral tradition at the root of Western academic life. The adversarial, agonistic element was central to the Greek's use of logic, and this element was intensified in the Middle Ages when learning became a process of disputation; knowledge was defined through verbal contests that were similar to the medieval jousts. The learning of Latin, the language of knowledge, was seen as a kind of male puberty rite. It was a process that was oral, agonistic and exclusively male. Until very recently the process of knowledge acquisition was one in which men disputed with each other in their exclusive tongue, Latin.

Ong argues that the recent entry of women into universities has co-incided with the demise of Latin and, with it, the oral, agonistic culture that it defined.[6] This conclusion, however, is not the only significance of his work for the feminist critique of rationality. Ong's analysis explains one of the mechanisms by which the creation of knowledge has been preserved as a male domain. Latin, which was taught only to men, constituted the world of knowledge as an exclusively male world. Its contrast was the vernacular, the "mother tongue," that is taught by mothers to both sons and daughters. Another important element of Ong's work is that it appears to raise questions about Derrida's thesis regarding the privileging of speech over writing. As Ong himself points out, Latin is exclusively male and exclusively written.[7] This would seem to contradict Derrida's assertion that speech is privileged over writing in the West. But this contradiction is only apparent. In the academic world Latin was a spoken as well as a written language. And it was the specifically oral use of Latin that defined the agonistic culture that con-stituted the world of knowledge. The advent of women in academic life coincided with the demise of that orality – the introduction of written examinations – as well as the reduction of adversativeness – less combative teaching methods. Thus Derrida's thesis holds: women, who are associated with the disprivileged side of the dichotomy between speech and writing, represent a challenge to the domain of knowledge as it has been constituted in the West.

[. . .]

A second aspect of the literature that concerns academic knowledge creation and deployment deals with the connection between the real and the rational. Concepts formed from the male point of view create a male reality; both the real and the rational are defined in exclusively male terms. One consequence of the male definition of reality is that women's experiences become invisible, particularly to male academics. It also follows that women are inarticulate because the language they use is derivative of male definitions of reality. Although men would have us believe that the term "man" is generic, that is, that it includes the experience of both men and women, a simple example proves this false: the statement "man has difficulty in childbirth" is nonsense. This male definition of reality has been particularly problematic in history and the social sciences whose task it is to analyze and make sense of the experience of "mankind." Recent feminist critics of the discipline of history have argued that history has excluded women because "history" has been defined in terms of the public realm occupied exclusively by men. The same phenomenon has occurred in sociology. Dorothy Smith argues that we know the world sociologically through male categories. The categories of sociology are conceived in terms of man's experiences and leave women's reality "outside the frame."[8] The sociology of Max Weber is a good example of this phenomenon. Weber's system is built on the foundation of the rational, hence, male actor. Although Weber is blind to the gendered connotations of his system, it follows that, since only men are rational and only men can be subjects, only men are actors and hence the subjects of his sociology of action. Although the postmodern critique is sensitive to this connection between language and reality, feminist criticisms of the specifically masculine creation of language and reality such as these have significantly expanded that critique.

Although the theorists discussed above have very different solutions to the problems that they have outlined, their diagnosis of the problem is remarkably similar. All agree that the oppression of women is rooted in male-dominated language and a male definition of reality. What is significant about this agreement in the present context is that it is an extension of the point that the postmoderns argue in their connection between language and reality. The postmoderns assert that the discourses that create knowledge create reality as well. The feminists expand this by arguing that that definition and that reality are exclusively masculine. The two critiques reinforce and strengthen each other.

The discussion of the masculine domination of language sets the stage for the examination of a more specific discussion of one aspect of that domination: the association of the masculine with the rational, the feminine with the irrational. Most contemporary feminists agree on the diagnosis of this problem: since Plato, and most particularly since the

Enlightenment, reason and rationality have been defined in exclusively masculine terms; the "Man of Reason" is gendered, not generic. But although there is agreement on this diagnosis, the discussion of masculine definitions of rationality and a possible feminist alternative have been the source of a great deal of dissension among feminist theorists. Those who analyze the "Man of Reason" draw very different conclusions from their analyses and these differences have created what, for some feminists, constitutes a crisis in feminist theory. The modernism/postmodernism dispute generated by the crisis in Western epistemology has its parallel in feminist theory. The issues that divide feminist theorists on the issue of rationality reflect the modernist/postmodernist dispute in epistemology.

Most feminists who discuss the maleness of the "Man of Reason" focus on Enlightenment thought and its consequences for contemporary discussions. But several writers have traced the maleness of rational thought back to the Greeks and, consequently, claim that Western thought as a whole and not just the Enlightenment is the cause of this particular aspect of female oppression. In a brilliant analysis of Plato's allegory of the cave, Luce Irigaray shows that the masculine definitions of concepts of truth and rationality are central to Plato's concept of knowledge. In her analysis she carefully dissects the elements of the allegory and draws out their significance. She begins by observing that the prisoner is brought out of the cave as a child is brought out of the womb in a difficult delivery.[9] This statement sets up the basic interpretive elements she employs in her analysis. The feminine imagery is negative: the cave represents woman's womb; breaking out of the womb means breaking into truth and knowledge. Masculine images, on the contrary, are positive: throughout the allegory light and knowledge are associated with the masculine, earth and non-knowledge with the feminine. This dichotomy is clarified in Irigaray's statement that the earth is defined as "dark holes in which lucid reason risks drowning."[10] This connection between light and knowledge, furthermore, establishes an association that will come to dominate Western thought: vision is a "masculine" sense, while touch, on the other hand, is a feminine one. The certainty of knowledge is always associated with "seeing," a masculine way of knowing from which the feminine is excluded.

The association of the masculine with rationality, the feminine with irrationality in the history of Western thought has been extensively documented in contemporary feminist scholarship. That women should be excluded from the realm of knowledge scarcely needs documentation. The exclusion of women from the political sphere, although closely related, is less obvious. Okin's *Women in Western Political Thought*

(1979) and Elshtain's *Public Man, Private Woman* (1981) argue that the exclusion of women from the sphere of rationality is the cause of their exclusion from the political sphere. Since women are not rational they cannot be allowed to participate in the realm that is the highest expression of man's rationality: politics. The charge that women have been excluded from both politics and rationality since the inception of Western thought has become a commonplace that is rarely challenged. It is interesting to note that even those scholars who attempt to argue that women were not completely devalued in this tradition do not challenge this exclusion of women from the sphere of rationality. Both Saxonhouse and Slater, for example, argue that women figured prominently in Greek political life but agree that they were excluded from action in the political realm.[11] Saxonhouse in particular notes that Greek women were a respected, even integral, part of Greek life, but that they were not treated as men's equals in the political sphere.

In the course of her discussion, Saxonhouse also makes another point that has become a central theme of feminist scholarship in this area. She argues that it is only with the advent of liberalism that woman's inferior position became fixed through a strict division between the public and private realms.[12] It seems to be the consensus of most feminist writers that the dominance of the "Man of Reason" is most pronounced in the Enlightenment era and, particularly, under the aegis of liberalism. Feminist discussions of the implications of the masculinity of reason as it was defined by the Enlightenment in general and liberalism in particular are varied. It is possible, however, to summarize the principal arguments presented in these discussions by looking at three representative works: Lloyd's *The Man of Reason* (1984), Harding's "Is gender a variable in conceptions of rationality?" (1984), and McMillan's *Women, Reason, and Nature* (1982). Although each of these works discusses the implications of the masculine definition of reason in Enlightenment thought, each comes to a very different conclusion as to the significance of this fact for feminism. An examination of these works thus indicates the nature of the "crisis" that this issue has caused for feminist scholarship.

The central theme of Lloyd's account is her assertion that more is at stake in assessing our ideals of reason than "just" questions of truth. She argues that our conception of reason also informs our conception of personhood and what we identify as a good person.[13] Her argument in this respect reinforces the linguistic argument noted above. Concepts of gender and personhood are inextricably linked in the language that we employ. This language, first, links rationality with what it means to be a good, fully human person and, second, excludes women from that sphere because they are excluded from the realm of rationality. It follows that women can be neither fully rational nor fully human in a moral sense. This is a theme that figures prominently in the feminist indictment of liberalism. Another theme of Lloyd's discussion is the change that occurred in conceptions of reason at the time of the Enlightenment. Focusing on Descartes, Lloyd argues that the legacy of his thought is an association of women with the sensuous realm of the body, men with the non-sensuous realm of reason.[14] The association between women and the realm of the senses is closely related to an issue that has generated an extensive literature among feminists: the association between women and nature. In her discussion Lloyd attributes much of woman's exclusion from the sphere of rationality to this association. Not only are women deemed irrational and hence not fully human, but, because of their association with nature, they are also associated with unknown, dark and mysterious forces.

Lloyd's discussion is insightful and provocative. It convincingly documents how and why women have been excluded from the sphere of rationality and, hence, morality. But it is a curious argument in one sense: it is wholly descriptive. Lloyd does little more than catalogue the exclusion of women from rationality in Western thought. She does not present an argument as to the significance of her revelations, merely noting that the idea that women have their own mode of thought has surfaced in contemporary thought.[15] In a sense Harding's work picks up where Lloyd leaves off by arguing that we must move beyond the errors of masculine thought to a "feminine perspective." Harding wants to identify the errors of the mode of thought that produced the exclusion that Lloyd merely describes. In the history of Western thought, she argues, sex has been considered a variable in the distribution of rationality whereas, in fact, it is gender that is involved.[16] In this she is following what has become one of the central themes of feminist scholarship: the distinction between sex and gender.

Harding moves from this point to argue that the conception of rationality behind the "Man of Reason" is essentially flawed: it is both one-sided and perverse. She thus asserts that there would be little point to an effort to incorporate women into the masculine conception of reason. Harding's argument here is both important and one that has become increasingly common in feminist circles. She is attacking a notion that has been prominent among liberal feminists in both the nineteenth and twentieth centuries: that the liberal/Enlightenment conception of reason could simply be "opened up" to include women. Although liberal feminists do not deny that liberals, along with other Enlightenment thinkers, exclude women from the realm of reason, they do argue that

that definition of reason can and should be changed so as to include women. Harding is arguing that such a move is both futile and self-defeating because the liberal/Enlightenment conception of reason is distorted. Thus it cannot and should not be a conception that we, as feminists, seek to emulate.

In an argument that sounds very Gadamerian, Harding contends that while the masculine mode of knowing – rationality and abstraction – involved distortion, the feminine conception of epistemology involves a hermeneutic mode that does not.[17] This argument is not without its problems. Most importantly it raises questions regarding the validity of a feminist epistemology discussed above. But it is important for two reasons. First, Harding makes it clear that feminists must reject the rationalist epistemology that created the dilemma of the "Man of Reason" in the first place. Second, it is important because the argument has a great deal of affinity with the postmodern critique of rationality. Both identify the problem as Enlightenment rationality itself and reject the possibility of redefining that conception.

By far the most controversial approach to the question of women and the "Man of Reason," however, is that offered by McMillan. Like Harding, McMillan's argument has an affinity with the postmodern critique because she attacks the masculine conception of reason itself and offers an alternative to that conception. Unlike Harding, however, McMillan's argument focuses specifically on the moral connotations of the "Man of Reason." She asserts that the exclusion of feeling, emotion and intuition from the sphere of rationality is at the root of the Enlightenment's misconception of reason. The Enlightenment dichotomy between reason on one hand, feeling and emotion on the other, she claims, involves a fundamental misunderstanding of both reason and morality.[18] Like Gadamer she states that knowledge in general and morality in particular are contextual and relational. Armed with these insights she then goes on to argue that those who assert that women are not rational, which, she notes, even includes some feminists, are wrong because they misunderstand the nature of rationality. Those who exclude women from the realm of rationality are accepting the Enlightenment definition that associates rationality with scientific abstraction and irrationality with feeling and emotion. In a passage that could have been written by Gadamer she states: "It is more to the point, therefore, to show not that women too can excel in scientific activities but that science is not an absolute gauge of what counts as knowledge."[19]

It is at this point in her argument, however, that McMillan's discussion takes a startling turn. She asserts that feminists are alienating women from their "true nature" because they subscribe to the rationalist view that she is rejecting.[20] Because it enjoins women to adopt the masculine definition of reality, McMillan identifies and condemns the women's liberation movement as a rebellion against "nature."[21] She claims that women's realm, the private sphere of the home and childrearing, is just as human and therefore "rational" as the public sphere of men. She concludes that women need not and should not renounce this realm in favor of the male realm of rationality and abstraction. Although she does not go as far as Nietzsche in his assertion that women who engage in science are denying their nature, the implication of her argument is much the same. Like Nietzsche's work, furthermore, McMillan's argument is a curious amalgam of modernist and postmodernist themes that ultimately leads her to a contradiction. Like the postmoderns, McMillan rejects the Enlightenment conception of reason and, specifically, the dichotomy between reason and emotion. But, unlike the postmoderns, she then goes on to accept, even reify, that dichotomy in her attempt to define women's "true nature." Unfortunately for the logic of her argument, she cannot have it both ways. Either the dichotomy itself is flawed and thus cannot be an accurate description of either the masculine or the feminine (the postmodernist move) or it is accurate and describes essential masculine and feminine nature (the modernist move). McMillan's argument fails because she wants to adopt both arguments at once.

Despite its reactionary conclusions, however, McMillan's work illustrates very clearly the difficulties that the critique of the masculine definition of rationality poses for feminist thinking. Lloyd, who limits her critique to a description of women's exclusion from rationality, leaves open the question of the implications of this critique for feminist theory. Harding and McMillan move beyond this analysis to challenge the epistemological basis of the "Man of Reason" but come to radically different conclusions regarding what this critique entails for feminism. What is significant about both of their approaches, however, is the fact that they both assert the existence of a feminine "nature," perspective, or way of knowing. Although the appeal to the essentially feminine is muted in Harding and McMillan's anti-feminist use of the concept is one that most feminists would not find difficult to reject, this commonality between the two accounts is nevertheless noteworthy. It is representative of a strong tendency in contemporary feminist theory to appeal to a universal feminine nature, a feminist epistemology, a distinctive feminine way of knowing, or "maternal thinking." Postmodernism offers a number of convincing arguments as to why such a move in feminist theory is self-defeating. Before moving to a discussion of those arguments, however, it is useful to look again at the history of the methodological debate in the social sciences. The masculine definition of rationality has created problems in the social sciences that offer an instructive parallel to those encountered in feminist theory.

Since the Enlightenment the social sciences have taken great pains to prove their "scientific" status. In terms of the Enlightenment definition of science this means that they must show themselves to be rational, capable of abstract analysis, and able to generate universal laws. Each of these criteria have proved difficult for the social sciences to meet. Social scientific positivists or empiricists, accepting this definition of the scientific, have exerted great effort in the attempt to force the social sciences into this mold. Interpretive or humanist social scientists have taken a different tack. They argue that the social sciences cannot and should not attempt to meet these criteria. The result of their position, however, is that the social sciences must be excluded from the realm of scientificity. Since the scientific, rational realm is also the realm of the masculine, this entails that the social sciences, if they are excluded from this realm, must be declared "feminine."

The dilemma created by this dichotomy and its gendered connotations is particularly evident in the work of one social scientist, Freud, who was especially concerned with a specific aspect of scientific knowledge, its completeness. Freud, who was very anxious to create a *science* of psychoanalysis, was galled by the incompleteness of the knowledge that he acquired in his psychoanalytic studies. In a perceptive feminist examination of Freud's analysis in the Dora case, Toril Moi argues that Freud can define knowledge only as something that is "finished, closed, whole" and, as such, also the basis for the exercise of power.[22] Yet Freud also admits that psychoanalytic technique does not lend itself to complete knowledge; it can only produce knowledge that is fragmentary and incomplete. In a revealing passage he even admits that his knowledge of femininity in particular is "certainly incomplete and fragmentary." Moi puts Freud's dilemma this way: "To admit that there are holes in one's knowledge is tantamount to transforming the penis to a hole, that is to say, to transforming the man into a woman."[23] The conclusion that follows from this is that the social sciences are "feminine" sciences, or, as one commentator put it, psychoanalysis is doing "women's work."[24] This conclusion, unacceptable as it was to Freud, is nevertheless inevitable if we accept the masculine conception of rationality as definitive.

Freud's dilemma, and the dilemma of the social sciences that his work illustrates, is instructive for feminist theory. If the dichotomy between the rational and the irrational is accepted in the social sciences, then these sciences will remain inferior to the natural sciences and excluded from the realm of the scientific and the rational. The same is true for feminist theory. As long as the association between the rational and the masculine, the irrational and the feminine is maintained, the feminine "way of knowing" will be conceptualized as inferior to that of the masculine. Efforts to revalorize this realm are futile unless the dichotomy itself is displaced. It is this conclusion that points to the necessity for the postmodern critique in both the social sciences and feminist theory.

Notes and References

1 D. Spender, *Man Made Language* (Routledge and Kegan Paul, London, 1980), p. 23.
2 B. Fried, "Boys will be boys will be boys," in *Biological Woman*, ed. R. Hubbard, M. Henifin and B. Fried (Schenkman, Cambridge, Mass., 1982), p. 49.
3 E. Beardsley, "Referential genderization," in *Women and Philosophy*, ed. C. Gould and M. Wartofsky (G.P. Putnam, New York, 1976), p. 287.
4 R. Lakoff, *Language and Woman's Place* (Harper and Row, New York, 1975), p. 6.
5 W. Ong, *Interfaces of the Word* (Cornell University Press, Ithaca, N.Y., 1977), p. 1981.
6 W. Ong, *Fighting for Life* (Cornell University Press, Ithaca, N.Y., 1981), p. 135.
7 Ong, *Interfaces of the Word*, p. 29.
8 D. Smith, "A sociology for women," in *The Prism of Sex*, ed. J. Sherman and E. Beck (University of Wisconsin Press, Madison, Wis., 1979), p. 148.
9 L. Irigaray, *Speculum of the Other Woman*, tr. G. Gill (Cornell University Press, Ithaca, N.Y., 1985) p. 279.
10 Ibid., p. 302.
11 A. Saxonhouse, *Women in the History of Political Thought* (Praeger, New York, 1985); P. Slater, *The Glory of Hera* (Beacon Press, Boston, Mass., 1968).
12 Saxonhouse, *Women in the History of Political Thought*, p. 15.
13 G. Lloyd, *The Man of Reason* (University of Minnesota Press, Minneapolis, Minn., 1984), p. ix.
14 G. Lloyd, "Reason, gender and morality in the history of philosophy," *Social Research*, 50 (3) (1983), p. 508.
15 Lloyd, *The Man of Reason*, p. 75.
16 S. Harding, "Is gender a variable in conceptions of rationality?" in *Beyond Domination*, ed. C. Gould (Rowman and Allanheld, Totowa, N.J., 1984), pp. 43–4.
17 Ibid., p. 57.

18 C. McMillan, *Women, Reason, and Nature* (Basil Blackwell, Oxford, 1982), p. 21.
19 Ibid., p. 42.
20 Ibid., p. 153.
21 Ibid., p. 118.
22 T. Moi, "Representation of patriarchy," in *In Dora's Case*, ed. C. Bernheimer and C. Kahane (Columbia University Press, New York, 1985), p. 194.
23 Ibid., p. 197.
24 J. Miller, *Towards a New Psychology of Women* (Beacon Press, Boston, Mass., 1976), p. 26.

6

Radical Philosophies of Sexual Difference: Luce Irigaray

Rosi Braidotti

Luce Irigaray is one of the theorists most passionately interested in difference: differences between the sexes, differences among women, differences within the single individual woman. She adopts as her premise that feminine *jouissance*, that is to say, a specific female representation of the unconscious and of desire, is the non-said of all discourse, and develops a fundamental critique of discourse by trying to inscribe sexual difference in it. Her field of operation is essentially the history of metaphysics, and although her writing style is profoundly literary and very creative, the *corpus* she deals with is the master-texts of Western philosophy.

Irigaray's work can be read as a 'positive' reaction to the crisis of modernity; not only is it inscribed in this 'crisis', but also it may be read as a direct answer to the stance of the modern master-thinkers: Foucault's archaeological/genealogical method, Derrida's metaphysical deconstruction, Deleuze's desiring machines. Irigaray's thought engages in an in-depth dialogue with these theories, responds to them and adapts them to her project of expressing the positivity of sexual difference. As such, her thought stands as one of the most exhaustive and significant examples of reflection from a woman's perspective. As object/subject of her analysis she privileges the master-thinkers of Western ontology, those who have theorized human subjectivity in terms of a transcendental rationality, a rational essence which maintains a close link with the divine.

Considering the difficulty of the texts of the metaphysical tradition, the question of accessibility and of how to read Irigaray's complex and highly elaborate books has been raised; the most clear reply is given by M. Whitford[1] who warns us against reductive readings and takes a stand, especially against the charges of essentialism.

The question of the relation between writing as a space of subjective creation – *pathos* – and thought as a moment of elaboration and critical self-reflection – *logos* – is one of the axes of Irigaray's texts. The coherence of her varied and seemingly heterogeneous *corpus* rests on an effective, imaginary, and conceptual or theoretical bond between literature and philosophy. Irigaray operates on both registers at once, producing texts where theoretical elaboration is accompanied by textual performance. At times she may appear to be in suspension and, in a way, vacillating between the two, yet she never loses her focus.

At the outset, reading Irigaray's texts will pose the question of her place and mode of enunciation: whom is she addressing? For whom is she writing? As I understand it, her work plays on a double register: she affirms the subversive novelty and also the historical reality that is feminism, while keeping open an intense dialogue with the master-thinkers of Western philosophy. Her methodological stance seems to me to pose a crucial question: how can we nourish and develop what is most innovative and subversive in women's thought, while avoiding the classic traps awaiting the feminine: mimetism, dependency, denegation, hysteria, aporia? How can we speak, think and create, within structures that are misogynist and seem to feed off the exclusion and appropriation of the feminine? How can one be a conceptual thinker and not be contaminated by the 'femino-phobic' nature of theoretical thought? How can women repossess and recover the positivity of the feminine? In reply to these crucial issues Irigaray adopts a series of discursive tactics, in a set of discontinuous variations on the theme. In a double movement that combines denunciation and creation, she unveils the masculine character of discourse, while positing a new female feminist subject.

Consequently, one has to learn to read the images that mark Irigaray's texts and maximize their power of inspiration. For instance, challenging the zero-value, value as black hole that psychoanalysis attaches to woman, Irigaray overthrows the metaphorical code by opposing the notion of the 'close-by' to the conceptual void, or the 'nothingness' of the female sex. This 'closeness' or proximity is translated in new images of the woman's body, in the lips of her sex which touch each other, move apart, are each other's double. This image serves to crystallize Luce Irigaray's intuition about *écriture féminine* as sign of an other relation to meaning, and of a profound dislocation of the relationship to alterity.

> One would have to listen with another ear, as if hearing *an 'other meaning' always in the process of weaving itself, of embracing itself with words, but also of getting rid of words in order not to become fixed, congealed in them.* For if 'she' says something, it is not, it is already no longer, identical with what she means. What she says is never identical with anything, moreover; rather, it is contiguous. *It touches (upon).* And when it strays too far from that proximity, she breaks off and starts over at 'zero': her body-sex.[2]

If woman has always been outside the economy of the *logos*, it is because she is in herself an excess, a too much which cannot find its place in traditional discourses, 'whence this mystery she represents, in a culture which claims to enumerate and decipher everything in terms of unity, and to inventory everything in terms of individuality. She is neither one nor two.'[3] It is on feminine multiple, plural *jouissance* that Irigaray bases her revaluation of *écriture féminine*.

Women's coming into writing and, therefore, the expression of a specifically feminine speech in the text, is not a historical given which has already been achieved in the current context; no more is it a guaranteed future triumph, the glorious return of the repressed; but – and this is what seems to me important about Irigaray's articulation of the question – rather, an event which rests on a certain number of preconditions, including, in particular, the development of women's sociopolitical struggles. Textual practice cannot be severed from political practice: together they form the multiple nucleus of the struggles on which the consolidation of the women's movement depends.

The women's movement is for Irigaray the privileged space of elaboration of new discursive practices, which enables the political evolution of feminism. Her position on feminism is much more positive than that of the other *écriture féminine* women; Irigaray is also the only one to have been involved in feminist actions through the 1970s.

In other words, while committing herself to feminist struggles for equality, Irigaray defends the notion of 'difference' in a conditional mode. This means that woman does not yet exist and that she will be unable to come into being without women's collective efforts, which empower and symbolize her specific sexuality, *jouissance*, textual practice, and political vision. Sexual difference as the difference that women make has to be constructed and, for Irigaray, it is the task of the women's movement to set the conditions of possibility for this becoming.

In several of her writings, and most explicitly in *This Sex which is Not One*, Irigaray addresses the question of the relationship between equality and difference. She repeatedly warns women against the fact that emancipation leads to homologation to masculine modes: 'Woman could be *man's equal*. In this case she would enjoy, in a more or less near future, the same economic, social, political rights as men. She would be a potential man.'[4] The political danger of fitting into pre-established masculine canons is one of Irigaray's firmest points of critique of emancipatory feminism. In a recent article, called, appropriately, 'Egales à qui?', Irigaray compares the equality and difference positions on the issue of women's relationship to the divine and the problem of female priesthood. Taking her distance from the work of Mary Daly, Irigaray stresses the fact that, when dealing with issues such as religion and the divine, the revendication of equal rights is simply not enough. What is needed is the symbolic recognition of both sexes' access to the divine, both sexes' notion of the divine. A new symbolic system by and for women is needed and Irigaray proposes the image of the mother/daughter couple as the starting point. Attacking the monosexed image of the Christian God, Irigaray emphasizes the importance for women of defining their own relationship to the divine:

> We need not become 'other' in relation to ourselves. And yet there is a threshold we should be aware of. In my view, it is marked by sexual difference. Within the same sex, what usually rules is quantity. It is a question of leaving behind our comparative state, by perception, by the exercise and expression of our sexuality, our sensibility, and our minds, by living as subjects our relations to our mothers, to the universe, to other women, to other men.[5]

It is important to see, however, that this theory of difference leads Irigaray to provide further theoretical defence of feminism and its stakes; her justification of *écriture féminine* is articulated along with the search for women's unexplored possibilities and potentialities, so that this 'other' which is concealed by the masquerade known as femininity may be revealed. This project is developed in the privileged place that is the women's movement. The premise that women's entry into the cultural order was necessarily accompanied by radical political changes in their status serves to conclude her theory of difference in a defence of feminism as a political movement.

Women's movements, a separatist space, are essential if women are to speak their desires and to shatter the silence about the exploitation they have undergone; it is the theoretical and political building site for forms of expression and multiple struggles:

> What is happening in the women's liberation movement cannot simply be surveyed, described, related 'from the outside'.... I prefer to speak, in

the plural, of women's liberation movements . . . there are multiple groups and tendencies in women's struggles today, and to reduce them to a single movement involves a risk of introducing phenomena of hierarchization, claims of orthodoxy, and so on.[6]

The multiplicity of theoretical and political positions is the source of the very wealth of feminist consciousness. The aim is not to elaborate a single-minded and all-encompassing feminist politics, but rather to bring on the conditions of possibility of in-depth transformations, which themselves stem from the collective political struggle.

When women want to escape from exploitation, they do not merely destroy a few 'prejudices', they disrupt the entire order of dominant values, economic, social, moral and sexual. They call into question all existing theory, all thought, all language, inasmuch as these are monopolized by men and men alone. They challenge *the very foundation of our social and cultural order*, whose organization has been prescribed by the patriarchal system.[7]

Like all modern philosophy, she takes as her point of departure the dispersal of the classical subject into a multiplicity of 'discursive practices'. But although her critique is a party to the massive labour of demolition and cleaning-up of the classical system of representation, her aim is to denounce the implicit link between reason and masculinity. Written in the 'female feminine mode', her approach provides a theoretical basis for the radical transformation that feminism has brought about in our understanding of subjectivity.

That the subject is no longer the privileged link in the formation and legitimation of knowledge, but is, on the contrary, the effect of a system of signification is the idea which, as we have already seen, has inspired the whole structuralist generation. On a certain level, Irigaray is implicated in the post-structuralist condition, but her aim is the deconstruction of phallologocentrism through the affirmation of another symbolic system, based on female feminine specificity. For her, deconstruction only constitutes the most critical and most explicitly feminist stage in her re-reading of the history of Western philosophy: the heart of her work is about creating an alternative system.

The oppression of women is both real and symbolic, that is, it rests as much on material structures of repression as on philosophical presuppositions. Irigaray's discursive tactics aim to restore particularity and sex-specificity to discourse, against its universalizing claims. She sees in sexual in-difference the basis of masculine logic in its entirety, its tendency to reduce everything to the same, to the One:

> This domination of the philosophical logos stems in large part from its
> power to *reduce all others to the economy of the Same*. The teleologically
> constructive project it takes on is always also a project of diversion, de-
> flection, reduction of the other in the Same. . . . Whence the necessity of
> 'reopening' the figures of philosophical discourse – idea, substance, tran-
> scendental subjectivity, absolute knowledge – in order to pry out of them
> what they have borrowed that is feminine, from the feminine, to make
> them 'render up' and give back what they owe the feminine. This may be
> done in various ways, along various 'paths'; moreover, at minimum several
> of these must be pursued.[8]

In other words, the historical phenomenon that is the dissolution of the
classical subject of representation could and should lead us on to unveil
the possibility of a new non-logocentric way of thinking: this is the
philosophy of sexual difference. It is not enough to denounce the
obsessional narcissism of theoretical reason, as does one current in
modern philosophy; it is more a question of making a different discursive space available for the 'female feminine'.

It is this precise objective that orients Irigaray's critique of classical
philosophy. Her reading of Western philosophy rests on two premises:
she retraces the history first of the male sexed subject of knowledge and
second of the primacy according to Reason. The latter is analysed as the
'natural' light which allegedly illuminates all truth, but which for Irigaray
reflects more particularly the male subject's self-image in a mirror-game
of speculation: self-reflection.[9] This specular game essentially functions
at the expense of the woman's body; material body, matrix of being, it
is repudiated and devalued by the self-affirmation of the masculine logos
which uses pure Reason as its pretext.

[. . .]

The blind spot of Western Reason's dream of symmetry, woman as
non-place of Being, lack, absence and indeterminacy, also invests what
are known as the 'natural' sciences. Aristotle's theory of generation, in
which the biological conception of a female sexed being becomes an
accident of nature (since the only 'natural' form of human life is the
male), proves the power of the prejudice thus established at the heart
of the enterprise of philosophy.

Assumptions, yet they weighed heavily on the destiny of women, for
it was not until the twentieth century that they were 'scientifically' re-
futed. Irigaray emphasizes the consequences of this misogyny, and the
links between the 'blind spot' and the privilege philosophy accords to
pure luminous rationality. Reducing this universalizing claim to the most

specific of its prejudices, taking as her essential point of departure the Cartesian cogito, she retraces the development of the modern forms of phallocentrism.

Descartes's point of departure was irrefutable, namely that the relation between subject and predicate leaves no room for indeterminacy. In this correspondence theory of truth, the copula becomes the indubitable sign of the identity of subject and predicate, and the guarantee of a 'universal nature' inherent in individual propositions, which thus enables the rational to be assimilated to the real. Irigaray emphasizes that this correspondence relation between subject and predicate, which is the basis of the legitimation of the subject, corresponds to the subject's separation from matter.

> If there is no more earth to press down/repress, to work, to represent, but also and always to desire (for one's own), no opaque matter which in theory does not know herself, then what pedestal remains for the existence of the 'subject'?[10]

The Cartesian subject is transcendental – what he transcends is, precisely, his material basis, and he expels matter-earth. But at the time of Descartes – and this is what distinguishes him from his predecessors – the idea that the subject is necessarily the site of Being and Knowledge had become so essential to the order of discourse that it was indispensable to the Cartesian validation of the universal.

In a fundamental reversal, the singular authority represented by the Cartesian subject then turns into the way of attesting the (existence of the) universal. Not only does the Cartesian subject present himself as privileged moment of discourse, but also he passes himself off as the foundation of his own condition of being.

And so the Cartesian method traces an intellectual route which passes beyond doubt, beyond all possible speculation by the Other, or others. The cogito, which, precisely by doubting its universal knowledge, legitimates itself, is careful not to presuppose that some other being could also doubt:

> Representation here is auto-effective, auto-effecting solipsism. It embroiders its dream of potentiality alone in its chamber, indifferent, at least for a while, to the rest of (its) history that is still being woven. All alone, with an ever cautious *negativism*, it cuts up and rewords the *subject's links to his archives*. And *to his process/trial of engendering*. Once upon a time, something related to genesis and becoming used also to appear and even to precede the specific predicates attributed to the substance, the subjectum. But now, by a stroke of almost incredible boldness, it is the

singular subject who is charged with giving birth to the universe all over again, after he has brought himself back into the world in a way that avoids the precariousness of existence as it is usually understood. Once *the chain of relationships, the cord*, has been *severed*, together with ancestry and the mysteries of conception, then there is nothing left but the subject who can go back and sever them all over again whenever he likes. In a speculative act of denial and negation that serves to affirm his autonomy. By means of a verb (to think) that, as if by chance – or is it necessity? – can do without an object if need be, can also be predicated as an absolute, though at a price of some austerity, some effort of will. Speculation is 'pure', and as intransitive in its process as 'to live' or 'to be'.[11]

The universalizing claim of this solipsism partly derives from the process of self-affectation of the subject, his 'dream of potentiality alone in [his] chamber', but is constantly confirmed by his denigration of corporeal being.

The cogito's characteristic is to determine itself as here and now, and to put all into doubt, except for its own thought processes. The 'thinking tissue' being very significantly constituted by the other, all thought is reflected thanks to a screen; for Western thought, the privileged specular place is the woman's body: 'that all-powerful mirror denied and neglected in the self-sufficiency of the (self) thinking subject, her "body" henceforward specularized through and through'.[12]

Wholly reflected by the looking glass of the female body, the thinking subject no longer sees his mirror; nor does he see that his thought, all thought, rests on a fiction, this illusion of himself as a totality. Where does the cogito draw its absolute certainty from? From the fact that it confers existence on itself, purified of all sensory or passionate confusions. Alone at last, 'I' think, therefore 'I' *have* being: 'Therefore I am. Alone at last, the copula. I–me together in an embrace that begins over and over again.'[13]

This is a solipsistic dream which is played out at the expense of the woman's body, matter, and the corporeal roots of the human intellect. 'The "I" thinks, therefore this thing, this body that is also nature, that is still the *mother*, becomes an extension at the "I" 's disposal for analytical investigations, scientific projections, the regulated exercise of the imaginary, the utilitarian practice of technique.'[14]

God himself is not an infinite Being for the 'I' has accorded him this essence and his existence, according to the order of Reason. 'Speculative' philosophy is characterized by its desire to impose itself on matter and therefore on woman as creative principle: the supremacy of the intelligible over the sensory, idea over body. And although philosophical thought depends on the male sexed body, the male embodied subject is precisely that great non-said of Western philosophy.

Using psychoanalysis to dislocate philosophy's discourse of truth, Irigaray adopts a double strategy: according to a process of mimesis, she accepts the materiality which defines woman; but when she asks 'But what if this matter began to speak?', she radically subverts the specular relation which allows discursive production to feed symbolically and materially on the female body.

Reduced to unconsciousness (that is, to the negative of masculine consciousness), to the matter which upholds the masculine system of representation, woman incarnates the oblivion whence flows the forgetting of all matter, which alone makes possible the solipsistic dream of the philosophical subject. As soon as woman-matter begins to speak, the whole edifice of Western Reason begins to crumble.

> The 'masculine' is not prepared to share the initiative of discourse. It prefers to experiment with speaking, writing, enjoying 'woman' rather than leaving to that other any right to intervene, to 'act' in her own interests. What remains the most completely prohibited to woman, of course, is that she should express something of her own sexual pleasure. This latter is supposed to remain a 'realm' of discourse, produced by men. For in fact feminine pleasure signifies the greatest threat of all to masculine discourse, represents its most irreducible 'exteriority', or 'exterritoriality'.[15]

Notes and References

1 M. Whitford, 'Luce Irigaray and the female imaginary: speaking as a woman', *Radical Philosophy*, 43 (1986), pp. 3–8.
2 L. Irigaray, *This Sex Which is Not One* (Cornell University Press, Ithaca, N.Y., 1985), p. 29.
3 Ibid., p. 26.
4 Ibid., p. 84.
5 L. Irigaray, 'Equal to whom?', *Differences*, 1 (2) (1989), pp. 59–76.
6 Irigaray, *This Sex Which is Not One*, p. 164.
7 Ibid., p. 165.
8 Ibid., p. 74.
9 L. Irigaray, *Speculum of the Other Women* (Cornell University Press, Ithaca, N. Y., 1985), p. 148.
10 Ibid., p. 133.
11 Ibid., pp. 181–2.
12 Ibid., p. 183.
13 Ibid., pp. 189–90.
14 Ibid., p. 186.
15 Irigaray, *This Sex Which is Not One*, p. 157.

James Joyce between *Eros* and *Agape*

Julia Kristeva

Joyce's Catholicism, his profound experience of trinitary religion to the point of derision, confronted him with its centre, the eucharist, the rite *par excellence* of identification with the body of God, the fulcrum of all other identifications, including the artistic profusion of imagination favoured by Catholicism. This Catholic cultural context, intensely assimilated by Joyce, probably encountered a mechanism which is, moreover, the drive behind his fictional experiment, and allowed him to concentrate his efforts at representation and elucidation upon the identificatory substratum of psychic operation, placed so authoritatively at the centre of the last of the religions.

Quite emphatically, the many different ways in which Joyce – *the grace hoper* – insists on transsubstantiation or on the heresy of Arius, as well as on the consubstantiality of the father and the son in *Hamlet*, but also between Shakespeare, his father, his son Hamnet and the whole body of the playwright's work, as a real filiation, are the finest expression of the Joycian obsession, via the theme of the eucharist.

More indirectly, the orality of Bloom, avid consumer of livers, gizzards and other animal entrails; the vertiginous assimilation of knowledge by Mulligan or Stephen; the meal that constitutes the scene for the finally real encounter between Stephen and Bloom, leaving the way open for exchange, which extends to their sexual exchange of women; but also the assimilation by the narrator of the character of Molly, whose final monologue, more strikingly than any other use of the mask of a character by an author, indicates the displacement and realization, in the narrative themes as well as the very dynamic of the fiction, of the *topos* of identification.

In any case, it is probably in the two variants of amorous experience as they are illustrated by Stephen Dedalus and Leopold Bloom – in

Stephen's *Agape* and Bloom's *Eros* – that I would see the most perti-
nent and, analytically, the most *successful* attempt that Joyce undertook
in order to explain the identificatory movement specific to artistic existence. We should say immediately that, if the exposure of intra-psychic
identification in a literary text may be interpreted as a 'return of the
repressed' (we repress the processes which have governed the constitution of our psychic space, and it is only by means of a liberation of
repression or a modification of the barrier of repression that this repressed can manifest itself) and if, in this respect, the massive presence
of identificatory narrative themes or processes may be considered as a
symptom, then it is surely a proliferating, unstable and problematic
identification which is the symptom *par excellence* of the act of writing,
as described by Mallarmé.

But Joyce knows this, with a knowledge that is perhaps unconscious,
or at any rate with a knowledge illuminated by theological science, and
consequently he turns the symptom around, pours it out and claims its
profound logic as a necessary part of our everyday lives.

We need multiple, plastic, polymorphous and polyphonic identifications and, if the eucharist has lost the overarching power which gave us
the opportunity to have them, then two possibilities at least remain
open to us: let us read literature on the one hand, and attempt to
reinvent love on the other. Amorous experience and artistic experience,
as two interdependent aspects of the identificatory process, are our only
means of preserving our psychic space as a 'living system', that is, open
to the other, capable of adaptation and change. Such an integration of
polymorphism or perversion is inseparable from a practice of language
that is not restricted to calculation, however vertiginous, of pure signifiers,
but which integrates pre- or transverbal representations, embracing a
vast *semiotic* range which extends from gesture to colours and sounds,
and turns the use of language not into a logical exercise but into a ritual
theatre, a carnivalized liturgy.

Does this mean that this closeness to psychosis (in the manipulation
of words as if they were things), broached by an identificatory
polymorphousness of such extraordinary perversity, is due to one ultimate identification with an archaic mother, the supreme authority in
which the identity of the constantly defiant narrator takes refuge, and,
persistently, the law of paternal identity, the guarantee of all normative
identity? C.G. Jung seems to believe so when he asserts that Joyce
'knows the female soul, as if he were the devil's grandmother'. But it is
a strange grandmother who takes on the ways of a sensual Jew, and
whose phallic *jouissance*, not unfamiliar with real decantings into female bodies (e.g. Bloom's masturbation while facing Gertie), is still

finally inspired by the dominant power of the text and the sacred imposition of the proper name.

Or on the other hand is Joyce perhaps a 'holy man' who has turned the perverse symptom of identification with the woman inside out, like a glove, and brought out, in place of castration, the projection of style – as Lacan has it?

I would say instead that Joyce succeeds where Orpheus fails. Does his adventure not reveal the modern, post-Christian version of the Greek myth in which the hero-artist is forbidden to see something, to seek Eurydice in hell, to return to the mystery of femininity? For as we know, if he does so he loses his loved one, and this impossible love is paid for by a sacrifice (he is torn to pieces by the maenads) but also by an immortality (he lives on, scattered in his songs). On the contrary, Dedalus–Bloom does not divert his gaze from the infernal night that swallows Eurydice, but still does not disappear himself. Any more than Joyce, in spite of the difficulties of his existence, sacrificed his social being to the myth of *l'art maudit*, but rather ironically guided his boat between patrons and female guardians of literature. Only, and tragically, the madness of Lucia perhaps testifies to the ludic metamorphoses of a father who will not stay fixed in one place.

But the Joveian odyssey towards the fatherland of the work does not, on the other hand, release him from the task of returning to the invisible secret of femininity which Freud described as the inaccessible part of the personality in both sexes. The narrator watches her, his Eurydice–Molly, insolent, aggressive and obscene (we might consider, in counterpoint to this, the scatological letters between Joyce and Nora) and, without a hint of fear, he draws her from the inferno of passion . . . into his monologue-song.

People have mistakenly sought, in this ending of *Ulysses*, an acknowledgement or, on the other hand, a censure of female sexuality. It is more a matter of the male artist, gorged with an ultimate appropriation-identification, giving us back a Bacchante . . . swallowed by Orpheus. And it is then that Dedalus–Bloom fulfils the plenitude of his body-text, that he can finally leave us his text as if it were his body, his trans-substantiation. 'This is my body', the narrator seems to say, the narrator whose identifications with HCE will be remembered from *Finnegans Wake*. And the reader, this time like the maenads, assimilates through the signs of the text the real presence of a complex masculine sexuality. Entirely without repression.

Something that is doubtless the condition of an enigmatic *sublimation*: the text bars but does not repress the libido, and has its cathartic effect upon the reader. But this spiriting away of repression doubtless explains the horror, the embarrassment, the bewitchment and, crucially, the surrender of the reader. Everything is visible, and all positions are there to be taken. *Nothing is missing*; there is nothing hidden that could be actually present. Thus it is that the inferno of passion, diabolical femininity, is reabsorbed into the themes of representation as well as language, to become comedy or derision. The personal secret may remain within such an economy, but not the reserve of feelings that feeds psychological life: it is reabsorbed by the ubiquity of a greedy and unstoppable identificatory process.

The father lives so that the son may live, the son dies so that the father may be incarnated in his work and become his own son. In this truly Dedalian labyrinth, *cherchez la femme*. The Christian *agape* of transsubstantiation was opposed to the Greek *Eros* which, before being sublimated in the mystical quest for the good and the beautiful in the words of Diotima in Plato's *Symposium*, or in the second part of the *Phaedrus*, was announced in the Greek philosopher as a violent, sado-masochistic and, *in extremis,* murderous psychodrama, between the lover and the loved one whom Plato had no hesitation in describing as a wolf and a lamb.

In fact, the amorous swallowing of the father which concludes the act of identification should not conceal the violence of *underlying aggressiveness*. An aggressiveness against him, or rather against his body, in as much as he *is* the body and bears the memory of the body of the mother, that is, of an outer body, which arises from the period of archaic symbiosis between the ego and its narcissistic attributes. By imagining the decay, or simply the sexuality – weakness, *jouissance*, sin – of the *paternal* body, I rid myself of my dependence on the *maternal* body. Moreover, this act of imagination-transposition turns my own neotenic weakness . . . into the fate of another: it is not I but he who is the passionate invalid, the sacrificial victim. . . .

However, in the fantasm, and within the movement of identification-idealization with the father, it is the mother who receives the lightning bolts of rejection, at least for a while, from anyone, and finally from the perverse. In the end, identification, as a *heterogeneous transference* (body into meaning, mystical metaphor–metamorphosis), instead of the father, initially places me within the improbable and the uncertain: in *meaning*. But it is by separating myself from the *amor matris* (genitive subjective and objective) that I enter the legal fiction that constitutes my identity as a subject. In any case, this infinite erotic separation is the matrix of my eroticism – a constant double for my agapeian identifications.

Stephen's eroticism is cunningly mobilized around his mother, for whose death he is keen to believe himself responsible (who kills a mother: her son or cancer?). In any case, Stephen's malevolent passion is addressed to her: 'The corpsechewer! Raw head and bloody bones!'

Is Joyce sick? Or esoteric? Or postmodern? A host of questions present themselves, however non-normative we try and make our reading. I shall answer personally that his symptom and his obscurity, even in their most abstruse Dedalian puzzles, pose the crucial question of postmodernism: identification, representation. Without eliminating them as the vertiginous acceleration of *Finnegans Wake* will do, or the later poetic avant-garde, *Ulysses* confronts us with the very space in which an unstable image coagulates, for psychical linguistic and translinguistic experience, ready to turn into flesh *and* into meaninglessness. The themes of *Ulysses* are a perfect illustration of this incandescence of imaginary space which, because of its two-dimensionality – body and meaning – because of this transcorporeality, rivals the place of the sacred. Was this not Joyce's final ambition, which so much 'literature' makes us forget?

This practice of writing in Joyce – an extraordinary modern attempt to secularize transsubstantiation, with its joys and its deadly dangers – raises an important question for the analytic cure, which confronts problematic identifications (but is there any other kind?). In order to refer the subject to *one* identity, the analytic process perhaps assures him of a certain symbolic stability, but it must use the decisive and polymorphous qualities of the analyst's discourse, to avoid drying up the fluidity of the subject's imagination. And, finally, should the somewhat depressive disillusion that comes at the end of analysis not also take account of the real, however unattainable, as the ultimate motive for identification?

The lost father of the individual prehistory, a real body conditions my *jouissance* as a speaking being and, while making my analysis interminable, conditions my identificatory surges which simply ensure the act of living.

8

Feminism and the Question of Postmodernism

Seyla Benhabib

In her recently published book, *Thinking Fragments: Psychoanalysis, Feminism and Postmodernism in the Contemporary West*, Jane Flax characterizes the postmodern position as subscription to the theses of the Death of Man, of History and of Metaphysics.

The Death of Man. "Postmodernists wish to destroy," she writes, "all essentialist conceptions of human being or nature. . . . In fact Man is a social, historical or linguistic artifact, not a noumenal or transcendental Being. . . . Man is forever caught in the web of fictive meaning, in chains of signification, in which the subject is merely another position in language."[1]

The Death of History. "The idea that History exists for or is his Being is more than just another precondition and justification for the fiction of Man. This idea also supports and underlies the concept of Progress, which is itself such an important part of Man's story. . . . Such an idea of Man and History privileges and presupposes the value of unity, homegeneity, totality, closure and identity."[2]

The Death of Metaphysics. According to postmodernists, "Western metaphysics has been under the spell of the 'metaphysics of presence' at least since Plato. . . . For postmodernists this quest for the Real conceals most Western philosophers' desire, which is to master the world once and for all by enclosing it within an illusory but absolute system they believe represents or corresponds to a unitary Being beyond history, particularity and change. . . . Just as the Real is the ground of Truth, so too philosophy as the privileged representative of the Real and interrogator of truth claims must play a 'foundational' role in all 'positive knowledge.' "[3]

Flax's clear and cogent characterization of the postmodernist position will enable us to see why feminists find in this critique of the ideals of Western rationalism and the Enlightenment more than a congenial ally. But let me also note certain important discrepancies between my own formulation of the conceptual options made possible by the end of the classical episteme of representation and Flax's version of postmodernism. First, whereas in the course of the transition from "nineteenth century idealism to twentieth century contextualism" (R. Rorty),[4] I see a move toward the radical situatedness and contextualization of the subject, Flax follows the French tradition in stipulating the "death of the subject." Second, whereas I see a transformation in the object as well the medium of epistemological representation from consciousness to language, from claims about truth and reality to a more limited investigation of the conditions under which a community of inquirers can make warranted assertions about truth and the real, Flax maintains that "philosophy as the privileged representative of the Real" has not been transformed but has died off. As for the thesis of the Death of History, I shall argue below that, of all the claims associated with postmodernist positions, this one is the least problematical. Critical theorists as well as postmodernists, liberals as well as communitarians, could agree upon some version of the thesis of the "death of history," in the sense of a teleologically determined progression of historical transformations; but the controversial questions concern the relation of historical narrative to the interests of present actors in their historical past. These discrepancies between Flax's formulations and my own as to how to characterize the epistemic options of the present will play a larger role as the argument progresses.

Consider for the time being how, like postmodernism, feminist theory as well has created its own versions of the three theses concerning the Death of Man, History and Metaphysics.

The feminist counterpoint to the postmodernist theme of the Death of Man can be named the "Demystification of the Male Subject of Reason." Whereas postmodernists substitute for Man, or the sovereign subject of the theoretical and practical reason of the tradition, the study of contingent, historically changing and culturally variable social, linguistic and discursive practices, feminists claim that "gender" and the various practices contributing to its constitution are one of the most crucial contexts in which to situate the purportedly neutral and universal subject of reason. The Western philosophical tradition articulates the deep structures of the experiences and consciousness of a self which it claims to be representative for humans as such. The deepest categories of Western philosophy obliterate differences of gender as these shape and structure the experience and subjectivity of the self. Western reason posits itself as the discourse of the one self-identical subject, thereby blinding us to and in fact delegitimizing the presence of otherness and difference which do not fit into its categories. From Plato over Descartes to Kant and Hegel Western philosophy thematizes the story of the male subject of reason.

The feminist counterpoint to the Death of History would be the "Engendering of Historical Narrative." If the subject of the Western intellectual tradition has usually been the white, propertied, Christian, male head of household, then History as hitherto recorded and narrated has been "his story." Furthermore, the various philosophies of history which have dominated since the Enlightenment have forced historical narrative into unity, homogeneity and linearity with the consequence that fragmentation, heterogeneity and above all the varying pace of different temporalities as experienced by different groups have been obliterated. We need only remember Hegel's belief that Africa has no history. Until very recently neither did women have their own history, their own narrative with different categories of periodization and with different structural regularities.

The feminist counterpoint to the Death of Metaphysics would be "Feminist Skepticism Toward the Claims of Transcendent Reason." If the subject of reason is not a suprahistorical and context-transcendent being, but the theoretical and practical creations and activities of this subject bear in every instance the marks of the context out of which they emerge, then the subject of philosophy is inevitably embroiled with knowledge-governing interests which mark and direct its activities. For feminist theory, the most important "knowledge-guiding interest" in Habermas's terms, or disciplinary matrix of truth and power in Foucault's terms, are gender relations and the social, economic, political and symbolic constitution of gender differences among human beings.

Despite this "elective affinity" between feminism and postmodernism, each of the three theses enumerated above can be interpreted to permit if not contradictory then at least radically divergent theoretical strategies. And for feminists which set of theoretical claims they adopt as their own cannot be a matter of indifference. As Linda Alcoff has recently observed, feminist theory is undergoing a profound identity crisis at the moment.[5] The postmodernist position(s) thought through to their conclusions may not only eliminate the specificity of feminist theory but place in question the very emancipatory ideals of the women's movements altogether.

I will now formulate two versions of the three theses enumerated above with the goal of clarifying once more the various conceptual options made available with the demise of the episteme of representations. Put in a nutshell, my argument is that strong and weak versions of the theses of the Death of Man, of History and of Metaphysics are possible. Whereas the weak versions of these theses entail premises around which critical theorists as well as postmodernists and possibly even liberals and communitarians can unite, their strong versions undermine the possibility of normative criticism at large. Feminist theory can ally itself with this strong version of postmodernism only at the risk of incoherence and self-contradictoriness.

1   Let us begin by considering the thesis of the Death of Man for a closer understanding of the conceptual option(s) allowed by the end of the episteme of representation. The weak version of this thesis would *situate* the subject in the context of various social, linguistic and discursive practices. This view would by no means question the desirability and theoretical necessity of articulating a more adequate, less deluded and less mystified vision of subjectivity than those provided by the concepts of the Cartesian cogito, the "transcendental unity of apperception," "Geist and consciousness," or "das Man" (the they). The traditional attributes of the philosophical subject of the West, like self-reflexivity, the capacity for acting on principles, rational accountability for one's actions and the ability to project a life-plan into the future, in short, some form of autonomy and rationality, could then be reformulated by taking account of the radical situatedness of the subject.

The strong version of the thesis of the Death of Man is perhaps best captured in Flax's own phrase that "Man is forever caught in the web of fictive meaning, in chains of signification, *in which the subject is merely another position in language.*" The subject thus dissolves into the chain of significations of which it was supposed to be the initiator. Along with this dissolution of the subject into yet "another position in language" disappear of course concepts of intentionality, accountability, self-reflexivity and autonomy. The subject that is but another position in language can no longer master and create that distance between itself and the chain of significations in which it is immersed such that it can reflect upon them and creatively alter them.

The strong version of the Death of the Subject thesis is not compatible with the goals of feminism. Surely, a subjectivity that would not be structured by language, by narrative and by the symbolic codes of narrative available in a culture is unthinkable. We tell of who we are, of the "I" that we are, by means of a narrative. "I was born on such and such a date, as the daughter of such and such . . ." etc. These narratives are deeply colored and structured by the codes of expectable and understandable biographies and identities in our cultures. We can concede all that, but nevertheless we must still argue that we are not merely extensions of our histories, that *vis-à-vis* our own stories we are in the position of author and character at once. The situated and gendered subject is heteronomously determined but still strives toward autonomy. I want to ask how in fact the very project of female emancipation would be thinkable without such a regulative ideal of enhancing the agency, autonomy and selfhood of women.

Feminist appropriations of Nietzsche on this question can only be incoherent. In her recent book, *Gender Trouble: Feminism and the Subversion of Identity*, Judith Butler wants to extend the limits of reflexivity in thinking about the self beyond the dichotomy of "sex" and "gender." Her convincing and original arguments rejecting this dichotomous reasoning within which feminist theory has operated until recently get clouded, however, by the claim that to reject this dichotomy would mean subscribing to the view that the "gendered self" does not exist; all that the self is, is a series of performances. "Gender," writes Butler, "is not to culture as sex is to nature; gender is also the discursive/cultural means by which 'sexed nature' or a 'natural sex' is produced and established as 'prediscursive,' prior to culture, a politically neutral surface *on which* culture acts."[6] For Butler the myth of the already sexed body is the epistemological equivalent of the myth of the given: just as the given can only be identified within a discursive framework, so too it is the culturally available codes of gender that "sexualize" a body and that construct the directionality of that body's sexual desire.

But Butler also maintains that to think beyond the univocality and dualisms of gender categories, we must bid farewell to the "doer behind the deed," to the self as the subject of a life-narrative. "In an application that Nietzsche himself would not have anticipated or condoned, we might state as a corollary: There is no gender identity behind the expressions of gender; that identity is performatively constituted by the very 'expressions' that are said to be its results."[7] Yet if this view of the self is adopted, is there any possibility of transforming those "expressions" which constitute us? If we are no more than the sum total of the gendered expressions we perform, is there ever any chance to stop the performance for a while, to pull the curtain down, and only let it rise if one can have a say in the production of the play itself? Isn't this what the struggle over gender is all about? Surely we can criticize the "metaphysical presuppositions of identity politics" and challenge the supremacy of heterosexist positions in the women's movement. Yet is such a challenge only thinkable via a complete debunking of any concepts of selfhood, agency and autonomy? What follows from this Nietzschean position is a vision of the self as a masquerading performer, except of course we are now asked to believe that there is no self behind the mask. Given how fragile and tenuous women's sense of selfhood is in many cases, how much of a hit-and-miss affair their struggles for autonomy are, this reduction of female agency to a "doing without the doer" at best appears to me to be making a virtue out of necessity.

The view that gendered identity is constituted by "deeds without the doer," or by performances without a subject, not only undermines the normative vision of feminist politics and theory. It is also impossible to get rid of the subject altogether and claim to be a fully accountable participant in the community of discourse and inquiry: the strong thesis of the death of the subject undermines the discourse of the theorist herself. If the subject who produces discourse is but a product of the discourse it has created, or better still is but "another position in language," then the responsibility for this discourse cannot be attributed to the author but must be attributable to some fictive "authorial position," constituted by the intersection of "discursive planes." (I am tempted to add that in geometry the intersection of planes produces a line!) Butler entertains this possibility in the introduction to her work: "Philosophy is the predominant disciplinary mechanism that currently mobilizes this author-subject."[8] The "subject" here means also the "object of the discourse"; not the one who utilizes the discourse but the one who is utilized by the discourse itself. Presumably that is why Butler uses the language of "a discourse mobilizing an author/subject." The center of motility is not the thinking, acting and feeling self but "discourses," "systems of signification," "chains of signs," etc. But how then should we read *Gender Trouble*?

The kind of reading I am engaging here presupposes that there is a thinking author who has produced this text, who has intentions, purposes and goals in communicating with me; that the task of theoretical reflection begins with the attempt to understand what the author meant. Certainly, language always says much more than what the author means; there will always be a discrepancy between what we mean and what we say; but we engage in communication, theoretical no less than everyday communication, to gain some basis of mutual understanding and reasoning. The view that the subject is not reducible to "yet another position in language," but that no matter how constituted by language the subject retains a certain autonomy and ability to rearrange the significations of language, is a regulative principle of all communication and social action. Not only feminist politics, but also coherent theorizing becomes impossible if the speaking and thinking self is replaced by "authorial positions," and if the self becomes a ventriloquist for discourses operating through her or "mobilizing" her.

Perhaps I have overstated the case against Butler. Perhaps Butler does not want, any more than Flax herself, to dispense with women's sense of selfhood, agency and autonomy. In the concluding reflections to *Gender Trouble* Butler returns to questions of agency, identity and politics. She writes:

> The question of locating "agency" is usually associated with the viability of the "subject," where the subject is understood to have some stable existence prior to the cultural field that it negotiated. Or, if the subject is culturally constructed, it is nevertheless vested with an agency, usually figured as the capacity for reflexive mediation, that remains intact regardless of its cultural embeddedness. On such a model, "culture" and "discourse" *mire* the subject, but do not constitute that subject. This move to qualify and to enmire the preexisting subject has appeared necessary to establish a point of agency that is not fully *determined* by that culture and discourse. And yet, this kind of reasoning falsely presumes (a) agency can only be established through recourse to a prediscursive "I," even if that "I" is found in the midst of a discursive convergence, and (b) that to be *constituted* by discourse is to be *determined* by discourse, where determination forecloses the possibility of agency.[9]

Butler rejects that identity can only be established through recourse to an " 'I' that preexists signification."[10] She points out that "the enabling conditions for an assertion of 'I' are provided by the structure of signification, the rules that regulate the legitimate and illegitimate invocation of that pronoun, the practices that establish the terms of intelligibility by which that pronoun can circulate." The narrative codes of a culture then define the content with which this pronoun will be invested, the appropriate instances when it can be invoked, by whom and how. Yet one can agree with all that and still maintain that no individual is merely a blank slate upon whom are inscribed the codes of a culture, a kind of Lockean tabula rasa in latter-day Foucaultian garb! The historical and cultural study of diverse codes of the constitution of subjectivity, or the historical study of the formation of the individual, does not answer the question: what mechanisms and dynamics are involved in the developmental process through which the human infant, a vulnerable and dependent body, becomes a distinct self with the ability to speak its language and the ability to participate in the complex social processes which define its world? Such dynamics and mechanisms enabled the children of the ancient Egyptians to become members of that cultural community no less than they enabled Hopi children to become social individuals. The study of culturally diverse codes which define individuality is not the same as an answer to the question as to *how* the human infant becomes the social self, regardless of the cultural and normative content which defines selfhood. In the latter case we are studying *structural processes and dynamics of socialization and individuation*; in the former, historical processes of signification and meaning constitution. Indeed, as Butler observes, "to be constituted by discourse is not to be determined by discourse." We have to explain how a human infant can become the speaker of an infinitely meaningful number of sentences in a given natural language, how it acquires, that is, the competence to become a linguistic being; furthermore, we have to explain how every human infant can become the initiator of a unique life-story, of a meaningful tale – which certainly is only meaningful if we know the cultural codes under which it is constructed – but which we cannot predict even if we knew these cultural codes.

Butler writes "that 'agency' then is to be located within the possibility of a variation on that repetition" (the repetition of gender performances).[11] But where are the resources for that variation derived from? What is it that enables the self to "vary" the gender codes? to resist hegemonic discourses? What psychic, intellectual or other sources of creativity and resistance must we attribute to subjects for such variation to be possible?

The answers to these questions, even if they were fully available to me at this point, which they are not, would go beyond the boundaries of this analysis. Yet we have reached an important conclusion: the issues generated by the complex interaction between feminism and postmodernism around concepts of the self and subjectivity cannot be captured by bombastic proclamations of the "Death of the Subject." The central question is how we must understand the phrase: "the I although constituted by discourse is not determined by it." To embark upon a meaningful answer to this query from where we stand today involves not yet another decoding of metaphors and tropes about the self, but a serious interchange between philosophy and the social sciences like sociolinguistics, social interactionist psychology, socialization theory, psychoanalysis and cultural history among others. To put it bluntly: the thesis of the Death of the Subject presupposes a remarkably crude version of individuation and socialization processes when compared with currently available social science reflections on the subject. But neither the fundamentalist models of inquiry of the tradition, which privilege the reflective I reflecting upon the conditions of its reflexive or non-reflexive existence, nor the postmodernist decoding of the subject into bodily surfaces "that are enacted *as* the natural, so [that] these surfaces can become the site of a dissonant and denaturalized performance" (Butler) will suffice in the task of explaining how the individual can be "constituted by discourse and yet not be determined by it." The analysis of gender once more forces the boundaries of disciplinary discourses toward a new integration of theoretical paradigms.

2   Consider now the thesis of the Death of History. Of all positions normally associated with postmodernism this particular one appears to me to be the least problematical. Disillusionment with the ideals of progress, awareness of the atrocities committed in this century in the name of technological and economic progress, the political and moral bankruptcy of the natural sciences which put themselves in the service of the forces of human and planetary destruction – these are the shared sentiments of our century. Intellectuals and philosophers in the twentieth century are to be distinguished from one another less as being friends and opponents of the belief in progress but more in terms of the following: whether the farewell from the "metanarratives of the Enlightenment" can be exercised in terms of a continuing belief in the power of rational reflection or whether this farewell is but a prelude to a departure from such reflection.

Interpreted as a *weak* thesis, the Death of History could mean two things: theoretically, this could be understood as a call to end the practice of "grand narratives" which are essentialist and monocausal. It is futile, let us say, to search for an essence of "motherhood," as a cross-cultural universal; just as it is futile to seek to produce a single grand theory of female oppression and male dominance across cultures and societies – be such a theory psychoanalytic, anthropological or biological. Politically, the end of such grand narratives would mean rejecting the hegemonial claims of any group or organization to "represent" the forces of history, to be moving with such forces, or to be acting in their name. The critique of the various totalitarian and totalizing movements of our century from National Socialism and Fascism to Stalinism and other forms of authoritarianism is certainly one of the most formative political experiences of postmodernist intellectuals like Lyotard, Foucault and Derrida. This is also what makes the Death of History thesis interpreted as the end of "grand narratives" so attractive to feminist theorists. Nancy Fraser and Linda Nicholson write for example:

the practice of feminist politics in the 1980s has generated a new set of pressures which have worked against metanarratives. In recent years, poor and working-class women, women of color, and lesbians have finally won a wider hearing for their objections to feminist theories which fail to illuminate their lives and address their problems. They have exposed the earlier quasi-metanarratives, with their assumptions of universal female dependence and confinement to the domestic sphere, as false extrapolations from the experience of the white, middle-class, heterosexual women who dominated the beginnings of the second wave. . . . Thus, as the class, sexual, racial and ethnic awareness of the movement has altered, so has the preferred conception of theory. It has become clear that quasi-metanarratives hamper rather than promote sisterhood, since they elide differences among women and among the forms of sexism to which different women are differentially subject.[12]

The *strong* version of the thesis of the Death of History would imply, however, a prima facie rejection of any historical narrative that concerns itself with the long durée and that focuses on macro- rather than on micro-social practices. Nicholson and Fraser also warn against this "nominalist" tendency in Lyotard's work.[13] I agree with them that it would be a mistake to interpret the death of "grand narratives" as sanctioning in the future local stories as opposed to global history. The decision as to how local or global a historical narrative or piece of social science research need be cannot be determined by epistemological arguments extraneous to the task at hand. It is the empirical researcher who should answer this question; the philosopher has no business legislating the scope of research to the empirical scientist. To the extent that Lyotard's version of postmodernism seems to sanctify the "small" or "local narrative" over the grand one, he engages in unnecessary apriorism with regard to open-ended questions of scientific inquiry.

The more difficult question suggested by the strong thesis of the Death of History appears to me to be different: even while we dispense with grand narratives, how can we rethink the relationship between politics, historiography and historical memory? Is it possible for struggling groups not to interpret history in light of a moral–political imperative, namely, the imperative of the future interest in emancipation? Think for a moment not only of the way in which feminist historians in the last two decades have discovered women and their hitherto invisible lives and work, but of the manner in which they have also revalorized and taught us to see with different eyes such traditionally female and previously denigrated activities like gossip, quilt-making, and even forms of typically female sickness like headaches, hysteria and taking to bed during menstruation.[14] In this process of the "feminist transvaluation of values"

our *present* interest in women's strategies of survival and historical resistance has led us to imbue these *past* activities, which were wholly
uninteresting from the standpoint of the traditional historian, with new
meaning and significance.

While it is no longer possible or desirable to produce "grand narratives" of history, the Death of History thesis occludes the epistemological interest in history and in historical narrative which accompany the
aspirations of all struggling historical actors. Once this "interest" in
recovering the lives and struggles of those "losers" and "victims" of
history are lost, can we produce engaged feminist theory?

Defenders of "postmodern historiography" like Fraser and Nicholson
who issue calls for a "postmodern feminist theory" look away from
these difficulties in part because what they mean by this kind of theorizing is less "postmodernist" but more "neopragmatist." By "postmodern
feminist theory" they mean a theory that would be pragmatic and
fallibilistic, that "would tailor its method and categories to the specific
task at hand, using multiple categories when appropriate and forswear-
ing the metaphysical comfort of a single feminist method or feminist
epistemology."[15] Yet this even-handed and commonsensical approach
to tailoring theory to the tasks at hand is not postmodernist. Fraser and
Nicholson can reconcile their political commitments with their theoretical sympathies for postmodernism only because they have substituted
theoretical pragmatism for, in effect, the "hyper-theoretical" claims of
postmodern historiography. Let me illustrate with an example from recent feminist debates.

The Summer 1990 issues of the journal *Signs* carried an exchange
between Linda Gordon and Joan Scott which involved reviews by each
of the other's recent books and the authors' responses.[16] This exchange
contains a very succinct statement of the kinds of political cum theoretical issues currently facing feminist theorists who may or may not want
to adopt postmodernist methodologies in their own work. Central to
postmodernist methodology in historiography no less than in philosophy and cultural analysis is the status of the subject and of subjectivity.
After reviewing Linda Gordon's presentation of the history of family
violence as it was treated and defined by professional social workers in
three child-saving agencies in Boston from the 1880s to the 1960s, Scott
observes that Gordon's book "is aimed at refuting simple theories of
social control and rejecting interpretations that stress the top-down nature
of welfare policies and the passivity of their recipients.'[17] Instead Gordon
proposes an interactive model of relationships, according to which power
is negotiated among family members and among the victims and state
agencies. Joan Scott sees little evidence for women as "active agents"

in Gordon's book; the title of Gordon's book – *Heroes of their Own Lives: The Politics and History of Family Violence* – Scott observes "is more a wish than a historical reality, more a politically correct formulation than anything that can be substantiated by the sources."[18] And the methodological difficulty is stated succinctly, in terms which immediately remind us of Butler's claims examined in the previous section concerning the "social and cultural construction of agency." Scott writes:

> A different conceptualization of agency might have avoided the contradictions Gordon runs into and articulated better the complex relationship between welfare workers and their clients evident in the book. *This conceptualization would see agency not as an attribute or trait inhering in the will of autonomous individual subjects, but as a discursive effect, in this case the effect of social workers' constructions of families, gender, and family violence. It would take the idea of "construction" seriously, as something that has positive social effects. (For the most part Gordon uses "construction" as if it were synonymous with "definition," but definition lacks the materiality connoted by "construction.")* It was, after all, the existence of welfare societies that not only made family violence a problem to be dealt with but also gave family members a place to turn to, a sense of responsibility, a reason for acting, and a way of thinking about resistance.[19]

What one sees in Scott's critique of Gordon's book is a clash of paradigms within women's historiography – a clash between the social history-from-below paradigm used by Gordon, the task of which is to illuminate the gender, class and race struggles through which power is negotiated, subverted as well as resisted by the so-called "victims" of history, and the paradigm of postmodernist historiography, influenced by Foucault's work, in which the emphasis is on the "construction" of the agency of the victims through mechanisms of social and discursive control. Just as for Michel Foucault there is no history of the victims but only a history of the construction of victimization, a history of the agencies of victim control, so too, for Scott as well, it is the "social construction of family violence" rather than the actual lives of the victims of family violence which is methodologically central. Just as for Foucault every act of resistance is but another manifestation of an omnipresent discourse–power complex, for Scott too, women who negotiate and resist power do not exist; the only struggles in history are between competing paradigms of discourses, power–knowledge complexes.

Let me tread lightly here: not being a professional historian, it is beyond my competency to arbitrate the dispute between Joan Scott and

Linda Gordon. What I am calling attention to here are some of the conceptual issues involved, and which have their source in a version of the Death of the Subject thesis considered above. We see in Scott's critique of Gordon how Foucaultian premises about the social "construction of agency" are juxtaposed to the history-from-below approach espoused by Gordon. If we go along with Joan Scott, one approach to feminist historiography follows; and another, if we are with Gordon. Of course, it could also be that there is no either/or here, that each method and approach should learn from and benefit from the other. Yet before we can issue a Pollyanna call to all parties of the debate, we should get clear on what the conceptual constraints of postmodernist historiography are for feminists. Linda Gordon I think puts the matter very succinctly:

> In fact Scott's and my differences go to the heart of contemporary controversies about the meanings of gender. Scott's determinist perspective emphasizes gender as "difference," marked by the otherness and absolute silencing of women. I use gender to describe a power system in which women are subordinated through relations that are contradictory, ambiguous, and conflictual – a subordination maintained against resistance, in which women have by no means always defined themselves as other, in which women face and take choices and action despite constriction. These are only two of many versions of gender, and they are by no means opposite, but they may illuminate the relevant issues here.[20]

We see once more that the Death of History thesis as well allows conceptual alternatives: agreement on the end of historical metanarratives either of the Marxian sort which center around class struggle or of the liberal sort which center around a notion of progress is not sufficient. Beyond such agreement begin difficult questions on the relationship between historiography, politics and memory. Should we approach history to retrieve from it the victims' memories, lost struggles and unsuccessful resistances, or should we approach history to retrieve from it the monotonous succession of infinite power–knowledge complexes that materially constitute selves? As Gordon points out, these methodological approaches also have implications for how we should think of "gender." Postmodernist historiography too, then, poses difficult alternatives for feminists which challenge any hasty or enthusiastic alliance between their positions.

3   Finally, let me articulate strong and weak versions of the Death of Metaphysics thesis. In considering this point it would be important to note right at the outset that much of the postmodernist critique of

Western metaphysics itself proceeds under the spell of a metanarrative, namely, the narrative first articulated by Heidegger and then developed by Derrida that "Western metaphysics has been under the spell of the 'metaphysics of presence' at least since Plato. ..." This characterization of the philosophical tradition allows postmodernists the rhetorical advantage of presenting what they are arguing against in its least defensible versions. Listen again to Flax's words: "For postmodernists this quest for the Real conceals the philosophers' desire, which is to master the world" or "Just as the Real is the ground of Truth, so too philosophy as the privileged representative of the Real ..." etc. But is the philosophical tradition so monolithic and so essentialist as postmodernists would like to claim? Would not even Thomas Hobbes shudder at the suggestion that the "Real is the ground of Truth"? What would Kant say when confronted with the claim that "philosophy is the privileged representative of the Real"? Would not Hegel consider the view that concepts and language are one sphere and the "real" yet another merely a version of a naive correspondence theory of truth which the chapter on "Sense certainty" in the *Phenomenology of Spirit* so eloquently dispensed with? In its strong version, the Death of Metaphysics thesis suffers not only from a subscription to a grandiose metanarrative, but more significantly, this grandiose metanarrative flattens out the history of modern philosophy and the competing conceptual schemes it contains to the point of unrecognizability. Once this history is rendered unrecognizable then the conceptual and philosophical problems involved in this bravado proclamation of the Death of Metaphysics can be neglected.

The weak version of the Death of Metaphysics thesis which is today more influential than the strong Heidegger–Derrida thesis about the "metaphysics of presence" is Richard Rorty's account. In *Philosophy and the Mirror of Nature* Rorty has shown in subtle and convincing manner that empiricist as well as rationalist projects in the modern period presupposed that philosophy, in contradistinction from the developing natural sciences in this period, could articulate the basis of validity of right knowledge and correct action. Rorty names this the project of "epistemology";[21] this is the view that philosophy is a metadiscourse of legitimation, articulating the criteria of validity presupposed by all other discourses. Once it ceases to be a discourse of justification, philosophy loses its *raison d'être*. This is indeed the crux of the matter. Once we have detranscendentalized, contextualized, historicized, genderized the subject of knowledge, the context of inquiry, and even the methods of justification, what remains of philosophy? Does not philosophy become a form of genealogical critique of regimes of discourse and power as they succeed each other in their endless historical monotony? Or maybe philosophy becomes a form of thick cultural narration of the sort that hitherto only poets had provided us with? Or maybe all that remains of philosophy is a form of sociology of knowledge, which, instead of investigating the conditions of the validity of knowledge and action, investigates the empirical conditions under which communities of interpretation generate such validity claims?

Why is this question concerning the identity and future and maybe the possibility of philosophy of interest to feminists? Can feminist theory not flourish without getting embroiled in the arcane debates about the end or transformation of philosophy? The inclination of the majority of feminist theorists at the present is to argue that we can side-step this question; even if we do not want to ignore it, we must not be committed to answer it one way or another. Fraser and Nicholson ask: "How can we conceive a version of criticism without philosophy which is robust enough to handle the tough job of analyzing sexism in all its endless variety and monotonous similarity?"[22] My answer is that we cannot, and it is this which makes me doubt that as feminists we can adopt postmodernism as a theoretical ally. Social criticism without some form of philosophy is not possible, and without social criticism the project of a feminist theory which is at once committed to knowledge and to the emancipatory interests of women is inconceivable. Sabina Lovibond has articulated the dilemma of postmodernists quite well:

> I think we have reason to be wary, not only of the unqualified Nietzschean vision of an end of legitimation, but also of the suggestion that it would somehow be "better" if legitimation exercises were carried out in a self-consciously parochial spirit. For if feminism aspires to be something more than a reformist movement, then it is bound sooner or later to find itself calling the parish boundaries into question.
>
> . . .
>
> So postmodernism seems to face a dilemma: either it can concede the necessity, in terms of the aims of feminism, of "turning the world upside down" in the way just outlined – thereby opening a door once again to the Enlightenment idea of a total reconstruction of society on rational lines; or it can dogmatically reaffirm the arguments already marshalled against that idea – thereby licensing the cynical thought that, here as elsewhere, "who will do what to whom under the new pluralism is depressingly predictable."[23]

Faced with this objection, the answer of postmodernists committed both to the project of social criticism and to the thesis of the death of philosophy as a metanarrative of legitimation will be that the "local narratives," "les petits récits," which constitute our everyday social practices or language games, are themselves reflexive and self-critical enough to pass judgments on themselves. The Enlightenment fiction of philosophical reflection, of *episteme* juxtaposed to the non-critical practice of everyday *doxa*, is precisely that, a fiction of legitimation which ignores that everyday practices and traditions also have their own criteria of legitimation and criticism. The question then would be if among the criteria made available to us by various practices, language games and cultural traditions we could not find some which would serve feminists in their task of social criticism and radical political transformation. Following Michael Walzer, such postmodernists might wish to maintain that the view of the social critic is never "the view from nowhere," but always the view of the one situated somewhere, in some culture, society and tradition.

Notes and References

1   J. Flax, *Psychoanalysis, Feminism and Postmodernism in the Contemporary West* (University of California Press, Berkeley, Calif., 1990), p. 32.
2   Ibid., p. 33.
3   Ibid., p. 34.
4   R. Rorty, "Nineteenth-century idealism and twentieth-century contextualism," in *Consequences of Pragmatism* (University of Minnesota Press, Minneapolis, Minn., 1982), pp. 139–60.
5   L. Alcoff, "Poststructuralism and cultural feminism," *Signs*, 13 (3) (1988), pp. 4–36.
6   J. Butler, *Gender Trouble: Feminism and the Subversion of Identity* (Routledge, London, 1990), p. 7.
7   Ibid., p. 25.
8   Ibid., p. xiii.
9   Ibid., p. 143.
10 Ibid., p. 143.
11 Ibid., p. 145.
12 N. Fraser and L. Nicholson, "Social criticism without philosophy: an encounter between feminism and postmodernism," in *Feminism/Postmodernism*, ed. L. Nicholson (Routledge, London, 1990), p. 33.
13 Ibid., p. 34.
14 R. Bridenthal, C. Koonz and S. Stuard (eds), *Becoming Visible: Women in European History* (Houghton Mifflin, Boston, Mass., 1987).
15 Fraser and Nicholson, "Social criticism without philosophy," p. 35.
16 Cf. J. Scott's review of L. Gordon, "Heroes of their own lives: the politics and history of family violence," L. Gordon's review of J. Scott, "Gender and the politics of history," and their responses, all in *Signs*, 15 (4) (1990), pp. 848–60.

17   Ibid., p. 849.
18   Ibid., p. 850.
19   Ibid., p. 851, emphasis added.
20   Ibid., p. 852.
21   R. Rorty, *Philosophy and the Mirror of Nature* (Princeton University Press, Princeton, N.J., 1979), pp. 131ff.
22   Fraser and Nicholson, "Social criticism without philosophy," p. 34.
23   S. Lovibond, "Feminism and postmodernism," *New Left Review*, 178 (1989), p. 22.

9

The Dangers of a Woman-Centred Philosophy

Moira Gatens

One way in which some feminists have responded to philosophy may be characterized as a form of Radical Feminism or theoretical separatism. These feminists present two kinds of arguments. The first is that there is no relation between feminism and philosophy or more generally between feminism and *theory*. Feminism, on this view, is pure *praxis*, the very activity of theorizing being somehow identified with masculinity or maleness. Perhaps the view of Solanas would be appropriate to quote here. She writes:

> The male's inability to relate to anybody or anything makes his life point-less and meaningless (the ultimate male insight is that life is absurd), so he invented philosophy.... Most men, utterly cowardly, project their inherent weaknesses onto women, label them female weaknesses and believe themselves to have female strengths; most philosophers, not quite so cowardly, face the fact that male lacks exist in men, but still can't face the fact that they exist in men only. So they label the male condition the Human Condition, pose their nothingness problem, which horrifies them, as a philosophical dilemma, thereby giving stature to their animal-ism, grandiloquently label their nothingness their 'Identity Problem', and proceed to prattle on pompously about the 'Crisis of the Individual', the 'Essence of Being', 'Existence preceding Essence', 'Existential Modes of Being', etc., etc.[1]

These problems are described by Solanas as specifically *male* problems. The female, on her account, exhibits no such perverse relation to her being which she grasps intuitively and without lack. Philosophy, or theory, on this view is a male enterprise, arising out of an inherent inadequacy of the male sex.

The second argument of feminists, still within this first approach, is that the relationship between feminism and philosophy is historically, and *necessarily*, an oppressive one. This group argues that philosophy is, necessarily, a masculine enterprise that owes its existence to the repression or exclusion of femininity and as such it is of no use to feminists or their projects. In fact, philosophy may be seen, on this view, as a dangerous and ensnaring trap.[2] Both Spender and Daly may be taken as representatives of this response. They do not advocate the abandonment of theory or philosophy *per se*; rather they recommend the rejection of *patriarchal* theory and *patriarchal* philosophy in favour of 'woman-centred' theory. What is clear in their accounts of patriarchal scholarship is that they believe that patriarchal scholars were/are motivated by conscious and malicious intentions which they held/hold towards women. I am not arguing for the inverse view: that misogynistic cultures create misogynistic scholars; rather I am arguing against the viability of any such simplistic causal relation. Unfortunately, neither cultures nor people are as conveniently transparent as this relation implies. The tendency of both Daly and Spender to impute oppressive *intentions* to patriarchal theorists is simply naive. M. le Doeuff has made this point well. She writes:

> Whether we like it or not, we are within philosophy, surrounded by masculine–feminine divisions that philosophy has helped to articulate and refine. The problem is to know whether we want to remain there and be dominated by them, or whether we can take up a critical position in relation to them, a position which will necessarily evolve through deciphering the basic philosophical assumptions latent in discourse about women. *The worst metaphysical positions are those which one adopts unconsciously whilst believing or claiming that one is speaking from a position outside philosophy.*[3]

The failure of Daly to recognize the unconscious determinations of our culture's attitudes towards women and femininity creates problems not only for her appraisal of patriarchal scholarship but also for her faith in the 'True Self' of women and the patriarchally uncontaminated theory/practice/life she thinks them capable of producing. There is an assumed purity and an originary element to her descriptions of this 'True Self' that place it outside of history, language and culture. For example, she argues that:

It is axiomatic for Amazons that all external/internalized influences, such as myths, names, ideologies, social structures, which cut off the flow of the Self's original movement should be pared away.[4]

Unless we assume a soul or an essence to being, Daly's 'True Self', the timeless kernel at the centre of women's being, is an empty fiction. Women no less than men, though undoubtedly in a different fashion, are products of culture and cannot coherently claim for themselves an *a priori* purity or absence of contamination by its values, its language or its myths.

Spender's thesis concerning the generation of new, woman-centred, meanings suffers from similar problems. She seems to believe that conscious volition is at work both in the 'male-hold' on language and in the feminist attempt to break this hold. The battle over language is presented by Spender as a battle between the wills of men and women. Concerning men and language she writes:

it is obvious that those who have the power to make the symbols and their meanings are in a privileged and highly advantageous position. They have, at least, the potential to order the world to suit their own ends, the potential to construct a language, a reality, a body of knowledge in which they are the central figures, the potential to legitimate their own primacy and to create a system of beliefs which is beyond challenge (so that their superiority is 'natural' and 'objectively tested').[5]

The feminist response to this male privilege and power should be as follows:

We can *choose* to dispense with male views and values and we can generate and make explicit our own: and we can make our views and values *authentic* and *real*.[6]

It is not clear what would give these woman-centred views and values their authentic or real status. Spender's views on language and value involve an implicit assumption which constructs women's perceptions and values as automatically sound. I fail to see the rationale, let alone the justification, for this judgement. The refuge she takes in a pluralistic relativism, where everyone's meanings are valid, for them, only confounds this issue further.

The major source of my disagreement with both these writers is their tendency simultaneously to include and exclude women from (patriarchal) culture, language and values. Women suffer oppression, exploitation and effacement in culture at the same time as they stand apart from culture. That part of female consciousness that is enmeshed in culture is corrupt (Daly's fembots, painted birds, daddy's girls, etc.) but that part that somehow stands apart from culture is the source and guarantee for the authenticity of feminist insight and woman-centred meaning. This false/true dichotomization of women is untenable. It results in the positing of a hierarchy of *types* of women: the oppressed woman who cannot, because she lacks education or opportunity, see through her condition; the complicit woman who chooses not to acknowledge her condition through fear of losing class privilege and having to accept responsibility for her own life; and the authentic woman who recognizes her oppression and chooses to struggle to overcome it. This pattern of describing women was noted in the work of de Beauvoir and is also clearly present in the work of Daly and Spender. The problem is that empirical women rarely, if ever, fit neatly into one or other of these categories and rarely experience their lives as the result of conscious choice. The lived condition of most women tends to be rather more complex than this hierarchy allows. In terms of this first approach, then, the response to the perceived relation between feminism and philosophy is to choose feminism – understood either as pure praxis or as uncontaminated theory – *over* philosophy. This approach to philosophy has several problems.

First, it is dependent for its rationale on an unspoken and unexamined proposition that philosophy, as a discipline or an activity, coincides with its past. It assumes that philosophy is and will be what it was. This reification of philosophy misses the point that philosophy is, among other things, a human activity that is *ongoing*. It is a cultural product that, as Marx observed, reflects the values, concerns and power relations of the culture which produces it.[7] The objects of philosophical enquiry typically include such things as human being, its cultural, political and linguistic environment. Given that these are not static entities, the project of philosophy is necessarily open-ended. The conception of philosophy as a system of truths that could, in principle, be complete, true for all time, relies on the correlative claim that nature or ontology and truth or epistemology are static. In that feminists in the first approach accept the picture that philosophy often presents of itself, it allows this dominant characterization free rein. My argument against this first approach towards the question of the relation between feminism and philosophy, then, is that if it is presented as a long-term programme, it is utopian and runs the serious risk of reproducing elsewhere the very relations which it seeks to leave behind. As other feminists have pointed out, one of the most worrying dangers of this approach is the unwitting affirmation, duplication or repetition of past philosophers' descriptions of women. To affirm women's nature as 'naturally' or 'innately' nurturing, sensitive or biophilic is to ignore the ways in which those qualities have been constructed by social, political and discursive practices.

Whereas the first response sees philosophy as antithetical to feminist aims, the second response identifies the problem as lying with the attitudes of particular (male) philosophers rather than with philosophy itself. This response may be typified by the stance of liberal feminists, although it is not limited to them. Feminists in this category agree that, historically, philosophers have had oppressive relations to women (of misogyny, of omission) but that such relations are not a *necessary* feature of philosophy. They argue or assume that philosophy as a discipline and as a method of enquiry is entirely neutral with regard to sex. Researchers adopting this approach view the history of philosophy as male-dominated, but argue that women are at present in a situation of being able to correct this bias. In this case, the relation between feminist theory and philosophy is envisaged as complementary, one in which feminist theory adds to, or 'completes', traditional or existing philosophy, by filling in the 'gaps' in political, moral and social theories. By adding an analysis of the specific social, political and economic experience of women, this approach seeks to transform philosophy from a male-dominated enterprise into a *human* enterprise.

The response of these feminists sees the relation between feminism and philosophy as complementary but short-lived. Implicit in much of their work is a notion of the 'inbuilt obsolescence' of feminism. Eventually, they suppose, it will be unnecessary to retain a specifically feminist perspective.

[...]

What this approach usually entails is the adoption of a particular philosophical theory as a method of analysis, and then taking 'woman' as the object, as the philosophical problem. This is what Wollstonecraft attempts, using egalitarianism, in *A Vindication of the Rights of Woman*; what J.S. Mill and Taylor attempt, using liberalism; what de Beauvoir attempts, using existentialism, in *The Second Sex*; and what Mitchell attempts to do by employing both psychoanalysis and Marxism, in *Psychoanalysis and Feminism*. It is work done under the rubric of this second approach that epitomizes the dominant relation between feminism and philosophy since Wollstonecraft. We see that Wollstonecraft's views on the education of women reveal a theoretical pre-commitment to egalitarianism. She writes that:

> the most perfect education, in my opinion, is such an exercise of the
> understanding as is best calculated to strengthen the body and form the
> heart. Or, in other words, to enable the individual to attain such habits of
> virtue as will render it independent. In fact, it is a farce to call any being
> virtuous whose virtues do not result from the exercise of its own reason.
> This was Rousseau's opinion respecting men; I *extend* it to women....[8]

So, we see that the general outline of the theory employed by these
feminists is considered unproblematic. The problem of how these philosophical theories relate to women is located in a particular male theorist's prejudice, in this case Rousseau's poorly controlled sexual appetite.
These feminist theorists attempt to subtract the surface sexism of philosophers and include women in the theory on an equal footing with
men. This project is doomed to failure. Rousseau's texts may well contain many overtly sexist notions, but the simple removal of these does
not allow the equitable inclusion of women. His theory of social contract *requires* the privatization of sexual relations, reproduction and
domestic work, along with the confinement of women to the role of
wife/mother in the private sphere. The role he assigns to women is
pivotal to his ideal society.

The failure to question the necessity of women's exclusion from liberal political life places feminists in paradoxical situations. It is crucial
to examine the way in which the public and the private spheres are
sexually specified and, in particular, to examine the unacknowledged
but crucially supporting role that wives/mothers play in the maintenance
of the public sphere. Such examination in turn requires a more critical
approach to the dichotomies that dominate Western conceptualizations
of human life. We need to be much more sceptical of the reason/pas-
sion, mind/body, nature/culture splits and their apparent neutrality and
universality with regard to sexual difference. We can no longer assume
that these categories are descriptions of *human* being. Rather, we must
recognize the ways in which, both historically and discursively, each half
of a single dichotomy has been more closely associated with one sex
than with the other.

There is a marked lack of reciprocity in philosophical accounts of the
complementarity between male and female human being. It is woman
who, conceptually and literally, acts as the 'bridge' for man between
nature and culture, the mind and the body, the private and the public
spheres. Whilst she acts as bridge, she herself cannot cross from nature
to culture, from body to mind or from private to public. Or, at least, she
cannot enjoy both sides of the dichotomy since there is no one, and no
concept, to act as her bridge. This problem is partly what is at stake

when feminists point out that notions of sexual equality often involve little more than women 'becoming-men' or mimicking men.

[...]

Women most often emerge from such accounts as less than human, as bound to their bodies and the exigencies of reproduction, as incapable of a certain kind of transcendence or reason that marks the *truly* human individual. Clearly, the dichotomies which dominate philosophical thinking are not sexually neutral but are deeply implicated in the politics of sexual difference. It is this realization that constitutes the 'quantum leap' in feminist theorizing. It allows a quite different, and more productive, relation to be posited between feminist theories and philosophical theories.

Whereas feminists who adopt the 'woman-centred' approach argue that women should ignore or avoid philosophical tradition, those who adopt the critique of philosophy approach argue that this tradition must be confronted. As it is a tradition that has helped form our conceptions of masculinity and femininity, to affirm the value of femininity or female experience without analysing the historical construction of this experience is to invite failure and repetition. It is the dichotomies of philosophical thought that have been especially targeted for feminist scrutiny.

Dichotomous categories of thought can be traced to the beginnings of philosophy in ancient Greece. The earliest records we have, from the Ionians, show a table of dichotomous distinctions: good/bad, light/dark, unity/plurality, limited/unlimited and male/female. An important point to note about these distinctions is the associations at work between the left- and right-hand sides of these dichotomies. Maleness is associated with good, light, unity and limitation, all of which have positive connotations. Conversely, femaleness is associated with the negative, right-hand side of these distinctions. Even in the modern period, in the work of Descartes, for example, dichotomies dominate philosophical reflections on the world, human knowledge and human nature. Descartes sought to explain all that exists in terms of one or other of two substances: mind and matter. These dichotomies may be presented by philosophers as logical or theoretical tools, as useful or effective ways of dividing up and understanding the world. Alternatively, they may be seen as neutral, objective or true descriptions of actual divisions in the world, as was the case with Descartes.

The claim here is *not* that dichotomous thought is bad or oppressive *per se*, but rather that it can covertly promote social and political values by presenting a conceptual division as if it were a factual or natural division. Nancy Jay in 'Gender and dichotomy'[9] offers an excellent analysis of the way in which social and political values may be contained in dichotomies that present themselves as objective distinctions. Take the mind/body distinction as an example: it presents itself as a self-evident distinction; there is nothing to suggest that mind and body are given unequal value and each seems as if it is defined interdependently. However, a close examination of the way these terms function in, say, the philosophy of Descartes shows that mind is given a positive, and body a negative, value. What appears to be a distinction between A (mind) and B (body), in fact, takes the form of A (mind) and Not-A (body). When we understand the actual functioning of an apparently neutral distinction, the values and the meanings implicit within it become accessible to scrutiny. In this case the term occupying the position A has a primacy and a privilege in relation to defining its partner.

In this way a dichotomy may function to divide a continuous field of differences (A, B, C, D) into an exclusive opposition with one term being singled out to define all the rest: A defines the entire field of Not-A. A is here defined in positive terms, as possessing x, y, z properties, whereas its 'opposite' is negatively defined. Not-A becomes defined by the fact that it *lacks* the properties x, y, z, rather than being defined in its own right. Not-A becomes the privation or absence of A: the fact that it is Not-A is what defines it rather than the fact that it is B. Moreover, as Jay points out, dichotomous thought is structured such that there is an 'infinitation of the negative', the Not-A. What she is referring to here is that because it is only the category A that is positively defined, the category of Not-A can have a potentially infinite number of entities fall under it. Returning to our example, if A is mind then, harking back to Descartes's ontology, Not-A, the field of bodies, includes not only human bodies but also celestial bodies, animal bodies, plants, rocks, and so on, in fact virtually everything that is not-mind. The privileging of A in defining its partner, Not-A, involves a certain lack of coherence in the character of Not-A, or, as Jay puts it, Not-A has no *internal* boundaries.

If Jay's central thesis is correct then the use of dichotomies cannot always be understood as simply a neutral way of dividing up the world into categories. Rather, dichotomies may contain a set of implicit assumptions that assign a prominence and a dominant value to the term in the position of A at the expense of Not-A. This is crucially important in the context of feminist critiques of philosophy, given the predominance of dichotomous thought in that discipline and its tendency to *sexualize* the two sides of any given dichotomy. Jay remarks:

Hidden, taken for granted, A/Not-A distinctions are dangerous and, because of their peculiar affinity with gender distinctions, it seems important for feminist theory to be systematic in recognizing them.[10]

An examination of the case of the male/female distinction in the history of Western thought, and especially in philosophy, shows that although men and women are different (say A and B) they are commonly defined, openly or implicitly, in a dichotomous fashion.

Jay notes the way in which, in all known cultures, there are ceremonies or rituals whereby (especially male) children make their entry into the community of adolescent males or females. This ceremony is thought to serve two primary purposes: the child is symbolically, or actually, separated from the mother by joining him or her to non-familial structures or social institutions; and through this process the child gains a specific sexual identity and a knowledge of sex-appropriate behaviour. That this ceremony is often exclusively male is telling in itself. It is often only the male child who is publicly defined and acknowledged as male – the female taking on her identity almost by default, that is, by being not-male. There are strong resonances of this structure in Freud's theory of the Oedipus complex.

Chodorow, too, has remarked on the definitive break that the male child has with the mother compared with the continuity of identity experienced by the female child.[11] Clearly, then, this pattern is not peculiar to tribal societies. Our culture exhibits its own forms of sexual initiation. These forms are reflected in our linguistic and conceptual history. Aristotle, for example, regarded women as 'deformed men'. From Ancient Greece to our own time women have been defined not so much in terms of any positive qualities that they possess but rather in terms of the male qualities that they lack. For the Greeks it was lesser reason; for others it was lesser strength; for Freud women lack (or have only an atrophied) penis. The important feature to note is that there is a history of women being defined only in terms relative to men, who are taken as the norm, the standard or the primary term. This structure mirrors the structure of dichotomy as outlined by Jay. Moreover it is a structure that cannot be explained simply in terms of conscious or unconscious male prejudice or *sexism*. It is typical of a form of thought that has been termed *phallocentric*. It is sufficient to note here that phallocentrism operates by way of dichotomous thought, where one central term defines all others only in terms relative to itself.

A recent example of feminist critique which confirms the foregoing analysis of the way dichotomies function in the history of Western philosophy is Genevieve Lloyd's *The Man of Reason: 'Male' and*

'*Female' in Western Philosophy.*[12] Lloyd's careful analysis of the history of conceptions of reason aims to demonstrate that 'the maleness of the Man of Reason . . . is no superficial linguistic bias'.[13] Rather, she argues, the latent conceptual connections between reason, masculinity, truth and the intellect, on one hand, and sense, femininity, error and emotion, on the other, are so entrenched and pervasive in the history of philosophy that they virtually prohibit women from reason. Women have experienced, and often still do experience, practical limits to their participation in reason: such things as lack of access to institutions, illiteracy, forced confinement to the domestic sphere, and so on. Lloyd argues that there are also *discursive* barriers between reason and femininity.

Two major theses of her work are important here: first, she argues that reason has defined itself in opposition to femininity; and second, femininity as a discursive category, and as lived by women, is constituted, at least partly, by this exclusion. This last claim is of obvious importance to the viability of the claims of a woman-centred perspective. If this perspective is partly constituted by women's exclusion from male-defined norms, then in what sense could it be said to be 'authentic' or 'real'? Lloyd aims to concentrate mainly on conceptions of reason but her general analysis can be made to hold good in relation to other distinctions important in political and ethical philosophy. In what follows it will be argued that an analysis of the nature/culture and public/private dichotomies reveals a similar pattern to the one deciphered above. Women's supposed close association with nature and the private sphere will be shown to be, at least partly, an effect of the way these distinctions are dichotomously conceived.

Eighteenth-century political philosophy furnishes an interesting series of constructions of nature and the supposed affinity that women and the family have with it. In *Emile*, for example, Rousseau writes that 'Natural relations remain the same throughout the centuries.'[14] This sentiment sits very uneasily in the broad thesis of *Emile* which purports to be concerned with the inevitable and corrupting alterations to nature and natural relations that accompany a highly developed civilization. In order to penetrate the meaning of this sentence we must understand that for Rousseau it is only by the rational and artificial *reconstruction* of nature that the uneasy relations between nature and culture, the man and the citizen, the family and the state, can be harmonized. Woman is crucial to this harmonization. By fulfilling her 'natural' role as wife/mother she acts as a pivotal point around which the tensions in these dichotomies are resolved. They are resolved, however, at considerable cost to the woman who is neither citizen nor, strictly speaking, woman at all. Rather, she is reduced to the role of wife/mother. By privatizing familial concerns and making them the special province of women, Rousseau leaves men free to move between the private world – where 'natural' relations between the sexes and between fathers and children are conducted – and the public world of culture, citizenship and politico-ethical relations with other men. These two self-contained spheres allow him to split his own, possibly inconsistent, needs and desires into two domains. Since these are separated, they present little danger to his enjoyment of both.

The story of his wife, however, is quite different. She is not a citizen, she does not share the (theoretically) equitable relations of the free market, in fact she is not a political animal at all. She has been defined only in terms relative to men and male needs. In the case of Rousseau this is evident from the layout of *Emile*. Sophy makes her appearance in book 5, the last book, at that point where Emile needs to marry, to have children and to become a head of a household, which he must if he is to take up his rightful place in culture. What Sophy represents for Rousseau is the natural base and guarantee for the artificiality of culture. The significance of the claim that natural relations are timeless is clear. If relations between men and women do change, these changes are the result of artifice and corruption since natural relations are *by definition* static.

The seventeenth-century philosophers, Hobbes and Locke, both argue that men and women were equal in the state of nature. In the *Discourse*[15] Rousseau also allows that women in the state of nature possess equal capacity with men in fending for themselves. Why then do these philosophers consistently claim that women are naturally inferior in culture? An adequate response to this question requires the consideration of another philosophical construction, the social contract. Whatever disagreements philosophers have concerning the form and the legitimacy of the social contract, they universally agree that it is a contract entered into by men only. The significance of this is that women are, conceptually at least, still in a state of nature. Even contemporary theorists, such as Rawls, make this assumption. Women, therefore, lack a political existence and the benefits of such an existence, such as the protection of the state. This makes women vulnerable to the 'whims' of men, who are not bound by the usual laws of the body politic in their treatment of women. Ironically this arrangement also presents a threat to the state since women are internal to its operations yet not bound, by contract, to its rules and ideals. Hence, it is common, in the eighteenth century, to find women being conceptualized as uncivilized and hostile to reason and law. Rousseau remarked on the 'disorder' of women[16] and Hume on their propensity to the violent and socially disruptive passions.[17] The coercion required to ensure that women do not disrupt the political body created by men is not seen as political since men's relation to women is regarded as having its basis in *natural* rather than *political* authority.

The difficulty involved in trying to demonstrate, in terms consistent with eighteenth-century political discourses, that the relation of men to women is one of political dominance is evidence of the power of the dichotomies which dominate those discourses. Man's relation to woman is familial and families are not appropriate objects of study for political philosophy. What is appropriate to political philosophy is the relationship of the family, as a structure, to the state. Or, put another way, the relationship between a man as head of a household and the state. This philosophical construction of nature and the associations between nature, women and the family is important to address for at least two reasons. First, the particular construction of nature in the eighteenth century was an important underpinning to the viability of the social contract and women's exclusion from it. The construction of private, familial interests as natural, and political and economic interests as cultural, allows the identity of man to be split into a private paternal authority and a fraternally constituted public citizen. These identities are both spatially and conceptually separated. Second, this construction of nature allows the depiction of women as the enemies of civilization – which, of course, means *patriarchal* civilization. The response of Rousseau to this situation is typical. He recommends the segregation of female and male concerns and asserts that the masculine public sphere should be invested with the ultimate authority in cases of conflict. In other words, it is masculine interests which take precedence over both familial and feminine ones.

The particular manner in which woman is constructed as the guardian of familial interests, and the opposing of these interests to the public sphere, actually predisposes women to be the enemies of public life. The theoretical justifications for women's exclusion from the public sphere and the consequent collapsing of familial and female interests are circular or self-fulfilling. Woman is constructed as close to nature, subject to passion and disorder, and so excluded from the rational body politic, which then constructs her as its internal enemy, or as Hegel phrases it, as its 'everlasting irony'.[18] Feminist theorists, at least from Wollstonecraft, have tried to point out that much of the irony involved in the contradictions between women's public and private existence stems from the contradictory demands put upon them by the masculine body politic. A discursive analysis of how political philosophy constructs

its objects of study goes some way toward grasping how these para-
doxes and ironies of female existence are created. It also shows why,
when a political theory is treated as sex-neutral, women will figure, in
those theories, as deficient. In this way this approach to various philosophical theories reverses the tendency of philosophy to pose women as
the problem.

This third approach, which has here been called the feminist critique
of philosophy, inverts the traditional understanding of the relation between human nature and culture. One such traditional understanding
can be found in *The Principles of Philosophy* where Descartes describes
philosophy as being like a tree: metaphysics being the roots that are not
visible but essential; physics being the trunk and the branches being all
the other aspects of philosophy, including ethics and politics.[19] His point
in using this metaphor is that the extremities of the tree, including its
fruit, cannot be understood or improved without a thorough knowledge
of the tree as a complete organic system. The ethico-political theory of
Descartes is notoriously spare and, according to the philosopher himself, this is because ethics and politics are, necessarily, the last objects
of knowledge to be reached by reason. Put another way, if we are to
understand and improve human social and political existence then we
must first understand the principles of human nature, initially as a particular and then in relation to the regulative system of nature as a
whole. This is the way that Hobbes, Locke, Hume, Rousseau and Mill
all proceed. The answer to the first query, 'what essentially is a human
being?', sets determining limits to what kind of social, political and
ethical organization is thought to be suitable to it.

In these theorists' work human nature is thought to have an essentially constant and universal character that is, in differing degrees, considered to be mutable: improvable or corruptible. The kind of social
and political organization and the ethical and legal principles that are
to govern that organization are deduced from what a human being is
thought to be, what its needs, desires, capabilities and limitations are.
Once this problem is fathomed, the management of groups of such
beings is largely a matter of deduction from these first principles. What
must be kept in mind here, however, is that this mode of philosophizing
involves a *formal* conception of human nature or human essence.

The introduction of the notion of a socially constructed subject, which
is a notion absolutely central to feminist theory, undermines the coherence of much traditional political philosophy. To view human being as
a social product devoid of determining universal characteristics is to
view its possibilities as open-ended. This is not to say that human being
is not constrained by historical context or by rudimentary biological

facts but rather that these factors set the outer parameters of possibility only. Within these constraints, if they can be called that, there is a variety of possibilities.

The third response of feminists to philosophy affirms the possibility of a productive relation between the two. This developing feminist philosophy involves the obsolescence neither of feminism nor of philosophy, but hopefully the transformation of both. The salient point to make here is that, *contra* Daly and Spender, there cannot be an unadulterated feminist theory which would announce our arrival at a place where we could say we are 'beyond' patriarchal theory and patriarchal experience. Nor, *contra* Richards, can there be a philosophy which would be neutral, universal or truly *human* in its character, thus rendering feminism redundant.

This developing perspective, informed by both feminist theory and philosophy, offers the means of beginning to conceptualize and live – in an intertwined way – other forms of political and ethical being. In particular, a feminist philosophy can offer an integrated, though not closed, conception of being that acknowledges the connections between being and knowing, between politics and ethics, and between bodies and minds. This project, for feminists, has an urgency that prohibits its depiction as an ideal or merely abstract theoretical exercise. Compliantly living the social significance of the female body is no longer even a *practical* possibility for many women. The traditional ideals of womanhood and femininity conflict with the lived reality of women today.

Some feminists are engaged in the deconstruction of these traditional ideals and the construction of other meanings and other significances of female experience. The further erosion of dominant modes of interpretation of life and values is necessary. It has been argued here that the disjunctive relations internal to the reason/passion, mind/body and nature/culture dichotomies must be eroded. Feminist utilizations of psychoanalytic theory and deconstruction have opened one path which offers a means of conceptualizing reason and emotion, the mind and the body, nature and culture, without assuming a dichotomous structuring to these distinctions.

Notes and References

1   V. Solanas, 'The S.C.V.M. Manifesto', in *Masculine/Feminine*, ed. B. Roszack and T. Roszack (Harper and Row, New York, 1969), p. 265.
2   M. Daly, *Gyn/Ecology: The Metaethics of Radical Feminism* (Beacon Press, Boston, Mass., 1978).

3   M. le Doeuff, 'Women and philosophy', *Radical Philosophy*, 17 (1977), p. 2.
4   Daly, *Gyn/Ecology*, p. 381.
5   D. Spender, *Man Made Language* (Routledge and Kegan Paul, London, 1985), p. 142.
6   Ibid., p. 4, emphasis added.
7   K. Marx, 'The German ideology', in *The Marx–Engels Reader*, ed. R. Tucker (Norton, New York, 1972), pp. 136–7.
8   M. Wollstonecraft, *A Vindication of the Rights of Women* (Penguin, Harmondsworth, 1975), p. 103, emphasis added.
9   N. Jay, 'Gender and dichotomy', *Feminist Studies*, 7 (1981), pp. 38–56.
10 Ibid., p. 47.
11 N. Chodorow, *The Reproduction of Mothering: Psychoanalysis and the Sociology of Gender* (University of California Press, Berkeley, Calif., 1978).
12 G. Lloyd, *The Man of Reason* (Methuen, London, 1989).
13 Ibid., p. ix.
14 J.-J. Rousseau, *Emile* (Dent, London, 1972), p. 354.
15 J.-J. Rousseau, 'Discourse on the origin of inequality', in *The First and Second Discourses*, ed. R. Masters and J. Masters (St Martin's Press, New York, 1964).
16 J.-J. Rousseau, *Politics and the Arts: A Letter to D'Alembert on the Theatre* (Cornell University Press, Ithaca, N.Y., 1968), p. 109.
17 D. Hume, *A Treatise of Human Nature*, ed. L.A. Selby-Bigge (Clarendon Press, Oxford, 1968), book III, part II.
18 G. Hegel, *The Phenomenology of Mind*, tr. J.B. Baillie (Harper and Row, New York, 1967), p. 496.
19 R. Descartes, 'The principles of philosophy', in *The Philosophical Works of Descartes*, tr. E. Haldane and G. Ross (Cambridge University Press, Cambridge, 1970), vol. I, pp. 211–13.

10

The Disorder of Women

Carole Pateman

In his essay, *Politics and the Arts*, Rousseau proclaims that 'never has a people perished from an excess of wine; all perish from the disorder of women'. Rousseau states that drunkenness is usually the sole failing of otherwise upright, decent men; only the immoral fear the indiscretion that wine will promote. Drunkenness is not the worst of the vices since it makes men stupid rather than evil, and wine turns men away from the other vices so it poses no danger to the polity. In contrast, the 'disorder of women' engenders all the vices and can bring the state to ruin.[1]

Rousseau is not the only social or political theorist to regard women as a permanently subversive force within the political order. Freud (to whose arguments I shall also refer) argues in Chapter 4 of *Civilization and Its Discontents* that women are 'hostile to' and 'in opposition to' civilization. In a similar vein, Hegel writes that the community 'creates its enemy for itself within its own gates' in 'womankind in general'. Women are 'the everlasting irony in the life of the community', and when 'women hold the helm of government, the state is at once in jeopardy'.[2]

[...]

This belief in the essential subversiveness of women is of extremely ancient origin and is deeply embedded in our mythological and religious heritage. However, it is only in the modern world that 'the disorder of women' constitutes a general social and political problem. More specifically, it is only with the development of liberal individualism and the arguments of its democratic and socialist critics that beliefs about women become an acute, though not always acknowledged, problem in social and political theory and practice. In pre-modern conceptions of the world, animal and human life were seen as part of a divinely or 'naturally' ordered hierarchy of creation; individuals were conceived as born into a natural order of dominance and subordination. Nature and culture were part of a whole in which the hierarchy of social life was grounded in natural differences such as age, sex and strength. Rulers were those whose 'natural' characteristics fitted them for the task. From about the seventeenth century a new and revolutionary conception of social life developed within which the relationship between 'nature' and 'society', and between women and society, became inherently problematic.

Individuals began to be seen as rational beings, born free and equal to each other – or as naturally free and equal – and as individuals who create their social relationships and institutions for themselves. Political institutions, in particular, began to be seen as, properly, based on convention – on contract, consent and agreement. The conception of a conventionally grounded socio-political order brought with it a complex of problems concerning its relation to nature that, three centuries later, is still unresolved. The nature of the individuals who create and take their place within conventional or 'civil' associations is one of these problems. Do all individuals have the requisite nature or natural capacities? Or are there some who lack, or cannot develop, the capacities required for participation in civil life? If these individuals exist, their nature will appear as a threat to social life and there has been wide agreement that women are dangerous for this very reason. Women, by virtue of their natures, are a source of disorder in the state.

'Disorder' can be used in either of two basic senses: first, there is the socio-political sense of 'civil disorder' as in a rowdy demonstration, a tumultuous assembly, a riot, a breakdown of law and order. Second, 'disorder' is also used to refer to an internal malfunction of an individual, as when we speak of a disordered imagination or a disorder of the stomach or intestines. The term thus has application to the constitution of both the individual and the state. In addition, its moral content can also be made explicit when it is used to describe a 'disorderly house' in which decency and propriety are cast aside. Women, it is held, are a source of disorder because their being, or their nature, is such that it necessarily leads them to exert a disruptive influence in social and political life. Women have a disorder at their very centres – in their morality – which can bring about the destruction of the state. Women thus exemplify one of the ways in which nature and society stand opposed to each other. Moreover, the threat posed by women is exacerbated because of the place, or social sphere, for which they are fitted by their natures – the family. Another of the problems thrown up by the individualist, conventionalist conception of social life is whether *all* social relations are conventional in character. The family is seemingly the most natural of all human associations and thus specially suited to women, who cannot transcend their natures in the manner demanded by civil forms of life. However, if the family is natural, then it is a form of association that stands in contrast to, and perhaps in conflict with, (conventional) social and political life. These two aspects of the problem of the disorder of women are revealed in the writings of the social contract theorists and especially in Rousseau's theory.

The social contract theorists set out the individualist and conventionalist conception of social life with particular clarity. Their arguments depend on, and thus illustrate, all the ambiguities and complexities inherent in the antinomy between nature and 'convention'. Popular contemporary beliefs about women, no less than seventeenth-century patriarchal arguments, rely on an appeal to nature and also on the fact that what is natural or 'ordered according to nature' is widely believed to be good and desirable. The contract theorists appealed both to conceptions of individuals' natures and to the state of nature which natural individuals inhabited – but exactly in what form they inhabited it, and what kind of relationships existed between them, is one of the key questions in the contract story.

Rousseau's version of contract theory highlights the problems in an acute form. He was the only contract theorist willing to pursue the revolutionary implications inherent in the doctrine, but he also believed that women posed a permanent threat to political order. Rousseau's theory contains some profound sociological insights precisely because he was concerned with the interrelations of different dimensions of social life and with transformations of human consciousness. In the *Discourse on Inequality* he attacks the abstract individualism of the liberal contract theorists who postulated a familiar yet natural condition original to humanity. Rousseau argues that, strictly, a natural state is asocial, inhabited only by animals of various kinds, one species of which has the potential to develop into human individuals. That is to say, Rousseau denies that one can draw political conclusions from assertions about the natural characteristics of isolated individuals or individuals seen severally, not collectively. His basic premise is that human life is social life, or sociality is natural to humans. According to Rousseau, and here he agrees with Locke, the social state of nature is inhabited not by (isolated) individuals but by families. He writes that 'the oldest of all societies, and the only natural one, is that of the family'.[3] This is another way of saying that the family precedes, or can exist in the absence of, wider social institutions or 'civil society'; it exists in the natural condition. The family is also grounded in the natural ties of love and affection (which are natural because they are within human capacities as, say, flying is not) and it has its origin in the biological process of procreation, in the natural difference between the sexes. Rousseau argues that the family provides us with a major example of a social institution that follows the order of nature because, in the family, age naturally takes precedence over youth and males are naturally in authority over females. For Rousseau, the family is necessarily patriarchal.

The state of nature stands in contrast to civil society, but the family is common to both forms of existence. The family spans the divide between a condition grounded in nature and the conventional bonds of civil life. Few social and political theorists, with the notable exception of Hobbes, have been willing to present the family as a conventional association. Indeed, in the *Philosophy of Right*, Hegel claims that it is 'shameful' to see marriage and the family as merely contractual associations. The family is widely regarded as the natural basis of civil life. Familial, or domestic, relations are based on the natural ties of biology and sentiment, and the family is constituted by the particularistic bonds of an organic unity. However, the status of the family as the foundation of civil society means that the contrast between the different forms of social life in 'the state of nature' and 'civil society' is carried over into civil life itself. The distinction between and separation of the private and public, or particularistic and universal, spheres of association is a fundamental structural principle of the modern, liberal conception of social life. The natural, particularistic family nestles at the centre of the private sphere, and it throws into prominence and stands opposed to the impersonal, universal, 'conventional ' bonds of public life.

[. . .]

[Crucial to this opposition – according to Rousseau and Freud – is the incompatibility of womankind with a fundamental bond of civil (public) society, that is, justice.] Rousseau and Freud offer a remarkably similar diagnosis of why women are incapable of developing a sense of justice. Both agree that, for women, anatomy is destiny. The biological (natural) differences between the sexes influence and are reflected in their respective moral characters. Rousseau argues that the source of the disorder of women lies in their boundless sexual passion. Women, he claims, foreshadowing Freud, are unable to subdue and sublimate their sexual desires in the same manner, or to the same extent, as men. Men are the active and aggressive sex and are 'controlled by nature'; passive and defensive women have only the control of modesty. There must therefore be a double standard of sexual conduct. If both sexes gave equal rein to their passions 'the men . . . would at last become [the women's] victims, and would be dragged to their death without the least chance of escape'.[4] Modesty is natural to women, but it provides a weak and uncertain control of their sexual desires. Moreover, as Rousseau argues in *Politics and the Arts*: 'even if it could be denied that a special sentiment of chasteness was natural to women, would it be any the less true that in society . . . they ought to be raised in principles appropriate to it? If the timidity, chasteness, and modesty which are proper to them are social inventions, it is in society's interest that women acquire these qualities. . . .'[5] However, even an education specifically designed to foster modesty is not sufficient guarantee against the disorderliness of women. Rousseau spells out this lesson in graphic fashion in *La Nouvelle Héloise*. Julie desires nothing more than to be virtuous and lead an exemplary life as a wife and mother, but she is unable, despite all her efforts and apparent success in passing through the trials set for her by Wolmar, to overcome her passion for Saint Preux. If the good order of Clarens is not to be fatally disrupted, Julie must take the one course left to her; the only solution to the problem of the disorder of women is her 'accidental' death.

Rousseau and Freud argue that this fundamental difference between the sexes has existed since the very beginning of social life and, indeed, has structured it. Both claim that the creation of civil society, or 'civilization', is the work of men. For Rousseau the sexes are equal only when isolated from each other among the animals in the true (asocial) natural condition. Social life develops as family life, and while charting its emergence Rousseau suddenly announces that 'the first difference was established in the way of life of the two sexes, . . . women . . . grew accustomed to tend the hut and the children'.[6] His conjectural history of the development of civil society and the transformation of human nature then continues as a history of male activity and male nature. Freud also presents a conjectural history of the development of civil society (civilization) in *Civilization and Its Discontents*. He argues that once 'the need for genital satisfaction no longer made its appearance like a guest who drops in suddenly',[7] males had a reason for keeping females close at hand and the latter, in their turn, were obliged to comply in order to care for their helpless young. Once the family was established, the development of civilization was the work of men alone because it requires the 'instinctual sublimations of which women are little capable'. Only men are capable of sublimating their passions and thus capable of the justice that civil life demands. Furthermore, men's involvement in public life, and their consequent dependence on other men, means that they have little energy left for their wives and families:

'thus the woman finds herself forced into the background by the claims of civilization and she adopts a hostile attitude towards it'.[8]

No explanation was available of why women are less able than men to sublimate their passions or how the 'special stamp to the character of females as social beings'[9] comes about until Freud formulated his psychoanalytic theory. Rousseau can only tell us that men and women differ in this respect – and he prescribes an education for girls that will reinforce their disorderly natures and indifference to justice. Women are 'naturally' made to be 'at the mercy of man's judgement' and 'to endure even injustice at his hands'.[10] (Hegel, it might be noted, was content to leave women in their natural state; women, he says with resignation, are 'educated – who knows how? – as it were by breathing in ideas, by living. . . .')[11] Freud argues that the explanation for women's lack of, or deficiency in, a sense of justice is the differential passage of the two sexes through the Oedipus complex and a consequent difference in the development of their super-egos. The super-ego is the 'representative for us of every moral restriction'[12] and, especially, of the restrictions that justice demands.

Civilization is the work of men in the most profound sense, for it is men alone who possess a fully developed super-ego. The emergence of the super-ego is bound up with (the conjectural history of) the 'original' momentous move from the family to wider communal life. Freud argues that 'originally' the 'first' sons killed the 'first' father, whom they simultaneously loved and hated. Out of the awful act of hatred, remorse and guilt grew from their love, and their subsequent identification with their dead father led to the emergence of the super-ego. The brothers, Freud argues, imposed on each other the mutual restrictions necessary to prevent a repetition of their dreadful deed. Thus the public virtue of justice, or 'the first "right" or "law" ' necessary for civil life, was established – by men; women had no part in this development.[13] In our own time the different manner in which little boys and girls pass through the Oedipus complex harks back to the purely masculine 'origin' of justice, political right and the super-ego.

[. . .]

In contrast, women lack or, at best, have a much weaker super-ego than men. [The result is the comparative disorder of women.]

[. . .]

Turning now back to Rousseau, he presents us with many insights into the problem of the disorder of women. However, he is, very surprisingly, far less aware of the problem posed by the family. Rousseau's political theory highlights the conflict between the private interests of sectional associations and the general will (or principles of justice) that governs the political order. However, he fails to see that the family, too, is a sectional association that threatens justice. Rousseau pictures the family, the little commonwealth with the father at its head, as the foundation of the state: 'Will the bonds of convention hold firm without some foundation in nature? Can devotion to the state exist apart from the love of those near and dear to us? Can patriotism thrive except in the soil of that miniature fatherland, the home? Is it not the good son, the good husband, the good father, who makes the good citizen?'[14] Perhaps – if the father's sense of justice is strong enough to override his love for his family, his desire to protect its interests and the baleful influence of his wife. Freud argues that the conflict between love, whether sensual or 'aim-inhibited', and public life cannot be avoided: 'love comes into opposition to the interests of civilization; . . . civilization threatens love with substantial restrictions'. The more closely that family members are attached to each other, the harder it is for them to enter into public life.[15] Freud might have added that the more diligently husbands and fathers work for the interests of their families, the more likely it is that they will put those interests before the requirements of justice. There can be no easy reconciliation of the virtues of love and justice.

Paradoxically, because the family is the 'foundation' of social life in the sense that it is the point of 'procreative origin'[16] of society and because it stands directly at the border with nature, women are seen as guardians of order and morality as well as inherently subversive. It is women who reproduce and have the major responsibility for educating the next generation; it is the mother who turns asocial, bisexual babies into little 'boys' and 'girls'. Rousseau glorifies women's task as mothers. He was one of the first writers to emphasize the moral implications of breast-feeding, and he is careful to stress, for example, that when Julie constructs her natural garden retreat she does not allow the work to interfere with her duties as a mother. (However, it should be noted that the mother's task is completed in the early years; a male tutor takes over from her.) Women's guardianship of order reaches beyond motherhood. Within the shelter of domestic life women impose an order, a social pattern, and thus give meaning to the natural world of birth and death and other physical processes, of dirt and raw materials, that is integral to domestic life. Women are direct mediators between nature and society. However, because women face nature directly, and because, in giving birth and in their other bodily functions, they appear as part of nature, they exemplify the ambiguous status of the family as both natural and social. Women impose order and foster morality; but they are also in daily contact with dirt and with natural processes only partly under our control. They cannot escape being tainted by this contact or completely transcend the naturalness of their own being. Hence they represent both order and disorder, both morality and boundless passion.

It is worth remarking here that one way in which women (and their male kin and keepers) attempt to hide this contact with nature, their own natural functions, and hence their potential for disorder, is through cleanliness – presented as purity. In the *Persian Letters*, the chief eunuch stresses to Usbek that he has always been trained to keep the women in the seraglio 'absolutely clean ... and [to take] an infinite amount of care over it.'[17] Rousseau proclaims that 'nothing could be more revolting than a dirty woman, and a husband who tires of her is not to blame'. Emile will never find this fault in Sophy: 'things are never clean enough for her. ... She has always disliked inspecting the kitchen-garden ... the soil is dirty, ... absolute cleanliness ... has become a habit, till it absorbs one half of her time and controls the other; so that she thinks less of how to do a thing than of how to do it without getting dirty. ... Sophy is more than clean, she is pure.'[18]

The profound insights into the contradictions and antagonisms in the dialectic between individuals and their social relations, and between the family and civil society, to be found in the work of thinkers of the stature of Rousseau and Freud, are sadly neglected (or not even recognized) in most contemporary work on the subject of justice and in much feminist writing. In part, this reflects the consolidation of liberal theory over three centuries as the ideology of the liberal capitalist state, centred on the separation of the political and private spheres. The problems which appear explicitly at the origins of liberal theory in the arguments of the social contract theorists and their critics are now either ignored or regarded as unproblematic. In particular, the tension between nature and convention or love and justice is continually glossed over or suppressed.

Early liberal feminist writers such as Mary Wollstonecraft and John Stuart Mill, for example, who agree that women lack a sense of justice, offer a much more superficial diagnosis of the problem than Rousseau (though that is not to underestimate their achievement). They see it primarily as a matter of extending the liberal principles of freedom, equality and rationality to women through a process of education. In the *Vindication*, Wollstonecraft appeals for the 'rights of men and citizens' to be extended to both sexes; reason has no sex. It appears that the virtues are sexually differentiated because women have been turned into 'artificial' creatures. Their education (or, more accurately, lack of it) enforces their dependence on men and makes them mean and selfish, narrowing the range of their concerns to exclude the wider community so that they cannot develop a sense of justice. Similarly, in *The Subjection of Women*, Mill argues that we cannot say that women are 'naturally ' fit only for subordination because we know nothing of what they might become if the principles of freedom and equality, now governing the rest of our social institutions, were extended to sexual relations. Mill argues that individuals develop a sense of justice through participation in as wide a range of public institutions as possible; confined to the family – which the law allows to be a 'school of despotism' – women can never learn to weigh the public interest against selfish inclination.

The obvious problem with Mill's and Wollstonecraft's arguments is that although they both advocate a proper education for women and a widening of opportunities to enable them to be economically independent of men, they also assume that the opportunities will be largely irrelevant for the majority of women. Most women will continue working within the home since childrearing will remain their major responsibility. But this means that, despite legal and educational reforms, men's moral understanding will continue to be more highly developed than women's. Women will not obtain within the family the breadth of social experience and practical education that will develop their sense of justice and allow them, with safety, to participate in political life. The problem of the disorder of women, while mitigated by education, remains unresolved. These feminist arguments assume that the family can become the bedrock on which the liberal state is raised, but they also contain a hint that love and justice can conflict. Mill implies that education is the answer here too; educated persons of both sexes should be able to control and subdue their 'lower' passions. Wollstonecraft contrasts love, that is, sexual passion, with friendship and mutual respect between equals, and she argues that the latter is the only true basis for marriage and family life. Rousseau, also, thought it 'an error' to see sexual passion as the basis of domestic life (he makes it clear that Saint Preux, Julie's lover, would not make a good husband). He claims that: 'people do not marry in order to think exclusively of each other, but in order to fulfill the duties of civil society jointly, to govern the house prudently, to rear their children well. Lovers never see anyone but themselves, they incessantly attend only to themselves, and the only thing they are able to do is love each other.'[19]

However, given Rousseau's conception of women's nature and his plan for their education, it is impossible that marriage could be placed on this footing – as he shows clearly enough in his story of Wolmar's virtue and Julie's love. To state that sexual attraction is not the proper foundation for marriage solves nothing if it is also believed that women are naturally creatures governed wholly by their sexual passions. More generally, the liberal feminists' recognition that the relationship between the sexes contradicts basic liberal principles and their proposals for social reforms fail to get to the heart of the problem of the disorder of women. Their argument is undercut by the acceptance of the separation of domestic from civil life, which is also a sexual separation; women and love are irrevocably set in opposition to justice. Liberal theory presupposes the opposition between nature and convention but the opposition can be neither admitted nor its implications pursued. The account of the development of the sense of justice in Rawls's extremely influential *A Theory of Justice* shows how liberal theorists consistently obscure one of the major problems in their arguments.

Rawls states that he has drawn on both Rousseau and Freud, but he gives no indication that he has appreciated the relevance of their insights into sexual relationships for the question of justice. Rawls presents an apparently sexually undifferentiated account; arguing that 'our moral understanding increases as we move in the course of life through a sequence of positions'.[20] The sense of justice develops in three stages; first, the child learns the 'morality of order' from its parents. Then the 'morality of association', a morality characterized by the co-operative virtues of justice and impartiality, is developed when the individual occupies a variety of roles in a range of institutions. Finally, we reach the stage of the 'morality of principles' in which we understand the fundamental role of justice in the social order and we wish to uphold it; the sense of justice is attained. Now this account, of course, has the same obvious failing as the liberal feminist arguments – only if men *and* women can move 'through a sequence of positions' will both sexes develop the sense of justice. Rawls, not surprisingly, rejects cries to 'abolish the family', but he has nothing to say about the sexual division of labour or the conviction that domestic life is the proper sphere for women. On the contrary, he remarks that if a publicly recognized concept of justice regulates social life it will 'reconcile us to the dispositions of the natural order'.[21] And what is more natural, or in accordance with the order of nature, than the division of social life and its virtues between the sexes: conventional political life and justice belong to men; domestic life and love belong to women?

One reaction from the feminist movement to the problems sketched in this analysis has been a call for the last vestiges of nature to be swept away. In the *Dialectics of Sex*, Firestone claims that the problem of women and nature can be solved through artificial reproduction which will allow all relationships, including those between adults and children, to be based on convention or to be freely chosen. However, this is to argue that the whole of social life could be fashioned in the image of a philosophically and sociologically incoherent abstract, possessive individualism. It is a 'solution' based on a continuing opposition between nature and society rather than an attempt to recreate this relationship. Another feminist response to claims about the disorder of women has been to argue that, since 'justice' is the work of men and an aspect of the domination of women, women should reject it totally and remake their lives on the basis of love, sentiment and personal relations. But this no more solves the problem than a declaration of war on nature; neither position breaks with liberal conceptions or can take account of the dialectic between individual and social life, between the particular or personal and the universal or political. To attempt technologically to banish nature or to deny that justice has any relevance is to try to wish away fundamental dimensions of human life. Rather, the extraordinarily difficult and complex task must be undertaken of developing a critique of the liberal and patriarchal conception of the relation between nature and convention that will also provide the foundation for a theory of a democratic, sexually egalitarian practice.

The insights and failings of the theorists discussed in this analysis provide one starting point for such a critique. I have concentrated on 'love', that is to say, sexual passion. However, one of the most urgent tasks is to provide an alternative to the liberal view of justice, that assumes that 'a' sense of justice presently exists, developed through the smooth passage of all individuals through social institutions. This claim rests on the uncritical acceptance that the structure of liberal capitalist institutions allows both men and women, working class and middle class, to develop in the same fashion. It ignores the reality of institutions in which the subordination of women and the 'despotic organization of production'[22] are seen as natural. Rousseau's critique of abstract individualism and the liberal theory of the state can assist in building a critical theory, just as his many insights into the relationship between sexual and political life, disentangled from his patriarchalism, are essential to a critical theory of the relation between love and justice. Similarly, Freud's psychoanalytic theory is indispensable, but must be used carefully as part of an account of the historical development of civil society – which includes a specific form of domestic association and 'masculine' and 'feminine' sexuality – and not, as Freud presents it, as an abstract theory of the 'individual' and 'civilization'. This project may sound daunting, even completely overwhelming. Yet once the problem of the disorder of women begins to be seen as a question of social life, not as a fact that confronts us in nature, the reality of the structure of our personal and political lives is beginning to be revealed within the appearance presented in liberal and patriarchal ideology, and the task has already begun.

Notes and References

1   J.-J. Rousseau, *Politics and the Arts: A Letter to D'Alembert on the Theatre*, tr. A. Bloom (Cornell University Press, Ithaca, N.Y., 1968), p. 109.
2   G. Hegel, *The Phenomenology of Mind*, tr. J.B. Baillie (Allen and Unwin, London, 1949), p. 496; G. Hegel, *Philosophy of Right*, tr. T.M. Knox (Oxford University Press, Oxford, 1952), addition to para. 166.
3   J.-J. Rousseau, *The Social Contract*, tr. M. Cranston (Penguin, Harmondsworth, 1968), book I, p. 50.
4   J.-J. Rousseau, *Emile*, tr. B. Foxley (Dent, London, 1911), p. 322.
5   Rousseau, *Politics and the Arts*, p. 87.
6   J.-J. Rousseau, 'Discourse on the origin and foundations of inequality', in *The First and Second Discourses*, ed. R. Masters and J. Masters (St Martin's Press, New York, 1964), p. 147.
7   S. Freud, 'Civilisation and its discontents', in *The Standard Edition of the Complete Psychological Works*, tr. J. Strachey (Hogarth Press, London, 1961), vol. 21, p. 99.
8   Ibid., pp. 103–4.
9   S. Freud, 'Female sexuality', in *On Sexuality*, ed. A. Richards (Penguin Freud Library, Harmondsworth, 1977), vol. 7, p. 377.
10   Rousseau, *Emile*, pp. 328, 359.
11   Hegel, *Philosophy of Right*, addition to para. 166.
12   S. Freud, 'The dissection of the psychical personality', in *New Introductory Lectures on Psychoanalysis*, ed. J. Strachey (Penguin Freud Library, Harmondsworth, 1973), vol. 2, p. 98.
13   Freud, 'Civilisation and its discontents', pp. 101, 131–2.
14   Rousseau, *Emile*, p. 326.
15   Freud, 'Civilisation and its discontents', pp. 102–3.
16   A. Yeatman, 'Gender ascription and the conditions of its breakdown: the rationalization of the "domestic sphere" and the nineteenth-century "cult of domesticity" ', unpublished.
17   Montesquieu, *Persian Letters*, tr. C. Betts (Penguin, Harmondsworth, 1973), letter 64, p. 131.
18   Rousseau, *Emile*, pp. 357–8.
19   J.-J. Rousseau, *La Nouvelle Héloise*, tr. J. McDowell (Pennsylvania State University Press, University Park, 1968), part 3, letter 30, pp. 261–2.
20   J. Rawls, *A Theory of Justice* (Oxford University Press, Oxford, 1971), p. 468.
21   Ibid., p. 512.
22   B. Clark and G. Gintis, 'Rawlsian justice and economic systems', *Philosophy and Public Affairs*, 4 (1978), pp. 302–25.

PART II

Gendered Work and Gendered Identity

IN THIS PART we turn away from abstract theory and philosophy towards more empirical assessments of gender divisions and inequalities. Reading 11, by Natalie Zemon Davis nevertheless has interesting connections with themes introduced in the concluding contributions to Part I. The identifying of femininity with disorder, she shows, has deep historical roots. The disorder of women supposedly derived from their physiology. The female personality was thought to result from the influence of 'cold and wet humours', making women unpredictable and emotional. The male, by contrast, was 'hot and dry', making him more consistent and reasoned in his life. The womb was thought of like a hungry animal; when not continuously involved in reproduction it would supposedly wander about the body producing disorientation and anxiety. As Davis points out, European males were asserting the biological 'inferiority' of women long before they did so of Africans.

Women's disorderliness meant they were receptive to the arts of witchcraft, in itself thought of as a fundamental threat to the world of men. Female unruliness was to be brought under control by education producing modesty and humility, by honest work and the subordination of the wife to her husband. In the period of the early development of modernity, in the seventeenth and eighteenth centuries, the subjection of wives to their husbands actually became greater than it had previously been. Married women were deprived of certain forms of independence they used to possess in law and their right to decide about the disposal of their dowries and possessions was made more restricted. Thus we find that at the very period at which 'universal' democratic rights were being pioneered, women were being confined in the domestic sphere more thoroughly than before. Rulers and political theorists alike saw the increasing subjection of wives to husbands as a means of securing female obedience in a political order that was becoming more fully centralized.

Reading 12, by June Purvis, discusses a later period of modern social developments. Her theme is the invisibility of women in interpretations of the nineteenth century made by contemporary historians. Orthodox histories of the period, she says, mostly speak of women in relation to the struggle for the vote. Until recently this was just as true of leftist historians as of more liberal or conservative writers. Thus E. P. Thompson's celebrated study, *The Making of the English Working Class*, has little to say about women. He defines the main dynamic of his analysis, social class, in terms that refer more or less exclusively to men. Leftist historians place much more emphasis than others upon the writing of history 'from the bottom up'; but their studies of the lower classes usually say little about working-class women. The recent work of Eric

Hobsbawm gives more attention to women, but concentrates mainly upon the activities and experiences of middle-class women.

Feminist historians have sought to correct these emphases and to interrogate the assumptions made by male-centred history. One somewhat unfortunate consequence of this, however, Purvis says, is that feminist history has developed largely in separation from the mainstream subject, many of whose representatives continue largely to ignore the contributions of feminist authors.

In Reading 13 Philip Pacey discusses just such a historical domain left unexplored until fairly recently: the association of women with a renewed domesticity in the nineteenth century. The late eighteenth and nineteenth centuries were the time at which the 'home' in the modern sense was invented. Prior to that period, for most of the population, the household dwelling was also a place of work: a farm or workshop. The idea of the home developed as part of the separation of the household from the workplace, coupled to the idea that the first of these was an environment to be nourished and cherished.

Beginning among the middle classes and later spreading downwards, women's role increasingly came to be seen as bound up with 'home-making'. 'Home-making' in the literature of the period was usually presented in a positive way, but was connected to the legal restrictions upon the rights of wives mentioned above. Home-making, Pacey points out, allowed female creativity some outlet, but at the same time smothered and constricted that creativity. For many middle-class women, up to the turn of the twentieth century, the more routine forms of housework were undertaken by servants. From the early point of the present century onwards, servants began to disappear; the home increasingly became mechanized and, as it did, the position of 'housewife' became more clearly shaped. Even though substantial proportions of women were in paid labour, in the poorer classes particularly, women were still expected to be responsible for the running and cultivation of the home.

The separation of home from workplace, Harriet Bradley notes in Reading 14, framed not just domestic labour but the type of paid work that women were expected to undertake if they were employed outside the domestic milieu. During the nineteenth and early twentieth centuries many men began to insist that their wives should stay in the home and not take on work outside. Those who did go out to work, particularly younger single women, were frequently subject to close supervision by fathers and male employers. In many working-class homes young women had to hand over their pay packets to their parents and accept the parents' rulings about what sort of jobs they should have and how they should behave in them.

The legal grounding of domestic patriarchy started to break down with the passing of the Married Women's Property Act in 1882, which reinstated various property and political rights for women. Yet even today patriarchal elements in family organization continue to exert a major influence over women in paid labour. A high proportion of married women now go out to work, but it is still mostly their responsibility to make adequate provision for childcare and they continue to do most of the housework. Women's careers are typically interrupted, as they retreat from the labour force to care for young children, at the very stage at which ambitious males are taking the first key steps up a promotion ladder.

The majority of men today are not hostile towards their wives going out to work, but in most households it is the man's work that determines where the couple lives and how much of their lives are organized. In the domain of work itself, what Connell would call 'gender regimes', or in Bradley's phrase 'gendered work cultures', are still firmly embedded. Some types of work are believed to be 'appropriate' for women; and women are debarred from various types of occupations by informal barriers and restrictions.

Reading 15, by Christine Delphy and Diana Leonard, concentrates directly upon the household environment. Women's concern with domesticity provides a comfortable environment from which the male can issue out to take on the wider world. The domestic work of women allows soldiers to go off to fight wars, businessmen to work twelve hours a day in the office, and teachers to acquire extra qualifications in the evenings and at weekends. Delphy and Leonard quote studies indicating that where men become unemployed or retired their role in household work does not increase – in fact it seems to decline further. Women in their mid-60s do three times as much domestic work per day as do their spouses.

Marriage, say Delphy and Leonard, is a gendered and unequal division of labour. Where a husband does take over activities from his wife within the home he is likely also to want control of them. It is quite uncommon for husbands to work alongside wives or under their supervision. Where husbands and wives possess similar work skills, it is unusual for husbands to help wives to the same degree to which the reverse occurs. Among those engaged in academic research, for instance, wives help husbands with research activities, interviewing and proof-reading much more frequently than is true the other way around.

The advent of new forms of domestic technology – household appliances and commercially produced services, such as pre-prepared food, disposable nappies and so forth – has only partially reduced the amounts of time women spend on domestic chores. Some such innovations have

actually allowed tasks which used to be undertaken outside the home
to be reincorporated within it – such as laundering. Other chores, such
as the cleaning and the servicing of the home, are now generally expected to be carried out to higher standards than once was the case.

Christina Hardyment (Reading 16) looks specifically at the impact of
'labour-saving' machinery in the home. The domestic appliance market,
she argues, has changed rather little since the early part of the present
century. New domestic machinery has been invented with great frequency over this period, although often the changes are more of style
than substance. Virtually all such innovations encourage an essentially
private mode of housekeeping, rather than integrating the tasks of the
household into wider communal services. The invention and marketing
of domestic machinery thus presumes, and actively sustains, the assumption that the typical consuming unit is a self-sufficient household
cared for by a wife.

At the turn of the century, Hardyment says, other technological possibilities still remained open. At that time there were those who sought
to professionalize domestic service and take it out of the home, rather
than confine it there. Cooking, cleaning and laundry, for example, could
all in principle be done outside the home – either provided in a communal way or bought in as services. Various feminists promoted such a
possibility as desirable, on the basis that it would free women from
subjugation to housework. Thus the radical feminist Charlotte Perkins
Gilman suggested that each local community should have a central
kitchen; families could either eat in restaurants supplied by the kitchen
or have food sent over to the home.

Hardyment agrees with Delphy and Leonard that women's concern
with childcare and domestic tasks blocks their opportunities for achieving equality with men in the workplace. There is a vicious circle involved here. Women will never be able to claim full equality alongside
men until they have comparable levels of earnings and until men participate equally in parenthood and domestic labour. Yet the one form
of inequality is kept in place precisely by the other. Far more women
in paid work are in part-time employment than men; most part-time
jobs are poorly paid and have low promotion prospects. These very
factors serve to drive women back towards the home and the whole
cycle is repeated. Hardyment concludes that some of the suggestions
made by Perkins might still be relevant today to help to break this
cycle. It would be quite feasible to remove a good deal of domestic
labour from the home by the provision of external commercial services.

In Reading 17 Michael Mann takes up the vexed question of the
relation between patriarchy and stratification. The social sciences, he

points out, have been dominated by theories of stratification which place the main emphasis upon social class, status and political power. Gender divisions are acknowledged as important, but not really integrated into the core of stratification theory. Mann identifies five main arenas of stratification that have influenced and been influenced by gender. These are the following: the 'individual', understood as the creation of a liberal market society; the family and household; the division of labour between the sexes; social classes; and nation-states. The relations between gender and stratification are mediated by each of these different 'nuclei'.

The emergence of modern industry, as the various contributors mentioned above also stress, gave patriarchy a new form. Most women became confined to the domestic sphere while men either controlled industry or sold their labour-power to employers to achieve a living wage. Unlike Bradley, who rejects this term, Mann refers to such a development as the emergence of 'neo-patriarchy'. The control of men over women became more indirect and filtered through different institutions from the past. The various 'nuclei' shifted in their connection with one another: for instance, classes became much more significant collective actors than they had been previously. Women, like men, became 'individuals', but gendered individuals through their connection with domesticity. While still involved in patriarchal family systems, they also became members of social classes and affected by such class stratification. Women and men belong essentially to different, but overlapping, stratification hierarchies. Their occupations cannot be meaningfully combined into a single scale, because few occupations are filled interchangeably by men and women and their typical career patterns also differ.

The relative position of women and men, Mann says, is also directly affected by the state. After much struggle, women achieved formal political equality, but are far from fully represented in political organizations or legislative bodies. Politically ordered gender stratification thus intersects with the other institutional arenas.

The resulting picture is a complex one, but Mann concludes that gender and stratification can no longer be kept in separate compartments; 'stratification is now gendered and gender is stratified'.

In Reading 18 Anne Phillips takes up the issue of the representation of women in political organizations. Like Mann, she points out that liberal democracy treats women as equal in so far as there is now universal suffrage, but neglects the highly imbalanced composition of elected assemblies. In all Western countries such assemblies tend to be staffed mainly by white middle-class males. The concern that women should be equally represented in parliaments and other legislative bodies corresponds to a simple demand for justice. But if greater equality for women were achieved in constituent assemblies what difference would this make to the content of political life? For the case for equal representation says nothing about what women would do if elevated to leading political positions.

Democracy in modern societies, Phillips points out, involves, as currently understood, a mixture of accountability and autonomy. The members of elected assemblies are supposed to represent the views of those who put them there, but also to act with a certain amount of independence from the vagaries of public opinion. Not only with regard to gender, but in other respects also, political leaders do not represent the general population – representation is skewed in terms of ethnicity, type of occupation and age. It clearly would be absurd to suppose that political assemblies should exactly mirror the main categories of people in the general population. The important thing is that there is sufficient representation for the various different interests within that population to have some kind of voice. At the moment, Phillips argues, white masculinity casts a shadow over other interests struggling to be heard. Increased representation of women in political bodies would certainly expand the range of concerns those bodies have. There are not many political questions which are specifically and wholly 'women's issues', but there are many problems to which women would probably bring fresh perspectives.

11

Gender and Sexual Temperament

Natalie Zemon Davis

The female sex was thought the disorderly one par excellence in early modern Europe. "*Une beste imparfaicte,*" went one adage, "*sans foy, sans loy, sans craincte, sans constance.*" Female disorderliness was already seen in the Garden of Eden, when Eve had been the first to yield to the serpent's temptation and incite Adam to disobey the Lord. To be sure, the men of the lower orders were also believed to be especially prone to riot and seditious unrest. But the defects of the males were thought to stem not so much from nature as from nurture: the ignorance in which they were reared, the brutish quality of life and conversation in the peasant's hut or the artisan's shop, and their poverty, which led to envy.

With the women the disorderliness was founded in physiology. As every physician knew in the sixteenth century, the female was composed of cold and wet humors (the male was hot and dry), and coldness and wetness meant a changeable, deceptive, and tricky temperament. Her womb was like a hungry animal; when not amply fed by sexual intercourse or reproduction, it was likely to wander about her body, overpowering her speech and senses. If the Virgin Mary was free of such a weakness, it was because she was the blessed vessel of the Lord. But no other woman had been immaculately conceived, and even the well-born lady could fall victim to a fit of the "mother," as the uterus was called. The male might suffer from retained sexual juices, too, but (as Doctor François Rabelais pointed out) he had the wit and will to control his fiery urges by work, wine, or study. The female just became hysterical. In the late seventeenth century, when vanguard physicians were abandoning humoral theories of personality in favor of more mechanistic notions of "animal spirits" and were beginning to remark that men suffered from emotional ills curiously like hysteria, they still maintained that the female's mind was more prone to be disordered by her fragile and unsteady temperament. Long before Europeans were asserting flatly that the "inferiority" of black Africans was innate, rather than the result, say, of climate, they were attributing female "inferiority" to nature.

The lower ruled the higher within the woman, then, and if she were given her way, she would want to rule over those above her outside. Her disorderliness led her into the evil arts of witchcraft, so ecclesiastical authorities claimed; and when she was embarked on some behavior for which her allegedly weak intellect disqualified her, such as theological speculation or preaching, that was blamed on her disorderliness, too. The rule of a queen was impossible in France by the Salic law, and mocked by the common proverb *"tomber en quenouille."* For Pastor John Knox it was a "monstrous regimen," "the subversion of good order . . . all equitie and justice," whereas the more moderate Calvin "reckoned it among the visitations of God's anger," but one that should be borne, like any tyranny, with patience. Even a contemporary defender of queenship, John Aylmer, still had to admit that when he thought of the willfulness of women he favored a strong role for Parliament. As late as 1742, in the face of entomological evidence to the contrary, some apiologists pretended that nature required the rule of a King Bee.

What were the proposed remedies for female unruliness? Religious training that fashioned the reins of modesty and humility; selective education that showed a woman her moral duty without enflaming her undisciplined imagination or loosing her tongue for public talk; honest work that busied her hands; and laws and constraints that made her subject to her husband.

In some ways, that subjection was gradually deepening from the sixteenth to the eighteenth centuries as the patriarchal family streamlined itself for more efficient property acquisition, social mobility, and preservation of the line, and as progress in state-building and the extension of commercial capitalism were achieved at a cost in human autonomy. By the eighteenth century, married women in France and England had largely lost what independent legal personality they had formerly had, and they had less legal right to make decisions on their own about their dowries and possessions than at an earlier period. Propertied women were involved less and less in local and regional political assemblies. Working women in prosperous families were beginning to withdraw from productive labor; those in poor families were increasingly filling the most ill-paid positions of wage labor. This is not to say that females had no informal access to power or continuing vital role in the economy in these centuries; but the character of those relations was in conflict.

Which side of the conflict was helped by the disorderly woman? Since this image was so often used as an excuse for the subjection of women, it is not surprising to find it opposed by one strain in early feminist thought, which argued that women were *not* by nature more unruly, disobedient, and fickle than men. If anything it was the other way around. "By nature, women be sober," said the poet Christine de Pisan, "and those that be not, they go out of kind." Women are by nature more modest and shamefaced than men, claimed a male feminist, which is demonstrated by the fact that women's privy parts are totally covered with pubic hair and are not handled by women the way men's are when they urinate. Why, then, did some men maintain that women were disorderly by nature? Because they were misogynists – vindictive, envious, or themselves dissolute.

These claims and counterclaims about sexual temperament raise questions not merely about the actual character of male and female behavior in pre-industrial Europe, but also about the varied uses of sexual symbolism. Sexual symbolism, of course, is always available to make statements about social experience and to reflect (or conceal) contradictions within it. At the end of the Middle Ages and in early modern Europe, the relation of the wife – of the potentially disorderly woman – to her husband was especially useful for expressing the relation of all subordinates to their superiors, and this for two reasons. First, economic relations were still often perceived in the medieval way as a matter of service. Second, the nature of political rule and the newer problem of sovereignty were very much at issue. In the little world of the family, with its conspicuous tension between intimacy and power, the larger matters of political and social order could find ready symbolization.

Thus, Jean Calvin, himself a collapser of ecclesiastical hierarchies, saw the subjection of the wife to the husband as a guarantee of the subjection of both of them to the authority of the Lord. Kings and political theorists saw the increasing legal subjection of wives to their husbands (and of children to their parents) as a guarantee of the obedience of both men and women to the slowly centralizing state – a training for the loyal subject of seventeenth-century France or for the dutiful citizen of seventeenth-century England. "Marriages are the seminaries of States," began the preamble to the French ordinance strengthening paternal power within the family. For John Locke, opponent of despotic rule in commonwealth and in marriage, the wife's relinquishing her right of decision to her husband as "naturally ... the abler and stronger" was analogous to the individual's relinquishing his natural liberties of decision and action to the legislative branch of government.[1]

Indeed, how could one separate the idea of subordination from the existence of the sexes? Gabriel de Foigny's remarkable fictitious land of Australie (1673), a utopia of hermaphrodites, shows how close the link between the two was perceived to be. The Australian, in whom the sexes were one, could not understand how a conflict of wills could be avoided within the "mutual possession" of European marriage. The French traveler answered that it was simple, for mother and child were both subject to the father. The hermaphrodite, horrified at such a violation of the total autonomy that was the sign of complete true "men," dismissed the European pattern as bestial.[2]

The female's position was used to symbolize not only hierarchical subordination but also violence and chaos. Bruegel's terrifying *Dulle Griet*, painted during the occupation of the Netherlands by Spanish soldiers, makes a huge, armed, unseeing woman, Mad Meg, the emblem of fiery destruction, of brutal oppression and disorder. Bruegel's painting cuts in more than one way, however, and shows how female disorderliness – the female out of her place – could be assigned another value. Next to Mad Meg is a small woman in white on top of a male monster; it is Saint Margaret of Antioch tying up the devil. Nearby other armed women are beating grotesque animals from Hell.

Bruegel's Margarets are by no means alone in pre-industrial Europe. In hierarchical and conflictful societies that loved to reflect on the world-turned-upside-down, the *topos* of the woman-on-top was one of the most enjoyed. Indeed, sexual inversion – that is, switches in sex roles – was a widespread form of cultural play in literature, in art, and in festivity. Sometimes the reversal involved dressing and masking as a member of the opposite sex – the prohibitions of Deuteronomy 22, Saint Paul, Saint Jerome, canon law, and Jean Calvin notwithstanding. Sometimes the reversal involved simply taking on certain roles or forms of behavior characteristic of the opposite sex. Women played men; men played women; men played women who were playing men.

It is the uses of sexual inversion, and more particularly of play with the image of the unruly woman in literature, in popular festivity, and in ordinary life, that will be the subject of the rest of this essay. Evidently, the primary impulse behind such inversion in early modern Europe was not homosexuality or disturbed gender identity. Although Henri III expressed special wishes of his own when he and his male "mignons" masked as Amazons in the 1570s, and although the seventeenth-century Abbé de Choisy, whose mother had dressed him as a girl through adolescence, had special reasons for using a woman's name and wearing female clothes until he was 33, still most literary and festive transvestism at this time had a wider psychosexual and cultural significance than this.

Anthropologists offer several suggestions about the functions of magical transvestism and ritual inversion of sex roles. First, sexual disguise can ward off danger from demons, malignant fairies, or other powers that threaten castration or defloration. Second, transvestism and sexual reversal can be part of adolescent rites of passage, either to suggest the marginality of the transitional state (as when a male initiate is likened to a menstruating woman) or to allow each sex to obtain something of the other's power (as in certain initiation and marriage customs in early Greece). Third, exchange of sex can be part of what Victor Turner has called "rituals of status reversal," as when women in certain parts of Africa usurp the clothing, weapons, or tasks of the superior males and behave in lewd ways to increase the chance for a good harvest or to turn aside an impending natural catastrophe. Finally, as James Peacock has pointed out, the transvestite actor, priest, or shaman can symbolize categories of cosmological or social organization. For instance, in Java the transvestite actor reinforces by his irregularity the importance of the categories high/low, male/female.

However diverse these uses of sexual inversion, anthropologists generally agree that they, like other rites and ceremonies of reversal, are ultimately sources of order and stability in a hierarchical society. They can clarify the structure by the process of reversing it. They can provide an expression of, and a safety valve for, conflicts within the system. They can correct and relieve the system when it has become authoritarian. But, so it is argued, they do not question the basic order of the society itself. They can renew the system, but they cannot change it.

Historians of early modern Europe are likely to find inversions and reversals less in prescribed rites than in carnivals and festivities. Their fools are likely to escape the bounds of ceremony, and their store of literary sources for inversion will include not only the traditional tales of magical transformation in sex, but also a variety of stories in which men and women *choose* to change their sexual status. In addition, there are comic conventions and genres, such as the picaresque, that allow much play with sexual roles. These new forms offered increased occasions and ways in which topsy-turvy could be used for explicit criticism of the social order. Nevertheless, students of these festive and literary forms have ordinarily come to the same conclusion as anthropologists regarding the limits of symbolic inversion: a world-turned-upside-down can only be righted, not changed. To quote Ian Donaldson's recent study *Comedy from Jonson to Fielding*: "The lunatic governor . . . , the incompetent judge, the mock doctor, the equivocating priest, the henpecked husband: such are the familiar and recurrent figures in the comedy of a society which gives a general assent to the necessity of entrusting power to its governors, judges, doctors, priests, and husbands."[3]

I would like to argue, on the contrary, that comic and festive inversion could *undermine* as well as reinforce that assent through its connections with everyday circumstances outside the privileged time of carnival and stage-play. Somewhat in contradistinction to Christine de Pisan and the gallant school of feminists, I want to argue that the image of the disorderly woman did not always function to keep women in their place. On the contrary, it was a multivalent image that could operate, first, to widen behavioral options for women within and even outside marriage, and, second, to sanction riot and political disobedience for both men and women in a society that allowed the lower orders few formal means of protest. Play with the unruly woman is partly a chance for temporary release from the traditional and stable hierarchy; but it is also part of the conflict over efforts to change the basic distribution of power within society. The woman-on-top might even facilitate innovation in historical theory and political behavior.

Notes and References

1   John Locke, *The Second Treatise of Government*, ed. T.P. Peardon (Liberal Arts Press, New York, 1952), ch. 7, para. 82; ch. 9, paras 128–31.
2   [Gabriel de Foigny], *Les avantures de Jacques Sadeur dans la découverte et le voyage de la terre australe* (Amsterdam, 1732), ch. 5, especially pp. 128–39.
3   Ian Donaldson, *The World Upside-Down, Comedy from Jonson to Fielding* (Clarendon, Oxford, 1970), p. 14.

12

Hidden from History

June Purvis

Liberal histories of the nineteenth century have concentrated predominantly on the activities of 'great' individuals in political, economic, intellectual, literary and artistic circles. However, as Matthews points out, this emphasis upon individualism has been restricted to great men and powerful male elites.[1] Indeed, some assert that the 'dirty linen' of great men attracts more attention than the great deeds of unfamous women. When women are mentioned in general histories of the period, it is mainly in relation to the struggle for suffrage; even then, the focus is usually upon one middle-class woman, Emmeline Pankhurst, and upon the organization she founded, the militant Women's Social and Political Union. Thomson, for example, in a popular history of nineteenth-century England first published in 1950 and reprinted up to 1969, limits his discussions to the following observations:

> The demand for extension of the vote to women was nineteenth-century in origin. John Stuart Mill had come to favour it. In 1903 the Women's Social and Political Union was founded at Manchester by Mrs Pankhurst with strong affiliations with the Independent Labour Party.[2]

Working-class women's part in such activities has been largely ignored.

Liberal histories also tend to adopt a 'Whiggish' approach, i.e. they tend to study the past with reference to the present and to classify 'historical personages . . . into the men who furthered progress and the men who tried to hinder it'. Such a division between Whig reformers 'fighting the good fight' against Tory defenders of the status quo provides a rule of thumb by which the historian tends to select and reject evidence according to implicit or explicit assumptions about notions of 'progress' and 'advance'. Feminist historians are critical about the concept of 'progress', especially when applied to women's lives.

The interpretative framework of liberal history has been consistently challenged by Marxist historians who offer, in contrast, a materialist analysis in which political and cultural events are related to the economic mode of production and its historical development. Such an approach derives mainly from the work of two nineteenth-century writers, Frederick Engels and Karl Marx. Social class relations and, in particular, class conflict and class consciousness are central features of such historical analyses. For example, E.P. Thompson, in his epic study *The Making of the English Working Class*, covering the period 1780–1832, defines social class as a relationship that happens 'when men, as a result of common experiences ... feel and articulate the identity of their interests as between themselves, and as against other men whose interests are different from (and usually opposed to) theirs'.[3]

From a Marxist perspective, the contradictions that may arise within the economic mode of production and the compromises made between class interests are also key concerns. Thus the Centre for Contemporary Cultural Studies (CCCS) Education Group, utilizing a Gramscian perspective, identifies various compromises and settlements in education which are interpreted as a result of confrontations between different social classes and various power struggles. Such settlements, however, are unstable and contradictory arrangements which may easily develop into political crises. For the CCCS group, one way of understanding the history of educational policy is in terms of 'the succession of crises and settlements'.[4]

Where Marxist history differs from liberal history is, on the one hand, in its relative lack of emphasis on constitutional matters and on the activities of elites and, on the other hand, in its commitment to revealing the economic and social life of different social classes. There is an emphasis upon providing a 'history from below' or 'history from the bottom up' as it is often called, concentrating especially on the lives of the working classes in nineteenth-century England – for example, the development of community life, trade unionism, education and work. Unfortunately, however, these studies are limited in their usefulness in discovering the experiences of working-class women. Even the most illustrious of Marxist historians seem to take the lead in the 'omission' of women from their accounts. For E.P. Thompson the main focus is upon the way working-class men were active in creating a social class identity.[5] Hobsbawm, in his book specifically entitled *Labouring Men*, includes a range of topics relevant to the working classes, especially to working-class men in the nineteenth century. In a later piece of research, Hobsbawm admits that 'male historians in the past, including Marxists, have grossly neglected the female half of the human race'[6] and attempts to remedy this by examining images of men and women in painting and emblems associated with revolutionary and socialist movements of the nineteenth and early twentieth centuries. His account, however, attracted much criticism. Alexander, Davin and Hostettler, for example, point out that Hobsbawm assumes that the sexual division of labour within the working class is straightforward, since he states that 'typically' only men went out to work while 'conventionally' women stayed at home; Hobsbawm remains firmly within the tradition of labour history, say these critics, in that he ignores the paid and unpaid work that working-class women engaged in within the home.[7]

More recently, in *The Age of Empire 1875–1914*, Hobsbawm devotes a whole chapter to women, especially the so-called emancipated 'new women' of the 1880s onwards, who entered the masculine preserve of the professions, took part in competitive public sports (such as competition tennis) and fought for women's rights. The main focus, however, is upon the lives of *middle-class* women. Some limited attention is given to working-class women but it is assumed that a working-class wife and mother stayed at home, since industrialization brought about a 'separation' between homeplace and workplace that made it difficult for her to earn money in the 'publicly recognized economy': once again, Hobsbawm assumes that 'habitually' women went to work until they married and 'did not usually do so when married'.[8] Although one paragraph is devoted to the poorly paid work that many married working-class women undertook within their own homes, no mention is made of their unpaid work in looking after the men who would form the healthy soldiers and sailors necessary for the maintenance of an empire. Rule's study of the labouring classes in early industrial England from 1750 to 1850 appears exceptional among Marxist histories in that about 6 per cent of the total text is devoted to discussing working-class women's lives in relation to such themes as the family, paid work, sexual exploitation, sexual freedom and prostitution:[9] furthermore, Rule hopes that 'soon a history of the working people will be able to fully incorporate working women'.[10]

This concentration on male experiences is found also, with a few notable exceptions, in contemporary histories of education in the nineteenth century. The education of women, especially working-class women, where visible, is all too often represented as peripheral to the mainstream educational concerns of this period. The majority of histories of nineteenth-century education, mainly written within a progressive, Whiggish framework, have tended to focus upon the administration of education and upon those educational institutions that boys and men were likely to attend, such as state-aided schools, secondary schools, public schools, technical institutions and universities.

Sheldon Rothblatt's history of Cambridge university academics is a typical example of such research. Concentrating solely on male academics, he fails to refer either to the women who fought to enter this male stronghold or to the small number of female lecturers in the various colleges in Cambridge. Although he titled his book *The Revolution of the Dons: Cambridge and Society in Victorian England*, the 'revolution' being waged between the sexes at Cambridge is ignored.[11] Similarly, a 1977 collection of readings edited by Reeder, *Urban Education in the 19th Century*, assumes that working-class boys are the reference point; indeed, in one of the papers, the sparse references to working-class girls are sometimes made in parenthesis, e.g. 'the problem of boy (and girl) labour', 'the discovery of the boy (and girl) labour problem'.[12]

Some histories of nineteenth-century education for working-class children have offered limited discussion of the education of working-class girls, but often this represents a small part of the total work. Hurt, for example, in his study of state-aided elementary schooling and the working classes from 1860 to 1918, devotes at a generous estimate only twelve pages to this topic, and even then it is mainly in relation to the teaching of domestic subjects such as needlework, sewing and cookery. Furthermore, Hurt's language helps perpetuate the idea that most pupils in the educational system are male:

> for the greater part of historical time children have received their education outside the classroom. Schooling has been the experience of the minority of *mankind* before the present century. Such phrases as 'got *his* book-learning' or 'got *his* schooling' vividly demonstrate the way in which the distinction between formal and informal education lives on in the minds of the elderly.[13]

The use of such language tends to hide or marginalize the presence of girls in educational institutions. In contrast, the work of Stephens and of Horn[14] appears exceptional in the attention given to the schooling of working-class boys *and* girls.

Marxist historians of working-class education in the nineteenth century, such as Silver, Johnson and Simon,[15] equally pay little attention to the education of females. One of the aims of Silver's *The Concept of Popular Education* is to explore the role of education in establishing 'a popular or working-class consciousness', while Simon attempts to relate the ideas of reformers and educational provision to 'social and political conflicts' of the period. Although both writers broaden the concept of 'education' to include adult education and various self-help educational ventures, references to working-class women in these activities are conspicuous by their absence.

One might expect general histories of adult education to pay at least some attention to the experiences of working-class women in the nineteenth century, if only because at that time adult education was clearly associated with men and women in the 'lower' orders. Yet if Roderick and Stephen's comparative account of the development of post-school education in England and America in the nineteenth century is an example, it is disappointing that coverage of the activities of working-class men is made with no reference to those of their womenfolk.[16] The same pattern can be found in Harrison's account of adult education in Yorkshire from 1790 to 1960.[17] Kelly's history of adult education in Great Britain does include some mention of working-class women as students in the nineteenth century but the amount of space given to the theme is minimal, e.g. a paragraph on women in an adult Sunday school, a paragraph on women in the working men's college movement.[18]

Male-centred histories of the nineteenth century are now being scrutinized by feminist historians, who question the assumptions made, the boundaries within which such knowledge is produced and the lens through which such events are interpreted. Some account of the development of this critique is necessary before we define what is meant by 'feminist' history and consider its relevance for this study.

Some writers, such as Norris, Lewis and Purvis,[19] trace the development of recent interest in feminist history to the so-called second wave of the organized women's movement in Britain, Western Europe and the USA from the late 1960s. In England such an interest was fuelled by the presence within the women's movement of several socialist/Marxist feminists who, like many on the left, had an enthusiasm for investigating historical patterns; disillusioned with the male bias of socialist/Marxist history and with the way they were treated by the male left, many of these women became immersed in feminist debates, theorizing and research.

An influential figure in England at this time was Sheila Rowbotham, whose book *Hidden from History: 300 years of women's oppression and the fight against it*, published in 1973, is usually regarded as the catalyst for the growth in the history of women, and especially of nineteenth-century women.[20] Other texts published since then, with words such as 'liberating', 'making visible', 'exploring' or 'rewriting' women's history in their titles, capture the spirit of Rowbotham's book. It was a path that was forged overwhelmingly by women, though it was specifically feminists who set the pace. Feminist history therefore developed as separate from mainstream history, and still has only an indirect relationship with it today. In particular, some historians in the academic world will not accept the 'academic status' of feminist history; Professor Sir Geoffrey Elton, for example, refers to women's history and the history of minorities as 'non-existent'.[21]

As feminist historians developed their perspective in the 1970s, the approach became more complex. For some, studying women was not a sufficient justification for being a 'feminist' historian. And the debate about the concept of 'feminist' history continues today, linked, as it was in the 1970s, into theoretical divisions within the women's movement and different definitions of 'feminism'.

Various interpretations of 'feminism' are available. Radcliffe Richards, for example, argues that the essence of feminism is the belief that women suffer from systematic social injustice because of their sex. Oakley suggests that feminism is about putting women first, about judging their interests to be important and insufficiently represented and accommodated within mainstream politics and the academic world. Spender claims that a feminist is a woman who does not accept man's socially sanctioned view of himself and that feminism refers to the alternative meanings put forward by feminists. Stanley and Wise emphasize that the central core of feminism is the belief that women are oppressed by the sexual political system and by men. Smith stresses that feminism is the political theory and practice that struggles to free all women: women of colour, working-class women, poor women, disabled women, lesbians, old women – as well as white, economically privileged, heterosexual women. For Jaggar feminism refers to all those people seeking to end women's subordination.[22]

What unites such definitions, despite their differing emphases, is the view of feminism as being not only about women and for women but also about sexual, class and racial oppression. It is also clear that feminism cannot easily be defined purely as a set of beliefs or a particular perspective – it is a political movement involving political actions. And like many political movements it is complex, with a number of internal divisions that do not easily separate. These divisions have roots which may be traced back, claims Banks, to three intellectual traditions that had their origins in the eighteenth century – evangelical Christianity, Enlightenment philosophy and communitarian socialism.[23] The divisions between feminists today are hard to classify, given the variety of perspectives *within* each division as well as the overlap between divisions. However, the following six groupings are commonly identified: radical feminism, Marxist feminism, socialist feminism, liberal feminism, black feminism and cultural feminism. Such differentiation, especially between the two main groupings – radical feminism and socialist feminism – has profound implications for the way history is interpreted.

It is important to note that whatever the definition of feminism and its divisions, not all female historians studying women wish their work to be placed under the umbrella of 'feminist' history. There are also a number of male historians studying women's experiences who have no connection to feminist debates and feminist circles. Women's history is not therefore necessarily feminist history; neither does feminist history just concentrate upon women. Feminist history is not defined by its subject matter but by the ideas and theories that inform a feminist analysis.

Clearly feminist history has involved questioning the form and content of historical knowledge since the majority of historical works are written by men and, as discussed earlier, generally *about* men. As Davin notes, men's activities – in war, courts, politics, diplomacy, administration and business – were the stuff of the drama. Women's activities were unrecorded at the time, and later were excluded as an area for study by the male-oriented definition of history.[24] Similarly, Lerner observes that men have defined their experiences as '*history*' and left women out.[25] Obviously, a problem exists if 'Men's histories' have been portrayed as 'universally human'.[26] Feminists, therefore, often call this perspective *man-made* or *male-stream* history – a historical view within which women have been ignored or hidden.

Notes and References

1 J. Matthews, 'Barbara Bodichon', in *Feminist Theorists*, ed. D. Spender (Women's Press, London, 1983), p. 118.
2 D. Thomson, *England in the Nineteenth Century* (Penguin, Harmondsworth, 1950), p. 187.
3 E.P. Thompson, *The Making of the English Working Class* (Penguin, Harmondsworth, 1974), pp. 9–10.
4 Centre for Contemporary Cultural Studies Education Group, *Unpopular Education* (Hutchinson, London, 1981), p. 32.
5 Thompson, *The Making*.
6 E. Hobsbawm, *Labouring Men* (Weidenfeld and Nicholson, London, 1964); E. Hobsbawm, 'Man and woman in socialist iconography', *History Workshop*, 6 (1978), p. 121.
7 S. Alexander, A. Davin and E. Hostettler, 'Labouring women', *History Workshop*, 8 (1979), p. 175.
8 E. Hobsbawm, *The Age of Empire 1875–1914* (Cardinal, London, 1987), pp. 197–8.
9 J. Rule, *The Labouring Classes in Early Industrial England* (Longman, London, 1986).
10 Ibid., p. 393.

11 S. Rothblatt, *The Revolution of the Dons* (Faber, London, 1968).
12 D. Reeder, 'Predicaments of city children', in his *Urban Education in the 19th Century* (Taylor and Francis, London, 1977), pp. 89–90.
13 J.S. Hurt, *Elementary Schooling* (Routledge and Kegan Paul, London, 1979), p. 136, emphasis added.
14 P. Horn, *The Victorian Country Child* (Alan Sutton, Stroud, 1990); P. Horn, *Education in Rural England* (Gill and Macmillan, Dublin, 1978); W. Stephens, *Education, Literacy and Society* (Manchester University Press, Manchester, 1987).
15 R. Johnson, 'Education policy and social control in Victorian England', *Past and Present*, 49 (1970), pp. 96–119; R. Johnson, 'Notes on the schooling of the English working class 1780–1850', in *Schooling and Capitalism*, ed. R. Dale, G. Esland and M. MacDonald (Routledge and Kegan Paul, London, 1976).
16 G. Roderick and M. Stephens, *Post School Education* (Croom Helm, London, 1984).
17 J. Harrison, *Learning and Living* (Routledge and Kegan Paul, London, 1961).
18 T. Kelly, *A History of Adult Education in Great Britain* (Liverpool University Press, Liverpool, 1962), pp. 80, 187.
19 J. Norris, 'Women's history', *North West Labour History Society Bulletin* (1980–1), p. 7; J. Lewis, 'Women lost and found', in *Men's Studies Modified*, ed. D. Spender (Pergamon, Oxford, 1981), p. 58; J. Purvis, 'A feminist perspective on the history of women's education', in *The Education of Girls and Women*, ed. J. Purvis (History of Education Society, Leicester, 1985), p. 1.
20 S. Rowbotham, *Hidden from History* (Pluto Press, London, 1973).
21 This remark was made at a meeting of the Historical Association in January 1986; *The Guardian* (14 January 1986).
22 J. Richards, *The Sceptical Feminist* (Penguin, Harmondsworth, 1980), p. 1; A. Oakley, *Subject Women* (Fontana, London, 1981), p. 335; D. Spender, *Women of Ideas and What Men Have Done to Them* (Pandora, London, 1982), p. 7; L. Stanley and S. Wise, *Breaking Out* (Routledge and Kegan Paul, London, 1983), pp. 51–2; B. Smith, 'Racism and women's studies', in *All the Women are White, All the Blacks are Men, But Some of Us are Brave*, ed. G. Hull, P. Scott and B. Smith (Feminist Press, New York, 1982), p. 49; A. Jaggar, *Feminist Politics and Human Nature* (Rowman and Allanheld, Totowa, N.J., 1983), p. 5.
23 O. Banks, *Faces of Feminism* (Martin Robertson, Oxford, 1981).
24 A. Davin, 'Women and history', in *The Body Politic*, ed. M. Wandor (Stage 1, London, 1972), p. 216.
25 Lerner, 'Placing women in history: a 1975 perspective', in *Liberating Women's History*, ed. B. Carroll (University of Illinois Press, Urbana, Ill., 1976), p. 365.
26 J. Matthews, *Good and Mad Women* (Allen and Unwin, Boston, Mass., 1984), p. 18.

13

Homemaking

Philip Pacey

Much of the nineteenth-century literature on 'homemaking' (like that on childcare) was either addressed directly to women or defined, elevated, yet confined woman's role by designating her 'the presiding spirit of home'. 'It is the province of woman to make home', wrote one gentleman in 1837; 'If she makes that delightful and salutary – the abode of order and purity, though she may never herself step beyond the threshold, she may yet send forthe from her humble dwelling, a power that will be felt round the globe.'[1] Such was the role propagated for women by men and women too, accepted or absorbed into their way of life by many housewives. It was a role which, in particular, both lauded, and *limited*, female creativity, smothering it with advice and instruction as well as restriction; yet creativity could win through, sometimes in open rebellion, sometimes through covert expression of frustration, and sometimes – as we shall see – by bringing to 'homemaking' a truly innovative spirit, transforming it by making of it a 'labour of love', and by winning from it family art.

[...]

The ideal of woman as homemaker and mistress of arts (or crafts) was grafted onto the housewifely role. From the fifteenth century, when Mary and the female saints began to be depicted as gentler and more maternal than their queenly and aristocratic bearing in medieval iconography, as befitted the relatively domestic settings in which they now appeared, a clear division opened between professional embroidery and the activities of women in the home who were responsible for an 'extraordinary spread of domestic embroidery':

> Every conceivable surface became a site for embroidery: sheets, valances and coverlets, table carpets, cupboard carpets, cushions for benches and chairs, coifs, stomachers, sleeves, handkerchiefs, bags, hawking gear, needlecases, book covers, book marks, book cushions, shoes, gloves and aprons.[2]

Embroidery became part of a woman's education, if that can possibly be the right word for a strictly limited, vocational training for a lifelong occupation; as such, and because of its domestic applications, it was downgraded to a mere 'craft' among the arts. Thus Nicholas Hilliard in *A treatise concerning the art of limning* of c.1600 carefully and deliberately distinguished painting by *dis*association:

> It tendeth not to common men's use, either for furnishing houses or any patterns for tapestries.

In the seventeenth-century Dutch town house, the physical separation of (male) 'work' from the home, and a very modest use of servants, consolidated and enhanced the responsibilities of married women who had 'the whole care and absolute management of all their Domestique'; paintings of Dutch interiors made this housewifely role visible in such a way as to make it seem timeless and inevitable. In painting after painting we see a wife, or a wife and a servant, putting away clean linen, sweeping the floor, bent over needlework, or playing a musical instrument.

But it was with the nineteenth century and the ideal of the 'artistic house' in particular that a powerful image of the housewife as a mistress of arts was created, its roots in historical precedent imaginatively enriched – Roszika Parker has shown how an idea of the medieval noblewoman, chastely and patiently embroidering in her secluded rooms in the safety of the castle, became a 'blue-print for the middle-class Victorian wife . . .'.[3] Woman as 'presiding spirit' of the home needed to be equipped with an array of skills, including needlework which

> brings daily blessings to every home, unnoticed, perhaps, because of its hourly silent application; for in a household each stitch is one for comfort to some person or other and without its ever watchful care home would be a scene of discomfort indeed.[4]

To support this womanly role, the literature of 'homemaking' was expanded to include 'how to' and 'hobby' books; magazines provided patterns for needlework from the late eighteenth century; suppliers marketed materials, kits, and patterns. Indeed, this is still the case:

'Knit his 'n hers sweaters', 'A pretty layette for baby' and 'Bean bags for the boys' are typical titles of craft projects to be found in women's magazines which serve to reproduce and support the 'norm' of the nuclear family unit and the place and function of woman within it.[5]

Not only is there nothing creative about slavishly following patterns, but ill-conceived projects, promoted as part of an urging of the housewife to make, make, make, have yielded some dire results, provoking Charles Kingsley, for instance, to speak of 'the abomination of "Fancy work" . . .'.[6] But at the same time we should beware of identifying creativity purely and simply with extrovert self-expression or 'originality'. Folk art produced subtle variations on established themes:

Quilt patterns were published and passed along in the 19th century (just as fashionable art styles are in today's art world). The innovative quilt maker or group of makers would come up with a new idea that broke or enriched the rules, just as the Navajo rug maker might vary brilliantly within set patterns (and modern abstractionists innovate by sticking to the rules of innovation).

Just so:

The shared or published pattern forms the same kind of armature . . . for freedom of expression within a framework as the underlying grid does in contemporary painting.[7]

And indeed it is right and proper that quilting, embroidery, and other products of women's creativity in the home have been subject to reassessment, by feminist art historians in particular, and have inspired, and been celebrated by, some contemporary women artists. Miriam Schapiro, for instance, has made artworks from scraps of material like those to be found in a thrifty housewife's rag-bag, cutting out and incorporating patchwork shapes of a heart and a house, in conscious tribute to her own mother's 'labour of love'.

'Homemaking' defined women's creativity in a way that limited it from the outset; it also added to the burden of housework. The effect this could have on a woman's innate creativity is movingly and illuminatingly told by a nineteenth-century American housewife, Jane Swisshelm:

During all my girlhood I saw no pictures, no art gallery, no studio, but had learned to feel great contempt for my own efforts at picture-making. A traveling artist stopped in Wilkinsburg and painted some portraits; we visited his studio, and a new world opened to me. Up to that time painting had seemed as inaccessible as the moon – a sublimity I no more thought of reaching than a star; but when I saw a portrait on the easel, a palette of paints and some brushes, I was at home in a new world. . . .

Bard, the wagon-maker, made me a stretcher, and with a yard of unbleached muslin, some tacks and white lead, I made a canvas. In the shop were white lead, lampblack, king's yellow and red lead, with oil and turpentine. I watched Bard mix paints, and concluded I wanted brown. Years before, I heard of brown umber, so I got umber and some brushes and began my husband's portrait. I hid it when he was there or I heard any one coming, and once blistered it badly trying to dry it before the fire, so that it was a very rough work; but it was a portrait, a daub, a likeness, and the hand was his hand and no other. The figure was correct, and the position in the chair, and, from the moment I began it, I felt I had found my vocation. . . . I forgot God, and did not know it; forgot philosophy, and did not care to remember it; but alas! I forgot to get Bard's dinner, and, although I forgot to be hungry, I had no reason to suppose he did. He would willingly have gone hungry, rather than give any one trouble; but I had neglected a duty. Not only once did I do this; but again and again, the fire went out or the bread ran over in the pans, while I painted and dreamed.

My conscience began to trouble me. Housekeeping was 'woman's sphere', although I had never then heard the words, for no woman had gotten out of it to be hounded back; but I knew my place and scorned to leave it. I tried to think I could paint without neglect of duty. It did not occur to me that painting was a duty for a married woman! Had the passion seized me before marriage, no other love could have come between me and art; but I felt that it was too late, as my life was already devoted to another subject – housekeeping.

It was a hard struggle. I tried to compromise, but experience soon deprived me of that hope, for to paint was to be oblivious of all other things. In my doubt, I met one of those newspaper paragraphs with which men are wont to pelt women into subjection: 'A man does not marry an artist, but a housekeeper'. This fitted my case, and my doom was sealed.

I put away my brushes; resolutely crucified my divine gift, and while it hung writhing on the cross, spent my best years and powers cooking cabbage. . . .[8]

It is noteworthy that Jane began by painting a portrait of her husband – family art that ought to be reconcilable with housekeeping. But Jane's creative impulse could not easily submit to restraint; clearly she was a born artist who should have had the opportunity to explore and develop her gift as freely as any man. When such opportunities were at last granted to women, they came, significantly, in the area of craft and design education in the first instance, and only later in the 'fine' arts; initially conceived as an extension of the educating of women as homemakers, and of the tuition which better-off families had been able to buy in for their daughters, art school classes for women were presented conservatively:

> We may remark, at the risk of repetition, that there is here no question of the introduction of women to new employments, or of the danger of tempting them from their homes.[9]

Yet many women have somehow been able to reconcile their innate creativity with a domestic role, sometimes happily, sometimes with mixed feelings but in ways which, rather than confronting domesticity head-on, transform it more or less successfully into a 'labour of love'. Just how much of a woman, and of a family, could be stitched into a quilt, even into a geometric design that on the face of it does not give anything away, is revealed in this recollection:

> It took me nearly twenty years, nearly twenty-five, I reckon, in the evening after supper when the children were all put to bed. My whole life is in that quilt. It scares me sometimes when I look at it. All my joys and all my sorrows are stitched into those little pieces. When I was proud of the boys and when I was downright provoked and angry with them. When the girls annoyed me or when they gave me a warm feeling around my heart. And John too. He was stitched into that quilt and all the thirty years we were married. Sometimes I loved him and sometimes I sat there hating him as I pieced the patches together. So they are all in that quilt, my hopes and fears, my joys and sorrows, my loves and hates. I tremble sometimes when I remember what that quilt knows about me.[10]

Such a quilt is an example of what Melissa Meyer and Miriam Schapiro have called 'femmage' – a collage-like reassembling of bits and pieces, inspired or necessitated by a thrifty using of what is to hand and might otherwise be wasted.[11] 'Necessity is the mother, not the father of invention,' says Lucy Lippard.[12] And indeed the very materials available inspired innovation, where a kit would have produced imitation; not only that, but their associations – the fact that, as dresses, shirts, curtains, or whatever, the scraps of material had already been part of the family's visual world and might be identified with particular members of the family – made of their reassembly the creating of a special kind of family chronicle and archive, an embellishing of home with memories of itself.

The improvising of various artefacts, from bits and pieces, was often praised as 'making something from nothing', but did not invariably demonstrate the miracle of creativity which that phrase suggests. However, Robert Roberts's tribute to his mother, who had poverty and a husband prone to drunkenness to contend with in the insalubrious environment of the Salford slums, bears eloquent witness to motherhood at its most creative:

> Skill seemed to flow through my mother's fingers. . . . My sisters said she could stare a few minutes at any garment in a shop window, then come home and make a replica. Did I, or another child, catch her at ease and want a kite that flew, a castle from a sauce box, a bow that really shot arrows? She turned them out, and well. . . .[13]

Where imitation was required, she achieved it without help from a pattern or kit; given a free hand, she didn't hesitate to originate and invent. The creativity which childcare requires, and that children themselves can inspire, sometimes doesn't call for more than perceiving a possibility and allowing it to happen. Such an incident was recorded by Mrs Almira Phelps in a diary of observations of her own child in the 1830s. She gave her boy a box of wafers and let him shake and pull at the box until he was able to open it. When 'hundreds of bright round pieces fell about him in glorious confusion' she felt that he 'had conquered a difficulty and had made a discovery'.[14] Undoubtedly *my* mother's creativity, including her activities as an amateur artist (and a willingness to let things happen – as I write this I suddenly and vividly recall free-ranging explorations and tippings-out of her bag of assorted buttons), account for my becoming interested in art at an early age, while sadly and ironically my interest in art certainly contributed to my becoming a harsh judge of much of what she actually produced. At the same time I detected, and reacted against, the 'stink of poverty'[15] associated with the necessarily homemade – money was short, and we often had to 'make do'; the results seemed a poor substitute for what money could buy. (Happily, what I regard as by far my mother's best painting is a portrait of our eldest son, done from a photograph recording a memorable occasion – a notable example of family art.)

In sometimes 'making something from nothing', or allowing marvels to happen as if out of nothing, Woman continues an ancient tradition, of priestess, mediator between Nature and Man; she re-enacts a revelation, teaches how to see by showing what is there to be seen, in a context in which

> the idea is no longer to make nothings into somethings, but to transform and give meanings to all things.[16]

Something of this same role comes into play in her involvement, as 'presiding spirit' and tutelar, in breadmaking, the preparation of food, the ceremonies which attend its eating and which bless the house:

> It is easy to make of love
> these ceremonials. As priests
> we fold cloth, break bread, share wine,
> hope there's enough to go round.[17]

Yet what is being referred to here is surely a 'femininity' that women and men share, if not in equal part?

Notes and References

1   J. Stearns, 'Female influence, and the true Christian mode of its exercise', quoted in *Artists in Aprons: Folk Art by American Women*, ed. K. Dewhurst, B. MacDowell and M. MacDowell (Dutton, New York, 1979), pp. 38–9.

2   R. Parker, *The Subversive Stitch* (The Women's Press, London, 1984), p. 69.

3   Ibid., p. 24.

4   E. Warren and Mrs Pullan, 'Treasures of needlework', quoted in Parker, *The Subversive Stitch*, pp. 154–5.

5   P. Dalton, 'Housewives, leisure crafts and ideology: de-skilling in consumer crafts', in *Women and Craft*, ed. G. Elinor, S. Richardson, S. Scott, A. Thomas and K. Walker (Virago, London, 1987), pp. 31–6.

6   C. Kingsley, 'Glaucus: or the wonders of the shore', quoted in Parker, *The Subversive Stitch*, p. 65.

7   L. Lippard, 'Making something from nothing: towards a definition of women's "hobby art" ', *Heresies*, 4 (1978), pp. 62–5.

8   J. Swisshelm, 'Half a century', quoted in Dewhurst, MacDowell and MacDowell, *Artists in Aprons*, pp. 42–3.

9   'Art-works for women III', *Art Journal*, 34 (1872), p. 130.

10 M. Ickis, *The Standard Book of Quilt Making and Collecting* (Dover, New York, 1960), p. 270.

11 M. Meyer and M. Schapiro, 'Waste not want not', *Heresies*, 4 (1978), pp. 66–9.

12 Lippard, 'Making something from nothing'.

13 R. Roberts, *A Ragged Schooling: Growing Up in the Classic Slum* (Manchester University Press, Manchester, 1976), p. 30.

14 A. Phelps, 'Observations on an infant', quoted in C. Hardyment, *Dream Babies: Child Care from Locke to Spock* (Cape, London, 1983), p. 75.

15 A. Walker and K. Walker, 'Starting with rag rugs: the aesthetics of survival', in Elinor et al., *Women and Craft*, p. 27.

16 Lippard, 'Making something from nothing', p. 65.

17 G. Clarke, *Letter from a Far Country* (Carcanet New Press, Manchester, 1982).

14

Gendered Jobs and Social Inequality

Harriet Bradley

The pre-industrial family was patriarchal. Despite the importance of women's economic contribution to the household unit, their work was framed by male authority and household requirements. Although a few took female careers and became independent craftswomen, the majority of married women worked in subordination to men's needs. Many worked with their menfolk in a family business and here they often took on the roles and tasks which, however important they really were, were conventionally *seen* as subsidiary. Women were *seen* as assistants and 'helpmeets' to men. Patriarchy did not preclude an appreciation of the complementarity of male and female economic activities; and the informality of the household economy meant that there was a flexibility in the sexual division of labour which permitted greater varieties than under the new system of production which was to supplant it.

Industrial capitalism brought many changes to the family, but not an immediate end to patriarchy. This epoch is one of 'neo-patriarchy' but the continuities are so marked that the name change seems unnecessary. For a start men clung on to their political and public supremacy in their persona of head of household, with women still lacking a political and public voice. Middle-class women by and large had their economic roles constricted and, becoming confined to the home, fell more firmly under male control. Indigent women of the middle classes, especially those who failed to find a husband, escaped this but were often forced into demeaning and ill-paid forms of work subject to the tyranny of employers. In some industries household working systems continued well into the nineteenth century and it is surely right to see these as an alternative type of patriarchal control strategy to the trade unions' exclusionary strategies which we have also seen so frequently in evidence. Once the household systems broke down, many working men took up the call for politics which would permit them to keep wives at home, under their patriarchal control as in the middle-class family. Although many working-class women, especially single girls, did 'go out' to work, thus escaping supervision by fathers and husbands, they were nonetheless usually subject to male authority when at work and in most homes the word of the father was still law. Indeed, in many working-class homes, young girls were still required to hand over their wage packets to their parents, and to accept their parents' decisions about when they left school and what jobs they should take, right up until the Second World War. Although mothers often took charge of such arrangements they themselves were subject to male decisions (sometimes violently enforced) and in running the household they shaped things to fit the father's activities and requirements, always seen as the first priority. Women's work through the nineteenth century continued to be framed in terms of either the family's or society's needs. It was only men, historically, who could take account of their own personal bents, needs and satisfactions.

However, by the end of the nineteenth century patriarchy had, more generally, come under attack. Middle-class feminist campaigners were fighting their way back into economic life. The legal backing of patriarchy was beginning to crumble as the Married Women's Property Act of 1882 paved the way for women's rights and female suffrage. In their famous (or infamous!) book *The Symmetrical Family* Willmott and Young argued that these developments, along with increased labour market opportunities for women and improved contraceptive technology, have culminated in the twentieth century in the appearance of the symmetrical family, where sex roles are less differentiated, with both spouses going out to work and men sharing in domestic work, and power is equalized.[1] But more recent studies of the family hardly sustain such a view.

If families are no longer strictly patriarchal they are still transmitters of sex inequalities. The ideals of the family wage, the male breadwinner and the full-time mother are nourished within the family and these ideals are highly supportive of segregation. Despite Willmott and Young's curious findings, more recent surveys of domestic labour have shown that women still bear the brunt of housework and childcare and, most importantly, bear responsibility for it. This is perhaps even more true of America than Britain. If married women go out to work, it is up to them to make alternative arrangements to cover housework and childcare. This, in turn, restricts their entry into employment. Jobs have to fit in with their domestic duties (part-time work, perhaps, located near to the home, homeworking in some cases). Their careers are broken to look after young children, typically at the key stages in which male colleagues are starting on the promotion ladder; as a result their chances of promotion and of further training are limited. Exhausted by the burden of looking after children and bearing responsibility for the home on top of a full-time job, women lack the energy to perform as well as men or to engage in the social and political wheeler-dealing essential for success in competitive jobs. All this traps women in a vicious circle of dependence. Domestic responsibilities prevent them from getting jobs which pay as well as men; it then becomes rational for the person with lower economic prospects to become the domestic worker, full time if necessary; this further limits their prospects. And so on.

Modern marriages may be 'companionate' rather than 'patriarchal', in Stone's terminology, but by and large, I would argue, families remain 'androcentric'. Arrangements within them are still moulded to the requirements of men. Families move around the country because of men's career choices and potentials. Women fit their choices in round this. Although most men in the 1980s no longer express hostility to the idea of their wives going out to work, as they have so often done in the past, there is often an implicit assumption that a wife can only take on a job if she can arrange matters so that the everyday management of the home is not disrupted. Modern families are extremely variable and flexible in their form and in their internal arrangements. But, where there is an adult male within them, economic choices revolve upon him. Family arrangements now, just as in pre-industrial societies, promote and support segregation in work.

Segregation and sex-typing, then, pre-date capitalist industry. Many of the gender arrangements of early capitalist production sprang directly from the patterns of work that existed in the pre-capitalist economy. However, capitalism has had a crucial role in maintaining, consolidating and reconstructing patterns of segregation and sex-typing. The employment of women in jobs designated as 'women's work' was a key part of the development of a degraded capitalist labour process. This served two purposes for capitalist employers. Women could be employed more cheaply, because of the lower social value already put on their work, thus leading to the accumulation of more profit. In addition the use of female labour helped in the struggle to break the control of male workers which was founded in their knowledge of and mastery over traditional craft techniques. When men fought back by claiming that certain jobs must remain 'male', this only served to deepen segregation, a process I define as 'resegmentation'. Women were driven into low-paid female jobs, thus posing less threat to the male workers while simultaneously satisfying the desire of capitalists for cheap labour. At times, capitalist employers and trade unions colluded in maintaining sex-typing, as patriarchal ideologies and interests overrode class divisions. Notions of skill and technology and their different application to the sexes have been used to ensure that technological change confirms the allotment of prime jobs to men, while women are pushed into the mindless machine-minding jobs produced by mechanical advance and 'rationalization'.

However, there is no *logical* necessity within the capitalist dynamic for sexual divisions to be created or maintained. Capitalism thrives on dividing the workforce, but there are other ways of doing this, as the example of South Africa shows. Further, let us note the flexibility of capitalist production, its ability to adapt to circumstances and make use of whatever is at hand in the search for profit. The attempt to show that capitalist production must *necessarily* be founded on gender divisions and the marginalization of women, that these are 'an essential and fundamental characteristic' of capitalist production relations, is therefore mistaken.[2] However, since sex divisions are the most fundamental and primary within human societies apart from age divisions (in the sense that being derived in part from biology they inevitably pre-date those that are purely cultural) and since family relations and social ideologies have so persistently emphasized gender differences, there can be no doubt that historically capitalist production has *always* developed, in each and every case, on the basis of sex-typed jobs. The consistency of segregation in capitalist nations around the world is clear. However, though capitalist production must historically be seen as gendered and although the reproduction of capitalist production relations means the reproduction of gender divisions, this does not mean that an end to capitalism will bring an end to sex-typing. As the examples of Russia and China show, family relationships together with ideologies of gender will ensure that segregation continues unless those, too, change. Since we argue that gender relations must be seen as separate from economic ones (although everywhere interpenetrated with them and acting upon them and being acted upon by them) there is no justification for the claim that socialism (even 'true' socialism) would, by itself, bring an end to sexual inequality, as long as socialism is defined as a type of economic arrangement.

A contrasting view comes from Elshtain. She believes that it is possible to achieve sex parity within a framework which accepts that men and women are different and will thus be found doing different things. To my mind such an account seriously overlooks the way in which gender relations are interpenetrated by capitalist relations. In a type of production system based on the assumption that hierarchies are necessary and that people at different levels in the hierarchy should be rewarded differently, any type of visible difference (gender, ethnicity) is prone to be seized upon and incorporated into the hierarchies of work. To this extent Marxists are right in their assertion that capitalism promotes racial and sexual divisions. For example, the Confederation of British Industry is currently campaigning for the abolition of British anti-discrimination legislation on the grounds that having to pay women as much as men makes British industry 'non-competitive'. While I am trying to ram home the message that stratification is gendered, we must not forget that the converse is equally true: as Mann says 'gender is stratified'.[3]

The importance of gender ideologies must be emphasized. The ideology of domesticity and of separate spheres is usually seen as emerging within the family as a response to the disruptions brought by industrialization, which destroyed traditional family roles and required in particular the specification of new social functions for women, but social meanings of masculinity and femininity were also negotiated *within the workplace itself* in the course of changes and conflicts. Despite the doctrine of 'separate spheres' many women took part in economic activity inside and outside the home and would continue to do so. Therefore it was necessary to establish notions of 'suitable' work for women and of the proper type of work environment in which this should take place. Moral panics involving the constant reiteration of these notions drove women out of some jobs (mining, farmwork and fishing) and into others (nursing, shop work and food processing). Thus ideas about feminine and masculine nature and behaviour were highly involved in the gendering of jobs and resulted in the formation of gendered work cultures. Matthaei has emphasized this strongly in her study of sex-typing in America; she also makes the point that such definitions were not simply imposed on male and female workpeople, but that they shared in their construction: 'a basic force behind sex-typing of jobs was the workers' desires to assert and reaffirm their manhood or womanhood and hence their difference from the opposite sex'.[4]

This continues to be a 'force' today in steering boys and girls into 'appropriate' career choices, especially in the teenage phase when sexual identity appears very fragile. Gendered work cultures then continue the process, helping to perpetuate notions of distinct sexual identities as has been well documented by Cockburn; as she says, work-based gender ideologies specify

> What a man 'is', what a woman 'is', what is right and proper, what is possible and impossible, what should be hoped and what should be feared. The hegemonic ideology of masculism involves a definition of men and

women as different, contrasted, complementary and unequal. It is powerful and it deforms both men and women.[5]

Employers have used the perception that women prefer working with
women, men with men, to justify both sex divisions and discriminatory
practices. But it should be emphasized that this perception appears
basically correct. Both women and men have accepted the idea that it
is more pleasant to work among your own sex. Many men prefer male
exclusivity at work and have fought over the years to keep women out
and developed ways to keep them in their place when they get in. Fine
has demonstrated some of the tactics used by males against women seen
as intruders in their cheerful and companionable male environments.[6]
Women are considered potentially disruptive and are made to feel
outcasts unless they are prepared to join in the male culture with its
swearing, boozing and sexist banter. Equally many women seem prepared to accept social definitions of what they can or cannot do and are
happy to find themselves in a feminized work environment. Only a
minority have rejected prevailing expectations. Here again ideas of the
skills specific to each sex and of the different aptitudes of men and
women with regard to technology are at play and are largely accepted;
in this way sex distinctions are seen as necessary and unavoidable.

Gendered work cultures are still well entrenched today. Many female
work groups in factories and offices 'bring home into' the work environment, both domesticating it (making boring work more tolerable, making the office a pleasant, sociable and cosy place to be in) and also being
domesticated by it (as once again the 'inbuilt' domestic orientation of
women is emphasized and made visible to men). Women in the traditionally female professions have no need to import the home into work,
for it is already there! Hospitals and schools mirror family relationships
and in them women practice their 'inbuilt' feminine skills for the public
good. As long as most comprehensive schools are headed by men, while
men teach boys football, women teach girls netball, men teach physics
and woodwork, women teach English and domestic science, it is hardly
surprising that overt messages of sex equality put forward by teachers
in lessons make little impression.

The position of the minority of women who enter male-dominated
trades and professions is rather different. They are faced, by contrast,
with the problem of fitting into a male occupational culture. This presents them with a double bind; if they take men on in their own terms,
they are denying their femininity, which may diminish their private status
as women; if they assert their femininity they risk being labelled as
inferior and inadequate workers. American women, too, face the same

dilemma; in one researcher's words 'the fear of a threat to femininity through successful achievement is the result of cultural learning so prevalent as to affect most women'.[7] However, in the work context, the former choice seems preferable, and many individual women succeed conspicuously in such jobs by outplaying the men at their own games of toughness and competitiveness. Yet even these women may privately confess to feelings of isolation and vulnerability. The setting up of female support or 'networking' groups is one way that some women have tried to counterpoise some element of female culture to the male work environment.

Scott's survey of several contemporary societies, both more and less industrialized, revealed that in all of them 'notions that women constituted a special category of labour persisted even where they could no longer be differentiated from men in terms of their supply characteristics'.[8] Women and men are viewed by employers in terms of their 'appropriateness for a job, rather than their actual abilities to do it'.[9] Thus even when the conditions of the labour market change, when production processes require different abilities, when family relations are in flux, gender ideologies persist. They must be seen as having, as it were, a life of their own. Without doubt they are one of the most important props for continued segregation and sex-typing.

If gender ideologies are to be considered as having their own independent reality, this does not mean of course that they will not alter in form over time as work and family relationships change. But I am arguing that there should be no expectation that they will directly reflect those changes. Thus current gender ideologies seem to me without doubt to be descended from the Victorian ideology of domesticity and of separate spheres. In consequence, as others have argued, these ideologies can legitimately be seen as patriarchal, even in a society where families are no longer strictly governed by patriarchy. This returns us to the issue of patriarchy and its relation to work. Walby has recently developed an account of phases of patriarchy, arguing that the private family-based form characteristic of pre-industrial and nineteenth-century societies has been replaced by a public form in which patriarchal control is maintained by work relations and the state:

> Private patriarchy is based upon the household, with a patriarch control-ling women individually and directly in the relatively private sphere of the home. Public patriarchy is based in sites other than the household, although this still may be a significant patriarchal site. Rather institutions conventionally regarded as part of the public domain are central in the maintenance of patriarchy.[10]

Walby believes that private patriarchy reached its peak in the mid-nineteenth century in middle-class families and that there has been since a movement away from it, largely as a result of feminist politics.

We may go further than Walby has and assert that many, if not most, contemporary families in Britain and America are no longer patriarchal in the strict sense; they may more aptly be described as 'androcentric'. The power of the father in the family now receives little social and legal sanction (although social security regulations are one exception here, giving support to Walby's view of the state). However, most social institutions are shaped around male definitions, priorities, requirements, preferences; men run most of them, if not all; the political and social ideas that rule our epoch come from men; in sum society revolves round men, is literally 'androcentric'.

Walby is correct in seeing the work sphere as crucial in maintaining male supremacy; and Prather has argued for America, too, that 'the concept of work is defined in masculine terms'.[11] Work relations are a paramount example of 'androcentrism'. For example, the arrangements of the traditional working week, nine to five and the weekend off, fit well with the male life routine (work all day, home for meal cooked by wife, evening at the pub or in front of the television, weekends spent in the garden or at sporting functions). It fits *not at all* with the life routine of the woman responsible for feeding and clothing children and taking them to school. On her free days she wants to be able to go to the shops and banks, not football matches. Yet part-time work, flexible hours or job-sharing schemes which fit with her requirements are seen as inferior forms of working and carry penalties in terms of deprivation of rights and benefits. Promotion prospects too, are based on assumptions of a normal male career, as the case studies demonstrate. Companies often require employees to move round the country to gain promotion, a thing impossible for most married women. Even in the traditional female profession of teaching, promotions have usually to be gained by moving to a new school or college, which again handicaps women and may well be one reason why, it is claimed, women do not apply for top posts. There are even some companies which require their managers to have a non-employed wife, so that she is available for entertaining and can give him the domestic support necessary to ensure his total dedication to the firm. The assumption, of course, is that *all* managers *must* be male. No company would dream of asking that a female manager have a non-employed husband! Social rituals of work, trade union activities and so forth reflect male timetabling and interests and priorities. We could go on *ad infinitum*. Finally, on top of this, it is at least feasible to argue (with Walby) that not only are current work arrangements androcentric, they are also correctly described as patriarchal at least if we apply the analogy of the household and authoritarian father to the enterprise or organization. All over the world, men give orders, women obey. The patriarch may have lost his seat in the drawing-room; he is still comfortably lodged in the office or behind the boardroom table.

Notes and References

1   P. Willmott and M. Young, *The Symmetrical Family* (Routledge and Kegan Paul, London, 1973).
2   I. Young, 'Beyond the happy marriage', in *Women and Revolution*, ed. L. Sargent (Pluto, London, 1981), pp. 58, 61.
3   M. Mann, 'A crisis in stratification', in *Gender and Stratification*, ed. R. Crompton and M. Mann (Polity, Cambridge, 1986), p. 56.
4   J. Matthaei, *An Economic History of Women in America* (Harvester, Brighton, 1982), p. 194.
5   C. Cockburn, 'The relations of technology', in Crompton and Mann, *Gender and Stratification*, p. 85.
6   G. Fine, 'One of the boys', in *Changing Men*, ed. M. Kimmel (Sage, London, 1987).
7   J. Laws, 'Work aspiration of women', in *Women and the Workplace*, ed. M. Blaxall and B. Reagan (University of Chicago Press, Chicago, Ill., 1976), p. 46.
8   A. Scott, 'Industrialisation, gender segregation and stratification theory', in Crompton and Mann, *Gender and Stratification*, p. 181.
9   Ibid., p. 160.
10 S. Walby, 'The historical periodisation of patriarchy', paper presented at the BSA Annual Conference.
11 J. Prather, 'Why can't women be more like men', in *Women in the Professions*, ed. L. Fidell and J. Delameter (Sage, London, 1971), p. 19.

15

The Variety of Work Done by Wives

Christine Delphy and Diana Leonard

The comfortable environment provided for a husband by a good wife is based on her taking on most of the household tasks. He is thereby fit for his occupational work and leisure and able to give them his undivided attention. 'A "normal" day's work is that of a person who does not have to do his own domestic work'.[1]

Women's 'keeping the home fires burning' allows soldiers to wage wars, senior executives to work twelve hours a day and to fly off abroad at a day's notice, skilled manual workers to be called out to do overtime at short notice, (male) teachers to gain higher qualifications at evening and weekend courses, and trade union officials and local politicians to cope with emergency meetings. Wives' coverage of domestic work also, of course, enables husbands to devote themselves to leisure – it allows sportsmen to go away on rugby tours or to play golf on Sundays.

Women's coverage of domestic work also allows men to do nothing when they are unemployed or retired. French time-budgets in 1985 showed that in couples where both are employed, men did 2 hours 41 minutes of domestic work per day (20 minutes more than in 1965) and wives 4 hours 38 minutes, but the difference actually increased when men were retired. Women at 65 do three hours more domestic work a day than their husbands.[2]

The availability of utilities (running water, gas and electricity), domestic appliances (washing machines, vacuum cleaners, food processors) and industrially produced commodities (cook-chilled food, disposable nappies, ready-made easy-care clothes and spray furniture polishes) have not reduced the time spent on household work, although they have reduced some of the hard physical effort involved. Rather they have (a) enabled some tasks formerly contracted out to be taken back and done within the home (for example, laundry); (b) other tasks to be done to higher standards and more frequently (for example, cooking, cleaning, laundry and particularly childcare); and (c) middle-class housekeeping standards to be maintained despite the departure of servants. Almost all the increased purchasing, transporting and domestic management has fallen to wives. They have taken on not only most of the work formerly done by servants in middle-class households, but also, in all households, work formerly done by other members of the household, including husbands.

Time-budget studies show not only that the amount of time women spend on domestic work has not declined this century and that they still do twice as much each day as men in all Western and Eastern bloc countries even when they have paid employment, but also that women do the more highly organized domestic work (for example, in the morning, from waking to 9 a.m., to get everyone off to work and school). When men spend time on housework, it does not involve the same kind of strain.

The fact that husbands may now offer increased help in the home has thus very rarely affected their freedom to take any form of employment or to enjoy leisure outside the home. Men have a 'right' to time off, to some regular leisure time spent away from home and family each week; and they can also be absent from home for long periods, for days or weeks or even months to pursue a whole range of manual, managerial and professional occupations and/or a range of leisure activities.

But of course men do not necessarily have to be away from home for their wives to take charge of housework and childcare. On the contrary, women's domestic work enables men to work at home while being assured of protection from disturbance – and in fact such men usually do less domestic work and childcare than those who work elsewhere. Employers benefit from their (male) employees' wives' labour because they can assume that none of their workers has responsibility for the physical care of any dependants or needs to do much domestic work for themselves. But in fact it is men who are self-employed who most rely on their wives – who leave them to do the domestic work single-handedly. And it is not only men's occupational work at home which relies on women's domestic labour – so too does men's ability to spend undisturbed leisure time at home, whether playing with train sets in the attic or reading the paper in the sitting room, and their being able to find 'going out with the wife and kids' a pleasure.

When wives have servants, even part-time cleaners a few days a week, they may appear to do less domestic work, and they are certainly often reviled as lazy parasites when they rely on paid help with childcare and housework (even if they are in full-time employment). But women are actually only given servants or *au pairs* when their workload simply cannot be carried by one person (for example, when they have several small children and no kin living nearby) or when their husbands want their time to be shifted elsewhere. For instance, when their husbands prefer them to earn an extra (professional-level) income, and/or to undertake the extra work needed for a higher standard of living and more consumption: buying and maintaining more things (more houses, more rooms, more interior decorating, more suits of more elaborate clothes), more entertaining and more involvement in a particular cultural milieu. Husbands may want their wives to have time to organize frequent, elaborate kin reunions or weekends with friends in their country cottages. Or to do more good works for charity. Or to learn another foreign language, and to visit exhibitions and go to the opera and read the latest books so they can talk confidently to guests. Or to be conspicuously leisured – showing-off the men's wealth by demonstrating that they do not need their wives to work and that they can afford for them to play bridge, or to keep horses and go hunting, or to play tennis and ski, or to have beauty treatments and buy clothes, or to create an elaborate garden.

However, having servants in itself involves work for women. Servants have to be hired, trained and managed. (Management and training in industry are not usually seen as idleness!) They also require emotional work: helpers have to be listened to, praised, made to feel important, and to have their anxieties soothed, etc. This is especially true of *au pairs*, who are in many ways yet another member of the family whom the wife looks after, albeit they are family members who contribute labour.

In any case, most women do not have servants. Rather they are themselves, as J.K. Galbraith says, 'crypto-servants'.[3]

In considering the suggestion that marriage is an equal partnership and that what wives do for husbands, husbands also do for wives, one is forced to conclude from the limited research on husbands' contributions to their wives' occupations that the evidence does not support the hypothesis of equality. 'The implications . . . a man's paid work has for his wife are much more significant and far reaching than vice versa.'[4]

Although marriage is a joint endeavour in the sense that both spouses benefit if their household prospers, and although most husbands do help their wives in various ways, husbands and wives do not get identical benefits if their household 'goes up in the world', nor do they do equal things for each other to achieve this end. Marriage is precisely a gendered and unequal division of labour, with most wives working more hours a day than their husbands in a subordinate role. Even when married women have full-time paid employment, they are still required to work for their husbands. They may even be required to provide a better service than if they were not employed, in order to justify having a job.

Men are of course physically and intellectually as capable of doing direct work for their wives' occupations or leisure activities as the other way about. But the chances they actually routinely do so are slim, first, because very few women occupy the sorts of jobs or do the sorts of voluntary work, sports or hobbies that require or enable the direct use of a spouse's labour. There are few women entrepreneurs or women in senior management and professional jobs. There are few women public figures, or politicians, or heads of state, or great artists. The division of labour in the labour market and discrimination in other parts of society thus supports the division of labour in marriage. Most women's activities outside the home neither assume nor offer the possibility of using another pair of hands.

But if a husband does get involved in his wife's occupation to the extent of becoming an 'additional worker' (that is, if her work makes such a big impact on his life), he will almost certainly take over direction from her and she will concentrate on just a part of it, for example, doing the designing while he runs the business (this applies to many successful firms founded by women, including Laura Ashley). Or he will coach and manage her if she is an athlete or a singer. Very few husbands work alongside and under their wife's direction. It is psychologically, socially or legally impossible.

A second reason why men do little for their wives' occupations is because if a married woman does become a senior manager, and even more if she becomes a head of state, her husband will have to keep well in the background if she is to stay visible – unlike a wife who can at least stand beside her husband on the platform without her status threatening his. Thus the Queen of England's Silver Jubilee had to be celebrated very much as a tribute to *her*, with incidental compliments and separate articles in magazines on Prince Philip alone, rather than as a tribute to their joint achievement – as it would have been if he had been king. In addition, a husband cannot act as a 'wife'. Consort roles are gendered: they presume their incumbents will undertake 'womanly' activities because it is presumed the position will be filled by a wife. And if men do take on tasks, they change their meaning anyway. Mr Thatcher did not act as a hostess for visiting dignitaries. He may have done some of the same *tasks* as Mrs Major, but being a host located him very differently from being a hostess.

Where husbands and wives have married spouses with similar skills, or where skills are deemed to be acquired 'over the breakfast table', it is a matter of fact that husbands give less help to wives than wives do to husbands. For example, among academic researchers, husbands almost never give as much help with interviewing and proof-reading as wives do – and they absolutely never do an amount that would challenge the centrality of their own careers. Husbands *could* be general backup workers for their wives but (a third reason why they usually do relatively little) they are not as likely to have the time, or to be as well placed, or due to sex stereotyping to have the social skills to help even if they want to. Husbands usually have occupations, generally higher status occupations, and leisure pursuits of their own, so they are unlikely to be on the spot and available to take messages, to keep people away while their wives are busy, or to run errands or do some typing. (They are even less likely to be 'available' to do this, according to the evidence, if they work at home than if they have a nine-to-five job outside their house.) But even when husbands are retired and their wives are self-employed, men offer only limited help. For instance, in one couple, interviewed in 1991 as part of a French study of wives' occupational work, the wife had a shop and her retired husband would unload the crates once a week and come and pick her up at closing time (since he had the use of the family car). He also helped to pull down the metal shutters over the shop window, but he did not do the books and he certainly did not do the housework.[5]

[. . .]

Further, women workers are not seen to have the same 'need' for home comforts and a listening ear as men – and to the extent that they do need comfort and support, they are thought to be able to provide it for themselves or to get it from other people (women) rather than necessarily from their husbands. (However, continuing to rely on your mother and sister after you are married is not fully approved of. It may be regarded as a symptom of emotional immaturity, or downgraded as being 'traditional working-class' behaviour.) Certainly commercial companies do not vet husbands as they vet wives (on the rare occasions when women hold the sorts of job where such things happen), nor, until forced by the women's movement and equality legislation, did they see it as necessary to pay for husbands to accompany wives on trips when the wives of male executives travelled for free. Presumably any woman in a career is seen as tough enough to cope on her own.

Indeed most of the literature seems to interpret husbands' 'moral support' for wives in paid employment as being to do with men's basic acceptance of women's 'right' to have jobs at all. One large-scale survey in Britain suggested that,

> husbands could not be described as enthusiastic supporters of their wives working. . . . The overriding impression our findings give is that husbands of working wives in varying degrees tolerated their wives working though in many cases they did not want it to interfere or conflict with their own work or domestic life. Women's part-time working may be seen as an accommodation to this view of the desirable balance between paid and unpaid work.[6]

Others have found that one wife in ten who is employed full-time works despite her husband's disapproval or without his knowledge.[7] The nearest to support many women get is the rather small comfort of knowing that their husbands tolerate their working all day on an assembly line only because they believe 'it drives women crazy to stay at home all day'. Not surprisingly such women feel they cannot complain about anything that happens at work, nor can they ask for men's help with domestic work, because they 'chose' to work. Among professionals ('the talking classes'), a husband may well find his wife talking about her job more interesting than her talking about the neighbours (providing she does not 'go on about it' too much), and he may be an important mentor and morale booster for her – as Rosanna Hertz found in a study of high-flying couples working in large corporations in Chicago.[8] Or again, a husband who is an active Labour Party member but whose work does not allow him to become a local councillor may support his wife in getting elected and in day-to-day political activism.[9] But there are equally cases where husbands put down their wives' jobs and voluntary activities systematically – or whenever their wives forget to keep their heads always a little bit lower than their husbands'. Perhaps such deliberate withholding of emotional support is an important form of male control of (and psychic violence towards) wives.

Wives certainly do not seem to be owed the sexual unwinding which men 'need' so badly. Wives who have sought divorce in Britain because their husbands lost interest in sex have been refused it on the grounds that such men's behaviour is not 'unreasonable'.

Notes and References

1   C. Delphy, 'Continuities and discontinuities in marriage and divorce', in *Sexual Division and Society*, ed. D. Leonard Barker and S. Allen (Tavistock, London, 1976), p. 81.

2 G. Grimler and C. Roy, *Time Use in France in 1985–86* (Institut National de la Statistique et des Etudes Economique, Premiers Resultats, no. 100, 1987).
3 J. Galbraith, 'The economics of the American housewife', *Atlantic Monthly* (August 1973), pp. 78–83.
4 J. Finch, *Married to the Job* (George Allen and Unwin, London, 1983), p. 1.
5 C. Delphy, *Travail professionnel invisible des femmes*, report by the Centre National de la Recherche Scientifique, Paris (forthcoming).
6 J. Martin and C. Roberts, *Women and Employment* (HMSO, London, 1984), p. 115.
7 A. Hunt, *A Survey of Women's Employment* (HMSO, London, 1968).
8 R. Hertz, *More Equal than Others* (University of California Press, Berkeley, Calif., 1986).
9 J. Barron, G. Crawley and T. Wood, *Married to the Council* (Bristol Polytechnic, Report to the Leverhulme Trust, 1987).

16

The Domestic Mystique

Christina Hardyment

Since the Second World War, mass-production techniques have slashed the prices of household machinery and increased their availability. Thanks to such machines, the average home is far cleaner and more comfortable than it was at the time of the Great Exhibition of 1851. Together with the mains services of water, gas and electricity, machines have reduced the problems of vermin, dirt and damp to insignificant proportions. The health of the family has improved enormously as a result. Moreover, one person can now run a house furnished with luxuries as well as necessities, and still have time to spare. Living-in domestic staff are unusual – the home is now the province of the family and the family alone.

[. . .]

But why then do time-use surveys show remarkably little lessening of the hours worked by full-time housewives? How necessary is the huge current expenditure of households on domestic appliances? What effect have such machines had on liberating women from the ancient shackles of domesticity? The answers to these crucial questions can only be arrived at by looking more closely at the apparently rosy picture of technological progress and improved domestic conditions for working women that is most people's image of twentieth-century life.

Louise Peet and Lenore Salter's textbook *Household Equipment* was first published in 1934 and its successive editions up to 1979 offer a useful guide to the trends affecting domestic equipment since the 1930s. The huge post-war demand for appliances meant that there were few style changes in the late 1940s – attention to design only occurs in a buyers' market. The extension of electricity supplies to rural areas increased the interest of country housewives in automatic washing machines, freezers and dishwashers: with heavy calls on their time from farm and garden, such women could easily justify their need for machines still considered luxuries by urban women.

By 1961, there had been a rapid succession of new models of the familiar old appliances. They were easier to operate, and emphasized energy-saving automatic features. Safety became an issue after a United States survey revealed that there were more than a million accidents in the kitchen every year. A final chapter of advice on saving motion and energy was directed to handicapped housewives and, significant pointer to the future, the increasing number of mothers who had jobs outside the home.

The 1970 edition declared that 'modern space-age living has invaded the kitchen', and added an introductory chapter on the 'wide and greatly increased use of household appliances in the last thirty or forty years'. There was a section about machines with electronic solid-state controls, and another on the growing market for 'personal care appliances' such as razors, hair-dryers and electric toothbrushes. A new emphasis on reliability and longevity was supposed to be producing a reduction in the need for service calls, but less starry-eyed accounts of the market admitted that industrial machines were consistently longer-lasting and more reliable than domestic models. It remains true that the exteriors of machines designed to suit current kitchen fashions are often less durable than the machines themselves: dated colours, broken handles and hinges, chips and cracks in casings, encourage replacement sooner than necessary.

By 1979 the general saturation of the market for the most popular appliances, and a slower than estimated replacement rate, led to frantic style wars among manufacturers. 'Changes take place in equipment from month to month, sometimes almost from week to week.' Much more attention was being paid to what the elusive consumers wanted. New models emphasized savings on energy and water, and anti-pollution devices. In their later editions, Peet and Salter also added a chapter on 'maximising the satisfaction of work in the home', a reflection of the growing demoralization of the woman who was still 'just a housewife', and her need for the same recognition and reward as that earned by the dashing 'superwoman' who seemed to bound effortlessly between home and workplace.

It is worth noting the profound conservatism of these recent trends. The main thrust and direction of the domestic appliance market as a whole has apparently changed very little since the introduction of the small electric motor in the 1920s set it on course as aiming to replace servants in the home with machines in every home. It encourages an essentially private pattern of housekeeping and homemaking rather than one of community co-operation and specialization of labour. In this pattern the typical unit of consumption is a small family living in a self-sufficient household organized by a lone woman who has the time to do all the housework herself. For example, she needs to be at home to put the washing into a machine and take it out later on; in the evening she will take food out of a refrigerator, prepare it with the aid of a range of gadgets, and cook it on a stove of some sort. She will put the dishes in a dishwasher and empty it when it is clean. She will clear up the family's mess with a small portable vacuum cleaner. As currently structured, modern manufacturers aim to furnish every home with a complete range of specialized tools and appliances; the job of their marketing divisions is to sell the idea of such a life-style as well as the machines to fit it.

But the boom days are over. . . . The current virtual saturation of the market means that there is very little scope for anything more dramatic than gradual sales to new households and the occasional 'mini-boom' as some essential and rapidly introduced item comes up for replacement.

Are the manufacturers wise to remain so blinkered by tradition? . . . Women who work outside the home are likely to have more domestic appliances than those who stay in the home. But are such appliances actually the best way of saving time and labour in the home, or merely the best on offer at the moment?

It is worth looking more closely at that turn-of-the-century decision to create mechanical servants. At that time there was another fairly well-canvassed option: to professionalize domestic service and to remove it completely from the home. This fitted in with the long-term trends identified by Barbara Ehrenreich and Deirdre English. The household, 'once a tiny manufacturing centre' where women made bread, butter, cloth, clothing, candles, medicines and other things essential to their families' survival, became, they believe, 'a domestic void'.[1] 'Four-fifths of the industrial processes carried on in the average American home in 1850 have departed, never to return.' Given this pattern, it made sense to look to outside services to relieve the remaining chores of daily household life – cooking, cleaning and laundry.

The leading advocate of such a course was the radical feminist thinker and economist, Charlotte Perkins Gilman. While welcoming the exodus of the underprivileged and oppressed domestic servant from the home, she could see more clearly than many of her contemporaries the danger of taking on the housework herself.

> The increasing cost and decreasing efficiency of domestic service teaches most women nothing. They simply revert to the more ancient custom of 'doing their own work'. But the double pressure goes on. More and

more professional women who will marry and have families and will not
be house servants for nothing, and less and less obtainable service, with
the sacrifice of the wife and mother to that primal altar, the cook stove.[2]

Applying Adam Smith's doctrine of specialization of labour to the
home, she felt that some women ought to take up careers in cleaning
in order that most were freed from housework. She suggested that each
community could have a central kitchen, so that on evenings when a
family did not feel like preparing its own supper it could either eat in
a central restaurant or have a meal sent over to be eaten in relaxed
privacy. Babycare and kindergartens for everybody's children could be
run by those whose bent lay in that particular direction. Gilman never
saw 'womankind' in the mass – her basic assumption was that different
women would have different ambitions and talents – just as different
men had.

[. . .]

In her book published in 1921 Mrs Havelock Ellis asserted the essential unfairness of the lot of domestic servants, and accepted as inevitable their disappearance from the home. Her solution to the 'servant
question' which was being so hotly debated at the time was first to put
domestic service completely on a trade basis and second to organize
community co-operation:

> If every woman could have a minimum instead of a maximum of domestic
> spider-threads tugging at her brain year in year out through the mu-
> nicipalization of laundries, bake-houses and kitchens, and restaurants
> worked under well-trained and methodical civil servants, just imagine
> what a new life would be on earth. Woman's equality would be estab-
> lished almost as much by this as by her economic independence, as it
> would open up the way in many cases for that very independence; for
> many women would find their real life-work in the municipal domestic
> factory, and be paid their true earnings as citizens. . . . The professional
> woman, with special gifts and special hereditary equipment, would also
> have a fair chance under such a system: the work of a Jane Welsh Carlyle
> was practically lost to us because there was no common kitchen for the
> wants of dyspeptics.[3]

There were practical experiments as well as utopian theories. Mansion flats in both New York and London were built with communal
heating, waste-disposal and water facilities. Some offered deep-freezes
and laundries in the basements, and a piped vacuum-cleaner service.
'Dainty dinners' could be sent up from the Mansion's central kitchens,
according to Lilly Frazer[4] and when the famous novelist Countess

'Elizabeth' von Arnim lived in London's Whitehall Court in the 1900s, a visitor was impressed to see a menu slipped under the door each morning. But although the Countess had six children, most such apartments were seen as bachelor – male or female – affairs, a useful way for single professionals to live, but not particularly suited to families.

Many domestic services are amenable to professionalization. Today only commemorated by the old-fashioned packs of Happy Families, a small army of tradesmen once called at houses to offer their services. The coalman and the sweep, the ice-man and the baker, the knife-grinder and the fishmonger all tapped at the back-door and offered their wares and services in the most convenient manner possible. In this context, it was quite natural for Lilly Frazer to suggest that 'In time, no doubt, a front doorstep cleaning brigade will form in the style of window-cleaning companies, and we will thus by payment escape the rather heavy drudgery of doorstep cleaning.'

If the only reason for servants leaving the homes had been the democratic justice case argued by Edith Havelock Ellis and her like, such a pattern of professionalization would have been extremely logical, because the labour for such services would have been available. However, the primary reason for the exodus of domestic servants was a labour shortage caused by the attraction of quite new job options for women: jobs in offices, in schools and in factories mechanized adequately enough to make work light and pleasant in comparison with domestic service. Such jobs offered reasonable terms for employment and far more promising opportunities for social intercourse.

There was a second element too – one which remains crucial to the whole domestic issue today – that prevented private servants transferring to the 'Civil Servant trades' envisaged by feminist thinkers. Professional services require payment. When domestic servants became hard to find or ideologically unacceptable, middle-class women rolled up their sleeves and declared marriage a trade. They found it an attractively economical solution to simplify their life-style and use machines in the home rather than to call on outside services. Until the housewife both believes that working outside the home herself is a feasible option and also costs her time at the same rate as that of her husband or partner, professional services will seem prohibitively expensive.

[. . .]

However, nothing in history is neat. For all the intricate tangle of femininity, motherhood and homemaking in the well-publicized foreground of domestic bliss, what has actually been happening in the twentieth century is a steady trend towards women taking as much of a part in the labour force as men. Efficient birth control and increased life expectancy have changed the world for women dramatically.

Women have literally been given a second lease of life by their liberation from the old tyranny of childbirth and its attendant dangers. It is unrealistic not to accept that this revolutionary change in the conditions of their existence will affect the pattern of their lives profoundly. In 1975–80, the birthrate in the United States sank to the 'historic low' of 1.8 per cent.[5] At the same time, women's workplace participation reached the all-time high of 51.2 per cent. 'For the first time in American history, more women are in the labour force than out of it, and women are likely to continue to stream into the workplace in the coming years,' comments Gerson, in her lucid account of women's career decisions, *Hard Choices* (1986). 'Recent predictions suggest that by 1990 around 70% of all women of working age will be employed or looking for a job.' British trends echo those of the United States, although Britain's current unemployment problem makes a conservative backlash against women seeking employment highly likely.

What makes the statistics even more powerful indicators of far-reaching change is that it is younger women who are tipping the scales most dramatically in favour of women's employment: they no longer stop working when they marry, postpone childbearing or renounce it altogether, and continue to work while their children are small. 'Since the 1950s, the non-domestic woman has emerged to challenge the predominance of the homemaker mother. The traditional household composed of a breadwinning husband and homemaking wife dropped from 59.4 per cent of all American households in 1950 to only 30.3 per cent in 1980.[6]

Women use their newly acquired time in a number of ways. Some still opt for traditional nurturing roles and community support. For an increasing number the massive campaign to encourage the sale of consumer goods has been too persuasive. Many households feel that one wage is no longer enough to keep a family in the style to which a wage-earning couple get accustomed before they marry and have children. The housewife is beginning at last to cost the time she spends pottering around the home unpaid, and to look for ways of cutting away the 'domestic spider-threads tugging at her brain year in year out'.

The current development of domestic technology is much complicated by such variations in the labour-saving needs of households and such different attitudes to home management. As Kathleen Gerson points out, there is a deep ideological schism between women who stay at home and women who go out to work. Women with no other occupation than housework and motherhood find it attractive to have machines in the home which enable them to raise the standards of their work but do not dispense with the need for someone to be in the home. Their demands are for ever more sophisticated machines – zigzag sewing-machines on which to perform wonders of embroidery, food-mixers with all the appliances they need to emulate a Cordon Bleu cook. As Betty Friedan's succinct variation on Parkinson's law has it: 'Housewifery expands to fill the time available.' The views of such women on childrearing are strongly coloured by the fact that they are at home. They stress a small child's need for its mother's constant presence, and the irreconcilable conflicts of the demands of a career and the demands of bringing up a family 'properly'. These are the women who clock up extraordinarily long hours in the time-use surveys: Joann Vanek estimated that they worked on average 55 hours a week in 1960, several hours longer than their grandmothers in the 1920s.

New-style 'dual-career' households, in which no one is available to do housework all day have quite different attitudes. The women in them spend only half as much time on housework as non-working women, and find it quite acceptable to let somebody else look after the children, arguing that it is in the best interest of both mother and child to do so. Such a split in domestic points of view is nothing new, but until the 1980s the first category has always outnumbered the second, and substantial profits have been made by manufacturers who supply strictly domestic technology. Once the second category outnumbers the first – and estimates suggest that this will be so by the 1990s – we can expect much more entrepreneurial interest in the provision of extra-domestic aids to household management.

At the moment, in a society where half the women work outside the home and half do not, we are in a state of flux. The shops are still overflowing with seductively designed domestic technology, sophisticated advertising techniques link marital success to microwave ovens, and books on cooking and gardening outsell any other category of literature. Domestic appliance manufacturers want to hold on to their dominant market position, and they promote the woman-as-home-manager ideology in order to do so. There will continue to be advertisements featuring trim'n frilly homebodies salivating over the latest multi-programmed washing-machine.

[. . .]

There remain two broad areas where not nearly enough has changed, and where without change women can never take up the position in society that they now claim as their right. They are interrelated. One is the level of women's wages in comparison with those of men. The other is the matter of men sharing housework fairly and participating in parenthood.

Until women earn as much as men, there will always be a severely practical reason why it will be the mother rather than the father who breaks her career to look after their children. The most depressing aspect of the massive increase in the number of married women with children working in the last twenty years is that it is almost entirely an increase in part-time working. There is nothing inherently wrong with part-time working, especially in the context of family life, but there is something wrong in it being predominantly a woman's option, and in it offering low pay and poor-quality fringe benefits.

John Nicholson recently published an exhaustive examination of the myths surrounding human sex differences and the ascertainable facts. He came to the conclusion that the most obvious explanations for a woman's disadvantaged position in the workplace were that she took a chunk out of her career in order to look after children, and that she carried the major responsibility for household affairs, even when working as many paid hours a day as her husband. It was not just the actual time involved in such matters as good-enough motherhood and reasonable household management, but the whole attitude of mind which such an approach implied. Sights were pitched lower at the very opening of a girl's career, since she always had the mental reservation that she would be dropping it all sooner or later to be a wife and mother. Employers have treated women less well in the marketplace because they felt that, given a choice between domestic and work commitments, home would often come first (in fact, statistics on absenteeism show that this is simply not so).

Kathleen Gerson has broadened Nicholson's picture by taking a survey of women with different baseline commitments to careers, and examining the reason why some fulfilled their ambitions and others changed their plans. One of the most interesting of her revelations is the difference that chance opportunities made to the women. Unexpected appreciation in the workplace led several women who had planned to give up their jobs to persevere with working; more typically, dead-end low-status jobs led women who had originally hoped for permanent employment to take the 'domestic option' that many still look on as a woman's privilege. Privilege it may be, but until as many men as women find it an attractive option, it will have a suspect tinge of exploitation.

So to the vexed matter of men's participation in housework and parenthood – still staggeringly low according to surveys, for all the television sit-coms about house-husbands and boy nannies that suggest otherwise. The evidence is that it is a mistake to attempt to solve the problem of one woman doing two jobs (three if you count childrearing) by asking two people to do one and a half (or two) each. Modern domestic labour-saving appliances do make daily life far easier, cleaner and more comfortable – but they do not save enough time and effort in the home to allow both adults to be fully employed, to bring up a family and to enjoy some leisure and recreation. If Nicholson is right in claiming that housework and childcare disadvantage women in the workplace, then for men to take on more of the chores of a family will simply lead to heavy discrimination at work against those responsible for a family – men and women alike. It is possible that men need to be congratulated rather than nagged at for their clear-sighted refusal to fall into the trap of trying to be more than one person, of experiencing their children, in Bacon's classic phrase, as 'hostages to fortune . . . impediments to great enterprise'.[7]

In an ideal world, all employers will become as family-minded as some of the banks and insurance companies are becoming – they will offer several years leave to a parent of either sex, with the option of part-time work and refresher courses. Until that golden age, would-be successful dual-career families have two ways of solving their problems. Ironically, they are the same two options that were rejected by middle-class families at the turn of the century in favour of the glorious mirage of mechanical servants.

First, there has been some evidence of an unexpected increase in the numbers of domestic servants. It is unproven as yet, because Department of Employment statistics no longer aggregate domestics as a separate category, and many service jobs are unofficial. But domestic employment agencies report a significant rise in vacancies, although they say that in general there are more vacancies than suitable applicants. Many of the vacancies have been created by changes in work-permit regulations which have debarred the Filipino and Mediterranean migrants who used to fill a large proportion of domestic jobs. Jonathan Gershuny believes that the increase is 'a labour supply phenomenon – not so much the rich getting richer as the poor, especially women, desperately needing work'.[8]

Clearly, domestic service is no more popular than it ever was. Most jobs entail long hours and low pay. Most are filled by women with absolutely no alternative employment, who stay for as short a time as possible. The criticisms levied on the system by such democratic thinkers as Edith Havelock Ellis still hold good. Reviving domestic service is not a credible option today, for all the high rate of unemployment on the one hand, and the crying need of dual-career families on the other.

A distinction needs to be made between domestic service and what Gershuny has called the 'new service economy'. For the second option open to working couples is to rely more on services outside the home.

There are already signs of a revived interest in removing labour from the home altogether. More and more shops are opening up in the so-called 'unsocial' hours, making it possible for working couples to shop and eat with the minimum difficulty. Much of the labour has been taken out of cooking by the unholy alliance of frozen food and the micro-wave oven. Trends also show far more families buying 'take-aways' or eating out at realistically priced snack-bars during the week and buying a traditional Sunday lunch at a nearby pub at weekends. Entertaining at home is dying away entirely or becoming simplified. In large cities, where the numbers demanding such services make their provision viable, dinner parties are increasingly often supplied commercially by small teams of enterprising cooks, and the career woman who once rushed home from her office to pull on a pinny can now sink into a hot bath and wait for the doorbell to ring with an easy mind.

People who cost their own time realistically may stop buying washing-machines and tumble-driers and return to laundries or make use of service washes in launderettes: the success of the washing-machines installed in the 'family centres' on some large London estates show that the ancient sociable traditions of the communal washing ground can be revived and are experienced as welcome breaks from family life. Perhaps one day the fantasy world of My Beautiful Launderette will become a social commonplace. Because of generally improved quality of housing, decorations and furnishings, basic house-cleaning need no longer be a daily routine. Ultimately it may become a monthly blitz just like window-cleaning – left in the capable hands of mobile cleaning firms such as The Maids Ltd, Scrubbers, or Wombat and Mop, who use industrial cleaning methods to make houses considerably cleaner than any overworked and underpaid daily-help ever did. When garden contractors mow lawns during the week on a regular basis, suburban weekends will no longer be made hideous with the cacophony of a dozen rival machines.

[. . .]

Ultimately the potential of any machine should lie in the mind of its user rather than its maker. The tide is turning against isolated domesticity and the Dazzling Mums with hands that wash dishes as soft as their faces. Wives no longer want to be lonely garage attendants, however glamorous the setting of the pumps. Consumers are not indefinitely malleable nor totally undiscriminating, and hopefully the market will eventually follow their lead. Unnecessary machines – and the labour they entail – should leave the home. Instead, properly paid professionals can take over the drudgery of domesticity, and leave men and women enough time to make their houses satisfying homes.

Notes and References

1   B. Ehrenreich and D. English, *For Her Own Good* (Pluto, London, 1979).
2   C. Gilman, *The Home* (McClure Phillips, New York, 1903).
3   E. Ellis, *Democracy in the Kitchen* (Haslemere, London, 1894).
4   L. Frazer, *First Aid to the Servantless* (Heffers, Cambridge, 1913).
5   K. Gerson, *Hard Choices* (University of California, Los Angeles, Calif., 1985).
6   Ibid.
7   F. Bacon, 'Parents and children', *Essays* (1625); republished by World's Classics, Oxford, 1937.
8   J. Gershuny, *The Listener* (4 December 1986).

17

Persons, Households, Families, Lineages, Genders, Classes and Nations

Michael Mann

Society would be captured perfectly by sociological theory if it consisted merely of atomic particles clustering around the nuclei provided by our theoretical concepts. We know social reality is not so neat, but at some point we must act as if it were. After we elaborate our central theoretical concepts, we must assume that other social influences are randomly, contingently related to them. Social stratification, with its strong theoretical traditions, has done this fairly explicitly. Its two main orthodoxies, Marxian and Weberian, define three nuclei: social class, social status/ideology and political power. Though aware of the complexities of social life, theorists treat other aspects of stratification as ultimately contingent and non-structural. They may admit that gender relations are 'neglected', interesting and important. But gender relations are not part of the core of stratification. Beneath classes, status and political power lie actors who, in the last resort, resemble atomic particles.

Certain aspects of stratification have never fitted easily into this model – for example, ethnic and religious struggles have not usually been reducible to class and status as (respectively) the Marxian and Weberian traditions assert. My own unease has stemmed principally from nations and nation-states, which are not reducible to political phenomena (as both orthodoxies have it). Gender relations present a third area in which a set of properties intersects with the orthodox categories in a peculiar yet structured way. In this case, the orthodoxies have spawned what Popper would call an *ad hoc* auxiliary hypothesis, changing the basic atomic particles of the theory from individual persons to households. Thus women are said to obtain their position in social stratification from the dominant male of their household. Making that assumption we can proceed with the traditional model.

I believe that all three areas present fundamental difficulties for current stratification theory. I do not provide an alternative general theory here. I attempt a more limited, descriptive and historical task. I identify and trace the interrelations of five principal stratification nuclei – five collective actors who have impacted on gender/stratification relations over the recent history of the West. They are: the atomized 'person' (not strictly a collective actor, but nonetheless a social identity conferred by the core structures of liberal society); the connected networks of household/family/lineage; genders (the male and female sexes given social power-significance); social classes (viewed broadly in a Marxian perspective and so comprising principally capitalist and working classes and their fractions in modern Western society); and nations and nation-states. To adopt such a 'multidimensional building-block' approach to stratification theory reveals that I believe the theoretical crisis to be serious. It is not just a question of finding a theory to relate the two theoretical nuclei of capitalism and patriarchy. Capitalism is too limited a concept to deal with the totality of non-gendered stratification relations in modern society. And, as I will indicate, patriarchy no longer exists, even if a different form of gender domination does.

I have not the space either to define carefully all my nuclei or to document fully all my assertions regarding their interrelations. Much of the supporting material for my concepts and generalizations can be found in the first two volumes of my book, *The Sources of Social Power*. I start with the origins of modern gender relations, in patriarchal societies.

A patriarchal society is one in which power is held by male heads of households. There is also clear separation between the 'public' and the 'private' spheres of life. In the 'private' sphere of the household, the patriarch enjoys arbitrary power over all junior males, all females and all children. In the 'public' sphere, power is shared between male patriarchs according to whatever other principles of stratification operate. No female holds any formal public position of economic, ideological, military or political power. Indeed, females are not allowed into this 'public' realm of power. Whereas many, perhaps most, men expect to be patriarchs at some point in their life cycles, no women hold formal power. Within the household they may influence their male patriarch informally, but this is their only access to power. Contained within

patriarchy are two fundamental nuclei of stratification: the household/
family/lineage and the dominance of the male gender. These coexist in
any real society with social classes and other stratification groupings.

This is an ideal-type. Yet it has not been so far from historical reality,
from the first written records emerging from Mesopotamia around 2,500
BC to western Europe up to the eighteenth century AD. These historic
societies have distinguished the public from the private; in the public
sphere power relations have been overwhelmingly between male house-
hold-heads (patriarchs); and the private sphere has usually been ruled
formally by a patriarch. Families/households were the primary social
units. Their relations with their own broader lineage and with other
lineages constituted most of the formal structure of social stratification.
That is why the label 'patriarchy', though much disputed nowadays,
seems apposite to most of our history.

This must be qualified in three ways. First, in almost all societies
custom and law generally protected women from their patriarchs at
some basic level – and the woman's own lineage could uphold her rights
against an unjust husband. Second, less was in the public sphere in the
past than now, except amongst the highest social class. The 'private'
family was the main unit of economic production and of socialization,
and for almost the whole lifetime: there were few households of single,
childless, 'post-child' or retired persons. Far more was unpenetrated by
public power. Thus there was greater scope for private, informal power
according to personal influence and force of character. Modern studies
of comparable private activities (sexual relations, household budgeting
etc.) show greater variations in power between men and women than
do public power relations. This would matter more in historic societies
because more was private.

Third, and most significantly, women (and men) belonged (and still
do) to more than one household/family in their lifetimes. Power is
transmitted hereditarily through intercourse between a man and a woman
drawn from separate households, usually from separate lineages. So
power must make a journey, potentially fraught with difficulty, between
two families of origin and one family of procreation. Most historic societies, precisely because family and lineage are so crucial to their stratification, confer on the woman trusteeship over power resources
transferred from her family of origin. In early modern Europe spinsters
and widows could formally control most of the resources they inherited;
and married women could retain some control of land (but not of
moveable chattels) they brought into the marriage. In the upper classes
women could be legal agents, manage estates, defend castles and succeed to thrones; lesser, equivalent rights existed among merchants, guilds

and propertied peasants. Such women were not exercising power as 'persons' or even just as members of classes, but as trustees for their previous lineages. They were 'honorary patriarchs'.

These are qualifications, not refutations, of patriarchy. Customary protection, informal powers and exploitable spaces between families provided no basis for collective action by women. If they sought to influence public power, they had to go through patriarchs. Gender, though fundamental to stratification, was asymmetric: men could act, women could not. Exceptions can be found – but how many sociological generalizations spread out over 4,000 years of global history can do even half as well?

Social stratification was thus two-dimensional. One dimension comprised the two nuclei of household/family/lineage and the dominance of the male gender. The second dimension comprised whatever combination of 'public' stratification nuclei (classes, military elites etc.) existed in a particular society. The latter dimension was connected to the former in that public power groupings were predominantly aggregates of household/family/lineage heads. But apart from this, the two dimensions were segregated from each other. Thus, to analyse 'public' stratification in patriarchal society, we can largely ignore gender. We could write a history of power relations almost up to the eighteenth century and confine it to men, as long as we add the defensive proviso 'Oh, by the way, remember that this is a story of relations between male patriarchs. Underneath them all the time were women (and junior men, and children).' This can be validated with the aid of Acker's list of the assumptions made by orthodox stratification theory. She lists six.

1   The family is the unit of the stratification system.
2   The social position of the family is determined by the status of the male head of the household.
3   Females live in families.
4   Females' status is equivalent to that of their man.
5   Women determine their own social status only when not attached to men.
6   Women are unequal to men in various ways, and are evaluated differentially on the basis of sex, but this is irrelevant to the structure of stratification.[1]

These assumptions would be broadly true of most historic societies (later I shall agree with Acker that they are not true of modern societies). My only quibble would concern what we were to label 'social stratification'. For there were two incommensurate structures of stratification linked through families/households/lineages: the 'orthodox' structures of (male) classes etc., and the relations between the two genders. But as almost the whole recorded history of society concerns the first, public realm, perhaps we should concede even this point. The internal structure of public stratification was not gendered.

So the more patriarchal the society, the better orthodox theory performs. If orthodox theory does worse in modern societies, then they must be less patriarchal. As the particularism of agrarian societies gave way before the universal, diffused stratification of modern society, stratification became gendered internally. It is outside my scope here to weigh the many and varied causes of this transformation. It is sufficient to group them around three major power configurations of modern times – capitalism, liberal citizenship and the nation-state. I argue that these three configurations transformed gender/stratification relations in successive historical phases of modern Western society, the first two then becoming institutionalized, the third remaining unfinished. Cumulatively they add up to a contemporary stratification structure which has moved beyond patriarchy and become gendered internally in both its economic and political aspects.

I now deal with capitalism as a transformative.

[. . .]

From about the sixteenth to the nineteenth centuries in Western Europe, under the pressure of emerging capitalism, first in agriculture then in industry, more of economic life became a part of the public realm. Among the lower classes, the rise of wage labour and the loss of customary rights to land meant that the peasant family was no longer the main unit of production. People went out to work for others. The lineage weakened, the nuclear family grew stronger and became characterized by what Stone (1977) calls 'affective individualism' between husband and wife.[2] As labour was becoming an abstract commodity, it was possible that men and women could become interchangeable as labourers, so ending gender particularism in the economy. But, patriarchy was so well entrenched in European society that it withstood this capitalist pressure. Male workers and employers together contrived to create a labour market in which priority was given to males. Patriarchy acquired a new coloration: almost all men worked in the public sphere, at least half the women looked after the private household. The remaining women did work in the public sphere. But their wages could barely support a household; their occupations could be regarded as extensions of their private domestic roles – preparing and serving food, fashioning textiles and clothes, and caring for the young, the elderly, the indigent and the infirm, in educational, health and charitable occupations; they would fit employment around their family life cycles; and even if they worked they also undertook most domestic labour. The simple divide between the public and the private gave way to a more subtle gender segregation, diffused right through the traditional barrier between public and private spheres. We might well term these employment arrangements 'neo-patriarchy'.

Among the capitalist class parallel transformations occurred from the end of the eighteenth century. The business enterprise moved out of the household into the office, the exchange and the club. Women members of capitalist households lessened their active participation in the economy. They became domesticated. Because under law women could not retain control of moveable chattels they brought into marriage, they were also affected adversely by the change from land to capital. But this also meant that their own families of origin lost control over such capital. So a formidable lobby emerged to change matrimonial law to favour women. In Britain the Married Women's Property Act of 1870 was one of the first achievements of the feminist movement. Yet it was also assisted (and probably won decisively) by forces emanating from the heart of the old society. Lineage has remained fundamental to the inheritance of class position but, in this respect, classes reduced their patriarchal coloration.

By about 1850 in Britain the change in employment was virtually complete: more women in the public sphere, but under neo-patriarchal arrangements. These arrangements have subsequently become institutionalized. Looking back over employment trends it is astonishing how little has changed over the last 135 years. Occupational segregation and the confinement of most women to those 'semi-domesticated' occupational areas just mentioned still persists. The most significant general change has probably been the post-1940 increase in married women working before and after their childrearing phase. Most women now divide their lifetimes into private and part-public phases (I return to this later). Nor are women generally active users of capital. Their greater longevity, plus the Property Acts, ensure that they own more of capitalism than men do. Yet they tend to be passive rentiers, leaving managerial control of capital to publically employed men. If we followed Marxian orthodoxy and reduced stratification relations to direct 'relations of production' and to 'the labour process', we would have to conclude that little has changed and that at least a 'neo-patriarchy' remains.

But the adjustment of patriarchy to capitalism involved other changes.

The privacy of the household had diminished and in the public sphere the fourth of my nuclei – classes – became more significant collective actors. In place of 'classes' as aggregates of particularistic networks of lineages, in place of the asymmetry whereby only the ruling class was capable of extensive and political action, came universal symmetric classes. A conscious, organized capitalist class was in place in Britain by about 1880, a middle class slightly later, a working class by about 1914. Women, still dependent on their patriarchs, became members of such classes. This affected the character of nineteenth-century feminist movements (as we will see), intensifying middle-class liberal feminism, dividing it somewhat from a working-class socialist feminism around the beginning of this century. But it affected women in employment especially. Women were generally subordinate to men. But they also derived a class position from their patriarch, and this might raise them above other men. In an agrarian patriarchal society this had not mattered because men and women were largely kept apart in their spheres. But employment is public and waged. Wage hierarchies are institutionalized, and the large corporations and state departments of the twentieth century are organized with charts showing integrated hierarchies. Perhaps these would undermine the particularism of patriarchy and generate a single hierarchy covering at least occupational stratification and including both men and women?

Sociologists have long attempted to create a single hierarchical scale, normally based on occupation, along which to distribute the entire population. But they have had little success in combining men's and women's occupations in a single scale. Traditional orthodoxy has been to assign a woman's position in this hierarchy on the basis of the occupation of her relevant patriarch (husband or father). A recent polemic has illuminated the strengths and weaknesses of this approach. Goldthorpe has shown that, *if* you wish to construct a single scale based on occupation, the orthodox method is probably the best.[3] Yet Britten and Heath have also demonstrated that the woman's own occupation 'makes a difference', improving the prediction of voting behaviour, for example.[4] But men's and women's occupations cannot be combined meaningfully into a single scale. Few jobs are occupied interchangeably by men and women and their career patterns differ. Their jobs are just 'different'. They also aggregate into different social groupings as Murgatroyd shows.[5] She constructs indices of dissimilarity between the jobs of husbands and wives (data from the 10 per cent sample of the 1971 England and Wales Census). Whereas the Registrar-General's 'social classes' discriminate quite well between the men's occupations, they do not among the women's. Murgatroyd constructs a rather different set of 'women's social groups' to provide the best solution to the results of her multidimensional scaling. The orthodox scale does better where the woman's occupation contributes fewer resources to the household. It will do worse where the woman contributes as much as or more than the man. But it may also perceive incorrectly the hierarchical position of a woman who is effectively independent of patriarchs. How significant are these problems? How many are the women involved? I delay my answers until later because the questions introduce political as well as economic aspects of stratification.

But we should not become obsessed with constructing scales on which to distribute individuals. Stratification is more than the sum of individuals, or indeed of households. If our stratification theory sees its task only as assigning women as individuals to jobs or households, it will miss any collective impact women might have on stratification. And this has been considerable. There is a significant clustering of women's occupations. A kind of compromise between patriarchy and a more gendered stratification hierarchy has emerged. Women in the economy now form a number of quasi-class fractions. In each main case they occupy a 'buffer zone' between the men of their own class grouping and the men of the next class grouping down the hierarchy. At the bottom large numbers of women in part-time and unskilled manual employment are a buffer between the unemployed (who are mostly men, because many women are not registered as unemployed) and the 'skilled' manual workers above them (who are overwhelmingly male). The second largest female concentration is in clerical and sales work, inhabiting a buffer zone between manual and non-manual male workers. Third are the 'semi-professions', whose lower reaches are predominantly staffed by women with substantial educational qualifications in caring occupations. They form a buffer around an important educational divide within the middle class. Fourth – though this is a somewhat different distinction – are the passive rentier widows, spinsters and divorced women, and the 'sleeping-partner' wives and daughters, buffering capital from all labour. All told, this looks uncommonly like a systematic role for women in what many regard as the core of stratification – the economy and the occupational division of labour. Gender is no longer segregated from the rest of stratification: its segregating mechanisms have become a central mechanism of economic stratification.

Each one of these female buffer zones impacts upon social stratification in general and social class in particular. Here I touch on only one zone, the second. One of the 'hardy perennials' of stratification theory has been whether lower white-collar work has been 'proletarianized' during the twentieth century. The research of the Cambridge Department of

Applied Economics group enables us to see that this is a false issue.[6] Lower white-collar work is undertaken by three segregated groups of people: women, young men and older men. The older men are former manual workers who have moved sideways in the employment hierarchy; the young men are careerists expecting promotion. The lifetime trajectories of both differ from that of the women, who typically interrupt their employment for *seven* years while they rear children and who cannot expect promotion. Moreover, women would not have 'noticed' deskilling of white-collar work during most of the twentieth century, since – unlike the men – they are largely new to this employment. Women, new to the labour force, have predominantly staffed the expansion of lower white-collar employment. Gender has prevented the proletarianization of white-collar workers, both by dividing them from each other and by preventing deskilling having social significance for them. This is a definitive answer to a central concern of stratification theory, one that depends upon considering class stratification as being gendered. Explanations of comparable scope would follow from analysing the other gender buffers I identified. Economic stratification has become gendered.

I now discuss the rise of two more social nuclei, both more universal than the household/gender particularism of patriarchy. Both were conveyed primarily by Western liberalism and by the bourgeoisie. So their universalism was in practice restrained by the compromises which liberalism made with class and with particular national states.

The roots of individualism can be traced back to the early Christian notion of universal individual salvation. Christ's message in and immediately after his own time was broadly egalitarian, stressing that all were spiritually equal before God, capable of communicating directly with Him without going through the particularistic authority structures of Jewish or Roman society. There is some evidence of an early Christian 'feminist' movement. However, this was soon suppressed, and the famous doctrines of Saint Paul and of the pseudo-Pauline epistles took over. Women were to obey their masters to achieve salvation. According to Stone[7] and Hamilton[8] Protestantism at first gave ideological reinforcement to the patriarchy of the husband, while also increasing social respect for the status of the wife in her private sphere. But extreme Protestantism could stir up feminism, both in the Civil War period and at the end of the eighteenth century in the Evangelical movement. By 1800 many upper- and middle-class women were involved in moral-improvement projects among the masses. They began to see the implications for themselves of their faith in universal education. Evangelicals provided much of the leadership of the first feminist movements in Britain and the United States. Grimes argues that a Puritan ethic of moral individualism lay behind the women's suffrage movement in the western United States (where it was most successful) right up until 1914.[9]

But by this time Protestantism was not alone. Over several centuries institutions of political power had been developing away from the particularistic 'territorial federalism' characteristic of most agrarian societies, towards the emergence of universal 'ruling-class/nations'. Estates-General and Councils of the Realm gave way to enfranchised parliaments or massed courtiers; personal royal patronage gave way to the institutionalized sale of state offices; nobles, and sometimes merchants and yeomen, viewed themselves as a single 'nation' (even if still connected by lineage); monarchs ruled with the co-operation, and sometimes the formal consent, of this class/nation. Underlying much of the change was the growth of capitalism. The universal commodity form, the 'invisible hand' of the market, the 'free' wage labourer without particularistic ties to land or lord, the abstract rights of property – all encouraged the drift of Western culture toward 'individualism'.

This was reflected in political doctrine. Political rights and duties had hitherto been conceived predominantly in a particularistic way; obedience was due to a particular sovereign, ordained either by God or by original acclamation by the community and legitimized through dynastic succession. From him descended further networks of particularistic dynastic duties. But from about the time of Locke, there was greater interest in tracing political rights and duties to the qualities of abstract individuals. Free persons, not communities webbed together by custom, had entered into contracts to institute states. Sovereigns must uphold not custom, but the life, liberty and property of the individual, the abstract 'person'. And persons aggregated into a second novel nucleus, the nation. The nation became, not a community based on territory or blood, but a political community of free, participating citizens. Such theories were exemplified in the founding charters of the modern liberal era, those of the American and French Revolutions. Here we find declarations grounding all political rights in the sum of universal, abstract individuals – that is, in nations and persons.

It is true to say that most of the doctrines, when elaborated, made clear that the person and the nation were not universal: servants, almost always, and usually labourers and those without property, were not to be an active part of the political community. Thus liberalism was confined by class, just as was the parallel current of Evangelical Protestantism. Liberalism and moral improvement were opposed to the particularism of the old regime, called by them in Britain 'Old Corruption'. They sought a more universal basis for legal and political participation in the national state, but one confined by property. They wanted to enlighten and improve the morals of the lower classes, but through charity. Their legal and political universalism was the product of the emergence of a more extensive and universal bourgeoisie, but there, for the moment, it rested.

Women got similar treatment. Despite the rhetoric of liberalism women were not included in the nation. Was not the French founding charter entitled *Declaration of the Rights of Man and Citizen*? Nevertheless, from the 1680s to the 1980s the same liberal rhetoric has been used by radicals to achieve legal and political equality for all men and even for all women. Feminism, like socialism, built on top of the rhetoric. Each of the founding charters was rephrased in detail by leading feminists: for the text of Olympe de Gouge's 'Declaration of the rights of woman and citizen' see Riemer and Fout;[10] for the Seneca Falls Declaration (of Independence) see O'Neill.[11]

The main characteristic of the feminist movement in the late nineteenth and early twentieth centuries was its overlap with liberalism – added to at the end of this period by an overlap with socialism. Thus it was assisted by radical–liberal surges (e.g. the Progressives' surge in the western United States before 1914), but hindered by liberal defeats (e.g. the defeat of 'Reconstruction radicalism' in the United States in the 1870s). In Britain the switch from Asquith to Lloyd George as Liberal Party Leader was a considerable boost to the women's suffrage movement. Social democracy also shared social policies with the feminists (especially over education and recognition of workers' rights). So in the countries dominated by liberalism and contending with emerging socialism, feminists converted a considerable number of men who already had legal and political rights, especially the intellectuals. Liberalism was essentially universal within the bounds of the nation-state, and it could erect no powerful ideological defences against enfranchising either subordinate classes of women.

This was not sufficient, of course. To achieve suffrage, a widening of educational opportunities and legal equality, a large and troublesome women's movement was also required. This happened in two principal phases. From about 1870 the few feminist agitators acquired substantial numbers of middle-class followers, drawn principally from the expanding female occupations of teaching and social work. Then, from around 1910, we can talk of the emergence of 'mass' movements, as socialists and trades unions began to stir up women workers more generally, and as women's penetration of education and clerical work widened. By

1915 membership of the principal suffrage organization in the United States was 2 million. Though British numbers were smaller, the militancy of the suffragettes became far greater.

So by about 1912 legal and political citizenship for all men and women was only a matter of time. Liberalism and socialism had no good reasons for resisting feminist pressure, once this was brought to bear. The Great War probably sealed it, for women now contributed greatly to the national effort. The vital British Suffrage Acts came in 1918 and 1928; the United States Constitution was captured in 1919–20. Most accounts of the suffrage movement stress its slowness. But, considering that the vote had to be achieved from all-male legislatures and that the feminist movement could never wield anything like the mass numbers and violence of the male suffrage movements, this surely amounts to comparatively rapid and steady progress.

Full legal and political citizenship in the nation-state were achieved and then maintained comparatively easily by women. They have not been 'virtually represented' (in the words of the eighteenth-century conservative doctrine) for over fifty years in most of the West. Women have entered as 'individual citizens' into the legal and political institutions of social stratification. The Marxian tradition of analysis has played down the achievement of 'bourgeois democracy'. Feminists have generally followed this line when viewing modern gender relations, partly because of the fact that, having achieved the vote, the feminist movement seemed largely to disappear until the 1960s. However, as Banks points out, the most active remaining feminists in Britain transferred their energies into the politics of welfare.[12] This is the clue which moves us to the third phase of the story. National citizenship has indeed made a considerable impact on gender and by that route political stratification now also became gendered. As women were now a part of the state, and as the role of the state was enlarging enormously, gender became politicized, again subverting traditional patriarchy. Such is the argument I now want to discuss.

In 1880 state expenditure in the UK represented well under 10 per cent of GNP; by 1980 it was well over 40 per cent. Such a phenomenal rise, typical of advanced capitalist countries, indicates a sea-change in the life of the state, from a small specialized agency making laws and engaging in foreign wars, to a massive redistributor of the resources of (national) society. The state now co-ordinates most social activities, provides their infrastructures and redistributes between economic sectors, geographical areas, age- and life-cycle groups and social classes. The state became a nation-state, not merely in the liberal sense of political participation, but as the main collective nucleus of everyday life-experience. Gender was not an active agent in this transformation, but it could not help but be affected, and then react back upon the state. Gender became politicized.

The first main expansions, in the second half of the nineteenth century, were of transport and communications infrastructures, which did not particularly impact on gender, and of symbolic infrastructures (i.e. education) and care/control of the poor, which did. Both reduced the privacy of the household, removing some of its socialization functions, controlling the family life of the poor and expanding the occupations of teaching and social work. These immediately provided most of the activists of the first substantial feminist movements. Education and social welfare have continued as state growth areas through the twentieth century.

First, education has expanded enormously, to consume around 10–15 per cent of state budgets through the twentieth century and to play a substantial role in allocating persons to class positions. The history of what Parkin has termed 'credentialism' has been uneven.[13] The effects of its most recent spurt, the expansion of higher education in the 1950s and 1960s, are still working their way through social stratification. Meritocratic ideology claims that educational credentials are available to all talented persons. Of course, we know that class origins limit meritocracy quite substantially. But it has given a distinctive route up the stratification hierarchy to the *middle* class – distinct from the hereditary transmission of 'upper-class' capital. Though there is also gender discrimination, middle-class women have benefited from their traditional role as socializers within the family and from liberal ideology (which always saw literacy as necessary to citizen participation). Thus women have penetrated education as teachers and pupils more successfully than they have most other 'public' areas of society. Thus, where credentialism is strongest – in the professions and, especially, in education itself – women have become relatively well qualified, they have come closest to achieving equal pay and equal jobs and they continue to predominate amongst feminist activists. Segregation is not ended, equality not achieved, even here. But the growth of education has provided women with one of their furthest points of entry into the public sphere and into economic stratification.

Second, social welfare expanded as social democracy replaced liberalism, and as Poor Law became Welfare State. Social services, excluding education, consumed about 20 per cent of the state budget in 1920. Today it consumes over 40 per cent. What Marshall termed 'social citizenship' now covers all women as well as men.[14] It is still expressed in liberal terms – the rights of all persons in the nation to adequate subsistence. But persons also still live in households/families (though less in lineages). So the Welfare State has blown right through the private walls of the household. We subsist in the modern nation-state only by allowing state scrutiny of our income and wealth through taxation and by demonstrating our need and 'worth' for welfare. This is quite unlike the relationship between state and person-household in historic societies: states could not penetrate the locality or the household to know the incomes of their inhabitants, let alone tax them (except crudely) or provide generally for their welfare. But now my income and wealth, the value of my fixed property and moveables, the number and circumstances of other household members, my familial and/or sexual relations with them, and the sincerity of our attempts to find employment are all scrutinized by the nation-state.

State scrutiny implies that all these circumstances have become politicized. General rules are laid down by parliament concerning our welfare rights and duties, including familial and marital roles. These straddle a contradiction between the values of patriarchy and of citizenship. The result is again a sort of compromise between patriarchy and a more gendered stratification, in this case gendered political stratification. The state recognizes that a man should normally head the household, earn a family wage, be the public person. This is the neo-patriarchal aspect of the state, bringing notions of domesticity and femininity into politics. But the state also ensures that the woman-citizen can subsist, even if this contradicts the power of the patriarch. The state's dilemmas have been increased by the decline in infant mortality and birthrates, and the rise in divorce and remarriage. The duties of men to their ex-wives and absent children; the plight of single-parent families; who is to count as a 'dependant'? – these complex and contentious issues are now politicized, to generate perennial legislation. Sometimes the legislation protects women from men; sometimes it reproduces conditions of patriarchy. But it always generalizes and politicizes gender relations. Much legislation also recognizes *in extremis* the autonomy of women from any particular patriarch. Daughters have quite similar rights to sons in relation to their fathers; women who separate or divorce have a financial claim on their former joint household extending to their ex-spouse's present income; and single parents receive a state subsistence income. Subsistence is often meagre and embodies subtle discriminatory provisions against women, but most women derive some, and some derive most, of their subsistence from state welfare or legislative protection, rather than from a patriarch.

We can now put together economic and political transformations, to see the force of Acker's 'head-counting' criticism of the distributional scales of orthodox theory. Most of its six assumptions no longer apply to many women. For example, she says, 40 per cent of households in the 1960 US Census did not have a male head in the conventional sense – being female, or female-headed or husband–wife families in which the husband is retired, unemployed or working only part time. This proportion had become even higher by the time of the 1980 US Census. In such a context categorizing distributional scales by the occupations of male head will leave a lot out.

But the household types that do not fit into orthodox theory are extremely varied. Women who are relatively autonomous from, or equal to, their men might be thought unlikely to form a single collective actor. They are divided by class and by whether their situation results from employment or state dependence. Around 7 per cent of women in the UK earn more than their husbands, many doing well out of credentialism. About 10–15 per cent of employed women live alone or with someone not related to them. Their earnings (at least in the United States, with better census data in this respect) are not far short of the national average (and they are higher if we divide total household earnings by number of persons in the household), so they are comfortably off. About one in eight families with dependent children – the expected ideal-typical site of patriarchy – are headed by a single parent, of whom nine-tenths are women. Most are relatively poor, 40 per cent being below the current official poverty level (both here and in the United States).

Nevertheless, there are two common threads, one in employment, one outside of it, which together explain most of the economic circumstances of women. The first is that women receive less for their work than men in similar jobs. This is so transparent to all, so contradictory to liberal and social democratic notions of equality of all persons, and so economically disastrous to many autonomous women, that a new feminist politics of equal employment has arisen. This has a dual core of professional and trade-union women. The second is that women do the domestic work, especially childrearing. Yet this worsens a woman's job prospects in virtually every occupational category and makes her either more dependent on her husband or drastically reduces her standard of living. Childrearing now seems to lessen women's earnings more than direct gender discrimination does, at least in US Census figures. In 1980 the average household income in the United States was $24,656; that of households without children headed by a woman was $18,528 (and by a man $23,473); while that of households with children headed by a woman was only $11,639 – despite the fact that over half these women were working.[15] The number of childless women has declined greatly since the beginning of the century. Childrearing unites almost all women, for many of the variations between households, noted above, turn out to be between different phases of the life cycle. During the childrearing phase the rational economic strategy would seem clear: stick close to your patriarch, or face poverty. This strategy would place women within the protective cover of their husband's social class (and validate orthodox theory). But woman does not apparently live by bread alone. Divorce rates among couples with dependent children, and illegitimacy rates where the woman keeps her child, both continue to rise. But if women do want more bread, there is an alternative political strategy: include childrearing in social citizenship and reward it. This broad strategy also appeals to those whose success in employment is threatened by the childrearing phase.

This commonality of experience and political strategy among autonomous and/or state-dependent women is increasingly generating distinctive pressure-group politics. A 'social feminism' couples the old liberal 'person', claiming equality in education and employment, to state recognition of childrearing, centring on the provision of day-care facilities. In this country these pressure-group politics achieved an obvious impact on the manifestos of both major parties in the 1983 general election, especially on the Labour Party's. How effective are these new politics remains to be seen. But unless the variety of macrostructural trends, to which I have referred, are put into reverse, such pressures are likely to increase in stridency and mobilizing powers. Political stratification has become more gendered and this seems likely to continue. Though class of father and husband, and a woman's own occupational attainment, continue to divide women, the intersection of employment and Welfare State also provide gender solidarity. Gender is classed: but so too is economic and political stratification gendered.

So then, do we still have patriarchy? No, because the particularistic distinction between the public and the private sphere has been eroded, first by employment trends and the emergence of more universal classes, second by universal citizenship by all persons in the nation, and third by the nation-state's welfare interventions in the 'private' household/family.

Do we still have what I defined as 'neo-patriarchy'? Yes, to some extent, particularly in the extension of notions of 'domesticity' and 'femininity' into the public realms of employment and the Welfare State. Thus patriarchal values and practices still permeate many aspects of the culture of contemporary nation-states.

But we have also gone beyond even neo-patriarchy into two distinct and even opposite forms of gendered stratification. First, men and women have become in certain ways abstract, interchangeable 'persons' with equivalent rights as legal and political citizens, limited of course by the other stratification nuclei around which they might cluster – class and nation, but also (in some contexts not discussed here) ethnicity and religious affiliation. Persons have equality before the law and freedom of choice as individuals in few historic societies have done. One right that has expanded particularly for women is the right to choose a marriage partner, to terminate that marriage freely in divorce and to hold on to a portion of its material resources thereafter. These derivatives of liberalism, reinforced by social democracy and by feminist movements, represent fundamental changes in gender relations – whether or not feminists regard them as significant when compared to the transformations they would ideally like to see.

If this were the sole change, the other modern nuclei would be strengthened. Classes and nations would be homogenized and fortified by the collective experience and action of men and women together. Indeed, this has happened in certain respects, as, for example, in the gradual convergence of their rates of trade-union membership and their voting patterns.[16]

But such trends are contradicted by a second type of gendered stratification. Even where men and women are not interchangeable, the pattern of their segregation and inequality has become integral to the structure of 'public' stratification. In patriarchal society the dimension of gender stratification was largely segregated from the dimension of 'public' stratification (classes etc.). This still persists but has diminished greatly. The participation of women in the public realm, particularly in employment and through the Welfare State, now affects the core stratification relations in our society. I gave examples of groups of women 'buffering' and 'fractionalizing' economic and political stratification both in employment and out of it. Some sociologists who minimize the impact of gender on stratification point to the relative absence of collective action by all women, compared with the frequency of action by collectivities like classes. I have argued against this with respect to political stratification, where the politics of employment and childrearing unite a broader range of women. But to stress only this would be to miss the converse point: that the differential impact of gender in modern employment relations may reduce the impact of traditional (predominantly male) collectivities like class. Gender may cut across class; or gender and class may each fractionalize the impact of the other. As both trends are occurring simultaneously, a more complex form of stratification is now emerging.

To end thus is to end inconclusively, but it is also to report accurately on contemporary stratification. Patriarchy, even neo-patriarchy, was a relatively simple stratification structure. But modern capitalist nation-states present a more complex, uneven and probably unfinished array of stratification nuclei. Persons, families/households/lineages, genders, classes and nations (and others) all exist and interact. None can be assigned primacy, each has relevance for, and influences the shape of, the others and the whole. Two points are quite clear, however: stratification is now gendered and gender is stratified. We can no longer keep them in separate sociological compartments.

Notes and References

1   J. Acker, 'Women and social stratification', in *Changing Women in a Changing Society*, ed. J. Huber (University of Chicago Press, Chicago, Ill., 1973).

2   L. Stone, *The Family, Sex and Marriage in England, 1500–1800* (Weidenfeld and Nicholson, London, 1977).

3   J. Goldthorpe, 'Women and class analysis: in defense of the conventional view', *Sociology*, 17 (4) (1983); J. Goldthorpe, 'Women and class analysis: a reply to the replies', *Sociology*, 18 (4) (1984), pp. 465–88.

4   N. Britten and A. Heath, 'Women, men and social class', in *Gender, Class and Work*, ed. E. Gamarnikow, D. Morgan, J. Purvis and D. Taylorson (Heinemann, London, 1983); A. Heath and N. Britten, 'Women's jobs do make the difference', *Sociology* 18 (4) (1984), pp. 475–90.

5   L. Murgatroyd, 'Women, men and the social grading of occupations', *British Journal of Sociology*, 35 (4) (1984), pp. 473–97.

6   A. Stewart, R. Blackburn and K. Prandy, *Social Stratification and Occupations* (Macmillan, London, 1980).

7   Stone, *The Family, Sex and Marriage in England*, pp. 151–218.

8   R. Hamilton, *The Liberation of Women* (George Allen and Unwin, London, 1978), pp. 50–75.

9   A. Grimes, *The Puritan Ethic and Women's Suffrage* (Oxford University Press, New York, 1967).

10   E. Riemer and J. Fout, *European Women* (Harvester, Brighton, 1983), pp. 62–7.

11   W. O'Neill, *The Woman Movement* (George Allen and Unwin, London, 1969), pp. 108–10.

12   D. Banks, *Faces of Feminism* (Martin Robertson, Oxford, 1981), pp. 153–79.

13   F. Parkin, *Marxism and Class Theory* (Tavistock, London, 1979), pp. 54–60.

14   T. Marshall, *Citizenship and Social Class* (Cambridge University Press, Cambridge, 1950).

15   A. Hacker, 'Where have all the jobs gone?' *New York Review of Books* (30 June 1983), pp. 27–32.

16   J. Siltanen and M. Stanworth (eds), *Women and the Public Sphere* (Hutchinson, London, 1984).

18

The Representation of Women

Anne Phillips

Liberal democracy makes its neat equations between democracy and representation, democracy and universal suffrage, but asks us to consider as irrelevant the composition of our elected assemblies. The resulting pattern has been firmly skewed in the direction of white middle-class men, with the under-representation of women only the starkest (because they are half the population) among a range of excluded groups. The campaign for women's right to vote was always linked to a parallel campaign for women's right to be elected. Success in the first has not brought much joy in the second.

In even bothering to discuss this problem, I go against the grain of much contemporary feminism, and not only because of the theoretical challenges that have been levelled at liberal democracy. When the women's movement re-emerged in the late 1960s, there was a strong presumption in favour of direct democracy. This combined with a critical repudiation of party politics (returning the compliment to those parties who so long and happily ignored the women) to encourage scepticism towards orthodox channels. 'Getting women into politics', where politics meant parliament or national assembly, was very low down the list, and the real issues of democracy and participation were thought to lie elsewhere. Not that anyone would object if women were suddenly elected *en masse* to councils and parliaments: the celebrations would be boisterous enough for an achievement beyond most feminist dreams. But this then is part of the point. Until recently, no feminist in her right mind would have thought liberal democracy could deliver the goods, and since this coincided with a preference for more direct forms of participation, many just left it at that. The respectable agitations of bodies like the British 300 Group seemed to rest on a double naivety: the belief that substantially more women *could* get into Parliament without a prior revolution in social and sexual relations; and the equally odd notion that 300 women Members of Parliament would make a significant difference. In more academic circles, the literature on 'women in politics' (more accurately, women not in politics) operated perilously close to the threshold of boredom. For those who knew that women were oppressed, the dreary statistics lacked any element of surprise. The commonsense explanations for women's low profile held little appeal for minds still buzzing with the latest theoretical fashions.

The under-representation of women within conventional politics is nonetheless crucial in thinking about democracy and gender. The general critique of liberal democracy leaves a teasing vacuum on what could serve as alternatives, while the questions raised over the two most common alternatives suggest that neither can be simply adopted in its place. We can perhaps move on to more substantial ground if we examine more closely the weaknesses (and possibly strengths) of current liberal democratic practice. What does the under-representation of women add to the understanding of democracy? It shows that there is a problem undoubtedly, but is the problem then in the theory or application? Setting aside for the moment what may be more fundamental problems with liberal/representative democracy, can we anticipate a trend towards sexual parity? Is there a theoretical problem with the 'representation of women', an incongruity between this and the assumptions of liberal democracy? Does feminism provide us with a novel angle on these issues, a different way of conceiving either possibilities or limits? What are the theoretical issues implied in the notion of representation? What are the chances of electing more women?

In this context I now want to discuss 'mirror' representation. Confront people with the damning evidence on the number of women elected and they tend to divide into those who think this matters and those who say it does not. Much of the disagreement reflects the complacency, not to say dishonesty, of those who enjoy a monopoly of power, but there are more intriguing issues at stake. As with many feminist demands, the case for greater parity in politics has been made in three ways. Part of it relies on a notion of basic justice, and fits within a broad sweep of arguments that challenges sexual segregation wherever it occurs. Just as it is unjust that women should be cooks but not engineers, typists but not directors, so it is unjust that they should be excluded from the central activities in the political realm; indeed, given the overarching significance of politics, it is even more unfair that women should be kept out of this. But for the hundred years and more that access to political power has been an issue, women's organizations have combined the case for justice with at least one additional point. Sometimes the argument is that women would bring to politics a different set of values, experiences and expertise: that women would enrich our political life, usually in the direction of a more caring, compassionate society. A more radical version is that men and women are in conflict and that it is nonsense to see women as represented by men.

The case for justice says nothing about what women will do if they get into politics, while the two further arguments imply that the content of politics will change. All unite in seeing a sexual disproportion between electors and elected as evidence that something is wrong. The striking homogeneity of our existing representatives is proof enough of this, since if there were no substantial differences between men and women, or between black people and white, then those elected would undoubtedly be a more random sample from those who elect. Consistent under-representation of any social category already establishes that there is a problem. Such a marked variance from the population as a whole could never be an accidental result. Leaving aside as mere prejudice the notion that women are 'naturally' indifferent to politics, there must be something that prevents their involvement. The argument from justice then calls on us to eliminate or moderate whatever obstacles we find to women's participation, while the arguments from women's different values or different interests go one stage further. The sexual differentiation in conditions and experience has produced a specifically woman's point of view, which is either complementary or antagonistic to the man's. Any system of representation which consistently excludes the voices of women is not just unfair; it does not begin to count as representation.

All three arguments are at odds with what has become the orthodoxy, for while there are a number of competing versions on offer, the idea that representatives should in some way 'mirror' those they represent is probably the most contested. The near universal practice of electing representatives according to geographical constituencies suggests that those elected are meant to speak for an area or a place, the implication being that interests are relatively homogeneous within localities, but potentially at odds between them. Whether the representatives are male or female would then be deemed irrelevant, though where there are concentrations of rich or poor, or areas populated by particular racial or religious groups, the class, race or religion of the representative might well be seen as important. Party selectorates do, as we know, like to choose candidates who seem consonant with the locality but, with exceptions such as Northern Ireland where there is a clear conflict by religion, and perhaps inner city constituencies where the voters are more homogeneous in their class or their race, this version of representation is largely thought an anachronism.

The classic challenge to it derives from Edmund Burke's speech to the electors of Bristol, where he argued that representatives should serve not local interests but the nation, and should therefore be free to exercise their own judgement on political affairs. Here, too, sex is out of the picture, or perhaps, more precisely, enters to the disadvantage of women. The Burkean representative is a man of honour, integrity and breadth of vision. The process that produced him is merely the gesture meritocracy makes to democratic beliefs; what matters is that he should be 'better' than the voters who put him there.

The subsequent growth of the party system has legitimated yet another view: that those elected are to speak for their supporters' opinions or beliefs. The most radical versions of this will argue for strong mechanisms of accountability or recall, noting that if MPs and councillors are supposed to represent our political views, they should be bound or mandated to the policies we support. But except when issues of gender have entered into party programmes, there is no explicit presumption among either radicals or moderates in favour of either sex. The fact that most of those elected turn out to be men might be noted or deplored, but it is the ideas not the people that count.

The dominant practice in most contemporary democracies is a muddled combination of both accountability and autonomy. Our representatives are said to represent our views (political parties present us with alternative policies, and we make a choice between them), but only in the vaguest of ways (election manifestos offer bland generalities, and those elected then fill in the details themselves). Those elected are seen as carrying some responsibility for their area, but are not permitted to take this too far, for they are ultimately bound by party lines. On any of the major social or demographic characteristics (age, sex, race, class) they do not represent us at all. Taking the example of British MPs: lawyers make up the largest single occupational group; women have only just pushed beyond 5 per cent of the total; and the proportion of the population that is non-white is currently 'represented' by a mere handful of MPs, whose election in 1987 marked the first substantial breach in the white monopoly.

Those who challenge the system which produces this are usually faced with a form of *reductio ad absurdum* that queries how far the principle of proportionality should go. Are we supposed to elect students, pensioners, the unemployed, in numbers that mirror their proportion in society? Are we supposed to have proportional representation of every occupational classification, every religion, every racial and linguistic

minority? Are we supposed to do five-yearly investigations into the
number of lesbians and homosexuals in order to ensure their fair representation in parliament? And what about height, weight, hair colour,
tastes in music or sport or books? The whole idea is patently absurd.

Representative democracy cannot produce a perfect reflection of
society: the only guarantee of that would be all the citizens meeting
together in national assembly. Within the limits of representation, it
is hard to see how to get agreement on the categories to be covered.
Even where such agreement becomes possible, proportionality inevitably reduces local autonomy, for it must involve some form of national
party directive over the kind of candidates each constituency should
choose. But arguments that rely on the impossibility of one extreme
in order to justify its opposite are always suspect, and as long as those
who speak for us are drawn from such an *un*representative sample, then
democracy will remain profoundly flawed. The obstacles that deny certain people the chance of election are as undemocratic in their way as
the laws that once excluded them from the right to vote. And moving
on to the more positive point, different experiences do create different
values, priorities, interests; while we may all be capable of that imagi-
native leap that takes us beyond our own situation, history indicates
that we do this very partially, if at all. Those who regard the current
situation with complacency are not too far in spirit from the nineteenth-
century apologists of male suffrage, who claimed that a man spoke for
himself and 'his' woman, and thus that the woman had no need for a
separate voice. Where there are different interests and different experiences, it is either naive or dishonest to say that one group can speak
for us all.

What we see as the salient differences will of course vary through
history. In contemporary Britain, for example, it may not seem of much
moment whether the proportions of Catholics, Protestants or Jews
elected fairly reflect the proportions in society as a whole. It has certainly mattered in the past, and in the case of Muslims it is beginning
to matter a great deal. The prevailing terms of contemporary politics
suggest the triad of sex, race and class as the dominant fissures, but I do
not insist on these as exclusive. Political movements establish which
categories are important; comparisons of those elected with a random
sample of those who elect alert us to what is usually a yawning divide.
It does not detract from the seriousness of the case to note that this will
throw up the odd aberration. Until it was pointed out to me that those
elected to the presidency of the United States are not just white and
male but tall, it had not occurred to me that height could be a salient
consideration. I now take this as confirming the equation between politics

and men, which casts its shadow over those who fall short of the masculine ideal.

[. . .]

Continuing to discuss the problem of representation of women, one of the debates in contemporary feminist theory is whether women can be described as an interest-based group, whose interests then need representing. The argument began with Virginia Sapiro's 'When are interests interesting?'[1] which set out to establish that the key issue is no longer women's right to be represented as individual women (their right to vote and stand in elections) but their representation as a group. Because of their materially different position in society, women have objectively different interests from men, but the entry of women as individual actors on the political scene does not mean that these interests are actively pursued. Though research suggests that women politicians develop different styles of political engagement, it also suggests that they are wary of speaking for women. So when policies that favour women have been introduced, it is as often as not a by-product of changed circumstances (new labour market needs, for example) or of the fortunes of other social groups (equal opportunity policies were introduced in the United States with a view to tackling racial disadvantage, but they then applied to women as well). Getting more women elected may be a necessary but is certainly not a sufficient condition.

Later research offers more encouraging results on the stance of women politicians and raises interesting questions about the numbers threshold at which women acquire the confidence to speak for their sex. But the debate has moved in a different direction, falling into what I have noted as the division between those who seek to incorporate an understanding of women into existing frameworks and those who see women as more fundamentally subversive. Thus Irene Diamond and Nancy Hartsock argue that the very language of rights and interests is grounded in the individualism of market society, an individualism of rational economic *men*. Feminist theory offers a 'clean break with the assumptions of the interest group framework',[2] which they describe as centring on instrumental advantage and individual gain. The experience and concerns of women are said to transcend this, primarily because women's involvement in reproduction leads them to define themselves in more relational terms. It is not then a matter of representing the specific 'interests' of women (whether this means more women in politics, or parties devoted to women's concerns); the needs of women explode the whole politics of interest.

This is a risky case to argue, as is everything that relies on women's special qualities or their different relationship to the world. An emphasis on needs as opposed to interests can too readily facilitate the belief that participation does not much matter; or that getting into politics is a male-defined game and best left up to the boys. I am not saying that Diamond and Hartsock reach this conclusion, but writing in the context of the United States they are understandably disillusioned by the politics of women's lobbying, which in a system that has given little formal power to women as representatives, and few enough concessions in material terms, has been the main public face of women's 'interests'. Others who adopt the notion of a specifically 'women's culture' have fallen more definitely into the trap and explicitly advise women against sharing male power.

[...]

Does it make sense, however, to talk of an objective common interest, or to speak of 'the' feminist demands? The least controversial route follows general formulations: Jonasdottir's 'formal' interest in participation,[3] or Hege Skjeie's notion of access.[4] Since segregation is a fundamental ordering principle of gendered societies, women can be said to share at least one interest in common. They need improved access to every sphere. Beyond this we cannot too readily assume shared interests between women. We cannot say that women share a common 'interest' on such substantive issues as disarmament or ecology, or at any rate we cannot say they agree. We cannot even claim a clearly 'women's' perspective on such issues as abortion, for while surveys regularly report a difference in male and female attitudes, this is often that men are more liberal – or, to put it another way, more cavalier. The experience of being a woman increases both the importance women attach to legalizing abortion *and* the reluctance they feel towards abortion itself. Each of these is a 'women's' perspective. Which of them should our representatives represent?

This brings me to a further problem that has been very little discussed. Within the framework of liberal democracy, elections are conducted on the basis of party competition, and while we may bemoan the poverty of electoral debate, we are supposed to be voting not for people but ideas. In the continuing battle between accountability and autonomy, the more democratic have usually sided with the principle of rendering accounts, arguing that this is what representation should mean. If the vote is to have any substance it must entail more than a preference for an individual we can trust: it should be a preference for a programme we support. We do not expect our representatives to turn round and tell us they've just had a brilliant idea but forgot to mention it when they asked for our votes. Or more cynically, we may well expect it, but we regard such behaviour as undemocratic and would never promote it as an ideal. Candidates are supposed to tell us their plans before the election and give us a chance to make up our minds. The fact that we vote for parties rather than individuals reflects this: instead of choosing between individuals on the basis of trust we choose between parties on the basis of their policies and ideals. Strong democrats mostly want to enhance rather than reduce this feature, and there is a long tradition that seeks to make representatives more accountable, to let the electorate decide on as much as is feasible and set the boundaries within which representatives can move.

The arguments over the representation of women have tended to evade this issue. Much recent literature has explored whether women representatives do indeed act differently from men, whether they adopt a different style of political behaviour, identify a different range of priorities, are more liberal or radical than men. The implication is that we want them to be different, and that if they are not it undermines the case. As Vicky Randall puts it, 'it may be argued that we need to know more about the behaviour of women politicians, before deciding whether, as feminists, we want to increase their numbers'.[5] Yet within the general debates on democracy, this is an odd approach, for it suggests that once we have this evidence we will be happy to give our representatives a pretty free hand.

When a woman has been chosen as a candidate by her party and elected to carry through what her party represents, do we really want her to take it upon herself to say she 'speaks' for women, that she has a privileged understanding of women's special needs? Should she be setting herself up in opposition to her party, claiming a mandate derived from her sex? Is there not a tension between this and the accountability that democrats so widely espouse? As party activists and candidates, women can of course speak for women: they can agitate for party programmes or manifestos to include policies that reflect women's needs; they can make themselves experts in aspects of family or employment policy; they can serve as spokeswomen for feminist ideals. And on that vast range of topics that no party ever bothers to put before an electorate, women representatives can make themselves as free as the men to pursue the policies they favour. But we cannot have it both ways. We cannot challenge the Burkean notion of (non)-representation which sets the elected above the electors and lets them get on with what they know best; and at the same time treat women as if they have a special mission beyond party lines.

As long as the number of women elected is so pitiful, and the range of issues regarded as 'political' so male-defined, the dilemma will rarely emerge. Thus abortion has been considered a non-party issue in Britain, and feminists have been profoundly thankful for the handful of women MPs who have assumed a particular responsibility in debates on the topic. No one would accuse them of exceeding their representative role, or say that they were not elected to defend women's right to choose. In most cases the needs or interests of women have been so steadily overlooked by political parties that feminists are more anxious to hear women speak to these interests than to worry over their self-appointed role. What now seems an academic dilemma may, however, become important in the future. From the most minimalist to the most active, all theories of democracy deal with the question of popular control, and while the competition between political parties offers only limited mechanisms through which the electorate asserts its views (in the dourest versions, only the chance to say which party should govern), it does at least engage with the issue. In what sense, other than being women, can women say they represent women's views? Their legitimacy derives from election not nature, and any mandate in relation to women depends on the extent to which their parties – whether 'feminized' versions of existing parties or newly created women's parties – have argued explicitly for policies for women. Outside this mechanism, is it legitimate to say they represent their sex?

[. . .]

It is easy enough then to show that women are under-represented in politics, and not too much more difficult to make the case that women are oppressed. On both counts something should surely be done. The disproportion between those elected and those who elect is too astounding to be attributed to accident, while the fact that it serves those who are already advantaged is too striking for any democrat to ignore. The difficulties arise in the next stage, for within the framework of representative democracy it is political parties that have provided the vehicle for representation, and in its more substantial sense, the representation of women does not fit. 'Women' are not homogeneous and do not speak with a single voice.

Those who most vehemently opposed women's right to vote often feared that women would vote in a block and differently from men: that women's suffrage would disrupt the basis of party alignments by producing a new 'women's vote'; or, equally damning, that the new electors would prove more conservative than men and shift the previous balance between parties. This, of course, is why the leadership of the British Liberal Party was so resistant to votes for women, despite growing support within the Liberal rank and file; and why, in contrast, the leadership of the Conservative Party proved more sympathetic, despite horror and outrage in the party as a whole. As Millicent Fawcett put it, 'from the suffrage point of view, the [Liberal Party] was an army without generals, and the [Tory Party] was generals without an army'.[6] As events turned out, a relatively minor 'gender gap' emerged, with women at first more inclined to vote for conservative parties, and more recently the other way round. Those who resist an increase in women's representation no doubt harbour similar fears, anticipating that the women elected will alter the game. I hope there will be changes, but in the interests of democratic accountability these have to take place in the open, through the decision-making processes of each party and the publicity of electoral campaigns. We cannot jump too easily into the notion that there is an interest of women; and short of women's constituencies or women's elections, there is no clear mechanism for their representation.

Notes and References

1 V. Sapiro, 'When are interests interesting?', *American Political Science Review*, 75 (3) (1981), pp. 701–16.
2 I. Diamond and N. Hartsock, 'Beyond interests in politics', *American Political Science Review*, 75 (3) (1981), p. 720.
3 A. Jonasdottir, 'On the concept of interests, women's interests and the limitations of interest theory', in *The Political Interests of Gender*, ed. K. Jones and A. Jonasdottir (Sage, London, 1988).
4 H. Skjeie, *The Feminization of Power* (Institute for Social Research, Norway, 1988).
5 V. Randall, *Women and Politics*, 2nd edn (Macmillan, London, 1987), p. 151.
6 Quoted in A. Rosen, *Rise Up, Women!* (Routledge and Kegan Paul, London, 1974), p. 12.

PART III

Gender, Sexuality, Power

JUDY WAJCMAN (READING 19) analyses further connections between gender and technology. Is modern industrial production in some way specifically bound up with masculinity and, if so, how? That there is a relation between masculinity and military weaponry is readily understandable, for war has always been mainly a male affair. Certain more traditional industrial technologies became 'male' because they demanded physical strength to operate – or 'strength' was built into such technologies because they were previously conceived as male. Yet men today dominate the new microelectronic technologies – to which such traditional considerations appear largely irrelevant. Thus research studies indicate that computers are defined as predominantly male machinery at home, at school and in the workplace. Far more boys than girls are members of computer clubs and regularly use computer games.

Wajcman traces the connections between maleness and technology to the perpetuation of patriarchal relations via the educational system, youth culture, the family and the mass media. Research on sex stereotyping in schools provides ample evidence of how it comes about that girls and boys tend to move into different subject areas, and have different attitudes towards the subject areas which they share in common. The proportion of girls applying to study computer science at university is actually declining. The widespread introduction of microcomputers into schools has not helped readjust gender divisions affecting microtechnology. On the contrary, computers have tended to become a new male preserve, connected with male dominance of science and mathematics.

Most of this, Wajcman says, does not occur as a result of direct teaching but through the 'hidden curriculum': the attitudes and values conveyed in an implicit way by teachers and peer groups. Yet the rejection of microtechnology on the part of girls should not be seen, Wajcman claims, solely in a negative way; girls may use their femininity as a means of actively rejecting the dominant ethos of the school.

In the next selection, Reading 20, Michelle Stanworth analyses the different technological innovations that have influenced human reproduction in particular. She distinguishes four types of reproductive technology. First, there are those technologies concerned with contraception. These include diaphragms, condoms, sterilization, abortion and the contraceptive pill. The second type is bound up with the organization of labour and childbirth. Over the past century or so, childbirth has largely been taken out of the hands of female midwives and placed under the control of medical professionals, with various sorts of diagnostic and therapeutic technology being introduced.

A third form of reproductive technology concerns earlier phases of pregnancy. Techniques for monitoring foetal development and neo-natal care are now an intrinsic part of the experience of pregnant women. Finally, and most controversial of all, are the technologies designed to produce conception in the infertile. A wave of experimentation with 'fertility drugs' has been succeeded by the introduction of *in vitro* fertilization.

Reproductive technologies, Stanworth argues, have had a mixed impact upon women's lives. In the industrialized societies today, compared with previous generations, women have far fewer pregnancies, bear fewer babies against their wishes and die much less frequently in childbirth, and their infant children die much less often. These advances have mostly been brought about by developments in reproductive technologies.

Yet to suppose that such developments have given women more control over motherhood would be too oversimplified a view. Motherhood has become a much more absorbing, full-time occupation than it used to be; in many pre-modern cultures, for example, large families were a burden upon women, but at the same time older children and grandparents would very often care for infants and small children. Some reproductive technologies themselves carry new health risks. In addition, male medical personnel control decisions affecting women that previously were in the hands of female carers. Some have seen the history of reproductive technologies as a process by which men have taken control of reproduction from women. While there is a good deal of truth to this analysis, Stanworth concludes, we should also see that women have frequently been able actively to adapt reproductive technologies to their own purposes and contest the patriarchal relations with which they are faced.

Drawing upon the ideas of Michel Foucault, Jeffrey Weeks focuses on the role of sexuality in modern culture in Reading 21. Sexuality, he suggests, is at the intersection of two major sets of concerns in modern societies: with subjectivity or self-identity and with the health and prosperity of the social community. At the core of both lies the capacities and pleasures of the body. All sorts of modes of administration and management of the body, and of sexual activity, have arisen as moral discipline, hygiene and health have become part of social regulation.

The Victorian period was of pivotal importance here. That era has usually been thought of as one marked by puritanism and sexual repression. Such attitudes certainly existed, and were directed against women's sexuality in particular. Yet the Victorians, Weeks says, following Foucault, were absorbed with sex and engaged in many forms of public discussion of it. Even their repressiveness was a mark of the very fascination which the subject exerted. Public preoccupation with sexuality has developed further over the course of the present century. Although attitudes have varied over time, a number of persistent concerns and themes can be discerned. The relations between men and women, in respect of sexuality and morality, obviously form a central one. Others concern issues of sexual deviance, family relationships, relations between children and adults and racial or ethnic relations.

The moral concerns that shaped sexuality in the nineteenth century were mainly expressed by middle-class groups. The middle class wished to differentiate itself both from the 'immoral' activities of the aristocracy and what were taken to be tendencies towards promiscuity on the part of the working class. Victorian 'respectability' sought to remould the rest of society in its image. Such respectability was always gendered; men routinely engaged in sexual adventures from which 'respectable' women were barred. For the Victorian middle classes, not just women but the poorer classes as a whole were thought to be 'closer to nature' than the more educated groups.

The nineteenth century was a key period for the development of ideologies of female sexuality. Weeks refers to the research of the American historian Thomas Laqeur, which indicates that the nineteenth century saw a basic shift in the ways in which male and female bodies were typically thought of. Until the end of the eighteenth century there was essentially a 'one-sex' model of sexual physiology. The female body was interpreted as an inferior version of the male, although capable of producing sexual pleasure; in fact female sexual pleasure was seen as necessary to successful conception. In the nineteenth century this idea was replaced by a model of sexual physiology which emphasized the existence of two sharply different bodies, a radical opposition of male and female sexuality. In this newer view, women's reproductive cycle was taken to be linked to a dearth of sexual feeling. These definitions expressed new shifts in the balance of power between the sexes.

In Reading 22 Anthony Giddens discusses ideals of love and sexuality found among men and women today. The differences between the sexes remain substantial. He quotes a research study investigating the views of teenage girls and boys about sex and emotional feelings. The researcher discovered major contrasts between the ways in which the two sexes approached these topics. The girls talked about sex in the context of love and were able to develop fluent narratives about their personal lives and intimate involvements. The boys, on the other hand, were unwilling or unable to discuss sex in a narrative form, as connected to their likely futures; they spoke of the topic mainly in terms of a series of discrete sexual episodes or 'conquests'.

Ideals of romantic love on the part of girls today have become quite muted. Most of the girls interviewed accepted that relationships do not necessarily endure and that paid work was likely to be important to their future lives. Yet the theme of the connection between sex and romance came across very strongly. They saw sexual relationships in terms of equality. Boys, on the other hand, have by no means relinquished the double standard; they believe that what is normal behaviour in the male, the pursuit of sexual diversity, is inappropriate for the female. 'Loss of virginity' continues to be something girls 'give up', while boys see this as a talisman of achievement.

Women, Giddens argues, are pioneering major changes in the domain of personal relationships. The claim to equality lodged in the economic and political spheres spills over directly into the area of personal life and sexuality. Women are pressing for emotional democracy, a form of social relation in which there is emotional equality and communication. Achieving such a far-reaching transformation of personal life would involve many psychological as well as social changes; how far these will actually occur remains an open question. Male sexuality, with its inhibited forms of emotional communication, forms a major barrier. Giddens supports the thesis, mentioned above, that much male sexual violence today may not be so much an expression of pre-given patriarchy as a reaction to a world where women are no longer economically or emotionally compliant. It is more of an attempt to shore up a crumbling dominance than an expression of unchanging relations of power.

In Reading 23 Lesley Hall offers an interpretation of male sexuality that questions orthodoxies on the subject. Male sexuality plainly reflects the patriarchal relations of the wider society. Yet it would be mistaken, Hall shows, to suppose that men are universally confident in their assertion of sexual power. While the imagery of male sexuality suggests a confident dominance, the reality is often quite different. Male sexuality is frequently marked by prolonged anxieties and insecurities; the idea of rampant male sexuality is questionable.

Thus men in adolescence are frequently frightened by the development of their sexual impulses and uncertain about how to deal with them. Later, many men are worried by the threat of impotence, premature ejaculation and other problems of sexual functioning. In a manual written for general practitioners in the 1930s, men with sexual problems are spoken of as 'among the most miserable of all patients that the doctor is called upon to treat'. In her book from which this selection is drawn, Hall analyses letters men wrote to the sex educator Marie Stopes in the 1920s and 1930s. They are replete with anxieties that the correspondents felt unable to discuss either with their partners or in a more public way. Hall quotes the feminist author Gloria Steinem, who has written that if men suffered the problems women do with menstruation there would be enormous attention and financial resources dedicated to the subject. Yet in fact, Hall points out, the medical profession has been very loath to discuss the sexual and reproductive problems of the male. Partly because male sexuality is thought to be so 'straightforward', men's problems and anxieties have been largely kept under cover.

Seeing male sexuality as fraught and tensionful, Hall concludes, helps us understand male sexual behaviour more adequately than if it were assumed that it is unproblematic. Thus pornography and sexual violence can be seen as deriving as much from men's insecurities as from a confident assertion of untroubled male power.

The questions of how one should define 'pornography', and whether open access to pornographic materials is desirable, have been vexed questions for feminists. Conventionally, pornography is supposed to be different from 'art'. But what exactly is the nature of the difference? Susanne Kappeler takes up this issue in Reading 24. The literary establishment, and those whom she calls 'cultured feminists', see an opposition between the two. A book or a film recognized to have 'high artistic quality' is regarded in a different way, in respect of its sexual content, from others that do not possess such a quality.

Kappeler discusses the problems involved in making such judgements by taking as an example D.M. Thomas's novel *The White Hotel*. Regarded as a work of literary merit by many – and also a bestseller – the book contains a good deal of material that might appear 'pornographic' if it were found in another context. The claim of Thomas's work to be classified as 'artistic' depends upon the fact that he has written novels and poems to literary acclaim. Such a justification, Kappeler says, is necessarily circular and hardly bears upon the content of the novel itself. When we look at that content what we find is a theme of the extinction of woman as a human being and her reduction to an instrument of male sexual desire. This 'illusion of the woman as subject' gives the book a fundamentally pornographic structure. The novel, Kappeler argues, embodies a distorted sexual politics. Whatever literary merit it might have has no bearing upon this fundamental thematic.

Kappeler thus reads *The White Hotel* as an expression of male sexual violence. In Reading 25 Deborah Cameron and Elizabeth Frazer consider male violence against women in a more direct way. Feminists, they note, see a continuity between forms of violence by men against women such as rape or wife-battering and more 'minor' forms of male sexual harassment, like flashing or making obscene telephone calls. Men's sexuality is oriented to control and subordination of women: rape and flashing seem quite distinct, yet both are part of a variety of things that men (more accurately some men) do to reassure themselves of their potency and to induce fear and humiliation in their women victims. Male sexual violence, even if engaged in only by a minority of men, forms a general threat to women's security. To limit exposure to violence, women must take precautions well beyond those necessary for the average male. If rape does occur, the victim might find herself interrogated, shamed and even accused of perjury.

Sexual murder, Cameron and Frazer argue, is the desire for subjugation taken to its extreme – the destruction of the individual. The physical degradation inflicted by some killers, including mutilation of the victim's body, represents a final violation of the female sex. The sex murder creates a very real atmosphere of 'sexual terrorism' among the female population. 'Terrorism: the rule of fear', Cameron and Frazer conclude, and 'violence against women: the law of misogyny' can combine in an appalling 'lust to kill'.

The contribution from Barbara Sichtermann (Reading 26) concentrates specifically upon the phenomenon of rape. Rape, she agrees with Cameron and Frazer, is an assault upon a woman's moral as well as physical integrity. It should be treated, she says, as a violent crime like any other – and in this sense she moves the analysis somewhat away from the emphases of the two previous authors. The psycho-dynamics of rape are complex. Although writing as a feminist, Sichtermann controversially argues that the desire to be 'taken violently' is a common female fantasy. In sexual activity there is sometimes the desire to submit and an element of violence in pleasure itself.

Feminist theories of male sexual violence have usually tended to define this topic as taboo. After all, misogyny would thrive even more than it does if it were proclaimed that many women are actively willing to suffer. Sadism and masochism in fact, Sichtermann avers, are not specific to one sex or the other. The 'indivisible composite of pain and pleasure' cross-cuts the categories of female and male. In quite 'normal' sexual pleasure there is a component of pain; orgasm puts the individual in 'heaven' but is also a 'fall', a 'little death'. The notion of purely female masochism, and male sadism, should be abandoned.

None of this compromises the fact that rape is rape. Rape is an endeavour to establish, or re-establish, male dominance through the imposed use of physical force. It is patriarchal culture, Sichtermann says, which draws the pain–pleasure relation into the service of justifying male sexual aggression. The battle against rape does not pit one sex against the other, but separates patriarchy from its critics, whether these be female or male.

In Reading 27 Catherine Hall analyses images of masculinity in nineteenth-century Britain. The development of a new bourgeois middle class, consisting of professionals, traders and farmers, sought independence from the traditional values linked to the aristocracy and gentry. These new groups reinvented the 'gentleman', now defined in terms of middle-class morality and self-discipline. The traditional aristocratic male became seen as decadent, lazy and foppish. A man's individuality henceforth was tied to hard work and success. Along with this there went the 'invention of motherhood' for women; women were expected to devote themselves to the role of wife and mother.

Hall discusses these changing ideals of masculinity in the work of Thomas Carlyle and John Stuart Mill, two leading middle-class authors of the period. Each helped formulate notions of manliness and male cultural identity in the latter part of the nineteenth century. Carlyle saw masculinity as bound up with strength of purpose and independent action. Mill, who wrote from a much more liberal standpoint than Carlyle, saw masculinity as what was earned 'with the sweat of the brow'. They took opposing positions on the subject of slavery. Hall analyses these views in relation to a riot that occurred in Morant Bay in Jamaica in 1865. At issue in the debate was not only how Britain should treat her colonies but competing notions of manhood. For Mill and his followers racial equality was of paramount importance and directly connected to proper male behaviour. Mill pointed to parallels between slavery and the subjugation of women. For Carlyle, on the other hand, norms of masculinity, conceived of as the assertion of instrumental dominance over the world, produced a justification of power and hierarchy.

Power – in this case power transposed largely on a symbolic level – is the theme of the contribution from Carol Adams (Reading 28). Her thesis is an unusual one – the association between patriarchy and the eating of meat. Meat eating is almost everywhere associated with virility; and virility, Adams points out, has the dictionary definition of 'having the characteristics of an adult male, coming from the meaning "man" '. Cookery books, according to Adams, tend to address themselves to men when they discuss methods of preparing meat. Thus she refers to a section of one book called 'for men only', which consists of steak and beef dishes.

Historically, she shows, men have often eaten meat while women have made do with bread and vegetables. In times of war, government rationing has frequently reserved the right to eat meat for the soldier. During the Second World War the per capita consumption of meat in the US armed forces was about two-and-a-half times that of the average civilian. Meat, Adams concludes, is the 'literal evocation of male power'.

What is the nature of the link between male power and violence? Reading 29 by Josie O'Dwyer and Pat Carlen suggests that we should not oversimplify such connections. Women, for example, make up a far smaller proportion of the prison population, in all the developed societies, than do men; but women's prisons can be quite violent places. O'Dwyer came into contact with prison violence early on when she was in a borstal as a 17 year old. Here the violence to which she was subjected was at the hands of male warders. However, there were also female officers, known as the 'heavy mob', who made a speciality of using brutal force against the prisoners. These women were every bit as intimidatory as the men.

O'Dwyer experienced, and observed, a great deal of violence in Holloway prison, where the officers are all women. Violence and the threat of violence were used as part of a wider series of attempts to harass the prisoners. According to O'Dwyer, since the prisoners can rarely, if ever, escape the surveillance of the warders, they have little means of effective resistance.

The violent intimidation found in women's prisons probably directly reflects practices found in male prison environments. While women may be violent in some circumstances, violence is much more commonly associated with masculinity and with male power. Male violence against women – and some sorts of violence by men towards other men – is bound up with the sustaining of patriarchal power, but in ways which need some qualification.

Male violence, hierarchy and domination are the subject of Klaus Theweleit's discussion of military training procedures in the German army during the period of National Socialism (Reading 30). All the incoming cadets were placed in an order of ranks in which, save at the very beginning of the training period, there is always someone 'below' as well as 'above'. The trainee was taught to accept orders from above without question, but also that he had a duty to impose his will upon anyone lower in the hierarchy than himself. Conditions of life were harsh and privacy virtually non-existent. Anyone who gave signs of not being able to cope was a 'cissy' and liable to be put on report.

Theweleit describes in some detail the experiences of one recruit, a boy called Salomon. From his first day in the military academy, like his companions, Salomon was subjected to torments and humiliations by other cadets and by the training officers. The experience of bodily punishment was supposed to develop a 'thick skin', mental and physical toughness. Salomon endured the process with some success but saw others broken by it. In the end he 'surrendered with a zeal borne of desperation and unhappiness' to the aims of the academy.

The example of military training is important, because it indicates that for the large majority of men forms of violence expected in war do not derive from a natural male aggressiveness. The ordinary man, in other words, has to be taught to kill, as well as to have the discipline to face the threats of the battlefield. Military training is a dedicated regime that draws upon certain ideals of masculinity, but also actively represses warmer and more sentimental feelings. If Chodorow's theory is right, men do not so much lack emotions of sympathy and love as the capability to acknowledge them themselves and thereby to express them in a direct way to others. On both these accounts, along with many of the others discussed above, the relationship between the sexes is not something that is fixed and given; it is constructed – and can be transformed.

19

Technology as Masculine Culture

Judy Wajcman

Given the resilience of the association between technology and manliness, how do women think about and experience technology? What are the mechanisms, both formal and informal, that foster and reproduce the cultural stereotype of women as technologically incapable or indeed invisible in technical spheres?

The continuing male monopoly of weapons and mechanical tools is perhaps not so difficult to understand given the weight of male tradition and custom borne by these instruments of war and production. The old story that you had to be strong to work with machines had at least some credibility in this context. The male dominance of new technologies is, at first sight, much more puzzling. It was a commonly held expectation that with the development of microelectronics, and the decreasing importance of heavy industrial technology, the gender stereotyping of technology would diminish.

Computing is a crucial example, because as a completely new type of technology it had the potential to break the mould. In terms of sexual divisions, there are three distinct paths along which this technology might have developed. Computing could have been gender-neutral with no basic differentiation between female and male users. Or, it could have been a technology that women appropriated. After all, the image of new electronic computer technology fits with femininity in that it is clean, sedentary work involving rote tasks, detail, precision and nimble typing fingers. Yet recent evidence on the gender gap in access to computers at school, at play and at home supports the idea that our culture has already defined computers as preeminently male machines. Numerous British, American and Australian surveys show that boys vastly outnumber girls wherever there is discretionary use of these machines such as in school computer clubs, computer summer camps, at home and in games arcades. In response to this disturbing trend, a number of feminist researchers have recently investigated the relation of women and girls to computers. These studies afford useful insights into the marginalization of women from technology more generally.

Although work-related cultures have their own dynamics, they are also the result of cultural processes that take place outside of work and that are carried into it. Technologies, like people, are already sex-typed when they enter the workplace. Most women never approach the foreign territory of these masculine areas. This sex segregation at work reflects the fact that patriarchal relations are an integral part of our entire social system. In modern societies it is the education system, in conjunction with other social institutions, which helps to perpetuate gender inequalities from generation to generation. Schooling, youth cultures, the family and the mass media all transmit meanings and values that identify masculinity with machines and technological competence. These social contexts are intertwined and mutually reinforcing, but they should not be seen simply as external forces. Individuals actively participate in, resist, and even help reproduce by resisting, these social practices.

[. . .]

How does a completely new technology like computers, that may not automatically conform to preexisting patterns of gender differentiation, fit into these processes? Focusing on computers may enable us to see more clearly the social mechanisms through which a new technology becomes integrated into the masculine cultural system.

Schools are the most obvious places where young people first come in contact with computers. There is now an extensive literature on sex stereotyping in general in schools, particularly on the processes by which girls and boys are channelled into different subjects in secondary and tertiary education, and the link between education and gender divisions in the labour market. As with scientific and technological areas of tertiary education generally, the sex ratio of computer science is very marked. Since at least the mid-1970s there have been anti-discrimination legislation, equal opportunity programmes and other government and non-government initiatives in many countries to redress this imbalance. Despite all this effort, the number of girls taking computer science at British universities has been decreasing. The proportion of female applicants for undergraduate level computer science courses dropped from approximately 28 per cent in 1978 to 13 per cent in 1986.[1] In fact there are fewer women applying for computer science courses now than nine years ago although the subject has doubled in size. Similar situations are found in other countries.

This drop appears to be linked to the widespread introduction of microcomputers into schools. Here girls quickly learn that computers are 'just for the boys'. Numerous investigations into the under-representation of girls in science have indicated how the presentation of the subject alienates girls. Computers have been linked to things scientific and mathematical, traditionally male subjects. There has been a tendency to site school microcomputers in the science/maths department and computer studies is almost always taught by mathematics teachers, usually male. Even though it is now generally recognized that ability in mathematics is not an indication of aptitude for computing, it is still taken into account for entry to computing courses at school. 'Thus computers tend to be conceptually assimilated to the category of science, mathematics and technology and acquire some of the traditional qualities of differentiated interest amongst boys and girls.'[2]

Gender differences in educational experience are not simply the result of what is taught in courses of formal instruction. In a more profound way the culture of the school is involved in constructing gender and sexuality through the 'hidden curriculum' – teaching in an implicit way meanings and behaviours associated with femaleness and maleness, with femininity and masculinity. Studies of classrooms show that teachers behave differently to girls and boys, they speak to them differently, they require different responses and different behaviour from them. Gender identity is profoundly important to children's perception of themselves. Girls feel the need to display a set of behavioural patterns that are perceived as being feminine: these feminine qualities, however, are incompatible with the qualities supposed necessary for a 'mathematical mind'. Girls internalize the belief that boys possess something that they lack; difference is lived as inferiority. One study of primary school children reported, for example, that '[g]irls actually believed that boys were naturally ordained with a profusion of masculine esoteric skills such as being able to drive a car, tractor or helicopter'.[3] Computers are seen as belonging to the realm of machinery and mathematics – a daunting combination for girls.

However, there is a danger here of implying that, in conforming to the gender stereotype and thus rejecting technology, girls are their own worst enemy. Feminists have now challenged this passive model of female socialization, arguing that girls may well use their femininity as a form of resistance at school, or even resist feminine roles themselves. Some girls are interested in computers but it is difficult for them to pursue this because boys actively and aggressively capture computer time where, as is usually the case, there is insufficient computer supply in schools. This harassment of girls interested in computing continues into tertiary education. At this stage the harassment takes the form of obscene computer mail or print-outs of nude women. Women students in computer science at MIT found this problem so pervasive that they organized a special committee to deal with it.

Due partly to computer games, children today are more likely to develop their interest in information technology at home than at school. Schools reinforce the early socialization into gender roles that takes place within the family.

Many children's toys encourage boys to be assertive and independent, to solve problems, experiment with construction and, more recently, to regard the technological aspects of their toys with confidence and familiarity. The skills which children learn from these toys lay the foundations of mathematical, scientific and technological learning. By contrast, 'girls' toys' such as dolls foster different skills which are associated with caring and social interaction. Just as boys often come to school with the advantage of having played with mechanical toys, or connected an electric train set, they now have often played video games at home. Toys are an important part of the differentiated learning experiences between girls and boys. These toys in turn reflect the division of labour between women and men within the family. Household technologies are sharply gendered. Technologies of external household and car maintenance are traditionally the husbands' sphere, while women primarily use the technologies of the kitchen and cleaning. Moreover, control of technologies of entertainment such as the television and video recorder are also gendered male.

Computers all too easily fit into this sex-stereotyped view of technology. There is a tendency for the home micro to be bought for the sons of the family. This is encouraged by advertisements for computer games and home computers which are aimed at a male market and often feature pictures of boys looking raptly at the screen. Evidence collected by the Equal Opportunities Commission in 1985 revealed that of all British households owning microcomputers, boys are thirteen times more likely than girls to be using them. Moreover, only 4 per cent of micros are used by their mothers. Children quickly learn from their parents which are the appropriate spheres for them. In a California survey in which school children were asked to describe how they would use computers when they were 30 years old, 'the boys said they would use them for finances, data processing, and games; the girls thought they would use them for housework. Wrote one sixth grade girl: "When I am thirty, I'll have a computer that has long arms and that can clean the house and cook meals, and another to pay for groceries and stuff." [4]

Games are the primary attraction of computers for children. Given that it is men (often computer hackers) who design video games and software, it is hardly surprising that their designs typically appeal to male fantasies. In fact video games began at one of the places where computer culture itself got started. The first video game was Space War, built at MIT in the early 1960s. Many of the most popular games today are simply programmed versions of traditionally male non-computer games, involving shooting, blowing up, speeding, or zapping in some way or another. They often have militaristic titles such as 'Destroy All Subs' and 'Space Wars' highlighting their themes of adventure and violence. No wonder then that these games often frustrate or bore the non-macho players exposed to them. As a result, macho males often have a positive first experience with the computer; other males and most females have a negative initial experience.

It is this masculine narrative content of much computer game software that has received the most attention in explanations of the difference between female and male interest in video games. Many analyses focus on the private experience or 'intimate relation' with the machine ignoring the social dimension of interest in computing or in playing games. The predominantly male interest in games is a function of time and a legacy of male adolescent culture. Overall, girls simply have fewer opportunities to use computers than boys because the experience of leisure time is deeply divided along sex boundaries. Like their mothers, girls have a lot less time to play at home because of their domestic responsibilities. Young working-class daughters are expected to help with childcare and other household tasks in a way that their brothers are not. Boys learn from their fathers that it is their right to concentrate totally on the computer if they choose, oblivious of the surrounding domestic environment. Males are more easily allowed to follow up interests which do not have to be justified as benefiting anyone else.

In addition, girls' extracurricular activities are generally much more restricted than boys. Parents are cautious about allowing girls to stay after school in the unstructured environment of computer clubs. Public places like video arcades, which are central to the leisure culture of young male adolescents, are virtually off limits for most girls. They are populated almost exclusively by males; the few females in evidence are usually spectators. Leslie Haddon has shown that it was the continuity from pinball machines that helped shape the arcade game-playing world as a predominantly masculine one. Electronic games directly appropriated the role of pinball and, within a few years of their introduction, pinball sales had declined by two-thirds. The institutions that these young males had built up around pinball – the values, rules, and rituals – were transferred to the video game. '[T]he location of video games within the arcade and certain other contexts had meant that the new machines were incorporated into the existing social activities of this milieu. Amusement parks, and many of the other public sites where coin-operation machines were found, were part of street culture. They were mainly male, particularly young male, preserves.'[5] Thus the new technology was slotted into a preexisting male subculture and took on its masculine face.

We can conclude that the absence of technical confidence or competence does indeed become part of feminine gender identity, as well as being a sexual stereotype. It is now time to consider an argument that has been enthusiastically received by many Western feminists – that technical performance is a feature of fundamental cognitive difference between the sexes.

There have been endless variations on the theme that men's superior achievement demonstrates their greater physical and mental capacities. Traditionally, the significant discrepancy between the sexes in their ability to work with technology was attributed to physical strength or weakness and feminists spent the best part of the 1970s discrediting this doctrine of natural difference. I am prompted to wonder if it is merely an accident of history that, just as there is a major shift in the nature of technology from industrial to information technology, an increasing number of feminist accounts of women and computers are themselves emphasizing cognitive sex differences. These alleged differences between the sexes are conceptualized as opposed pairs which connect with other sets of oppositions. Males are portrayed as fascinated with the machine itself, being 'hard masters' in terms of computer programming, followers of rules and competitive. Females are described as only interested in computers as tools for use and application, as 'soft masters', as more concrete and co-operative in orientation. Thus it is argued that girls are less likely to achieve, not simply as the result of biological difference, but because of essential psychological differences. These arguments are reminiscent of two views that are by now somewhat discredited. One is the old sexual stereotype about women being too emotional, irrational and illogical, not to mention lacking the visual spatial awareness, to be good at mathematics: the other is the 1960s and 1970s belief that working-class and black children were naturally suited to less abstract or more concrete forms of learning. The new and fundamentally feminist twist in the argument, as we shall see, is that difference is no longer equated with inferiority or hierarchical ordering.

By far the best exposition of this view, and one which is drawn on widely by other authors, is to be found in the work of Sherry Turkle.[6] From her observations of young children programming at school, Turkle found that boys and girls tended to use two distinctive styles of computing, which she calls 'hard' and 'soft' mastery. Hard masters are overwhelmingly boys, imposing their will over the machine by implementing a structured, linear plan. The goal is to control the machine. Girls tend to be soft masters, having a more 'interactive', 'negotiating' or 'relational' style. They relate to the computer's formal system as a language for communication rather than as a set of rigid rules. Turkle draws a parallel with Claude Lévi-Strauss's distinction between Western science and the science of pre-literate societies in terms of the contrast between planning and *bricolage* or tinkering. 'The former is the science of the abstract, the latter is a science of the concrete. Like the *bricoleur*, the soft master works with a set of concrete elements. While the hard master thinks in terms of global abstractions, the soft master works on a problem by arranging and rearranging these elements, working through new combinations.'[7] Turkle is clear and emphatic that neither of these styles is superior for programming – they are different, and diversity or 'epistemological pluralism' should be celebrated. The problem for women then is the differential value accorded to the different styles. Computer expertise is defined as hard mastery; it is recognized as the only correct way to programme. Soft mastery is culturally constructed as inferior. Once more women are not up to hard male mastery.

Turkle is correct to point out that when gendered styles of computing are identified by teachers, they are valued accordingly. When women and girls do have a facility with programming, the categories for evaluating their performance are themselves gender-biased. They are designated as getting the right results by the wrong method. Only male mastery is identified as the rational, logical approach. However, I am uneasy when Turkle argues that male 'planners' versus female 'tinkerers' represent basic cognitive styles that are grounded in psychological sex differences, . . . an essential theory.

To the extent that this signals 'the return to conventional ideas of fundamental and comprehensive cognitive, emotional and moral difference between women and men'[8] I am unconvinced. First, on purely empirical grounds I am sceptical about the evidence provided for the existence of sex differences in cognitive styles. For example, Martin Hughes et al.[9] found no such differences. Previous research on sex differences with regard to mathematical ability has always stressed the lack of confidence and the conformity of girls and the resulting tendency for them to follow the rules diligently. This would lead one to suppose that girls would be the hard masters in computing. Are we now to believe that in computing boys follow the rules and girls are practising an alternative style?

More generally the search for 'significant' sex differences in this or that behaviour has a doubtful political pedigree and it is difficult to avoid the conclusion that such research finds what it has set out to find. Although studies do find evidence of differences between the sexes, the variation within the sexes is more important than the differences between them. Second, and more fundamentally, it is increasingly clear that cognition cannot be stripped of its social content to reveal pure logical reasoning.

Over the last ten years or so developmental psychology has recognized that the development of children cannot be understood outside the social context in which it occurs. Social relationships, understandings and practices play a constitutive role in the elaboration of the child's conceptual knowledge. To present differences in programming style as differences of individual psychology, as Turkle does, is to assume an individualized account of learning. Learning is a collective, social process. Turkle's predominantly psychological rather than sociological framework leads her to neglect the historical and cultural context in which computing education takes place. The pattern of boys being more independent and strategy-oriented, and girls being more concrete and dependent, bears a striking resemblance to the differences discussed by Valerie Walkerdine in the cognitive styles expected of, and encouraged in, boys and girls by teachers in the primary school.[10] In our society the computer has become socially constructed as a male domain; children learn from an early age to associate computers with boys and men. This means that girls approach the computer less often and with less confidence than boys. It may also mean that there are significant gender differences in how girls and boys relate to the machine and what it means to them. They may even have a tendency to want to use the machine for different things. But we should be extremely wary of saying that because women have different ways of proceeding, this indicates a fundamental difference in capacity. Rather, such discrepancies in cognitive style as can be observed are the consequence of major sexual inequalities in power.

In this connection it is salutary to note that the very first computer programmers were women. Between 1940 and 1950, many women were engaged in programming, coding, or working as machine operators. Again it was due to the exigencies of war that women were recruited by the military into both civilian and military positions to work as trained mathematicians to calculate firing tables by hand for rockets and artillery shells. When ENIAC (Electronic Numerical Integrator and Calculator), the first operational computer, was built in the United States in the early 1940s, these women were assigned to program it and became known as the 'ENIAC girls'. It was because programming was initially viewed as tedious clerical work of low status that it was assigned to women. As the complex skills and value of programming were increasingly recognized, it came to be considered creative, intellectual and demanding 'men's work'. Thus, depending on the circumstances, different cognitive styles may be characterized as 'masculine' or 'feminine' according to the power and status that attaches.

So technology is more than a set of artefacts. Technology is also a cultural product which is historically constituted by certain sorts of knowledge and social practices as well as other forms of representation. Conceiving of technology as a culture reveals the extent to which an affinity with technology has been and is integral to the constitution of male gender identity. Masculinity and femininity are produced in relation to each other and what is masculine, according to the ideology of sexual difference, must be the negation of the feminine. Different childhood exposure to technology, the prevalence of different role models, different forms of schooling, and the extreme segregation of the labour market all lead to what Cockburn describes as 'the construction of men as strong, manually able and technologically endowed, and women as physically and technically incompetent'.[11]

Gender is not just about difference but about power: this technical expertise is a source of men's actual or potential power over women. It is also an important part of women's experience of being less than, and dependent on, men. However, it should be remembered that the construction of masculinity is a complex process. There is not one monolithic masculinity and not all men are competent with technology. Rather, technical competence is central to the dominant cultural ideal of masculinity, and its absence a key feature of stereotyped femininity. The correspondence between men and machines is thus neither essential nor immutable, and therefore the potential exists for its transformation.

Notes and References

1   C. Hoyles (ed.), *Girls and Computers*, Bedford Way Papers 34 (Institute of Education, London, 1988), p. 9.
2   Ibid., p. 10.
3   K. Clarricoates, 'The importance of being Ernest ... Emma ... Tom ... Jane', in *Schooling for Women's Work*, ed. R. Deem (Routledge and Kegan Paul, London, 1980), p. 39.

4   G. Kolata, 'Equal time for women', *Discover,* January (1984), p. 25.
5   L. Haddon, 'The roots and early history of the British home computer market', PhD thesis (Imperial College, University of London, 1988), p. 211.
6   S. Turkle, *The Second Self* (Granada, London, 1984).
7   Ibid., p. 103.
8   L. Segal, *Is the Future Female?* (Virago, London, 1987), p. 146.
9   M. Hughes, A. Brackenridge, A. Bibby and P. Greenhaugh, 'Girls, boys and turtles', in Hoyles, *Girls and Computers.*
10 V. Walkerdine, *Counting Girls Out* (Virago, London, 1989).
11 C. Cockburn, *Brothers* (Pluto Press, London, 1983), p. 203.

20

Reproductive Technologies and the Deconstruction of Motherhood

Michelle Stanworth

Technologies designed to intervene in the process of human reproduction fall, roughly speaking, into four groups. The first and most familiar group includes those concerned with fertility control – with preventing conception, frustrating implantation of an embryo, or terminating pregnancy. ... Many of the technologies of fertility control – diaphragms, intra-uterine devices, sterilization, abortion, even the newly visible condom – have been known in some form for centuries. Hormone-suppressing contraceptive drugs are one of the few genuine innovations in contraceptive technology this century. Since by the late 1970s the market for 'the pill' in many Western countries was saturated, pharmaceutical companies now devote much of their research efforts to finding new ways of administering contraceptives that would open up expanding markets in the Third World.

A second group of reproductive technologies is concerned with the 'management' of labour and childbirth. In the course of the past 150 years in Europe and America, childbirth changed from a home-based activity, undertaken primarily with the assistance of female healers and friends, to an activity defined as the province of medical professionals. The extent of the shift is illustrated by the rising proportion of British babies born in hospital – from 15 per cent in 1927 to 99 per cent in 1985.[1] In its wake, a range of technologies for monitoring and controlling the progress of labour and delivery – instruments to assist delivery, caesarian sections, ways of inducing labour, episiotomies, techniques for measuring foetal heart-rate and movement – have been applied on an increasingly routine basis; the caesarian section rate in the United States, for example, rose from 4.5 per hundred in 1965 to 19 per 100 in 1982.[2] In many Western countries, the potential for effective intervention in the management of labour and childbirth is approaching saturation point, not only because of the high proportion of birthing women who are already subject to these techniques, but also because of objections to 'high-tech' deliveries from women themselves.

A current focus in terms of the development of reproductive technologies is upon extending obstetric services backwards into the antenatal period, through the use of more elaborate technologies and screening procedures for monitoring foetal development in the early stages of pregnancy; at least one-third of all pregnant women in the United States now experience ultrasound. The focus is also upon perfecting new techniques for neonatal care; and upon research that might eventually enable the modification of inborn 'defects' through human genetic engineering. In short, the third and one of the growth areas in reproductive technology is concerned with improving the health and the genetic characteristics of foetuses and of newborns – with the search for, as some have said, 'the perfect child'.

The fourth and perhaps most controversial group are the conceptive technologies, directed to the promotion of pregnancy through techniques for overcoming or bypassing infertility. Estimates for Britain suggest that 50,000 new cases of infertility present for treatment each year and the number of people requiring treatment at any one time may be as high as 2 million. Yet for much of this century, the treatment of infertility has been relatively static; apart from the clinical introduction of artificial insemination in the 1930s and the 'fertility drugs' of the 1960s, no new technologies were introduced until *in vitro* fertilization burst upon the scene in the late 1970s as a 'miracle cure'. Most research in the area of infertility is now devoted to the refinement of *in vitro* fertilization and to the development of new applications – through combination with, for example, egg donation, embryo donation, low–temperature storage of gametes and embryos, or surrogacy – rather than to alternative approaches to infertility. The conceptive technologies, often treated as if they were synonymous with 'high-tech' medicine, in fact are immensely varied; they range from surrogacy or artificial insemination – both of which can be and are practised in ways that require no medical intervention at all – to *in vitro* fertilization, which involves very sophisticated medical, surgical and laboratory procedures.

As the history of reproductive technologies is gradually being written, we have come to know more about the range of groups or institutions that have an interest in their development. Women themselves, as consumers of services concerned with reproductive care, have, to be sure, 'demanded' techniques that would help them to control their fertility, their pregnancies, their experience of birth and the health of their children. Yet it is clear that there is no simple cause-and-effect relationship between the 'demands' made by women and the 'supply' of reproductive technologies. For one thing, the 'demands' of those who can afford to pay are likely to be catered for far more assiduously than the 'demands' of those with smaller resources; and the greater the proportion of total health costs that is met by individuals, the more powerfully such inequalities are likely to assert themselves. For another, part of the 'demand' for reproductive technologies comes from state-subsidized programmes, and the objectives of the state in providing resources for the introduction of some technologies and withholding funding from others are not likely to reflect women's wishes in any straightforward way. The state responds to women's demands in the area of reproductive care selectively, in terms of its own priorities with respect to population policy, health expenditure and political pay-off. So, for example, in the context of rigorous insistence on reduction of public expenditure over the past decade, *in vitro* fertilization programmes have received virtually no public funding in Britain, while the Department of Health and Social Security viewed benignly – in the hopes of saving money on the care of handicapped children – the possibility of mass programmes of antenatal screening.

There are other reasons, too, why the demands of women for technologies to aid in reproductive care are insufficient to explain the technologies currently on offer. What we 'demand' (that is, what we are willing to tolerate) as consumers depends on the options available to us. Undoubtedly, the demand amongst heterosexual women who wished to avoid pregnancy for a 100 per cent reliable contraceptive technique that carried no risks to health or quality of life would be overwhelming; but in real life, women have to divide their 'demands' more or less grudgingly between a range of less-than-satisfactory options. Even our notions of what 'satisfactory' would be are shaped partly by our knowledge of existing or potential alternatives. If we come to believe that home births are dangerous (whether or not that belief is objectively 'true') we are unlikely to be able to articulate clearly our dissatisfactions with hospital confinements.

Many of the groups most directly responsible for developing and promoting reproductive technologies have an agenda in which women's 'demands' play only a small part. For obstetricians and gynaecologists, specific types of reproductive technologies may carry advantages quite separate from their impact on mothers and infants. Reproductive technologies often enhance the status of medical professionals and increase the funds they can command, by underpinning claims to specialized knowledge and by providing the basis for an extension of service. Such technologies may, in addition, help a profession in its attempts to dominate other competitors for control of an area of work; the application of new forms of technology has been one way that obstetricians have succeeded in reducing midwives to a subordinate status in the field of maternity services. Perhaps most significantly, new technologies help to establish that gynaecologists and obstetricians 'know more' about pregnancy and about women's bodies than women do themselves. When the majority of the profession is male, it is perhaps not surprising that medical practitioners have been attracted to techniques that enable them to brush aside a woman's own felt experience of menstruation, pregnancy and birth.

Medical practitioners are themselves dependent upon the research and development activities of pharmaceutical and medical supply companies, and many of these corporations have a vast financial interest in the manufacture and promotion of technologies concerned with reproductive care. The buoyant market for infertility treatment has attracted considerable private finance for research and development, but even this is probably outstripped by investment in the realm of genetic engineering. Feminists have raised troubling questions about the accountability and public scrutiny of reproductive technologies, the development of which is motored by private investment.

Precisely because of the different and sometimes conflicting interests at stake in the application of reproductive technologies, women have not been content to leave the evaluation of the impact of technology to 'the experts', who are often the very people involved in their promotion. Instead, they have highlighted the ambivalent effects of reproductive technologies on the lives of women. Women in Western Europe and North America today, compared with their foremothers, have fewer pregnancies, bear fewer babies against their wishes, are less likely to die in childbirth and less often experience the death of their babies. This is no small matter – and it is due, in some part, to technologies for intervening in human reproduction. But the view that reproductive technologies have given women control over motherhood – and thereby over their own lives – simply will not do.

First, this view takes insufficient account of the impact of changing social definitions of motherhood. While women today spend less time in pregnancy and breast-feeding than in the recent past, the care of children has come to be defined in a far more rigorous way; mothering involves responsibility not only for the physical and emotional care of children, but for detailed attention to their psychological, social and intellectual development. Motherhood is seen, more than in the past, as a full-time occupation. Mothers may be expected now to lavish as much 'care' on two children as they might previously have provided for six. In short, the reproductive technologies address themselves to only a small part of the experience of motherhood.

Second, reproductive decisions continue to be constrained by the shortcomings of existing means of fertility control. For example, the pill and the intra-uterine contraceptive device – heralded in the 1960s as instruments of women's liberation – appear now to carry worrying health risks and a range of distressing side-effects. Some contraceptive techniques, including some of the most reliable for preventing pregnancy, appear also to increase the risk of infertility, creating a catch-22 situation for women who wish to control the timing of childbearing. The failure to develop safer and more acceptable means of birth control is not simply a technical problem; in part, it reflects the low priority given to women's health and a tendency to disregard symptoms and issues that women themselves think are important.

Third, the way that access to means of fertility control is managed indicates how women's options regarding childbearing are linked to their location in the social structure. In Britain, the recent Gillick case represented an attempt to restrict through the courts the access of younger women to contraceptive information and supplies. Controversial contraceptives such as the injectable long-acting Depo-Provera, though considered unsuitable for the majority of women in Britain, have been used extensively on their Asian and black compatriots.[3] Although the 1967 Abortion Act entitles British women to legal abortion on medical and social grounds, access to safe abortion in many parts of the country – as in the United States – depends on ability to pay; the bulk of legal abortions in Britain today are performed outside the National Health Service.[4] Infertility, and especially the infections that lead to tubal closure, are particular problems for black women and women on low incomes in Britain and the United States, but these are precisely the women who have least access to new conceptive technologies like *in vitro* fertilization.

Fourth, the technical possibility of fertility control coexists with a powerful ideology of motherhood – the belief that motherhood is the natural, desired and ultimate goal of all 'normal' women, and that women who deny their 'maternal instincts' are selfish, peculiar or disturbed. At a conference in Oxford in 1987, Patrick Steptoe, the obstetrician who is credited with 'creating' the first test-tube baby, declared: 'It is a fact that there is a biological drive to reproduce. Women who deny this drive, or in whom it is frustrated, show disturbances in other ways.'[5] Many members of the medical profession share this view.

While many women wish to have children, the views of medical personnel are not simply a reflection of that fact. The idea of maternal instinct is sometimes used to override women's expressed wishes with regard to childbearing – discouraging young married women from sterilization or abortion, for example, while denying single women the chance to have a child. In other words, a belief in maternal instinct coexists with obstacles to autonomous motherhood – obstacles, that is, to motherhood for women who are not in a stable relationship with a man. According to ideologies of motherhood, all women *want* children; but single women, lesbian women (and disabled women) are often expected to forgo mothering 'in the interest of the child'.

Finally, technologies for 'managing' pregnancy and childbirth are often embedded in a medical frame of reference that defines pregnant women as 'patients', pregnancy as an illness and successful childbearing in terms that de-emphasize the social and emotional dimensions. In some respects, reproductive technologies have made childbearing safer for women and their infants, but they have also brought new dangers in their wake. Apart from medical risks and benefits, as the process of pregnancy and childbirth has come under the control of medical professionals, the majority of whom are men, many women are left with a sense of being mere onlookers in the important process of giving birth.

Thus, medical and scientific advances in the sphere of reproduction – so often hailed as the liberators of twentieth-century women – have, in fact, been a double-edged sword. On the one hand, they have offered women a greater technical possibility to decide if, when and under what conditions to have children; on the other, the domination of so much reproductive technology by the medical profession and by the state has enabled others to have an even greater capacity to exert control over women's lives. Moreover, the 'technical possibility' of choosing an oral contraceptive or *in vitro* fertilization is only a small aspect of reproductive freedom. For some women, motherhood remains their only chance of creativity, while economic and social circumstances compel others to relinquish motherhood altogether.

Against the stark backcloth of the history of technologies for controlling fertility, pregnancy and birth, how are we to analyse the emergent technologies concerned with promoting conception and with eliminating 'defects' in the unborn? One powerful theoretical approach sees in these new techniques a means for men to wrest 'not only control of reproduction, but reproduction itself' from women.[6] Following O'Brien,[7] it is suggested that men's alienation from reproduction – men's sense of disconnection from their seed during the process of conception, pregnancy and birth – has underpinned through the ages a relentless male desire to master nature, and to construct social institutions and cultural patterns that will not only subdue the waywardness of women but also give men an illusion of procreative continuity and power. New reproductive technologies are the vehicle that will turn men's illusions of reproductive power into a reality. By manipulating eggs and embryos, scientists will determine the sort of children who are born – will make themselves the fathers of humankind. By removing eggs and embryos from some women and implanting them in others, medical practitioners will gain unprecedented control over motherhood itself. Motherhood as a unified biological process will be effectively deconstructed: in place of 'mother', there will be ovarian mothers who supply eggs, uterine mothers who give birth to children and, presumably, social mothers who raise them. Through the eventual development of artificial wombs, the capacity will arise to make biological motherhood redundant. Whether or not women are eliminated, or merely reduced to the level of 'reproductive prostitutes', the object and the effect of the emergent technologies is to deconstruct motherhood and to destroy the claim to reproduction that is the foundation of women's identity.

The problem with this analysis is not that it is too radical, as some have claimed; rather, in seeking to protect women from the dangers of new technologies, it gives too much away. There is a tendency to echo the very views of scientific and medical practice, of women and of motherhood, which feminists have been seeking to transform. This analysis entails, in the first instance, an inflated view of science and medicine, the mirror image of that which scientists and medical practitioners often try themselves to promote. By emphasizing the continuities between technologies currently in clinical use, and those that exist merely in the fantasies of scientific commentators; by insisting that the practices involved in animal husbandry or in animal experimentation can unproblematically be transferred to human beings; by ignoring the ways in which women have resisted abuses of medical power and techniques they found unacceptable: by arguing this way, science and medicine have been portrayed as realms of boundless possibility, in the face of which mere human beings have no choices other than total rejection or capitulation. Any understanding of the constraints within which science and medicine operate, and of the way these can be shaped for the greater protection of women and men, is effectively erased.

Also integral to this approach is a view of women that comes uncomfortably close to that espoused by some members of the medical professions. Infertile women are too easily 'blinded by science';[8] they are manipulated into 'full and total support of any technique which will produce those desired children';[9] the choices they make and even their motivations to choose are controlled by men. In the case of doctors, it is the 'maternal instinct' that allows women's own assessments of what they want from their bodies or their pregnancies to be overlooked; in this analysis, it is patriarchal and pronatal conditioning that makes infertile women (and, by implication, all women) incapable of rationally grounded and authentic choice. The ideology of motherhood attempts to press women in the direction of childbearing, and in this sense women's motivations are socially shaped. But 'shaped' is not the same as 'determined'; and a rejection of childbearing (for infertile women or fertile) is not necessarily a more authentic choice. The very existence of a range of sanctions and rewards designed to entice women into marriage and motherhood indicates, not that conformity is guaranteed, but that avoidance of motherhood (and autonomous motherhood) are genuine options, which efforts are made to contain.

Finally, this approach tends to suggest that anything 'less' than a natural process, from conception through to birth, represents the degradation of motherhood itself. The motherhood that men are attempting to usurp becomes a motherhood that is biologically defined, and to which all women are assumed to have the same relationship. While it is the case that the lives of all women are shaped by their biological selves, and by their assumed or actual capacity to bear children, our bodies do not impose upon us a common experience of reproduction; on the contrary, our bodies stand as powerful reminders of the differentiating effects of age, health, disability, strength and fertility history. There is, moreover, little reason to assume that the biological potential to give birth has an identical meaning for women, regardless of their social circumstances or their wishes with regard to childbearing. How can the experience of women who have chosen to remain childfree be fitted into a framework that sees the continuous biological process that culminates in birth as the core of our identity as women? How can we make sense from this perspective of women (such as those interviewed by Luker[10]) who value children and childbearing highly, but who experience pregnancy itself as merely an unpleasant reality *en route* to raising children? How can we explain the fact that fewer working-class women in Britain attend antenatal clinics, demand natural childbirth or breast-feed their infants? Luker's analysis suggests the possibility that while for many middle-class women pregnancy may be a scarce resource – time out from a hectic professional life to enjoy the sensations of being a woman – for a greater proportion of working-class women pregnancy may be more a taken-for-granted prelude to social motherhood, not an experience to be cherished in itself. Far too many women have experienced the type of reproductive care that is insensitive to their own wishes and desires; but shared reaction against unsatisfactory medical treatment should not be allowed to mask differences in women's own sense of what authentic motherhood might be.

Notes and References

1 Office of Population Censuses and Statistics, *Birth Statistics* (HMSO, London, 1986).
2 R. Pfeufer Kahn, 'The reform of childbirth', *The Women's Review of Books*, *II* (3 December 1984), p. 15.
3 J. Rakusen, 'Depo-Provera', in *Women, Health and Reproduction*, ed. H. Roberts (Routledge and Kegan Paul, London, 1981); P. Bunkle, 'Calling the shots', in *Test-Tube Women*, ed. R. Arditti, R. Duelli Klein and S. Minden (Pandora, London, 1984).
4 WRRIC, *Women's Reproductive Rights Information Centre Newsletter*, June–July (London, 1986).
5 'Women, reproduction and technology', Conference of the History Workshop Centre, Oxford, 14–15 February 1987.
6 J. Raymond, 'Preface', in *Man-Made Women*, ed. G. Corea, R. Duelli Klein, J. Hanmer, H. Holmes, B. Hoskins, M. Kishwar, J. Raymond, R. Rowland and R. Steinbacher (Hutchinson, London, 1985), p. 12.
7 M. O'Brien, *The Politics of Reproduction* (Routledge and Kegan Paul, London, 1983).
8 J. Hanmer, 'Transforming consciousness', in Corea et al., *Man-Made Women*, p. 104.
9 R. Rowland, 'Motherhood, patriarchal power, alienation and the issue of 'choice' in sex preselection', in Corea et al., *Man-Made Women*, p. 75.
10 K. Lunker, *Abortion and the Politics of Motherhood* (University of California Press, Berkeley, Calif., 1984), pp. 168–9.

21

The Body and Sexuality

Jeffrey Weeks

Sexuality is shaped at the juncture of two major concerns: with our subjectivity (who and what we are); and with society (with the health, prosperity, growth and well-being of the population as a whole). The two are intimately connected because at the heart of both is the body and its potentialities. As society has become more and more concerned with the lives of its members – for the sake of moral uniformity, economic prosperity, national security, or hygiene and health – so it has become increasingly preoccupied with disciplining bodies and with the sex lives of its individuals. This has given rise to intricate methods of administration and management, to a flowering of moral anxieties, medical, hygienic, legal and welfarist interventions, or scientific delving, all designed to understand the self by understanding, and regulating, sexual behaviour.

The Victorian period is a key one in understanding the process in all its complexity. Traditionally, historians have commented on the repressiveness of the period, and in many ways this is an accurate picture. There was indeed a great deal of moral hypocrisy, as individuals (especially men) and society avowed respectability but did something else. Women's sexuality was severely regulated to ensure 'purity' at the same time as prostitution was rife.

[...]

But this repression, and the implied anxiety and delicacy about the body should not lead us to believe that the Victorians were averse to discussing sex. On the contrary, it is possible to argue that they, like their successors, were very nearly obsessed with it.

If we look at the key moments in British history since the beginning of the nineteenth century we see that, in one way or another, a preoccupation with sexual behaviour has been central to them. During the crisis of the French Revolutionary Wars early in the century, we see a concern with moral decline which, it was believed, was integral to the collapse of the *ancien regime*. Middle-class ideologies sought a new bourgeois morality to challenge the immorality of the aristocracy and the amorality of the labouring masses. In the 1830s and 1840s, with the first crisis of the new industrial order, there was a near obsessive interest in the sexuality of working women, and of children working in the mines and factories. The great series of Royal Commissions of the period reported in detail on the sexual licence of the new manufacturing centres.

By the mid-nineteenth century, fuelled by the spread of epidemics such as cholera and typhoid in the overcrowded towns and cities, attempts to reform society concentrated on questions of health and personal morality. From the 1860s to the 1890s, prostitution, venereal disease, public immorality and private vice were at the heart of debate, many choosing to see in moral decay a symbol of imperial decay.

Such preoccupations were not unique to the nineteenth century. If anything, sexuality became more and more a public obsession, particularly in relation to the integrity of the British population. In the years before the First World War, there was a vogue for eugenics, the planned breeding of the best. Though never dominant, it had a significant influence in shaping welfare policies and the attempt to reorder national priorities in the face of international competition. It also fed into a burgeoning racism in the inter-war years as politicians feared a declining population which would give dominance to 'inferior races'. In the 1940s, the key period for the establishment of the Welfare State, there was an urgent concern with the merits of birth control ('family planning') in ensuring that the right sort of people built families, and with the appropriate roles of men and women (especially women) in the family in the brave new world of social democracy.

Linked with this, by the 1950s, in the depth of the Cold War, there was a new searching out of sexual degenerates, especially homosexuals, who not only lived outside families but were also, apparently, peculiarly susceptible to treason. By the 1960s, a new liberalism ('permissiveness') seemed torn between relaxing the old authoritarian social codes and finding new modes of social regulation, based on the latest in social psychology, and a redefinition of the public/private divide. During the 1970s and 1980s there was, in effect, the beginning of a backlash against what were seen as the excesses of the earlier decade, and perhaps for the first time sexuality became a real front-line political issue as the emergence of the New Right identified the 'decline of the family', feminism and the new homosexual militancy as potent symbols of national decline.

What is at stake in these recurrent debates about morality and sexual behaviour? Clearly a number of different but related concerns are present: the relations between men and women, the problem of sexual deviance, the question of family and other relationships, the relations between adults and children, and the issue of difference, whether of class, gender or race. Each of these has a long history, but in the past couple of hundred years they have become central concerns, often centring around sexual issues. They illustrate the power of the belief that debates about sexuality are debates about the nature of society: as sex goes, so goes society.

It is important to recognize that sexuality is not a unified domain. Next we shall look at some of the forces that shape sexual beliefs and behaviour, complicating sexual identities.

The assumption here is that power does not operate through single mechanisms of control. In fact, it operates through complex and over-lapping – and often contradictory – mechanisms which produce domi-nation and oppositions, subordination and resistances. There are many structures of domination and subordination in the world of sexuality, but we shall discuss only two here: class and gender.

Class differences in sexual regulation are not unique to the modern world, but they have become more sharply apparent over the past 200 years. Foucault has argued that the very idea of 'sexuality' as a unified domain is essentially a bourgeois one, developed as part of the self-assertion of a class anxious to differentiate itself from the immorality of the aristocracy and the supposedly rampant promiscuity of the lower classes. It was basically a colonizing endeavour, seeking to remould both the polity and sexual behaviour in its own image. The respectable standards of family life developed in the nineteenth century ('Victorian values'), with the increased demarcation between male and female roles, a new emphasis on the need to bring public behaviour up to the best standards of private life, and a sharpened interest in the public policing of non-marital, non-heterosexual sexuality, became increasingly the norm by which all behaviour was judged.

This does not mean, of course, that all or even most behaviour con-formed to the norm. Historians have provided plentiful evidence that the working class remained extremely resistant to middle-class manners. Patterns of behaviour inherited from their rural predecessors continued to structure the sexual culture of working-class people well into the twentieth century. The fact that such patterns were different from those of the bourgeoisie does not mean that they were in themselves worse. Nevertheless, it is true that the patterns of sexual life of the present century are the results of a social struggle in which class and sexuality were inextricably linked. This is even reflected at the level of fantasy, particularly in the belief, evident in both heterosexual and homosexual upper-class male culture, that the working-class woman or man was somehow more spontaneous, closer to nature, than other people.

The result has been the existence of quite distinct class patterns of sexuality at various times. For example, attitudes to birth control varied considerably, with the professional classes leading the way in the adoption of artificial contraception from the 1860s, and working-class families on the whole having larger families until after the Second World War.[1] But it is also unwise to generalize about class patterns. Textile workers from early in the nineteenth century tended to have smaller families. In the inter-war years there were marked differences between the contraceptive activities of female factory workers, who had access to cultures of knowledge about birth control, and domestic workers, who often did not. As in the Third World today, to have large families was often economically rational in many social situations, and inappropriate in others. Geographical, religious, employment and other factors inevitably came into play.

The same is true in relation to many other aspects of sexual behaviour, for example in attitudes to masturbation, acceptance of casual prostitution, attitudes to homosexuality, and the like. Class, in other words, was a key factor, but not always a decisive one in shaping choices about sexual activity.

This leads us to the question of gender itself. Classes consist of men and women, and class and status differences may not have the same significance for women as for men. Gender is a crucial divide.

Gender is not a simple analytical category; it is, as feminist scholarship has increasingly documented, a relationship of power. So, patterns of female sexuality are inescapably a product of the historically rooted power of men to define what is necessary and desirable.

The nineteenth century was a key point in the definition of female sexuality in terms which have greatly influenced our own concepts, and not least our assumptions about the importance of bodily differences. Let us now look at a wider historical framework. Thomas Laqueur has argued that the political, economic, and cultural transformations of the eighteenth century created the context in which the articulation of radical differences between the sexes became culturally imperative.[2]

In a long and subtle examination of the evolution of concepts of the body and gender from the Greeks to the twentieth century, Laqueur suggests that there have been fundamental shifts in the ways we see the relationship between male and female bodies. He argues that, until the eighteenth century, the dominant discourse 'construed the male and female bodies as hierarchically, vertically, ordered versions of one sex'.[3] The hierarchical but single-sex model certainly interpreted the female body as an inferior and inverted version of the male, but stressed nevertheless the important role of female sexual pleasure, especially in the process of reproduction. Female orgasm and pleasure were seen as necessary to successful impregnation. The breakdown of this model, in political as well as medical debates, led to its replacement in the nineteenth century by a reproductive model which emphasized the existence of two, sharply different bodies, the radical opposition of male and female sexualities, the woman's automatic reproductive cycle, and her lack of sexual feeling. This was a critical moment in the reshaping of gender relations, because it suggested the absolute difference of men and women: no longer a single, partially differentiated body, but two singular bodies, the male and the female.

Laqueur argues that the shift he traces did not arise straightforwardly from scientific advance, nor was it the simple product of a singular effort at social control of women by men. The emergent discourse about sexual difference allowed a range of different, and often contradictory, social and political responses to emerge. But at the heart of the emerging definitions were new cultural and political relations, the product of shifts in the balance of power between men and women. The new perception of female sexuality and reproductive biology has been absolutely central to modern social and political discourse because it stressed difference and division rather than similarity and complementarity.

[...]

At the same time, it is important to remember that women have been active participants in shaping their own definition of need. Not only feminism, but the practices of everyday life have offered spaces for women to plot out their own lives. Since the nineteenth century, the acceptable spaces have expanded to include, not only pleasure in marriage, but also relatively respectable forms of non-procreative behaviour. The patterns of male sexual privilege have not been broken, but there is now plentiful evidence that such privilege is neither inevitable nor immutable.

Notes and References

1   A. McLaren, *Birth Control in Nineteenth Century England* (Croom Helm, London, 1978); J. Weeks, *Sex Politics and Society*, 2nd edn (Longman, Harlow, 1989).

2   T. Laqueur, *Making Sex* (Harvard University Press, London, 1990).

3   Ibid., p. 10.

22

Men, Women and Romantic Love

Anthony Giddens

In the late 1980s, Sharon Thompson carried out an investigation of the attitudes, values and sexual behaviour of 150 American teenagers from different class and ethnic backgrounds.[1] She found major differences between the ways in which the boys discussed sex (they did not often speak of love) in the course of her lengthy interviews with them and the responses of the girls. The boys appeared unable to talk about sex in a narrative form, as a connection to an envisaged future. They spoke mainly about sporadic sexual episodes, such as early heterosexual play or diverse sexual conquests. When she questioned the girls, on the other hand, Thompson found that almost every individual she talked to, with little prompting, could produce lengthy stories 'imbued with the discoveries, anguish, and elation of intimate relations'.[2] The girls, she says, had something approaching the skills of professional novelists in their ability to recount a detailed and complex tale; many talked for several hours with little contribution needed from the interviewer.

The fluent nature of these narratives of self, Thompson argues, derived in large part from the fact that they had been rehearsed. They were the result of the many hours of conversations teenage girls have with one another, during the course of which feelings and hopes are discussed and shaped. Thompson accepts that, as an individual from an older generation, the narratives recounted may have been partly edited for her benefit. But she was also drawn in as a sounding-board for reflexive interpretation on the part of the interviewees. She felt she 'had been entrusted with something as valuable, as telling and prophetic as a first love when the lover reads it, like an omen, for the future'. For, as a further reflexive resonance, she herself admits to an 'addiction to romance'.[3]

The main thematic device of the girls' stories was what Thompson labels the 'quest-romance'. Romance gears sexuality into an anticipated future in which sexual encounters are seen as detours on the way to an eventual love relationship. Sex is, as it were, a sparking device, with romance as the quest for destiny. The search for romantic love here, however, no longer means deferring sexual activity until the desired relationship comes along. Having sex with a new partner may be the start of the fateful encounter which is sought after, but more than likely it is not.

The following is a description given by an interviewee of a romance:

> We discovered that we lived sort of in the same neighbourhood, and we started taking the bus home together. Then we discovered we didn't want to take the bus home together. We wanted to walk because it meant more time talking. Both of us had our own ideas about the world.... We'd start talking about school, and we'd end up talking about the situation in China . . . and within three months, I was so in love . . . it was amazing.[4]

Amazing, yes – or it would have been to a researcher on teenage sexuality twenty-five years earlier – because the romance in question was a lesbian one. One of the findings that comes through strongly in Thompson's work is that sexual diversity exists alongside the persistence of notions of romance, although sometimes in an uneasy and conflictual relation. The lesbian girls among Thompson's interviewees appeared to find romance as compelling as did the heterosexuals.

'Loss of virginity' for a boy, as from time immemorial, continues today to be a misnomer: for boys, first sexual experience is a plus, a gain. It is a talisman which points to the future; not, however, in respect of core aspects of the self, but as one among other emblems of male capability. For girls, virginity is still something seen as given up. The question is not, for most, whether or not to do so as part of early sexual experience, but how to choose the right time and circumstance. The event connects directly to romantic narratives. Boys expect to force the issue of sexual initiation, girls to 'slow things down'. The query girls pose to themselves, as well as implicitly to their first partner, whoever he (or she) may be, is: will my sexuality allow me to determine the path of my future life? Will it give me sexual power? First sexual experience is for many a test of whether or not a future romantic scenario can be achieved.

As the term suggests, the quest-romance is not for these girls a passive set of aspirations – 'some day my prince will come'. Painful and anxiety-ridden in many respects, it is nevertheless an active process of engagement with future time. Thompson found that the girls she spoke to did not have to fight to achieve sexual freedom: such freedom exists, and the problem is to make something of it in the face of male attitudes which still carry more than an echo of the past. The girls therefore emerge as the main social experimenters here. Thompson expresses this very well:

> To an extent, teenage girls are struggling with the problem nineteenth-century feminists predicted when they argued against breaking the connection between sex and reproduction on the grounds that it constituted the only way women had to persuade men to commit themselves to a relationship. But it is, finally, not a problem of enforcement, but of vision. It demands facing the deconstruction of sex, romance and intimacy and renegotiating the bargain between the genders.[5]

Under the strain of these tasks, some girls try to retreat to pre-existing ideas and modes of behaviour – acceptance of the double standard, 'flypaper dreams of motherhood', hopes for eternal love. Most find themselves breaking away from earlier-established norms and taboos, adapting them in ways in which a great deal of emotional energy is invested, but which are quite provisional and open to restructuring in the light of possible future events.

By their late teens, many of the girls have already had experience of unhappy love affairs, and are well aware that romance can no longer be equated with permanence. In a highly reflexive society they come into contact with, and in their television watching and reading actively search out, numerous discussions about sex, relationships and influences affecting the position of women. The fragmentary elements of the romantic love complex with which these girls are grappling in seeking to take practical control of their lives are no longer linked wholly to marriage. Virtually all recognize that they will be in paid work for much of their lives, and most see the importance of work skills as a basis for their future autonomy. Only a few of the girls among Thompson's interviewees, however – mostly those from middle-class backgrounds – regard work as a major source of meaning for their future. Thus one girl said, 'My idea of what I want to do right now is to get a career that I love . . . if I marry somebody or even live with somebody and they leave me, I won't have anything to worry about because I'll be totally independent.' Yet, as Thompson found with others, she quickly reverted to matters of romance and sexuality: 'I want the ideal relationship with a guy. I guess I want someone to love me and care about me as much as I do them.'[6]

It is only over the past generation that striking out on one's own, for women, has meant leaving the parental home. In previous periods, for all but a small proportion of women, leaving home meant getting married. Compared with most men, the majority of women continue to identify entering the outside world with forming attachments. As many commentators have noted, even when an individual is still single and only anticipating future relationships, men normally speak in terms of 'I', whereas female narratives of self tend to be couched in terms of 'we'. The 'individualized speech' apparent in the above quotation is qualified by a surreptitious 'we' – someone who will 'love and care' and make a 'we' from the 'me'.

In contrast to those in younger age groups today, the experience of older women was almost always framed in terms of marriage, even if the person in question did not marry. Emily Hancock investigated the life histories of twenty American women, from various class origins, aged between 30 and 75 in the late 1980s. Some were still in their first marriages, others had remarried, were divorced or widowed. Marriage was to them the core experience of a woman's life – although many have had retrospectively to reconstruct their past because when they first got married, marriage was very different from what it is now.

Let us follow for a little while the history of Wendy, who was 39 when Hancock interviewed her. Wendy's life story demonstrates an increasing reflexive awareness of self, brought about partly by outside social changes and partly by personal crises and transitions that she has had to surmount. Wendy is the oldest of four children from an affluent New England family in which the parents followed fairly strict codes of 'proper behaviour'. She broke away from her parents' control by means of marriage, and did so actively and consciously, through an elopement (a term which, during a period of a few decades, has become archaic). Wendy saw marriage as equivalent to entry into adulthood. She thought of it as 'a re-creation of a cocoon at the same time that you're also a fully grown butterfly'.

Her attachment to her prospective husband facilitated her independence, at least as she saw things then: 'This relationship with a new person was the first really independent action I took. So many other things followed from that one.' Yet her act of autonomy was also one presuming material dependence. 'I suppose it would have been more radical not to have married at all. That would have been the most radical thing, but that was never an option for me. I never thought of myself as a person who would not be married. It was a given.' She didn't want only to be a housewife, and was determined not to have as parochial a life as her mother, whose prime concern had always been the home. Wendy became a schoolteacher and found the career satisfying. She did not give up the job when she became pregnant, but moved to half-time teaching.

Then her husband was killed in a freak accident. She underwent a severe crisis, and lost her grip on her sense of her adult self. It was not just the bereavement, but the loss of the attachment upon which she had based her feelings of security and accomplishment which was traumatic. She felt 'thrust back into adolescence', even though she had a child to look after. Her parents expected her to go back and live with them; she successfully resisted after having come to realize how much she had depended upon the marriage for a sense of integrity. Her second marriage, like her first, was entered into for love, and was 'part of putting myself back together'. But by this point she 'had more perspective' than when she married for the first time: 'It is doing these things with a self-consciousness that comes after scrambling that helps you realise potential. You shape it in a clearer way, like a sculpture.' Wendy had further children by her second marriage; she was content with her life, still found satisfaction in her paid work, but was not ambitious for further career achievement.

Compare Wendy's experience with that of Helen, aged 49 when contacted by the researcher. When she was growing up Helen had, in her own words, 'lacked self-confidence to a pathological degree'. At college, she met and married a professor who was rapidly making a reputation for himself in his chosen field. Having abandoned her education in order to get married, her sense of self-worth became largely dependent upon her involvement with the aspirations and achievements of her husband. She occupied part of his life, as she later put it, as 'a tenant' or 'a janitor'. She and her husband were living in university housing when he announced he wanted a divorce; since he was the one with the faculty position, she had to leave, taking their child to live with her. Unlike Wendy, her parents did not invite her to come back home or offer much moral or material support.

Overwhelmed at first by desperation and beset by loneliness. Helen eventually managed to go back to college part-time and finish her degree. None the less, she found herself for some while stuck in low-grade 'women's jobs' until she managed to get a post in publishing, and had at the time of the research become a successful editor. She is described by Hancock as a person with a sharp, sarcastic manner, given a sardonic wit. Yet her surface competence disguised attitudes of despair and self-hate with which the ending of her marriage had left her and from which she had never recovered. She felt caught up in a life that was 'empty and arid'. Rather than seeking to shape her future, she was continuing 'to drift toward infinity'. She concluded: 'You ask me what my adult life has been? A vacuum, that's what it's been. By the age of thirty-five, I was a corpse. And now I am almost fifty and I can't even account for the intervening fifteen years. I've brought up my child, but my sense of time has disappeared.'[7]

A reasonably contented and fulfilled woman, a lonely, embittered one: banal enough stories, each of them, although in both cases infused with considerable pain. What do they tell us about love, since love is not a dominating theme in the narratives of either individual? It would be easy to say, and impossible to dispute, that marriage was a trap for both women, even if a trap into which each deliberately plunged. Wendy was able to recover from the loss of her husband, whereas Helen could not do so, and became bowed down by the oppressive force of circumstances which women alone so often face. Each married for love – Wendy twice – but each, without fully realizing it, married as an assertion of independence and as a means of forging a definite self-identity. Who knows whether Wendy would still be able to take effective charge of her life if her second husband left her?

Like most of the women interviewed by Hancock, both sought to get away from the lives their mothers lived, which they identified with constrained domesticity. The process was tensionful, because each sought to distance herself from her mother without rejecting femininity. We do not see here the perpetuating of attitudes linking love and marriage as a 'final state'; but nor is there an attempt simply to enter a male world through the adoption of instrumental values. These women, as with the others portrayed in Hancock's book, are in a real sense pioneers moving through unmapped territory, who chart out shifts in self-identity as they confront and are confronted by changes in the nature of marriage, the family and work.

The paradox is that marriage is used as a means of achieving a measure of autonomy. Romantic love is a gamble against the future, an orientation to the control of future time on the part of women who became specialists in matters of (what now has come to be understood as) intimacy. There was an almost inevitable connection between love and marriage, for many women, in the earlier periods of modern development. But even then, quite apart from the interventions of foresightful feminist authors, women were *de facto* exploring other paths. The severance between marriage and its traditional roots in 'external' factors imposed itself much more forcefully upon women than men, who could find in marriage and the family primarily a refuge from economic individualism. For men, colonizing the future in terms of an anticipated economic career tended to push out of the reckoning the parallel, but substantively very different, form of colonizing time offered by romantic love. For them, on the surface at least, love remained closer to *amour passion*.

Marriage for Wendy and Helen, when they first entered it, was already contradictory, but also on the point of becoming infused with a higher level of reflexivity. It had not yet been prised free of its 'external' anchors, and provided a distinct status for women as wives and mothers. Yet, even in the early part of their lives, it was already not just for them a question of 'finding a man', but linked to tasks and concerns quite different from those of their mothers' generation. Women like Wendy and Helen helped prepare the way for a restructuring of intimate life. If the teenage girls do not speak much about marriage, it is not because they have successfully made a transition to a non-domestic future, but because they are participants in, and contributors to, a major reorganization in what marriage, and other forms of close personal tie, actually are. They talk of relationships rather than marriage as such, and they are right to do so.

The term 'relationship', meaning a close and continuing emotional tie to another, has only come into general usage relatively recently. To be clear what is at stake here, we can introduce the term *pure relationship* to refer to this phenomenon.[8] A pure relationship has nothing to do with sexual purity, and is a limiting concept rather than only a descriptive one. It refers to a situation where a social relation is entered into for its own sake, for what can be derived by each person from a sustained association with another; and which is continued only in so far as it is thought by both parties to deliver enough satisfactions for each individual to stay within it. Love used to be tied to sexuality, for most of the sexually 'normal' population, through marriage; but now the two are connected more and more via the pure relationship. Marriage – for many, but by no means all groups in the population – has veered increasingly towards the form of a pure relationship, with many ensuing consequences. The pure relationship, to repeat, is part of a generic restructuring of intimacy. It emerges in other contexts of sexuality besides heterosexual marriage; it is in some causally related ways parallel to the development of plastic sexuality. The romantic love complex helped carve open a way to the formation of pure relationships in the domain of sexuality, but has now become weakened by some of the very influences it helped create.

All this so far has been mostly about women. If the romantic love complex has been developed, and also later in some part dissolved, primarily by women, what has happened to men? Have men remained untouched by the changes which women have helped bring about, save in their role as reactionary defenders of entrenched privilege? That men are participants in the social changes influencing the rise of the pure relationship goes almost without saying. But I feel justified in offering an interpretation of the transmutation of romantic love which largely excludes men. Men are the laggards in the transitions now occurring – and in a certain sense have been so ever since the late eighteenth century. In Western culture at least, today is the first period in which men are finding themselves *to be* men, that is, as possessing a problematic 'masculinity'. In previous times, men have assumed that their activities constituted 'history', whereas women existed almost out of time, doing the same as they had always done.

Men, like women, fall in love and have done so throughout the recorded past. They have also over the last two centuries been influenced by the development of ideals of romantic love, but in a different way from women. Those men who have come too much under the sway of such notions of love have been set apart from the majority as 'romantics', in a particular sense of that term. They are, as it were, foppish dreamers, who have succumbed to female power. Such men have given up the division between unsullied and impure women so central to male sexuality. The romantic does not, nevertheless, treat women as equals. He is in thrall to a particular woman (or to several women in sequence) and he would build his life around her; but his succumbing is not a gesture of equality. He is not really a participant in the emerging exploration of intimacy, but more of a throwback to previous times. The romantic in this instance is not someone who has intuitively understood the nature of love as a mode of organizing personal life in relation to the colonizing of future time and to the construction of self-identity.

For most men, romantic love stands in tension with the imperatives of seduction. This observation means more than just that the rhetoric of romantic love is stock in trade for most Lotharios. Since the beginnings of the transformations affecting marriage and personal life, men by and large have excluded themselves from the developing domain of the intimate. The connections between romantic love and intimacy were suppressed, and falling in love remained closely bound up with access: access to women whose virtue or reputation was protected until, at least, a union was sanctified by marriage. Men have tended to be 'specialists in love' only in respect of the techniques of seduction or conquest.

There has always been a gulf between the sexes in terms of experience, upbringing and education. 'Those impossible women! How they do get around us! The poet was right: can't live with them or without them' (Aristophanes). In the nineteenth century, however, for reasons already discussed, women became opaque to men in a new way. They were rendered mysterious, as Foucault maintains, by the very discourses that sought to know them, which made female sexuality a 'problem' and treated their diseases as forms of social disqualification coming from murky depths. But they also became puzzling by virtue of the very changes they were helping to introduce.

What do men want? In one sense the answer has been clear and understood by both sexes from the nineteenth century onwards. Men want status among other men, conferred by material rewards and conjoined to rituals of male solidarity. But the male sex here misread a key trend in the trajectory of development of modernity. For men self-identity was sought after in work, and they failed – we always have to add, by and large – to understand that the reflexive project of self involves an emotional reconstruction of the past in order to project a coherent narrative towards the future. Their unconscious emotional reliance upon women was the mystery whose answer they sought in women themselves; and the quest for self-identity became concealed within this unacknowledged dependence.

Notes and References

1   S. Thompson, 'Search for tomorrow: or feminism and the reconstruction of teen romance', in *Pleasure and Danger. Exploring Female Sexuality*, ed. C. Vance (Pandora, London, 1989).
2   Ibid., p. 351.
3   Ibid., p. 351.
4   Quoted in ibid., p. 361.
5   Ibid., p. 360.
6   Ibid., p. 356.
7   Quoted in E. Hancock, *The Girl Within* (Pandora, London, 1990).
8   A. Giddens, *Modernity and Self-identity* (Polity, Cambridge, 1991).

23

Deconstructing the Monolithic Phallus

Lesley Hall

In the past two decades there has been an upsurge in historical writing about sex in history. Much of this has sprung from the interests of feminist and gay historians, although work by historians of demography and the family has also shed light on sexual conduct. Most of this work has looked at women or at 'deviant minorities' or at the rise of the birth control movement. Foucault, in *The History of Sexuality*, volume I: *An Introduction*, claimed that the rise of sexology in the later nineteenth century explicitly defined and categorized (for purposes of control) the hysterical woman, the onanistic child, the deviant and the Malthusian couple as the objects of this new, medicalized (as opposed to religious) discourse around sexual behaviour.

It is certainly to these groups that most historiographical attention has been paid. Unexamined by this trend, and often assumed to be monolithic, unchanging, unproblematic, stands the 'normal' male. The implication tends to be that sexual discourses operated exclusively for his benefit and that there was no ambiguity or ambivalence in his position, no possible constraint upon him. He and his sexuality have not been accorded the attention given to attitudes to female sexuality and the construction of deviant identities, or to examining changing reproductive behaviour within families.

[. . .]

The essentialist argument thinks of sex itself as a 'natural urge' or an instinct, and with regard to the two sexes promulgates a view of the natures of male and female as essentially different and unchanging throughout history and in all different societies. Under this schema (to be simplistic) males are forceful, aggressive, promiscuous, 'instrumental', while females are nurturing, maternal, monogamous, 'expressive'. At its most reductive, men have innate sexual desires and women have the innate capacity to arouse them. Any attempt to change this order of things given by either God or Nature is doomed to failure. Nature tends, in arguments of this kind, to mean either 'the way things are' or 'the way I think they ought to be'.

This notion of a constant natural and transcendent difference between the sexes is often merely an un-thought-out popular assumption, although it still has its academic defenders. There have been great variations throughout history and in different societies of what masculinity and femininity are expected to be and how they have been experienced. Even motherhood, often assumed to be the ultimate 'natural', has varied according to historical circumstance, as Fildes has shown in her study of infant feeding, and Hardyment in her account of changing ideas on childrearing.[1] The biological capacity of the human organism exists within symbolic environments which both act upon and can be manipulated by the individual, leading to a vast potential for variations. The experience of individuals does not necessarily match precisely with the roles prescribed for them at any particular point in time, as can be seen by contrasting the ideology of manhood with actual problems experienced by men. In most societies above a certain level of complexity any individual is likely to be receiving mixed and contradictory messages about the meanings of sex and appropriate gender-role behaviour. While eschewing, therefore, the more deterministic arguments of the 'socialization' theory of sex-roles, this analysis is located within a conceptualization of sex roles as being constructed and experienced within particular historical and social contexts.

I now define the 'normal male'. Too often he has been simply assumed to be someone who is not a woman, someone who is (at least consciously) not homosexual, someone who by his nature is privileged within society as women and homosexuals are not. The 'normal male' is a man who would define himself as heterosexual, wants to marry and lead a conventional conjugal life, and has no 'deviations of object' in his sex-life, beyond, perhaps, the odd mild fetishism. In fact, he is a man who would think of himself as 'normal', and for that reason perhaps not puzzle himself much about the wilder intricacies of sexual desire. The pioneer sexologist Havelock Ellis (1858–1939) remarked of the male sexual impulse

> To deal with it broadly as a whole seems unnecessary, if only because it is predominantly open and aggressive. Moreover, since the constitution of society has largely been in the hands of man, the nature of the sexual impulse in men has largely been expressed in the written and unwritten codes of social law.[2]

This idea of the simplicity and straightforwardness of male desire is part of the constructed package.

'Normality' does not exclude sexual anxiety. Because of these assumptions about male sexuality, its problems have often been ignored. The one problem that may be voiced is over the control of this potentially dangerous insurgent force. Control of women was, still is, often presented under rhetoric of the dangers of arousing masculine lusts by inappropriate dress or behaviour, with the prostitute seen as a temptress beguiling men into sin by playing on their vulnerability. In the later nineteenth and the early twentieth centuries, however, this fear of unbridled male sexuality led to the rise of anti-masturbation literature and other propaganda in favour of male purity. It might be supposed that only women had any vested interest in controlling male lusts, but men were also engaged by the problem of male purity. There was a certain class dimension to this question of control over male desire. Mastery over baser lusts was seen as appropriate and desirable behaviour (a form of internalized moral policing) for the middle classes or would-be respectable, but hardly to be expected of the lowest classes. The concept of the rampant nature of male sexuality, and the need for it to be controlled by women for the good of both sexes, is still to be found in writers on sociobiology and is at the heart of most essentialist arguments. It sometimes figures as a plea in mitigation in rape cases.

Male desire is not necessarily so rampageous as such fears would suggest. Men suffer from considerable anxieties around their sexuality. In adolescence they may be perturbed or even terrified by spontaneous nocturnal emissions, and worried about the consequences of masturbation, since folk 'wisdom' still carries all sorts of warnings about this practice even if sex-manuals have gone from condemnation to reassurance to advocacy. Men may be excessively concerned by what they perceive to be some abnormality of the external genitalia: smallness or largeness or lack of symmetry. The statistical frequency of impotence and premature ejaculation still seems to be a well-kept secret: to judge from the tenor of recent books written for general practitioners dealing with sexual problems,[3] men with these difficulties continue to feel themselves to be uniquely cursed: 'among the most miserable of all patients that the doctor is called upon to treat', as 'the young man with a disorder of sex' was described in 1930.[4] And not just young men, either. The sexual problems arising in middle-aged men are equally shrouded in silence, and cause despair. Doctors are often reluctant to discuss the implications for sexual life of certain common conditions or operations such as prostatectomy, or the effects on libido of some commonly prescribed drugs.

Apart from these perhaps solipsistic worries, men worry about sexual difficulties within relationships. During the nineteenth and early twentieth centuries, birth control was a major anxiety: this was a matter of concern to husbands as well as wives. Far from leaving the whole business up to the woman, many men were so concerned that it was the condom which was the most widely used form of artificial marital contraception, while in spite of the dire warnings about the effects of coitus interruptus, this continued to be a common practice. Men were not, either, indifferent to their wives' sexual pleasure. It could be argued that this was an essentially egotistical worry; mutually enjoyable intercourse being more pleasurable, women who enjoy sex will let their husbands have it more often, and satisfying his partner enhances a man's self-esteem. There is evidence, however, that men did care for their wives' well-being and health over and above any relation to their own gratification.

[. . .]

In a witty essay, 'If men could menstruate', the American feminist Gloria Steinem has advanced the conceit that if men rather than women had periods enormous attention and financial resources would be given to problems such as dysmenorrhoea.[5] The operation of power within society is not quite so clear-cut as this, as can be seen from a consideration of the interaction between (male) patient and (male) doctor over a crisis to do with the operation of sexual functioning. Such encounters raise fruitful questions about the construction of male sexuality within society as well as about the medical profession itself. This particular interaction provides a point where male power and medical power (in itself predominantly male) impinge upon one another, rather than intersecting in any simple graphic way. Foucault described sexuality as 'an especially dense transfer point for relations of power', although rather surprisingly did not cite the doctor–patient relationship in his list of the relationships in which sexuality particularly manifests this characteristic.[6]

A majority of the medical profession is still male, and it was male-dominated to an even greater extent earlier in this century. There has been a great deal of discussion, both sociological and historical, about the attitudes and behaviour of male doctors to female patients, particularly in the fields of gynaecology and obstetrics and of psychiatry. Doctors have been accused of reducing all female disorders to the sexual/reproductive, of unnecessary interventions, of colonizing and controlling the female sex in the bodies and minds of their patients.[7] Some doctors did keep their female patients in ignorance: married women with syphilis contracted from their husbands were not told of the nature of their disease. It has been suggested that doctors were far more forthright with men: for example, in discussing birth control. However, at least up to the 1930s, most doctors might tell husbands that their wives should have no more children but would be unlikely to suggest how, apart from abstinence, this might be accomplished, and would tend to evade any specific enquiries on birth control methods.

There is a general assumption that men were better served in medical encounters, that doctors were more at ease with them, treated them more like equals. However, the doctor–patient relationship involves a considerable imbalance of power, and medical sociologists have pointed out that the doctors' ideal patient has many 'feminine' characteristics, such as passivity and compliance. Given the dominance/submission dynamic within the relationship, doctors may be happier with situations where this is quite explicit in terms of general social relations. There are problems here to do with the nature of the doctor–patient relationship in general. It should not be presupposed that there was necessarily any alliance or sympathy between male doctor and male patient on grounds of shared gender. The very similarity of sex seems to have been a reason why in certain matters, such as dealing with sexual problems, doctors failed to meet their male patients' needs. Also, men had profound reservations about exposing sexual difficulties to other males, particularly those, such as doctors, who appeared to be in a position of authority.

Doctors were supposed, as a result of their medical training, to be privy to a whole body of sexual knowledge from which the lay person was excluded, a myth promulgated by lay and medical writers alike. Formal medical education was in fact remarkably lacking in even the most basic information about normal sexual activity. In spite of the prevalence of syphilis and gonorrhoea, venereology was not taught at the undergraduate level. Doctors shared with their patients preconceptions, indeed misconceptions and anxieties, about sex which seriously affected their professional efficacy in this field.

[...]

Doctors have been particularly reluctant to discuss the reproductive disorders of the male. Although it has been known since late in the nineteenth century that an examination of the semen would disclose whether a man was producing viable spermatozoa, during the earlier part of the twentieth century and even today doctors have proved reluctant to perform investigations into male fertility. Although this is a simple and non-invasive technique, requiring only a microscope and a fresh semen sample, doctors went on treating the female half of infertile couples without ever determining if the failure to conceive were in fact her 'fault' or that of her husband. This reluctance of doctors to contemplate sexual disorder in the male can have fatal consequences: although testicular cancer is the most common malignant tumour in men between the ages of 24 and 30, and on the increase, doctors do not routinely examine men's testicles in the way they do female breasts or cervixes, even though the disease is usually curable if diagnosed in time.

The medical refusal to contemplate male sexual and reproductive disorder with anything like the fervour it brings to gynaecological and obstetric problems is an outstanding example of the general reluctance in society to make explicit the difficulties of the male, in particular when the problem is that of malfunction of specifically masculine attributes. If men menstruated, it seems entirely probable that common wisdom and that of the massed ranks of the medical profession would concur that Real Men don't have period pains or PMT.

Notes and References

1   V. Fildes, *Breasts, Bottles and Babies: A History of Infant Feeding* (University of Edinburgh, Edinburgh, 1986); C. Hardyment, *Dream Babies: Child Care from Locke to Spock* (Cape, London, 1983).
2   H. Ellis, *Studies in the Psychology of Sex*, omnibus edn (Random House, New York, 1936), vol. III: *Analysis of the Sexual Impulse; Love and Pain; The Sexual Impulse in Women*, p. 189.
3   G. Freedmen, *Sexual Medicine* (Churchill Livingstone, Edinburgh, 1983); C. Fairburn, M. Dickerson and J. Greenwood, *Sexual Problems and their Management* (Churchill Livingstone, Edinburgh, 1983); J. Bancroft, *Human Sexuality and its Problems* (Churchill Livingstone, Edinburgh, 1983).
4   K. Walker, *Male Disorders of Sex* (Cape, London, 1930), p. 7.
5   G. Steinem, 'If men could menstruate', in *Outrageous Acts and Everyday Rebellions*, ed. G. Steinem (Cape, London, 1989), pp. 337–40.
6   M. Foucault, *The History of Sexuality*, tr. R. Hurley (Penguin, Harmondsworth, 1981), vol. 1: *An Introduction*, p. 103.
7   G. Parsons, 'Equal treatment for all: American medical remedies for male sexual problems: 1850–1990', *Journal of the History of Medicine and Allied Sciences*, 31 (1977), pp. 55–71.

Art and Pornography

Susanne Kappeler

Bernard Williams, as a member of the Committee on Obscenity and Film Censorship, asks a French official how to define a 'film's being pornographic'.[1] The Frenchman, dismissive of the philosopher's problem, replies: 'Everyone knows what a pornographic film is. There are no characters, there is nothing but sexual activity, and it is not made by anyone one has heard of.'[2] Williams insists: 'But . . . what if these criteria diverged? What if a film of nothing but sex were made by, say, Fellini?'[3] According to the Frenchman's criteria the case is clear: the film is (would be) made by someone one has heard of, hence not all of the defining criteria (would) have been fulfilled. The film would not be pornography.

What Williams is in fact asking is how we distinguish between pornography and art when there is a match of content: nothing but sex in both. A good question, considering that the commonsense definition of pornography rests on 'nothing but sex' in the content. Williams considered trying to distinguish between 'high' culture and 'mass-circulation' culture by having recourse to the size of the audience, since his feeling was that anything mass-circulated was faintly pornographic – or at least sexist. With the medium of cinema, however, we are beyond a doubt in the presence of a mass medium, and a distinction is now to be made within this mass-circulation medium between pornography and something more acceptable or even belonging to art. With this new problem, it is no longer the presence of 'pornographic material' – nothing but sex, no characters – that is the distinguishing characteristic of pornography (since this would not allow us to distinguish between pornography and art), but rather the context within which the work is produced and sold. To determine this context, the status of the producer is decisive. If 'one' has heard of him already as an artist, then the work is a work of art. If he is unknown, he is bound to be a producer of popular art or pornography.

While the British film censors may not be as happy to enshrine this criterion in law, it is precisely the criterion of the literary establishment, the liberal cultural elite, and emulated moreover by cultured feminists. It does not matter if the work is a table full of vaginas – great women represented through/as their genitals – if the creator is an artist, and in this case, if she is a woman. Leaving aside the fact that there is extensive room for argument over 'nothing but sex' (at what point does a character cease to be a character, or sexual activity cease to be/have plot), there have been films which pose precisely this dilemma, amongst them Pasolini's *Salo* and Oshima's *Empire of the Senses*. Film censors in different countries have responded with different measures, but the cultural establishment, by and large, has firmly adhered to its tradition of recognizing, and defending, its artists. The motive for defence is the recognition of the artist, but the argument of defence is then carried out in terms of seeing the artistic, literary, aesthetic and even profoundly true in the 'nothing but sex', some qualities of aesthetic execution which prevent us from seeing 'just sex' in the work. Yet there is trouble ahead for the critics, or at least for the more inclusive definition of a film's being pornographic, since the pornography industry, close at their heels, has decided to upgrade its products aesthetically and to develop a New Porn style: 'The old-time, 16 mm cheapies (boy meets girl, 15 seconds later they're in the sack, again and again and again) were replaced by costlier, 35 mm 'quality' films (better sound and colour reproductions, and some semblance of plot around the porn).'[4]

All the more reason for adhering to the 'someone one has heard of' criterion. The French censors' solution responded to this factor, for they did not banish *Salo* to the blue-movie houses with a 'P' certificate, but confined it by special decree to two art movie houses in Paris,[5] where, one presumes, it met only with a responsible metropolitan audience who appreciate the artistic Pasolini and where it was safe from abuse by the masses and the provincials. But the pornography industry is edging in this direction too: ' "The next big moneymaker," film director Chuck Vincent predicts, "will be celebrity porn. There won't be any more block busters like *Deep Throat* and *The Devil in Miss Jones*. No, the next big hit will star Farrah Fawcett, nothing less . . . That is the porn everyone is waiting for. Everyone." '[6] Except among the film buffs, the someones one has heard of in cinema are more likely than not the stars rather than the directors. And the reason why 'everyone' is waiting for this kind of pornography is that the quality actor will ratify the film as alright, just as for the more cultured the director (Fellini) ratifies the film as not only alright, but as art. So the industry, one might say, is going in the right direction.

The definition or categorization of something as 'literary' or artistic relies crucially, and in the end circularly, on the successful association of it with something else already classified as literary, and the identity of the author provides the easiest such association (never mind the lack of logic). The hypothetical case of Fellini pornography and the actual cases of *Salo* and *Empire of the Senses* obligingly illustrate the point. Critics will of course expend much energy and effort in arguing the literary or artistic qualities of the works in question; but the decision of the critic to put himself thus on the line and defend the daringly pornographic has been reached (a) beforehand, and (b) in the safe knowledge that Fellini, Pasolini, Oshima, *mean* 'literary', 'artistic', 'of quality'.

D.M. Thomas's *The White Hotel* is a similar case in point, and an excellent example for the study of the interaction between the literary and the pornographic, since it explicitly, 'daringly', places itself on the boundary between 'literature' and 'pornography' through the use of blatantly 'pornographic material'. This is nothing new in itself in the domain of literature, since the twentieth century has known a tradition of what is conventionally seen as an increasing liberalization of respectable art and literature. Thomas's novel is a more refined example, however, than the work of, say, Norman Mailer or Henry Miller, with a particular set of artistic and intellectual pretensions guaranteed to trigger the 'literary' responses from the cultured elite. I will examine the novel in the extended context of its critical acclaim, since we need for our analysis not only a text classified as literary, but all the attendant buttressing of literary critical appraisal which, more than the text itself, indicates the points of defence: the felt points of daringness which push the boundary, the points at which the category of the literary is invoked in order to salvage the pornographic, where the literary is said to neutralize or redeem the pornographic.

While Thomas may not have been quite as assuredly known as, say, Fellini, he nonetheless already belonged to, and participated in, the domain of the literary as a poet, translator of literature and novelist before the publication of *The White Hotel*. The publication of this novel by Victor Gollancz and as a King Penguin (Penguin's answer to Picador, the specialists in the 'contemporary literary'), and its presentation to the Booker Prize and the Cheltenham Prize (1981) are all indicators of its claim to the literary. The piquancy of the case, however, rests on its obvious, its 'daring' pornography. In fact, the British reception was somewhat hesitant at first, and the proper boom in this country started only after the book's stormy reception in the United States. Since then, it has been widely discussed in the media and prominently displayed and promoted by publishers and booksellers, and its rising sales figures quickly put it on the bestseller lists.

[. . .]

My argument is that it is due to the conjuncture of the pornographic with the literary that the novel enjoys such insistent acclaim, and that the arguments for its literariness 'in spite' of its pornographic qualities reveal the fundamental investment the literary has in the pornographic. The pornographic structure, however, extends far beyond the overtly 'obscene' 'sexual material' of its content and pervades the literary practice of author and critical reception alike. The literary arguments address only the changing quality of the obscene, the increasing explicitness and growing violence of the 'sex' represented, in accordance with the dominant view of pornography as a question of sexual content. But they are in fundamental agreement with the pornographic structure of representation, which is not only not criticized, but also replicated in the critical arguments.

I do not need to prove the conventionally pornographic presence in *The White Hotel*, as there seems to be general agreement that it is there, notably in the first two chapters, '*Don Giovanni*' and 'The Gastein Journal', and the Babi Yar section towards the end. The literary argument runs from there, namely that it depends on what Thomas 'does' with the pornographic element, what literary use he makes of it that moves it beyond 'nothing but sex' and gives it that 'meaning' which Susan Sontag finds in the 'meaninglessness' of *The Story of O*.[7] The expression 'nothing but sex' connotes gratuitousness and meaninglessness. The literary provides a frame in which this element, which otherwise might appear gratuitous and meaningless, may be anchored; it provides artistic purpose.

[. . .]

In *The White Hotel* we find the same 'meaning' that Susan Sontag finds in the meaninglessness of *The Story of O*, where 'O progresses simultaneously towards her own extinction as a human being and her fulfilment as a sexual being'.[8] And here is what 'sexual being' means: 'O does not simply become identical with her sexual availability, but wants to reach the perfection of becoming an object.'[9] 'It's alright to be a sex object,' or rather, it is 'perfection' to lose one's self, one's subjectivity,

to be extinct, and progress to the status of someone else's object, someone obviously still very much a subject. Selflessness: the definition of
perfect femininity, the goal of virtue for wife and mother, for womanhood
– today the double-bind of every mother in the country. Virtue: the
prerogative of 'women', men being content with less than sainthood for
themselves. Encouraging women to find their salvation in the extinction
of self, the evaporation of selfhood, the 'transcendence of personality',[10]
the loss of subjectivity, taking upon themselves the risk of a slower
salvation in the hereafter and the privilege of a selfish existence in the
here and now: the assertion of self, the egotism of *I am*, the exclusive
right to subjectivity. This spiritual altruism, this material egotism,
preaches to woman that 'her own extinction as a human being' means
her fulfilment as a 'woman' in the nineteenth century: the angel in the
house; her fulfilment as a 'sexual being', as 'sexual object' in the twentieth: the angel in the bed.

No one was selfish in the white hotel. This one is woman, rapidly becoming a no one herself. Everyone else, in the white hotel, is very
selfish: they all want to fuck her, have her. They assert their subjectivity
by means of her object-body and her evacuated humanity.

The assumption of the female point of view and narrative voice – the
assumption of linguistic and narrative female 'subjectivity' – in no way
lessens the pornographic structure, the fundamental elision of the woman
as subject. On the contrary, it goes one step further in the total
objectification of woman. It is indeed one of the well-tried pornographic
devices to fake the female's, the victim's, point of view and many pornographic books are published under a female author-pseudonym. It is
the narrative equivalent of Berger's 'hidden camera', giving access to 'a
domain which, although entirely visible to the camera, will never be
entered by the spectator' (*Inside Linda Lovelace*). The so-called female
point of view is a male construction of the passive victim in his own
scenario, the necessary counterpart to his active aggressor: whether 'she'
resists her own violation, whether she enjoys it in involuntary bodily
response and against her will, or whether she is voluntarily and infinitely
available to his impositions – all available alternatives serve to enhance
the pornographic pleasure, the active subjectivity of the male, his feeling
of life. The options are strictly defined within the one imperative that
it *will* happen to her; 'she' can choose an attitude. As Roland Barthes
defines it with characteristic oblique strokes:

> The scream is the victim's mark; she makes herself a victim because she
> chooses to scream; if, under the same vexation she were to ejaculate (sic),
> she would cease to be a victim, would be transformed into a libertine: *to*

scream/to discharge, this paradigm is the beginning of choice, i.e. Sadian meaning.[11]

Note how suddenly the passive female sufferer becomes an apparently active agent: *she makes herself* a victim because she *chooses* to scream. Note how 'the same vexation' she is under is beyond any choice, beyond alteration. The text, the scenario, is given, 'she' can choose to mark it. While the simple objectification, the straightforward victimization, annihilates the woman's subjectivity, denies, ignores and elides it, this second 'option' appropriates and fakes her subjectivity: her male master constructs and projects a man-made subjectivity onto the empty object vessel.

We have the whole spectrum of the victim's 'choices' in *The White Hotel*: from the resisting victim, who suffers pain from the struggle; through her involuntary 'pleasure' in spite of herself – 'his thrumming fingers filled me with a great gape of wanting', 'it was so sweet I screamed' – to her total conversion to his intentions.[12] The female gape of wanting, the void to be filled, the great emptiness waiting for the male stuffing, is one of the favourite male myths, tallying with the male obsession with the size of members and the male fear that 'the bigger, the better'.

Take this as sufficient illustration of the pornographic structure, of the sexism, of the sexual politics embodied in this female character's writings. I shall now look at one critic's response to, and reproduction of, the pornographic structure, the wholesale objectification of woman, the elision of female subjectivity. George Levine in his review of the novel in the high literary *The New York Review of Books* certainly recognizes the 'obscene' passages as conventionally pornographic: 'her first violent and pornographic "phantasy" is written in a loose blank verse'.[13] But he is safe in the knowledge that he will proceed to prove the novel's literary qualities, the desired remedy which salvages the pornographic from being pornography. Susan Sontag, in what remains one of the most influential apologias of literary pornography, her article 'The pornographic imagination', tells us that 'What makes a work of pornography part of the history of art rather than of trash is ... the originality, thoroughness, authenticity, and power ... incarnated in a work.'[14] These are not terms of very great precision, but we will find them echoed. 'Thoroughness', moreover, we might have thought to be a characteristic of pornography: 'nothing but sex', 'again and again and again'. 'Originality', on the other hand, is a key term of literary evaluation, and 'authenticity' a romantic inheritance.

The feminist critic, like the literary critic who looks beyond the overtly pornographic passages to identify literary originality and authenticity, finds in Thomas's use of the holocaust further proof of his bad faith. It may have seemed implausible already that a contemporary novelist should be unaware of the conventions of narrative and representation to the extent of thinking that he could 'speak through a woman', of believing that 'you are involving the feminine aspect of yourself in poetry', or that in creating a female character he would be writing 'from the point of view of a woman'.[15] It is inconceivable, however, that he should believe that linking sexual violence with the holocaust was a profound, original artistic achievement. Nazi sadism is a stock in trade of pornography, and one of the most marketable ones at that. Let us see what a literary man makes of this devastating conjunction.

George Levine finds *The White Hotel* 'a novel of immense ambition and virtuosity [what Thomas does with it]. With the strength [power] of its precise and risky use of language, it moves us from the self into history.'[16] Whose self? Whose history? Whom 'us'? Levine notes that the novel begins with Freud (and Jung) and 'ends somewhere beyond history. . . . Between these extremes, we follow the life of a fictional woman, Elisabeth Erdman.'[17] Lisa Erdman, alias Anna G., is, we noted, at the centre of the pornographic experience related in the two parts purported to be her writings, i.e. in the two pieces of acknowledged hard-core pornography; and she is at the centre of the experience of the sado-horrors of the holocaust narrative. For these narratives to be salvaged from the realm of the pornographic *per se*, the culture's rubbish bin, into the sanctuary of the literary would require something major to be 'done' by the rest of the novel, would require audacity as well as ambition, originality as well as power, to follow the literary argument. (Although in practice we know that nothing more needs to be 'done' than that it is written by someone one has heard of.) Levine senses the enormity of the task: 'The audacity of Thomas's achievement can be felt most immediately in its ambition.'[18] He obviously feels that the ambition has been fulfilled, the task accomplished. And how does he see it accomplished? Already in terms of the novel's structure he sees Lisa Erdman's life as the mere transition between the historic self (Freud) and the 'beyond history' of the holocaust. The focus, the point of attraction, is the self, the subject: 'Freud is one of the major characters, both investigating the experience and participating in it, speaking the reticent and revelatory language of his obsessive pursuit of scientific truth.'[19]

An affinity is obviously felt between the writer/reader and this major character Freud, and their joint project of 'investigating the experience' of horror, torture and sexual assault of Lisa Erdman; participating in her experience in the voyeuristic relation of the analyst/fictionalizer, participating vicariously in the experience of another by 'speaking the reticent and revelatory language' of representing her as an object, the one in his obsessive pursuit of scientific truth, the other in his obsessive pursuit of the (marketable) literary. The mutual glance of recognition between the white man and his guest, between author and reader, has been established, through the axis of identification with their represented representative, Freud, the major character. That this 'reticent and revelatory' relationship of language, of representation, to the particular 'experience' in question might be problematical, indeed is the problematic which might justify the task, seems hardly to dawn as a suspicion. The author, in his only narrative intervention that might represent an attempt to salvage the audacity of his endeavour, blithely calls Lisa Erdman's experiences (and those of all the other victims) in the Babi Yar massacre 'amazing experiences'.[20] His awareness of the problematic of his relationship to it finds expression in the triteness of 'Nor can the living ever speak for the dead.'[21] Yet speak he does.

Levine's assertion that 'neither Freud nor Babi Yar is cheapened or exploited by the fictionalizing, and [that] neither diminishes the fictional heroine, Elisabeth, who becomes a case study . . . and a victim of the slaughter,'[22] is a claim which goes without any proof or evidence and seems to me to betray a pointed unease. Already, from the centre of experience we have moved to the priority of Freud and Babi Yar, man and history, in our quick glance to check that neither has been cheapened; the 'fictional heroine' (no longer even 'woman') enters as an afterthought, and she enters in the conventional form of diminished identity, the feminine first name. 'Freud is one of the major characters . . . Elisabeth enters the book almost as an aside . . . in a letter . . . by Freud to his friend and disciple Hanns Sachs.'[23] Among this pantheon of historic men, Lisa Erdman is Elisabeth *tout court*, the fictional heroine, a mention in a letter, a case study, a victim of the slaughter, an aside, and if Levine cannot see any diminishment in this, it is because he cannot conceive of any stature for a woman in history. The critic's glance and the novel's structure in an harmonious homology.

After a quote from the letter, Levine continues: 'The images here (which will recur throughout the book) seem almost more important than the patient' (that is, Lisa Erdman).[24] The projects of 'Freud' (fictionalized) and of the writer/reader remain closely linked: in the one Lisa Erdman becomes a patient and a case study (no diminishment), in the other a fictional heroine of minor importance, subordinate to the imagery of the author and clearly distinguished from 'the subject of the novel' as established by Levine, that is Freud: 'these [letters] are often by Freud, and all of them imply that he is the subject of the novel'.[25] Moreover, the fictional heroine, in Levine's opinion, remains a 'mystery' despite her writings. However, 'her "writings"... alone (though they leave their author a mystery) are enough to justify the admiration this novel has already evoked from critics.'[26] (Remember that we set out to justify the 'writings' by the literary novel into which they were integrated.) 'Her' fantasy, represented by the dazzling 'virtuosity' and 'cleverness' of Thomas, becomes the delighted focus of this critic's obsessive pursuit of the literary, just as it does for the fictionalized Freud: 'a prose elaboration of her verse, carefully repeating images, developing them.... The language of the poem and the letter ranges from the merely vulgar, or banal, to a lush, romantic intensity, with a remarkable precision of imagery. Her writing is full of dislocation and surprise; it is seductive, frightening, and beautifully alive.'[27] It is in fact full of pain, violence and violation: 'whatever else the book is, it is a pleasure to read.'[28]

[...]

Levine reads the presented novel like the usual consumer of pornography, with the interest of the male experience to be got from it ('her' writing is 'seductive'); the woman in the piece reduced to object, means to a certain end, vehicle for his pleasure. His worry about the novel is not how the salaciousness of the pornography and the holocaust titillation might be justified: his worry is whether Thomas might stoop to discredit Freud. With a sigh of relief he observes: 'Discrediting Freud is neither a particularly interesting narrative enterprise, nor Thomas's true purpose. Thomas's Freud is both vulnerable and heroic, ambivalently confirmed in his unscientific guesses, made touchingly human in his reading of the death instinct into history.'[29] Lisa Erdman is both vulnerable and heroic, unambiguously condemned beyond the touchingly human in her experience of the death instinct manifested through Babi Yar. But Levine is immune to this side of the story. Freud, on the basis of his own persuasion, has become the uncontested hero of his reading ('But Freud is not merely a background figure here'); Freud 'is a hero of the quest for a world that makes sense, and he is himself a victim.'[30] Freud is the hero of this novel beginning with gratuitous pornographic exploitation, ending in gratuitous violence and horror laced with sexual sadism, whose plot, we understand, consists of the heroic quest for scientific truth, the vagaries of unscientific guesses, the touching vulnerability of the genius who explores 'virgin' territory of knowledge. The depth of the romantic intensity, of the emotional scope of this drama, lies in the reduction of the hero-genius to 'victim'. A most moving, stirring drama of humanity.

[. . .]

Lisa Erdman is dead many times over. Almost killed through the sexual violations by 'Freud's son' (Thomas's fantasy), mutilated through 'Freud's' forcing of her into the case study 'Anna G.', and dying a multiple death at the hands of her torturers at Babi Yar, she is buried once more by the literary reader Levine, who relegates her out of the novel, out of the plot, tossing her back at the hero Freud as a toy, an object, a means of stimulation for his fantasies. At best, the woman, Lisa Erdman, 'the neurotic "Anna G." ', in successive stages of fiction-alization at the hands of her fictionalizers, 'provides a moment of potential healing for Freud himself'.[31] The great hero, in his untiring fantasies, is 'vulnerable and heroic' in his supremacy, 'ambivalently con-firmed in his unscientific guesses' about women, made touchingly human in his reading of the death instinct into history, in his projection of sex and violence, the pornographic axiom, into the history of humanity, the culture of mankind.

Thomas, with his 'precise and inventive prose', 'his cleverness in mixing fiction with history',[32] which makes him join the pornographic fantasies with the atrocities of the history of Babi Yar, has become the snuff artist of the cultural establishment: he understands that Lisa Erdman is not just the fantasized victim of his narrative, the fantasized construc-tion of Freud's case history, but for true literary consummation has to be the real victim of authentic history. She must be a true woman and she must be truly dead to trigger the literary climax. He knows, because he has one as he writes:

> Writing is also a surrogate sexual pleasure, a sublimation of the sexual instinct. And what *does* happen is that you find yourself writing some-thing which you're enjoying sexually. Then you look back on it and say 'I enjoyed that, but it doesn't work in terms of the book'. . . . It was only when I read Kuznetsov's *Babi Yar* that it clicked. . . . So, from the poem I then wrote the prose expansion, taking each part of it and re-framing it as narrative. Then it went into realism.[33]

Writing is a surrogate sexual pleasure. It gives the feeling of life. Is it surprising, then, that this literary art is a reflection, a mirror image, of the conventional male-defined sexual act, the sexual assault on the sex object? 'My editor says my novels are like explosions, and I think that's right. It [sic] may go off like a damp squib, or it may make a nice bang, but it's not going to be one of those long drawn-out ... [sic] I can't work that way.'[34] What did the women say: 'that it is too fast, too rough, too phallic'. And as regards the reciprocity of that sex act, look at what happens to Thomas's 'partner': 'It's got ... to have ... impact, so that the reader is left shaken by it ... but over very quickly, or else it's just not going to interest me. ... The idea of writing a five-hundred, eight-hundred page novel would be inconceivable.'[35] I am quite sure.

The male literary reader, identifying with his hero Freud and his hero writer, turns on to this, responds to Thomas's realism and mistakes it for reality: 'Thomas suggests a reality at once vital and deadly, and more accessible than we – protected behind our documents and books – might care to know.'[36] And in his enjoyment he has 'no reservations' about this great work of art, 'its strengths remain'.[37] 'Its title suggests that life can be seen either as a matter of peace or of violence.'[38] Perhaps it depends on your point of view. Levine, at any rate, feels at peace, feels secure and protected in the literary sanctuary.

The feminist reader, by contrast, can find no place to take up in this literary romance. Hers would be the designated place of the victim, but if the truth be known, she does not wish for Thomas's impact, she has no desire for his big bang (however quickly it is over). This kind of reading, pornographic reading, is 'for men only'. For the woman reader has no part in Levine's 'we': *she* finds no protection behind his ('our') documents and books, the literary is no sanctuary to her. And she has every reason to 'care to know': how easily accessible this reality is, how easily accessible she is to this reality – deadly to her, but so vital to the patriarchs, our literary men.

Notes and References

1 Bernard Williams, 'Pornography and feminism', *London Review of Books* (17–31 March 1983), p. 23.
2 Ibid.
3 Ibid.
4 Henry Schipper, 'Filthy lucre: a tour of America's most profitable frontier', *Mother Jones* (April 1980), p. 60.
5 Williams, 'Pornography and feminism', p. 23.
6 Schipper, 'Filthy lucre', p. 62.
7 Susan Griffin, *Pornography and Silence* (Women's Press, London, 1981), p. 227.
8 *Susan Sontag Reader* (Farrar, Straus and Giroux, New York, 1982), p. 222.
9 Ibid., p. 220.

10 Ibid.
11 Roland Barthes, quoted in Andrea Dworkin, *Pornography: Men Possessing Women* (Women's Press, London, 1981), p. 94.
12 D.M. Thomas, *The White Hotel* (King Penguin, Harmondsworth, 1981), pp. 19, 23 and 22 respectively.
13 George Levine, 'No reservations', *New York Review of Books* (28 May 1981), p. 20.
14 *Susan Sontag Reader*, p. 214.
15 D.M. Thomas, 'Different voices' (an interview), *London Magazine* (February 1982), pp. 28, 30 and 30.
16 Levine, 'No reservations', p. 20.
17 Ibid.
18 Ibid.
19 Ibid.
20 Thomas, *The White Hotel*, p. 220.
21 Ibid., p. 221.
22 Levine, 'No reservations', p. 20.
23 Ibid.
24 Ibid.
25 Ibid.
26 Ibid.
27 Ibid.
28 Ibid.
29 Ibid., p. 22.
30 Ibid., p. 23.
31 Ibid., p. 23.
32 Ibid., pp. 23 and 20.
33 Thomas, 'Different voices', pp. 31–3.
34 Ibid., p. 36.
35 Ibid.
36 Levine, 'No reservations', p. 23.
37 Ibid., pp. 20 and 23.
38 Ibid., p. 23.

Masculinity, Violence and Sexual Murder

Deborah Cameron and Elizabeth Frazer

Male violence against women is defined broadly by feminists to include not just the most obvious abuses – rape, wife-battering and incest for instance – but also and importantly, a range of male behaviours that have often been dismissed as mere routine minor nuisances, like flashing, stealing underwear and making obscene phone-calls. Feminist analysis puts these various things together for two reasons.

First, they all enact very similar assumptions about male sexuality and women's relation to it. They say that men need, and feel entitled to have, unrestricted sexual access to women, even – sometimes especially – against women's will. They say that men's sexuality is aggressive and predatory. Superficially, flashing is quite different from rape, yet from the point of view of their function they are surprisingly similar: both are acts which men do in order to reassure themselves of their power and potency; both include, as a crucial factor in that reassurance, the fear and humiliation of the female victims.

Second, the myriad manifestations of male violence collectively function as a threat to women's autonomy. They undermine our self-esteem and limit our freedom of action – not only must we all live with the fear of sexual violence, society makes it our own responsibility to prevent it. If the worst does happen we may be blamed, not protected; our suffering will be trivialized, questioned or ignored. Thus a powerful incentive exists for us to police our own behaviour and acquiesce in the idea that men's sexuality is 'naturally' predatory, only to be contained by female circumspection.

These facts have led feminists to locate male violence against women in the realm of the *political*. It expresses not purely individual anger and frustration but a collective, culturally sanctioned misogyny which is important in maintaining the collective power of men. We can extend to all forms of male violence the phrase that is often used specifically about rape: 'an act of sexual terrorism'.

Is sex murder also a form of sexual terrorism? Certainly, we believe it can be given a partial analysis in those terms. It is relatively easy to see killing as male violence taken to its logical extreme, where humiliation becomes annihilation. Death is the ultimate negation of autonomy, and the kind of death inflicted by many sexual killers – the ripped breasts and genitals, the wombs torn out – is the ultimate violation of the female sex and body.

'Sexual terrorism', moreover, is a very apt description of the effect of sexual murder on the female population. A generalized fear of the lurking sex beast is instilled in women from their early years; it is death we fear, just as much as rape, and sadistic killers haunt our very worst nightmares. When a multiple killer is at large in our communities, we often end up living in a state of siege. Nicole Ward Jouve describes Yorkshire, her home, in the period of Peter Sutcliffe's 'reign of terror': 'Yorkshire Universities organized relays of buses and cars to see all female students home at night, and you didn't dare let your daughter go to the fair or even cross the village street in the dark.'[1] She also describes her feelings as a woman:

> One of the worst things about the panic that had set in was that, instead of feeling self-righteous, as you should have done if the high tone of indignation of the papers was anything to go by, you felt ... guilty. Apologetic. About going out in the dark. About wearing attractive clothes. Being out in the streets. Almost, about being a woman. Being a woman meant that you were murderable, and it was wrong of you so to be. In order to make up for it, you had to be specially good. Stay indoors. Not wander away from the protective side of a man: your man. For no other was safe and perhaps even he?[2]

These descriptions recall the words of Susan Brownmiller in *Against Our Will*, her study of rape, when she refers to it as a process of intimidation whereby all men keep all women in a state of fear: an institution. All men, because any man could have been the killer. An institution, because not only Sutcliffe but the whole weight of the culture colluded in the terror that affected women's existence in the North of England: the police who insisted we stay off the streets, the commentators who so callously devalued the lives of prostitutes, the football crowds who chanted and made jokes about the Ripper, those men who under cover of protecting frightened women found a golden opportunity to threaten and assault us. The killer even invaded our private thoughts and dreams, as Nicole Ward Jouve makes clear in her account of her own nightmares:

> A few nights later I saw him again. He was with a group of people I was quite happily going to join. He could not move, that is, he could not leave them. As soon as I saw he was there I tried to retrace my steps, creep out unnoticed, but before I was far enough, he turned his eyes and looked at me. His glance was terrifyingly blue. I woke up bathed in sweat.[3]

Terrorism: the rule of fear. Violence against women: the law of misogyny. No account of sexual murder could possibly be adequate which did not point out how perfectly the lust to kill exemplifies both.

Yet it is equally true that no account of sex murder could possibly be adequate if it ended there. There is more to sexual killing than misogyny and terror; and if this seems like a rather unorthodox conclusion, we can only reply that in the course of our research we were forced, despite initial resistance, to draw it.

Feminists have written little specifically about sexual murder and what they have written tends to focus on specific cases; as far as we know, there is no other feminist study of sexual killing as a general phenomenon. And this is probably an important reason why feminists tend to identify sex murder as another, extreme form of violence against women, motivated (like rape, only more so) by misogyny. We agree with this view – but only up to a point. It can only be a partial, incomplete account, for if one examines sexual killers *as a group*, it is evident that misogyny is not their only motive and indeed that not all are engaged in violence *against women*. Let us take these two points one at a time.

To begin with, the point that many sexual killers have desires and motivations that cannot be analysed as merely or exclusively misogynistic. We have to consider here the male quest for transcendence and the way in which murder has been used as an act of self-affirmation. To be sure, this may be mixed up with hatred for the victim, but often 'transcendence' is the dominant theme.

[...]

From the start of our research we have had to take seriously the existence of killers whose victims are *men*. We did initially consider the possibility that such killers were a totally different breed, but this idea did not stand up to scrutiny, since we found that men who murdered other men or boys were quite strikingly similar to those who murdered women. Furthermore, they fitted neatly into our definition of sex-killers as men who murder their objects of desire – the only difference being that their desires were homosexual ones.

Does homosexual murder present special problems for our thesis? Certainly, it does not challenge the generalization that sex-killers are male (like other women, lesbians have killed for motives of jealousy and revenge, but there has never been a lesbian Nilsen or Cooper). But it does challenge any simple equation of sex murder with violence against women.

If in this last remark we seem to be stating the obvious, it must be borne in mind that, for many psychoanalytically oriented writers, homosexual sex murder *is* directed against a woman. Like all sexual murder, it is really an act of revenge against the mother and male victims must therefore be analysed as symbolic woman-substitutes. We find this line of argument less than compelling, deriving as it does from an unquestioned assumption that homosexuality is nothing more than a distorted or pathological heterosexuality and that all sexual objects are by definition 'female'.

We can surely accommodate the striking resemblance between heterosexual and homosexual sex-murderers without pretending they are one and the same. Rather, what we need is a 'common denominator' which connects sexual killings of women and of men. Instead of focusing on the gender of the victim, we must look at what does not vary – the gender of the *killer*. The common denominator is not misogyny, it is a shared construction of masculine sexuality, or even more broadly, masculinity in general. It is under the banner of masculinity that all the main themes of sexual killing come together: misogyny, transcendence, sadistic sexuality, the basic ingredients of the lust to kill.

What is it, then, about masculinity that permits the emergence of these fatal themes? We believe the answer lies in the combination of two factors: first, the way that men have historically been defined as social and sexual subjects, and second, the particular notion of subjectivity that has been developed in Western culture. Let us take each of these factors in turn.

That Western thought has defined men as Subjects is often asserted, but it needs to be explained. After all, a philosophically minded sceptic might enquire, are not all human beings by definition subjects? Is this not the measure of what being human *is*? If so, surely women too possess subjectivity; it cannot be part of masculinity *per se*. In one sense the sceptic would be perfectly correct, for women like men are conscious actors in the world. Nevertheless, gender does make a difference. Although both men and women may be subjects in virtue of their shared humanity, culturally it is men who stand at the centre of the universe.

As Andrea Dworkin observes, the male subject is 'protected in laws and customs, proclaimed in art and in literature, documented in history, upheld in the distribution of wealth . . . when the subjective sense of self falters, institutions devoted to its maintenance buoy it up'.[4] Lacking these supports in social institutions and representations, women's subjectivity can easily slip away. Furthermore, in order to protect the centrality of the male subject, the not-male, the female, are defined by the culture as Other, objects. Thus subjectivity is at the heart of men's existence, whereas women's subject status is constantly being negated. Being treated as an object is a threat to male being in a way it can never be a threat to female.

Andrea Dworkin also points out that the importance of male self is part of male power. It is hard to challenge what she refers to as 'an *I am* that exists *a priori*, absolute', inscribed in every corner, every aspect of the culture.[5]

If the subject of Western culture is male, how has this male subjectivity been defined? We would pick out in particular the theme of man's *transcendence*, the struggle to free oneself, by a conscious act of will, from the material constraints which normally determine human destiny.

This theme has always been important in the Western philosophical tradition. 'Man' has been seen as a subject engaged in a struggle to master and subdue his object, nature, to know and act upon it (upon *her*, of course, in traditional parlance). This view is reflected in many ancient myths: the story of Prometheus who stole fire from the gods, of Faust and Satan, the overreachers, of quest narratives like the romance of the Holy Grail. Interestingly, myths about female seekers after knowledge, such as Eve and Pandora, have a different significance. Rather than being admired as tragic heroes and admitted to the category of transcendent subjects, these women are depicted as wicked or stupid, their feminine curiosity bringing nothing but trouble.

In the eighteenth century, however – the age of 'enlightenment' – Western philosophy came to understand man himself as an object, a part of nature and a proper object for scientific study. But this recognition of man's objectivity brought into sharper focus his striving for subjectivity. Many philosophers grappled with the problem of subjectivity. David Hume, the empiricist and sceptic, concluded that the 'self' was only an illusion. Immanuel Kant insistently wrote the self back in, arguing that we cannot have objectivity without subjectivity and vice versa. With Hegel and Nietzsche, transcendence of the body and bodily consciousness becomes a matter of overcoming the other – the overcoming of objectivity and the attainment of freedom and power. But one thing all these thinkers have in common is their conflation of the

Subject with the masculine subject, 'Man'. Transcendence has therefore come to be seen both as the project of the masculine and the sign of masculinity.

Since sexuality does not stand apart from the rest of culture, these themes have been echoed in erotic practice and in the definition of masculine sexuality. The motifs of that sexuality are *performance*, *penetration*, *conquest*. In the writings of Sade and his later admirers, the quest for transcendence is explicitly eroticized. Sexual acts and desires that transgress social or religious norms are redefined as inherently forms of transcendence, thus becoming the source of both power and pleasure, and paving the way for that male sexual sadism which becomes, at its most extreme, the lust to kill.

According to this argument, the lust to kill arose as part of a particular historical process, a transformation of sexual desire. Sexual murder once did not exist: will there be a time when it no longer exists?

Notes and References

1 N. Ward Jouve, *The Streetcleaner* (Marion Boyars, London and New York, 1986), p. 17.
2 Ibid., p. 25.
3 Ibid., p. 27.
4 A. Dworkin, *Pornography* (Women's Press, London, 1981), pp. 13–14.
5 Ibid., p. 13.

26

Rape and Sexuality

Barbara Sichtermann

In its discussions about rape, the women's movement indirectly out-lined a concept of (female) sexuality which bypasses too much for it to be complete. Certainly, the subject in question gives cause to emphasize the *peaceful* side of sexual experience and expression, but we cannot leave it at that because even this peaceful side has an element of vio-lence. Just as rape is an attack not just on peace but also on a woman's physical integrity, i.e. a plain violent crime like any serious physical assault, so sexuality is not simply a product of two bodies in harmony or an exchange of affirmations. It seems to me that there has been an implicit compromise on this point which was rather rash: a false, cosy sexuality where two smiling people fall happily into each other's arms. When feminists protest against the fact that rape is considered harm-less, their protest is based on a false idea of some kind of peaceful female sexuality which could be summed up in the catchphrase 'If a woman says no, then she means no.' As long as this continues to be the case, there will be no clear dividing line between physical assault and sexuality.

Peggy Parnass tried to kick against the prick – it did her no good. It brought her a nomination as 'male chauvinist pig' in *Emma*, a rare accolade for she was the first woman to get one.[1] 'Is it not true', she wrote on the subject of rape, 'that we have a desire to be "taken vio-lently" by a man?' Parnass might well have deserved a slight reproof from feminists for using this cliché, but she was on the right track with what she meant to say. Perhaps we do have such a desire, but we ought not to devalue it in terms like 'taken violently'. I even wonder whether it is feasible to mention it at all in the context of a discussion about rape, for if rape is real rape there can be no such desire present. The more I thought about it, the more it seemed impossible not to talk about this desire, about this and about other taboo expectations, impulses, ideas and fantasies which our bodies have. Otherwise, it is impossible to locate the borderline between assault and sexuality, between crime and pleasure, which is what makes rape such a grey area.

[. . .]

It has long been suspected that women's sexual fantasies include rape fantasies, that the idea of 'rape' turns women on as well as men; and it has subsequently been proved empirically. But after scientific investigation the interpretation has changed, thank goodness: rape fantasies are no longer considered to be evidence of women's elementary masochism but merely to be figurative transports, metaphors for the movements of flight and pursuit, hiding and finding, disappearing and reappearing and the feelings of curiosity and fear, pain and relief, deception and surprise which are part of 'normal' sexuality. All these movements and feelings constitute a ritual, a game, or a dance as it is sometimes called, where the consummation of sexuality is an integral part. It is in the various stages of this dance that we should look for those elements which will help us to draw the dividing line we seek.

If the dividing line between pleasure and pain really does become blurred at times, if Parnass was on the right track with her theory about 'violence', then there must be an element of (potential) injury and violence in pleasure itself, or to put it in the classic terminology, non-perverse sexuality must be bound up with an element of sadism and its complementary form, masochism. I think it has long been known that that really is the case. But the (new) women's movement, which after all started a feminist sexual revolution, avoids the implications of this realization. They have largely limited themselves to rejecting the theory of female masochism, a theory which as far as I know has never been given a complete theoretical formulation, but was sufficiently widespread as an opinion to be a contributory factor – making the crime of rape seem harmless in the public consciousness. The Viennese sociologists, Cheryl Benard and Edit Schlaffer, have had the last word so far in this dispute in their brilliant treatise on the widespread masochistic man figure in literature.[2]

The discussion, as far as it continues at all, hinges on 'who does what': which sex is the sadistic one and which is the masochistic one? Women protest about being told they are willing to suffer, and rightly so, when you think what sort of justifications were built in to the bold theory that women enjoyed pain. But even the next step, claiming a bit of sadism for women – after all, that is what happens indirectly when women discover an element of masochism in men – does not take us far enough from the question of who does what. Simplifying, there are three ways of either solving or getting rid of the problem. First, sado-masochism could be rejected as being perverted, and therefore need play no further part in any discussion of 'normal' sexuality. Second, sado-masochism could be projected away from women and onto men, the heterosexual men getting the sadism and homosexual men the masochism. Third – and the reader will have already guessed that this is the 'right' answer – we could allow ourselves to consider whether sado-masochism, pleasure derived from inflicting and suffering pain, is not an element inherent in a 'normal' individual's sexuality, an element which is part of the 'dance'. It is not gender-specific in itself and if it seems so that is because sadism and masochism were defined culturally and attributed to the sexes on a one-to-one basis. If this interpretation is correct, then it is worth examining more closely that indivisible composite of pain and pleasure itself which stands outside 'restrictive' categories such as 'male' and 'female'. By so doing, we will move beyond the prevailing categorization and its critique.

When I say that pleasure in suffering or inflicting pain is inherent in quite 'normal' sexuality, I do not mean that we are all repressed flagellants. I mean that in 'normal' sexual pleasure, in the orgasm, there is an element of pain. In striving to reach that pain we must be 'normal' masochists and in inflicting it we must be 'normal' sadists. (I would rather do without the concepts of 'sadism' and 'masochism' from now on because they are not quite applicable. In their narrowest sense, they are used to designate the pain experienced in the *pursuit* of pleasure, and not the pain experienced at orgasm.)

The pleasure experienced at orgasm does not only put the individual in 'heaven', it wounds that person too. All the paraphrases currently used to describe orgasm stand as proof of this: it is a 'little death', a 'fall', a 'transcendental experience'. This is nothing new but perhaps something which has been forgotten: we, particularly as women, and as part of a 'sexual revolutionary' generation, are as it were accustomed to expecting nothing but 'satisfaction', the release of tension, happiness and enjoyment from sexuality – so that we do not see the threat contained in 'fall', the 'little death', and the 'transcendental experience'. As feminists, we have come to the point where we consider this 'threat' as being something which men alone bring into play, and which women can – and ought to – avert, e.g. by boycotting the penis. The fact that this projection is possible throws light on the nature of lesbian relationships within the women's movement. A sexual relationship without 'militancy', without pain–pleasure, is something artificial, a nonentity.

[...]

Of course, in normal cases of sexual activity the individuals involved do not injure or kill one another, but they are aware of a certain 'threat' if they experience real pleasure. The 'threat' – and this is a very important point – does not come primarily from the partner, but from one's own sensation of pleasure, from one's own body, and it is only reflected in the partner. 'Only' is rather misplaced here, since the reflection is essential. The role it plays is so great that even in sexual interest there is an admixture of fear, or a kind of defensive reaction. The latter can become very strong if the interest is strong. Our pseudo-hedonistic culture cannot come to terms with this paradox and insists on trying to remove the element of suffering from the feeling of ecstasy in order to keep only pure pleasure. Instead of enjoying sensual pleasure to the full, we pick at it around the edge, the 'dance' becomes a little fling. If the women's movement wants to maintain its radical approach it must stop contributing to the domestication of sexuality by leading us to believe that sexual peace will break out as soon as men quit the field or at least begin to respect an unambiguous peace code laid down by women.

The crux of my argument about pain and pleasure is that 'pain' is an integral part of pleasure itself. There is no gender-specific desire to inflict or suffer pain, but there is a threat of pain for any individual who seeks or finds pleasure. Having once been forced to admit that women too are capable of experiencing orgasm, the patriarchy ought to have abandoned the notion of an elementary, purely female masochism (and the complement of that, a purely male sadism). The fact that it finds this so difficult shows just how easily shaken this new belief in women's ability to experience pleasure really is. You already hear all kinds of provisos. 'Women may well be able to reach orgasm but – their pattern of arousal is more even ... for that reason they want several orgasms ... they need more affection ... more feeling ...'; all this threatens to put too much pressure on men, making them impotent.

I am interested to see how long this list of projections and defence mechanisms will get in time. I would like to warn women that there is no use in singling out the 'flattering' things they attribute to us (several orgasms, more feeling, etc.) and turning them against men. These things are no use to us because they are incorrect. The more one sex tries to dictate its own conditions to the other in the field of sexuality – instead of seeing that there is only one set of conditions which apply to both sexes – the more remote pleasure becomes for us and the more scope there is for an outburst of violence which has nothing to do with pleasure. I'm trying to cut the Gordian knot with this argument: sexuality is bisexual, there is only one kind of sexuality, one form of it which is in each and every one of us. We are monosexual, but that says much less about us individually as sexual beings than was assumed before. I do not believe that sexual experience, the 'dance' in a narrower sense, differs very much from one sex to the other. Apart from the sexual functions connected with motherhood, which are the reserve of women alone, sexual arousal and sexual pleasure are the same, whatever the sex of the body experiencing them. It will gradually become clear that all the carefully fostered 'finer differences' (in the pattern of arousal, the need for affection) are consequences of the damage inflicted on each gender by the other, and not genetic codes. The explanation for men wanting to come straight to the point does not lie in any kind of greater biological or sexual aggression, but in a historically traceable distortion of their sexuality which has apparently made it difficult for them to follow a more roundabout route as a means of refining their experience of pleasure.

As for the characteristic elements which go to make up a ritual or 'dance', we can now go some way towards pinpointing them. For both sexes there are elements of withdrawal, refusal, flight and hiding. Yet since at the same time as fleeing from pain we pursue the pleasure bound up with it, there are also elements of venturing forth, resolution, pursuit, discovery, even aggression – for both sexes. These elements are played out not just in moving closer or further away from the partner's body, but also in moving closer or further away from one's own body. Certainly it is one of the most pernicious accomplishments of the patriarchy that, with its restrictive categorizations, it made it difficult for men to pursue pleasure by way of flight and made it practically impossible for women to seek pleasure by way of venturing forth.

Of course, individuals tend to favour certain elements because of their circumstances and because of their biological sex. But are they tied down to these? Our culture with its characteristic belief that everything and anything can be 'manufactured' becomes remarkably dogmatic on the question of opening sexual roles to all. What is missing here in my opinion is not just imagination and experimentation to extend the traditional boundaries, but also the ability to conceive of a particular role element as ambiguous or open to more than one practical interpretation. Most qualities have a complementary side – which may well be turned inward or downward but which is no less effective for that. 'However you twist it around', mutters the enlightened patriarchy eager to learn, 'the fact remains that women are more suited to passivity because of their anatomy.' If women ask what that is supposed to mean, alarmed by the revealing phrase 'the fact remains', they are told that passivity is equated with the willingness to allow something they do not want to happen to them. The desire for domination which every dominating force has to keep alive has, in the case of male domination, brought about a lasting perversion of the notion of sexual passivity. Even if women do have a stronger tendency towards passivity than men – why does 'the fact remain'? It would only mean that women are more able to let themselves go in a situation, not that they are more easily overcome. How fortunate it is to be able to be passive when involuntary physical sensations rule the hour. Old Freud was better at dialectics here than we who think we have come much further. 'It would be conceivable', he wrote, 'to characterize femininity in psychological terms as favouring passive goals.' But we must not misunderstand him. 'A great deal of activity may be required to achieve a passive goal.'[3]

What is the point of this long discussion for the subject of rape? A case of rape is only very indirectly a sexual act; it is, as the women's movement has repeatedly demonstrated, first and foremost a demonstration of power, of a will to assert authority and dominate, an attempt to (re-)establish male dominance by means of physical force, just like wife-battering. Using the sex organ in this act of violence does not make it a sexual act, but only serves to show that the rapist despises not just women but sexuality too and wants to dominate both. Confusing rape with the elements of 'flight' and 'aggression' in the sexual ritual would then be inadmissible by the very nature of the thing. It is the patriarchy which has suggested this confusion since time immemorial, and for itself it has been impudent enough to claim mitigating circumstances of sexual ecstasy in cases of rape. For this cold contempt of women and sexuality, it has deserved every kick in the groin it has ever received. But we are playing into its hands if, instead of redefining the borderline between violence and pleasure with reference to the element of 'flight and aggression' (pain–pleasure that is), we deny the existence of these elements. If we do that the patriarchy will go on using them as an excuse when it commits acts of violence.

It may well be that a woman says 'no' when she means 'yes', and it is just as likely that a man does the same. And yet they may not necessarily be hiding the truth. Their 'no' is a way of saying 'yes' for because of the double-sidedness of pleasure it is sometimes very difficult to distinguish a 'yes' from a 'no' – the one is expressed in the other and pleasure may be increased by mixing up, deceiving and confusing, provided these are 'honest' actions.

Yet in the final analysis it is impossible to mistake an answer of 'no' which is full of fear and expectation of pleasure, with the cry for help of a rape victim: and the fact that the patriarchy feels so damn sure of itself in this confusion is a severe indictment of the quality of the erotic culture which it has created – a non-culture, as nihilistic and brutal as a rapist's erection. Why are there not more men who are horrified by the concept of rape and that, by treating it as a *sexual* offence, the implication is that men's sexuality is depraved to the point of being an instrument of repression? At any rate, the ones who do express their horror are on our side: the front against rape does not divide the sexes, it separates the patriarchy from its critics, female and male.

Notes and References

1   P. Parnass, in *Emma*, 4 (1980).
2   C. Benard and E. Schlaffer, *Der Mann auf der Strasse, Uber das merkwürdige Verhalten von Männern in Ganz alltäglichen Situationen* (Reinbek, Rowalt, 1980).
3   S. Freud, *Gesammelte Werke* (S. Fischer, Frankfurt, 1961), vol. 15, p. 123.

27

Competing Masculinities

Catherine Hall

The antagonism of new class relations associated with the development of industrial capitalism in mid-nineteenth-century England had resulted in significant shifts in the balance of power and authority from the landed class to the industrial, professional and commercial classes. But the political power which the middle classes had achieved by mid-century, marked most spectacularly by the Reform Act of 1832 which gave middle-class men the vote, and the repeal of the Corn Laws in 1846 which marked an apparent defeat of the landed interest, was still seriously limited. Their formal representation at the national political level carried no guarantees as to their political effectiveness. The Cabinet, for example, remained until the end of the nineteenth century solidly dominated by the landed class. Middle-class men, however, were well used to the attempted exercise of power through influence and had perfected the art of pressure-group politics. The Utilitarians, for example, constituted themselves as a tightly organized grouping, ready to intervene with the full weight of their knowledge on whatever public issues they judged of concern. Thus the intellectual prestige of sections of the middle class was regularly mobilized to secure particular spheres of influence.

The rise of the new middle class had begun in the eighteenth century. The men of this middle class, whether professionals, manufacturers, merchants or farmers, increasingly sought independence from the paternalism and clientage relation into which they were tied with the aristocracy and gentry. Their claims for *independence* were associated with the rejection of older values linked with the gentry and aristocracy. Often scorched by the fire of religious enthusiasm, the new men of the middle class articulated a set of ideas about gentility, challenging land

and wealth as the key characteristics of the gentleman. Instead, they asserted that real gentility was rooted in religious belief. As that most favoured poet of the late-eighteenth-century religious revival, William Cowper, put it,

> My boast is not that I deduce my birth
> From loins enthroned or rulers of the earth
> But higher far my proud pretensions rise
> The son of parents passed into the skies.[1]

The middle-class challenge to the landed class was therefore first articulated in moral and religious terms. Their 'proud pretensions', contrary to those of the old landed class, depended on moral seriousness, expressed in daily life in their habits and demeanour. Their critique of the degeneracy and effeminacy of the aristocracy focused on its softness, sensuousness, indolence, luxuriousness, foppishness, and lack of a proper sense of purpose and direction. Central to their new and alternative set of values was the concept of the dignity of work, an old Puritan idea reworked in the smouldering flame of the dual revolutions. Men were to realize themselves in their occupations, women in the profession of wife and mother. Hard work and success in the market should be a marker of status, not something demeaning. A man's individuality, his male identity, was closely tied to independence. That independence, however, was no longer predicated on having the wherewithal not to have to work but rather on the dignity of work itself.

As Leonore Davidoff has argued, in the late eighteenth century the concept of the individual acquired new connotations. Constructed discursively as non-gendered, its meanings depended on a series of dualisms and gendered assumptions. The individual subject was central to political thought and action but that individuality was based upon difference and on 'others'. The male head of household who voted, therefore, spoke for and represented his dependants, whether wife, children or servants. 'Individuality thus implies mastery over things and people. The individual subject is both the subject who acts and the actor who acts on a subject.'[2] The individual subject, whether a captain of industry, a romantic artist, a rational intellectual or a town commissioner, was already male, whether he was active in the realm of economic activity, artistic representation, ethical responsibility or civic identity.

This conception of self reached its apotheosis in the early nineteenth century within a rich discursive formation linking Evangelical religion, romanticism and political economy. At its core was the notion of individual integrity, freedom from subjection to the will of another. 'A man must act', as the Evangelical clergyman Isaac Taylor taught his sons.[3] On the successful outcome of his actions depended his manliness, and failure in the public world could mean a loss of male identity. The Essex seed merchant, Jeremiah James Colman, a man who had experienced serious business fluctuations and had sometimes been unable to meet his creditors, expressed the fears of his generation when he noted in his diary one day, 'I may be a man one day and a mouse the next'.[4] Such a notion of individuality was premissed on the expansion of the free market which allowed individual men to break away from the clientage and paternalism of the aristocracy.

In a social world in which identity was always defined in relation to 'others', the 'others' of this manly independent individual were the dependent and the subjected – the woman, the child, the servant, the employee, the slave – all of whom were characterized by their personal dependence. Here, indeed, were the roots of the connections between the bondage of womanhood and the bondage of slavery which was richly explored both in politics and in literary and visual representations in the nineteenth century. One need only think of *Jane Eyre*, in which the heroine's search for individual freedom and independence from her subjection to men is represented as her escape from slavery, or John Stuart Mill's classic Liberal text entitled *The Subjection of Women*, with its analogy between marriage and slavery. In reality this independent man was himself dependent on those around him: his wife who managed the household and ensured his comfort, his servants who did the work within the household, tended the garden and cared for the children, his employees whose labour was essential to the running of his enterprise.

[. . .]

Thomas Carlyle and John Stuart Mill were two of the major male middle-class intellectuals and writers of their age. Both of them came from the new middle-class world. Both had the status to intervene as significant public figures in a political debate. Both were to play a critical part in reformulating ideas about manliness and about English identity in the 1860s. Both wrote extensively about themselves in their own lifetimes as well as being written about by others. Both had their portraits painted, Carlyle many times. Neither had any problem about recognizing themselves as individuals, subjects who could speak and act for themselves, though both came, in different ways, to recognize some of the problems involved in their subjection of others.

[...]

For Carlyle masculinity was associated with strength, with independence and with action for, like the Reverend Isaac Taylor before him, he believed that men, to be men, must act. His rugged, craggy physique and his look of intense, frowning concentration express a particular form of male strength and seriousness. His hatred of philanthropy was associated with the ways in which it weakened men and made them depend on others. Such a notion of manhood was underpinned by an insistence on the essential difference between the sexes. Some men were made to rule over others and men must be masters in their own house. Men were born to command, women to obey. In the words of Geraldine Jewsbury, quoting Carlyle as reported to her by his wife, and her great friend, Jane Welsh,

> a woman's natural object in the world is to *go out* and find herself some sort of *man her superior* and obey him loyally and lovingly and make herself as much as possible into *a beautiful reflex of him.*[5]

John Stuart Mill occupied in some ways a very different political position to that of Carlyle but he derived his authority from the same source – his writing. For Mill, too, there was no legitimacy in the world that was not earned by the sweat of the brow. Distinction, he believed, should be won, not inherited. He himself earned the major part of his living from the East India Company, as his father had before him, a job that left him with plenty of time for his own work.

[...]

Such public men would expect to take a position on the subject of slavery. The slavery issue had been a major debate in English society and the triumph of anti-slavery in the wake of the Reform Act of 1832 seemed to many to inaugurate a new era of progress. Mrs Craik represented the common-sense of middle-class 'Old England' when she evoked the 'soft, gray summer morning' breaking into brightness with the dawn of emancipation. The continued influence of the planters, however, ensured that the spectre of immediate emancipation was offset by the apprenticeship scheme which tied the freed slaves in the West Indies into labour on the plantations. This system was a failure and apprenticeship was abandoned in 1838. Emancipationists had been extremely worried as to how the plantation system would work once slavery was abolished. As far as Britain was concerned, the West Indian islands were an asset because of their sugar production and it was essential to find ways of maintaining that production with a free labour system. Meanwhile the planters were convinced that they would be ruined by emancipation. Neither group had foreseen the problems which were posed not just by the need to rethink the organization of the plantations in the wake of emancipation but also by the increased competition from other sugar-cane producers and from the production of beet in Europe and elsewhere.

[. . .]

It was the American Civil War which sharply divided English society on the issue of race and slavery. Carlyle was a strong supporter of the South, idealizing the conditions of the slaves, and could not understand why people should be 'cutting throats indefinitely to put the negro into a position for which all experience shows him unfit'.[6] Mill was convinced that it was the Civil War which decisively pushed the respectable into a position which implicitly, if not always explicitly, was pro-slavery. For him the war marked 'an aggressive enterprise of the slave-owners to extend the territory of slavery'. He was horrified at

> the rush of nearly the whole upper and middle classes of my own country, even those who passed for Liberals, into a furious pro-Southern partisan-ship: the working classes and some of the literary and scientific men, being almost the sole exceptions to the general frenzy. I have never felt so keenly how little permanent improvement had reached the minds of our influential classes, and of what small value were the Liberal opinions they had got into the habit of professing. None of the Continental Liber-als made the same mistake. But the generation which had extorted negro emancipation from our West India planters had passed away; another had succeeded which had not learnt by many years of discussion and exposure to feel strongly the enormities of slavery. . . .[7]

Furthermore, Mill argued, the habitual chauvinism of the English, a subject on which he could wax strong, meant that there was a profound ignorance as to what the struggles in the New World were really about. The existence of powerful pro-Southern feeling during the Civil War, however, was clearly an indicator of the shifts which had occurred in some sectors of public opinion on the subject of slavery and the rights of black peoples. It was to be the case of Governor Eyre of Jamaica, however, which brought these issues to the forefront of domestic politics.

News of a riot in Morant Bay [in Jamaica] and the subsequent reprisals reached England at the end of 1865 and the press reports which started to appear galvanized humanitarian and Radical opinion. After an initially favourable response to Eyre's success in dealing with the rebels, the Liberal Government became worried about some of the apparent irregularities which had taken place, particularly around the court martial and execution of George William Gordon. Gordon had been a member of the Jamaican House of Assembly; he was the illegitimate son of a white planter by a slave-woman but had himself become a landowner and married a white woman. Under pressure from influential sections of public opinion, the government announced that a Royal Commission would investigate what had happened and Eyre was called back to London.

The Jamaica Committee had meanwhile been established, an *ad hoc* association to co-ordinate the efforts of anti-slavery groups and others who were critical of the Jamaican events. The Jamaica Committee was led in the House of Commons by Thomas Hughes, Charles Buxton, and John Stuart Mill who had been elected as Liberal MP for Westminster in the election of 1865. By April the Royal Commission was ready and its findings made public. The Commission declared that there had been a genuine danger and that Eyre had been right to react vigorously. They also argued, however, that martial law had been maintained in Jamaica for too long and that the punishment meted out had been excessive and barbarous, the burning of houses wanton and cruel. Soon after the appearance of the Royal Commission the Prime Minister, John Russell, resigned when the House of Lords rejected his Reform Bill. With the Tories in power, led by Lord Derby, the Radicals were much less worried about embarrassing the government and prepared to press the issue of prosecutions hard. Mill and the activists on the committee wanted the government to prosecute Eyre. Failing this, they were prepared to proceed with a private prosecution.

The increasingly militant activity of the Jamaica Committee provoked a backlash and a growing public sympathy for Eyre. This sympathy for the wronged British Governor, as he was seen, linked into the growing fears amongst the middle class of working-class activity around the issue of reform. The dangers of democracy seemed all too imminent and anxieties about potential anarchy at home suffused the conservative discourses on the heroic Eyre who had saved the beleaguered whites. In this context a number of prominent public figures, led by Thomas Carlyle, organized a pro-Eyre defence group and for the next year a public debate was conducted over the events in Jamaica, with Mill and Carlyle as the two central public protagonists.

The Jamaica Committee and the Eyre Defence Committee were classic products of the time-honoured middle-class tradition of voluntary organization. In both cases a group of men got together over an issue on which they wanted to influence and orchestrate public opinion. They set up meetings, wrote to the newspapers, published pamphlets, arranged lecture tours, established committees with official positions, organized finances, sent delegations to the appropriate places, kept up pressure in Parliament and generally made themselves as publicly prominent as they could. Each organization boasted one of the doyens of the intellectual world as their leader: Carlyle, 'the universally acclaimed dean of Victorian letters'; Mill, 'the political instructor to the nation'.[8] Each of those leaders used every ounce of public influence which they possessed to maximal advantage in their search for publicity and support for their cause. But the debate between Carlyle and Mill was about more than the case of Governor Eyre or, indeed, an argument as to what kind of social and political organization there should be in Britain and her colonies. Also at issue between the two men and their followers were different notions as to what constituted a proper English manhood. In the course of the exchanges over Jamaica two different identities, two different subjectivities were being offered to English middle-class men. Both identities depended for their articulation on a sense of difference, not only from black men but also from black and white women. Both identities drew on the tradition of middle-class English manhood represented in *John Halifax, Gentleman*. But one of these identities was shown to be markedly more in favour than the other in 1866–7 and that particular vision of manhood was to contribute to the construction of popular imperialism in the late nineteenth century.

The Jamaica Committee drew its support from the cream of the Radical and scientific establishment – from Thomas Huxley, Herbert Spencer, Charles Lyall and Charles Darwin to John Bright, Leslie Stephen and Frederick Harrison. The committee was fundamentally a middle-class and urban organization with strong Unitarian representation. Their hallmarks were a commitment to dissent (in its widest meaning), rationality and scientific inquiry. The Eyre Defence Committee drew on a significantly different set of constituencies. Its members represented some of the cream of the literary establishment, including Charles Kingsley, Charles Dickens, John Ruskin and Alfred Lord Tennyson. The Defence Committee relied on support from landed society (their president was the Earl of Shrewsbury who owned land in Jamaica), from the army, and from the Church establishment. Their hallmark was a defence of what were constructed as traditional values.

John Stuart Mill and the Jamaica Committee focused their arguments around two central issues. The first was the question of the rule of law; the second the question of England's relation to her foreign dependencies. The arguments about the rule of law were provoked by what was seen as the terrible misuse of the law in Jamaica, particularly in the scandalous proceedings of the court martial which had hanged Gordon. One of the most effective propaganda weapons of the Jamaica Committee was Gordon's last letter to his wife, written on the eve of his death and very much in the manner of a Christian gentleman. Much of the public distress about the Jamaica controversy had centred on the hanging of a Christian member of the Assembly, with a trial that resembled a mockery of proper legal procedures. The use of martial law thus became a central issue. Mill and his allies maintained that this offered a threat not only to the subject-races of the Empire but to the rights of freeborn Englishmen themselves. As Mill put it in his *Autobiography*,

> there was much more at stake than only justice to the Negroes, imperative as was that consideration. The question was whether the British dependencies, and eventually, perhaps Great Britain itself, were to be under the government of law, or of military licence. . . .[9]

At public meetings across the country the protagonists of the prosecution of Eyre for his violation of the law demanded that it was essential to call for 'a prompt and effective vindication of the ancient guarantees of personal liberty in this country'.[10]

The appeal to ancient laws and English constitutionalism was one of the ways of constructing a particular version of England and making a particular appeal to the British people. Both sides in the debate tried to claim the support of 'the people' and constructed 'the people' rhetorically as the arbiters of the issue. Frequent recourse was made to ideas of the honour of England and how that honour could only be saved by specific courses of action. What was at stake in the debate were particular notions of Englishness and ethnicity, notions which were publicly contested in the two narrations of the Jamaican events. Mill had been horrified from the start at the lack of response to the butcheries in Jamaica, which, if they had happened under the aegis of another government, he was sure would have been abhorred. For him, the honour of England demanded that crimes committed under English law should be adequately and justly punished.

The notion was that the rule of law must stretch across the Empire for, of course, this view depended on a belief in equality between the races. Mill and his supporters insisted on the idea of formal equality between the races, equality before the law. It was necessary for the law to protect brown and black subjects because the only defence of a state in Liberal theory was as the protector of individual freedom. No individual should be forced into subordination to another and the state should ensure that this was not the case. One of the main worries of the abolitionists who had concerned themselves with conditions in Jamaica after emancipation was that they could not be confident that the Jamaican legal system was being used impartially. There were constant complaints that the magistrates were also the planters and that they misused their power. For Liberals, the issue of the impartiality of the law irrespective of race was clearly crucial. Indeed John Stuart Mill's classic defence of the rights of the female sex, *The Subjection of Women*, relied on a similar argument in relation to gender. Laws of marriage and inheritance which prevented women from achieving their full development as individuals must be bad laws.

The analogy between slavery and women's subordination was central to Mill and, as has already been pointed out, a common-place for some nineteenth-century thinkers. Mill's *Subjection* is suffused with the comparison between the bondage of slavery and the bondage of womanhood. His better knowledge of the second leads him to regard it as in some ways more complete a form of dependence since men demand emotional support from women as well as obedience. 'I am far from pretending', he writes, 'that wives are in general no better treated than slaves, but no slave is a slave to the same lengths, and in so full a sense of the word, as a wife is.'[11] Both slavery and the subordination of women were defended as *natural*, but both were rooted in the social practices of savage societies and the ways of barbarism could be civilized. Civilization, for Mill, was a key concept, and civilization meant the possibility of individuals acting together with a common purpose, the recognition of community, the development of a collective will (made possible by the immense advances of the middle classes) and a movement of power from individuals to the masses. One of the dangers of civilization, to his mind, was that it could lead to individuals becoming too dependent on society in general and this was something which must be struggled against.

For Mill, *dependence*, whether of grown men who should know better, of slaves or of women, is a primitive state, uncivilized. Unlike many men of his period he believed that if full personhood could be achieved by both women and blacks, they could become independent. He accepted the particular form of individuality, associated with masculinity, that was the common-sense of mid-nineteenth-century middle-class men, as being the norm to which all should aspire. But he built on the myth of independence which lay at the heart of masculinity and believed that others could achieve it, thus challenging the gender and ethnic specificity of the common-sense view of the individual.

The assumption that peoples should be subject to the laws in the same way, and able to develop their potential to the highest possible point, did not mean that Mill and his supporters believed the races were entirely equal. They emphasized the *potential* for equality rather than an equality which was yet fully realized. Women, blacks and browns, having been denied opportunities, must now have access to them but it would be necessary for them to learn civilization, just as working-class men would have to learn that civilization. This faith in the civilizing power of education, a characteristically nineteenth-century faith, was shared by missionaries and improvers of many kinds and one of the most common representations of the freed slave was as the child who needed help, guidance and support in the transition from freedom to manhood.

The analogy between race and gender and the assumption that different groups were differently positioned on the ladder of full personhood informed the organizational practice of the Jamaica Committee as well as the public declarations of its leaders and supporters. The committee itself was entirely male in the time-honoured tradition of voluntary organizations, especially when they required a high public profile. The national committee boasted Members of Parliament and numerous well-known provincial figures as well as intellectuals. The auxiliary committees, set up in provincial towns, had a similar structure with exclusively male committees composed of local bigwigs and dignitaries. Publishing their names in the newspaper, registering their activities in the public sphere, was itself part of the politics of prestige.

Women had no public profile in any of this, but undoubtedly, as in every similar organization, they did much of the backstage work and were crucial to the financial well-being of the campaign. However, their role was not simply to support the men in their more public endeavours. In organizations such as the Edinburgh Ladies' Emancipation Society the women were concerned to establish their special, and feminine, contribution. No one could deny, they argued,

> that Governor Eyre has been accessory to great cruelty and loss of life, flogging and slaughter of women as well as men, and a part of this after he had declared any fancied necessity at an end. It is disgusting to find English men, and especially English women, applauding the hero of such deeds as these.[12]

The reason, of course, for finding it particularly horrifying that Englishwomen should be supporting Eyre was that it challenged the ideal of woman as more sensitive and more open to morality than men. A special relation with religion and morality had long informed the practice of those middle-class women who were involved in anti-slavery and related issues. In the late eighteenth and early nineteenth centuries the issue that had especially engaged women was the attack on the slave family and the maternal relation. By mid-century, increasing involvement with the American movement was one of the reasons for the more explicit focus on questions of sexuality, which for the Edinburgh ladies, for example, was part of their thinking about Jamaica. For them, 'the deepest shame of womanhood' associated with slavery was the subjection of female slaves to the potential abuse of their masters.[13] Their horror at the hanging of Gordon was compounded by the fact that he had had a very close relationship with his mother and that he had bought his sisters out of slavery as soon as he could, thus demonstrating the depth of his familial affections.

For the Jamaica Committee and their allies the negroes belonged to the same human family as the whites, but for Carlyle and the Eyre Defence Committee, whites and negroes were not the same species. As Carlyle had argued in 1849, blacks were a lower order and should be treated as such. Eyre, in his evidence to the Royal Commission, had stated:

> That the negroes form a low state of civilization and being under the influence of superstitious feelings could not properly be dealt with in the same manner as might the peasantry of a European country. . . . That as a race the negroes are most excitable and impulsive, and any seditious or rebellious action was sure to be taken up by and extend amongst the large majority of those with whom it came in contact.[14]

Carlyle's view of the negroes as 'an ignorant, uncivilized, and grossly superstitious people', 'creatures' of 'impulse and imitation, easily misled, very excitable', full of 'evil passions' and 'little removed in many respects from absolute savages' became the orthodoxy of the campaign. The blacks, in other words, were not up to freedom. Nothing, then, could 'be more absurd than to compare a negro insurrection with a rebellion in England' and the Jamaica Committee's claim that negroes should be subject to the same laws as the English could not possibly be defended.[15]

The main efforts of Carlyle and the Defence Committee were focused on celebrating Eyre, his character and his actions. For Carlyle, Eyre was the man who had saved Jamaica from anarchy and horror and should be profoundly congratulated for it. As the narrator of heroism, he placed Eyre firmly in the great tradition of Cromwell and Frederick the Great. As a white man and an Englishman, with the memory of Haiti and the Indian Mutiny in the forefront of his mind, Eyre had been absolutely right to act resolutely and to use force. The double spectres of Haiti (when the blacks had driven out all the whites), and of the Indian Mutiny (when, according to the collective English myth, the Indians had brutally massacred, in the most treacherous circumstances, English men, women and children) were ever present in both the Jamaican and the English consciousness, shaping expectations and raising hopes and fears.

In Carlyle's view, Eyre had quenched a savage insurrection by prompt and skilful conduct. He had shown 'some of the very highest qualities that ever in a man . . . have been considered meritorious'.[16] Furthermore, Carlyle argued that far from Eyre transgressing the laws of England he had maintained the real and natural laws against the lawlessness of the black rebels. Carlyle called on the English to be grateful to Eyre for his actions. 'The English nation', he trumpeted, 'never loved anarchy; nor was wont to spend its sympathy on miserable mad seditions, especially of this inhuman and half-brutish type; but always loved order, and the prompt suppression of sedition.'[17]

After he met Eyre, Carlyle commented that he was 'visibly a brave, gentle, chivalrous and clear man, whom I would make dictator of Jamaica for the next twenty-five years were I now king of it . . .'.[18] For Carlyle, the death of a few hundred 'niggers' was not something to get agitated about. 'If Eyre had shot the whole Nigger population and flung them into the sea, would it probably have been much harm to them, not to speak of us,' he wrote.[19]

Carlyle's appeal to the English, for despite his Scottish origins he persisted in this usage, was pinned on the conviction that the English both valued order over anarchy and believed that strong men provided the best route to ensure this. He depended on the practical sense of the English. They were doers not talkers. 'Commend me to the silent English,' he wrote, 'to the silent Romans.' Their epic poems were written on the earth's surface. How much preferable to the 'ever-talking, ever-gesticulating French'.[20] Ask Mr Bull his spoken opinion of any matter, thought Carlyle, and there would be little benefit, but

> set him once to work, – respectable man! His spoken sense is next to nothing, nine-tenths of it palpable *non*sense: but his unspoken sense, his inner silent feeling of what is true, what does agree with fact, what is doable and what is not doable, – this seeks its fellow in the world. A terrible worker; irresistible against marshes, mountains, impediments, disorder, incivilisation; everywhere vanquishing disorder, leaving it behind him as method and order.[21]

Here was Governor Eyre, the true Englishman, impregnable against savagery and black barbarism. Here also were echoes of John Halifax, the man who did not mince words but acted.

Carlyle's celebration of Eyre rested in part on his notion of English 'doers' who knew what was 'doable' and did it. His critique of the effeminate moaners who complained about such action, who would allow the fire to utterly destroy rather than risk pouring on the water, drew on his long-established contempt for the groaning philanthropists who thought that the world could survive without pain. In 'Occasional discourse' the ostensible setting was a meeting of the 'Universal Abolition-of-pain Association', a bitter Dickensian touch from Carlyle.[22] For the prophet of the heroic, the Jamaica Committee were likened to 'a group or knot of rabid Nigger-Philanthropists barking furiously in the gutter'.[23] The barking, yapping little dogs lacked passion, feeling and humanity. Real manhood meant a capacity to act with authority and power.

The commitment to a particular variety of English masculinity and the denunciation of alternative forms as effeminate was linked with a specific set of ideas about sexual difference as well as about the fundamental nature of racial inequality. A profound believer in the proper spheres of men and women, Carlyle was convinced that mastery in the household meant mastery over wife as well as over servants. A properly hierarchical social order was infinitely preferable to the dangers of democracy. It was the collapse of hierarchy, the enfranchisement of large sections of the male working class, the spectre of feminism and the grotesque ambitions of the blacks in the wake of abolition that threatened to engulf right thinking and doing. Eyre was not only the hero who had saved Englishmen from a gruesome death, he had also protected Englishwomen and shielding 'the weaker sex' was, of course, a crucial aspect of independence and manliness.

As John Tyndall, the only major scientist to support the Defence Committee, argued, the negroes were lazy, profligate and savage. Eyre had the duty not only to preserve the lives of seven thousand British men, but also to preserve the honour of seven thousand British women from the murder and lust of black savages. Evoking the horrors of Haiti and Cawnpore, he approved:

> the conduct of those British officers in India who shot their wives before blowing themselves to pieces, rather than allow what they loved and honoured to fall into the hands of the Sepoys ... the women of England ought to have a voice in this matter, and to them I confidently appeal ... there is something in the soul of man to lift him to the level of

death, and to enable him to look it in the face. But there is nothing in the soul of woman to lift her to the level of that which I dare not do more than glance at here. . . .[24]

The reference was to the well-known horror stories of rape associated with the Haitian revolution. Such matters could not be discussed on public platforms in the 1860s. Eyre's own 'proudest recollection' of Morant Bay, he claimed, was that he had saved the ladies of Jamaica. In fact, the terrifying stories that gathered, and were repeated in the British press, about the brutalities done to women were shown in the evidence collected by the Royal Commission to be grossly overstated, but such empirical detail had little to do with the mythic qualities of the tales.

Englishmen's fears of black male sexuality and the threat it posed to 'their' women were linked with fears about the powers of black women unleashed. Eyre's reports to the Colonial Office had, from the start, stressed the atrocities committed by the rebels, which in his view justified his response. He, together with many others, commented on the women who were even more brutal and barbarous than the men. Such an image was harshly at odds with a Carlyle or a Ruskin view of the proper nature of womanhood. Large numbers of individual English-women were, indeed, involved in the activities of the Eyre Defence Committee, apparently fully supporting the manly ideal of the hero who would protect them from danger. As W.F. Finlason, a major protagonist of Eyre commented, they were delighted to count amongst their number some of the most distinguished of the women of England:

Their sex – whose perceptions of the *right* are, it has been observed, far more rapid than those of the other sex – and, in this respect, more resemble the rapid intuitions of genius than the slower processes of judgement – were, from the first, strongly in favour of the unfortunate ex-Governor.[25]

In the first months after the news of Morant Bay broke in England, public opinion was on the side of the critics. After the report of the Royal Commission and the decision by the Jamaica Committee to prosecute Eyre, a backlash formed, fuelled by Carlyle and his allies. There is little doubt that domestic political issues played a large part in the shift of the upper and middle classes away from a critique of a defender of order. The famous events in Hyde Park, when working-class reformers imposed their will by occupying the park, and the passage of the 1867 Reform Act, together with the alarms over the Fenians, frightened many. The connections between events in Jamaica and events in London began to appear much more dangerous. The Jamaica Committee had to rely increasingly on hard-core Radical and working-class support, but this did not enable them to prosecute successfully since no jury would agree that there was a charge to answer. Their pressure did stop the Government from reinstating Eyre, however, and it was not until the Tories were back in power in 1873 that he received a pension.

It was quite apparent to Mill that the failure of middle-class support was central to their lack of success. As he wrote in his *Autobiography*,

> It was clear that to bring English functionaries to the bar of a criminal court for abuses of power committed against negroes and mulattoes was not a popular proceeding with the English middle classes.[26]

Similarly *The Spectator*, in an article in June 1868 analysing why the middle classes had supported Eyre, noted that they were 'positively enraged at the demand of negroes for equal consideration with Irishmen, Scotchmen and Englishmen'.[27] The acute irony at the heart of this judgement, in a period when the English were beginning to reconstruct the meanings of Englishness in such a way as effectively to marginalize yet again the Irish and the Scots, was unfortunately lost on the author.

Carlyle, the Grand Old Man of English Letters, had played a significant part in articulating this rage and legitimating with Englishmen and Englishwomen the notion that negroes could not, and should not, expect equal consideration. In 1849 he had been a lone voice speaking in the wilderness, denouncing the hegemony of abolitionist and emancipatory discourses. By 1866 a new hegemony was in the making, not to emerge fully for quite some time. The optimism that had informed the Radical Liberal vision with its conviction that the great free market of the world would spread benevolence, civilization and happiness; that slavery was immoral and economically unnecessary; and that a free market economy would allow the negroes to rise to the heights of Englishness, was on the wane. It was Disraeli and Joseph Chamberlain who discursively constructed a new popular imperialism in the decades to follow, and who secured a base for a politics rooted in that imperialism. They could build on the legacy of Carlyle who, like Enoch Powell at a much later political moment, was central to the articulation of a new racism.

Mill and Carlyle both drew on the tradition of *John Halifax, Gentleman*. Both had a profound belief in the centrality of individual action and individual responsibility. Both had a deeply rooted sense of themselves as individual subjects, active in the world and able to act on others. Both were strong believers in the glory of work. Both were convinced that they must speak out when necessary and risk public unpopularity. Both had a deep conviction of their own public importance as writers and thinkers, doers in the prestigious world of letters. Both Carlyle and Mill were, like John Halifax, men of the middle class who saw themselves as effective actors in the great public theatre of life. But they built on that myth of individuality in significantly different ways, utilizing the same term but accenting and articulating it differently within Liberal and conservative discourses.

Both appealed strongly to an idea of England and a particular notion of Englishness, but they offered significantly different meanings to their ethnicities. Carlyle's Englishness was complacent and deeply chauvinistic. The England he evoked was unmitigatingly English. It was a nation which hated anarchy and loved order. Its epitome was to be found in John Bull, who might not be clever with words but who knew what was what when it came to deeds. The English people were born conservatives, but then 'All great Peoples are conservative; slow to believe in novelties', a noble, silent, peaceable people but one that could be roused to terrible rage.[28] Mill's view of his country was far more critical, his appeal to the English nation more to do with his profound belief in rationality than with a grasp of popular consciousness. As the child of an Enlightenment tradition he was deeply hostile to little Englishness, to the common English problem of 'judging universal questions by a merely English standard'.[29] Far from despising the French, he appreciated their less narrow-minded culture. He stood for the brotherhood of the free world, for England as the potential seat of reason and justice rather than custom, tradition and prejudice.

English manhood, in the eyes of Carlyle and Mill, had significantly different meanings. Carlyle's heroes were Cromwell and Hampden, men of action who could be roused to great emotion. Eyre, in Carlyle's narrative, was cast in this same mould. A man of passion rather than a man of reason. A man who acted first and sorted out the effects afterwards. A man of feeling. In the eyes of Carlyle, Mill was seriously lacking in such feeling. He described Mill's *Autobiography* as the 'Autobiography of a steam-engine', or 'the life of a logic-chopping engine'.[30] It showed, he felt, a chilling absence of humanity. Carlyle was not alone in this. Late-nineteenth-century critics of Mill were repelled by his account of his own relationship with Harriet Taylor and his insistence that a truly rational relation between a man and a woman could transcend mere sensuality. Mill's first biographer, echoing Carlyle's attack on the lack of manliness of abolitionists, commented that he was 'not singular in the opinion that in the so-called sensual feelings, he [Mill] was below average'.[31] Carlyle, then, was the man of passion, Mill the man of reason, a difference which can be traced in their very physiques; the one craggy and rugged, the other with the aquiline features of the classical.

Finally, the different views of manhood of Carlyle and Mill were to do with the different conceptions of authority and power associated with masculinity. While Carlyle clung to a notion of hierarchy and order, with white Englishmen as the ultimate arbiters in the interests of all, Mill dreamed of a more egalitarian society in the future in which all individuals, whether black or white, male or female, would have achieved 'civilization'. His relationship with Harriet Taylor provided his prefiguring of the potential between men and women, yet in the *Subjection* he still falls back on a notion of the natural division of labour between the sexes. Whether there were similar limitations on his conceptions of relations between the races, whether there would be in the end, whatever the degree of education achieved by the blacks, a *natural* division of labour between the races, remains a problem.

The debate over Eyre became a site of struggle over the dignity, sexual identity, hierarchic and legal status of whole categories of people – blacks as opposed to whites, Jamaican whites as opposed to the English, the middle class as opposed to the working class, men as opposed to women. In the process of that political struggle a particular definition of English manhood was triumphant, with consequences for all those defined as outside of, and alien to, it.

In December 1874 Disraeli, as Prime Minister, wrote to Carlyle. He offered him the Grand Cross of the Bath and a yearly income, saying, 'A Government should recognize intellect. It elevates and sustains the tone of a nation.'[32] This recognition, from the most powerful politician in the land, and one who was in the process of reconstructing the meanings of conservatism, marks one of the ways in which intellectual power is sustained and reproduces itself. Public distinction had been offered and, even though Carlyle refused it, he was of course highly gratified. Carlyle's intervention, with the full weight of his literary and political prestige, in the debate over the conduct of the authorities in Jamaica in 1865, could only be judged as elevating and sustaining the tone of the nation in a conservative, ethnocentric and racist conception of Englishness.

Notes and References

1   Quoted in L. Davidoff and C. Hall, *Family Fortunes: Men and Women of the English Middle Class 1780–1850* (Hutchinson and Chicago University Press, Chicago, Ill., 1987), p. 76.

2   L. Davidoff, ' "Adam spoke first and named the orders of the world": masculine and feminine domains in history and sociology', in *The Politics of Everyday Life: Continuity and Change in Work, Labour and the Family*, ed. H. Corr and L. Jamieson (Macmillan, London, 1990).

3   Revd I. Taylor, *Self Cultivation Recommended: or, Hints to a Youth Hearing School* (T. Cadell, London, 1817), p. 17.

4   Quoted in Davidoff and Hall, *Family Fortunes*, p. 229.

5   Quoted in N. Clarke, *Ambitious Heights. Writing, Friendships, Love. The Jewsbury Sisters, Felicia Hemans and Jane Carlyle* (Routledge, London, 1990), p. 99.

6   Quoted in B. Semmel, *The Governor Eyre Controversy* (MacGibbon and Kee, London, 1962), p. 105.

7   J.S. Mill, *Autobiography* (Oxford University Press, Oxford, 1924), p. 226.

8   Semmel, *The Governor Eyre Controversy*, p. 103; J. Vincent *The Formation of the Liberal Party, 1857–68* (Constable, London, 1966), p. 150.

9   Mill, *Autobiography*, p. 252.

10   Birmingham Jamaica Committee, *Jamaica Question* (Hudson, Birmingham, 1866), p. 7.

11   John Stuart Mill, *The Subjection of Women* (Virago, London, 1983), p. 57.

12   Edinburgh Ladies' Emancipation Society, *Annual Report and Sketch of Anti-Slavery Events and the Condition of the Freedmen* (H. Armour, Edinburgh, 1867), p. 3.

13   Edinburgh Ladies' Emancipation Society, *Annual Report*, Appendix, p. 19.

14   Parliamentary Papers, *Report of the Jamaica Royal Commission 1866*, vol. 1, pp. 1–3.

15   John Tyndall, quoted in H. Hume, *The Life of Edward John Eyre* (Richard Bentley, London, 1867).

16   Quoted in S. Olivier, *The Myth of Governor Eyre* (Leonard and Virginia Woolf, London, 1933), pp. 336–8.

17   Hume, *Edward John Eyre*, appendix D, p. 290.

18   W. Finlason, *The History of the Jamaica Case* (Chapman and Hall, London, 1869), p. 369.

19   Jane Welsh Carlyle, *Letters and Memorials of Jane Welsh Carlyle*, ed. James Anthony Froude (Longmans, Green, London, 1883), p. 381.

20   Thomas Carlyle, *Past and Present* (Dent, London, 1960), pp. 151–6.

21   Carlyle, *Past and Present*, pp. 155–6.

22   Thomas Carlyle, 'Occasional discourse on the Negro question', *Fraser Magazine*, 41 (January 1850).

23   Thomas Carlyle, 'Shooting Niagara: and after?', in *Critical and Miscellaneous Essays* (Chapman and Hall, London, 1899), vol. 5.

24   Quoted in Hume, *Edward John Eyre*, appendix C, p. 283.
25   Finlason, *History of the Jamaica Case*, p. 386 fn.
26   Mill, *Autobiography*, p. 253.
27   Quoted in Semmel, *The Governor Eyre Controversy*, p. 171.
28   Carlyle, *Past and Present*, p. 156.
29   Mill, *Autobiography*, p. 50.
30   Quoted in Emery E. Neff, *Carlyle and Mill. An Introduction to Victorian Thought* (Columbia University Press, Norwood, Mass., 1926), p. 52.
31   A. Bain, *John Stuart Mill* (Longmans, Green, London, 1882), p. 149.
32   Disraeli to Carlyle, December 1874, preserved in Carlyle's house.

28

The Sexual Politics of Meat

Carol Adams

People with power have always eaten meat. The aristocracy of Europe consumed large courses filled with every kind of meat while the laborer consumed the complex carbohydrates. Dietary habits proclaim class distinctions, but they proclaim patriarchal distinctions as well. Women, second-class citizens, are more likely to eat what are considered to be second-class foods in a patriarchal culture: vegetables, fruits, and grains rather than meat. The sexism in meat eating recapitulates the class distinctions with an added twist: a mythology permeates all classes that meat is a masculine food and meat eating a male activity.

Meat-eating societies gain male identification by their choice of food, and meat textbooks heartily endorse this association. *The Meat We Eat* proclaims meat to be "A Virile and Protective Food," thus "a liberal meat supply has always been associated with a happy and virile people."[1] *Meat Technology* informs us that "the virile Australian race is a typical example of heavy meat-eaters."[2] Leading gourmands refer "to the virile ordeal of spooning the brains directly out of a barbecued calf's head."[3] *Virile: of or having the characteristics of an adult male*, from *vir* meaning *man*. Meat eating measures individual and societal virility.

Meat is a constant for men, intermittent for women, a pattern painfully observed in famine situations today. Women are starving at a rate disproportionate to men. Lisa Leghorn and Mary Roodkowsky surveyed this phenomenon in their book *Who Really Starves? Women and World Hunger*. Women, they conclude, engage in deliberate self-deprivation, offering men the "best" foods at the expense of their own nutritional needs. For instance, they tell us that "Ethiopian women and girls of all classes are obliged to prepare two meals, one for the males and a second, often containing no meat or other substantial protein, for the females."[4]

In fact, men's protein needs are less than those of pregnant and nursing women and the disproportionate distribution of the main protein source occurs when women's need for protein is the greatest. Curiously, we are now being told that one should eat meat (or fish, vegetables, chocolate, and salt) at least six weeks before becoming pregnant if one wants a boy. But if a girl is desired, no meat please, rather milk, cheese, nuts, beans, and cereals.[5]

[. . .]

In technological societies, cookbooks reflect the presumption that men eat meat. A random survey of cookbooks reveals that the barbecue sections of most cookbooks are addressed to men and feature meat. The foods recommended for a "Mother's Day Tea" do not include meat, but readers are advised that on Father's Day, dinner should include London Broil because "a steak dinner has unfailing popularity with fathers."[6] In a chapter on "Feminine Hospitality" we are directed to serve vegetables, salads and soups. The *New McCall's Cookbook* suggests that a man's favorite dinner is London Broil. A "Ladies' Luncheon" would consist of cheese dishes and vegetables, but no meat. A section of one cookbook entitled "For Men Only" reinforces the omnipresence of meat in men's lives. What is for men only? London Broil, cubed steak and beef dinner.[7]

Twentieth-century cookbooks only serve to confirm the historical pattern found in the nineteenth century, when British working-class families could not afford sufficient meat to feed the entire family. "For the man only" appears continually in many of the menus of these families when referring to meat. In adhering to the mythologies of a culture (men need meat; meat gives bull-like strength) the male "breadwinner" actually received the meat. Social historians report that the "lion's share" of meat went to the husband.

What then was for women during the nineteenth century? On Sundays they might have a modest but good dinner. On the other days their food was bread with butter or drippings, weak tea, pudding, and vegetables. "The wife, in very poor families, is probably the worst-fed of the household," observed Dr Edward Smith in the first national food survey of British dietary habits in 1863, which revealed that the major difference in the diet of men and women in the same family was the amount of meat consumed.[8] Later investigators were told that the women and children in one rural county of England, "eat the potatoes and look at the meat."[9]

Where poverty forced a conscious distribution of meat, men received it. Many women emphasized that they had saved the meat for their husbands. They were articulating the prevailing connections between meat eating and the male role: "I keep it for him; he *has* to have it." Sample menus for South London laborers "showed extra meat, extra fish, extra cakes, or a different quality of meat for the man." Women ate meat once a week with their children, while the husband consumed meat and bacon, "almost daily."[10]

Early in the present century, the Fabian Women's group in London launched a four-year study in which they recorded the daily budget of thirty families in a working-class community. These budgets were collected and explained in a compassionate book, *Round About a Pound a Week*. Here is perceived clearly the sexual politics of meat: "In the household which spends 10s or even less on food, only one kind of diet is possible, and that is the man's diet. The children have what is left over. There must be a Sunday joint, or, if that be not possible, at least a Sunday dish of meat, in order to satisfy the father's desire for the kind of food he relishes, and most naturally therefore intends to have." More succinctly, we are told: "Meat is bought for the men" and the leftover meat from the Sunday dinner "is eaten cold by him the next day."[11] Poverty also determines who carves the meat. As Cicely Hamilton discovered during this same period, women carve when they know there is not enough meat to go around.[12]

In situations of abundance, sex role assumptions about meat are not so blatantly expressed. For this reason, the diets of English upper-class women and men are much more similar than the diets of upper-class women and working-class women. Moreover, with the abundance of meat available in the United States as opposed to the restricted amount available in England, there has been enough for all, except when meat supplies were controlled. For instance, while enslaved black men received half a pound of meat per day, enslaved black women often found that they received little more than a quarter pound a day at times.[13] Additionally, during the wars of the twentieth century, the pattern of meat consumption recalled that of English nineteenth-century working-class families with one variation: the "worker" of the country's household, the soldier, got the meat; civilians were urged to learn how to cook without meat.

[. . .]

During wartime, government rationing policies reserve the right to meat for the epitome of the masculine man: the soldier. With meat rationing in effect for civilians during the Second World War, the per capita consumption of meat in the army and navy was about two-and-a-half times that of the average civilian. Russell Baker observed that the Second World War began a "beef madness . . . when richly fatted beef was force-fed into every putative American warrior."[14] In contrast to the recipe books for civilians that praised complex carbohydrates, cookbooks for soldiers contained variation upon variation of meat dishes. One survey conducted of four military training camps reported that the soldier consumed daily 131 grams of protein, 201 grams of fat, and 484 grams of carbohydrates.[15] Hidden costs of warring masculinity are to be found in the provision of male-defined foods to the warriors.

Women are the food preparers; meat has to be cooked to be palatable for people. Thus, in a patriarchal culture, just as our culture accedes to the "needs" of its soldiers, women accede to the dietary demands of their husbands, especially when it comes to meat. The feminist surveyors of women's budgets in the early twentieth century observed:

> It is quite likely that someone who had strength, wisdom, and vitality, who did not live that life in those tiny, crowded rooms, in that lack of light and air, who was not bowed down with worry, but was herself economically independent of the man who earned the money, could lay out his few shillings with a better eye to a scientific food value. It is quite as likely, however, that the man who earned the money would entirely refuse the scientific food, and demand his old tasty kippers and meat.[16]

A discussion of nutrition during wartime contained this aside: it was one thing, they acknowledged, to demonstrate that there were many viable alternatives to meat, "but it is another to convince a man who enjoys his beefsteak."[17] The male prerogative to eat meat is an external, observable activity implicitly reflecting a recurring fact: meat is a symbol of male dominance.

It has traditionally been felt that the working man needs meat for strength. A superstition analogous to homeopathic principles operates in this belief: in eating the muscle of strong animals, we will become strong. According to the mythology of patriarchal culture, meat promotes strength; the attributes of masculinity are achieved through eating these masculine foods. Visions of meat-eating football players, wrestlers, and boxers lumber in our brains in this equation. Though vegetarian weight lifters and athletes in other fields have demonstrated the equation to be fallacious, the myth remains: men are strong, men need to be strong, thus men need meat. The literal evocation of male power is found in the concept of meat.

Irving Fisher took the notion of "strength" from the definition of meat eating as long ago as 1906. Fisher suggested that strength be measured by its lasting power rather than by its association with quick results, and compared meat-eating athletes with vegetarian athletes and sedentary vegetarians. Endurance was measured by having the participants perform in three areas: holding their arms horizontally for as long as possible, doing deep knee bends, and performing leg raises while lying down. He concluded that the vegetarians, whether athletes or not, had greater endurance than meat eaters. "Even the *maximum* record of the flesh-eaters was barely more than half the *average* for the flesh-abstainers."[18]

Meat is king: this noun describing meat is a noun denoting male power. Vegetables, a generic term meat eaters use for all foods that are not meat, have become as associated with women as meat is with men, recalling on a subconscious level the days of Woman the Gatherer. Since women have been made subsidiary in a male-dominated, meat-eating world, so has our food. The foods associated with second-class citizens are considered to be second-class protein. Just as it is thought that a woman cannot make it on her own, so we think that vegetables cannot make a meal on their own, despite the fact that meat is only secondhand vegetables and vegetables provide, on the average, more than twice the vitamins and minerals of meat. Meat is upheld as a powerful, irreplaceable item of food. The message is clear: the vassal vegetable should content itself with its assigned place and not attempt to dethrone king meat. After all, how can one enthrone women's foods when women cannot be kings?

Notes and References

1 T. Zeigler, *The Meat We Eat* (Interstate Printers and Publishers, Danville, 1966), p. 5, 1.
2 F. Gernard, *Meat Technology: A Practical Textbook for Student and Butcher* (Northwood Publications, London, 1977), p. 348.
3 W. Root and R. de Rochemont, *Eating in America: A History* (William Morrow, New York, 1976), p. 279.
4 L. Leghorn and R. Roodkowsky, *Who Really Starves? Women and World Hunger* (Friendship Press, New York, 1977), p. 21.
5 L. Shearer, "Intelligence report: does diet determine sex?" *Parade*, 27 (1982), p. 7.
6 Sunset Books and Sunset Magazines, *Sunset Menu Cook Book* (Lane Magazine and Book Company, Menlo Park, Calif., 1969), pp. 139–40.
7 *Oriental Cookery* (Chunking and Mazola Corn Oil).
8 E. Smith, *Practical Dietary for Families, Schools and the Labouring Classes* (Walton and Maberly, London, 1864), p. 199.

9   B. Rowntree and M. Kendall, "How the labourer lives: a study of the rural labour problem," quoted in L. Oren, "The welfare of women in labouring families: England 1860–1950," *Feminist Studies*, 1 (1973), p. 110.

10 Rowntree and Kendall, "How the labourer lives"; H. Reeves, *Round About a Pound a Week* (Virago, London, 1979), quoted in Oren, "The welfare of women," p. 110.

11 Reeves, *Round About a Pound a Week*, pp. 144, 97.

12 C. Hamilton, *Marriage as a Trade* (Women's Press, London, 1981), p. 75.

13 T. Savitt, *Medicine and Slavery: The Diseases and Health Care of Blacks in Antebellum Virginia* (University of Illinois Press, Urbana, Ill., 1978), p. 91.

14 R. Baker, "Red meat decadence," *New York Times* (3 April 1973), p. 43.

15 A.M. Altschul, *Proteins: Their Chemistry and Politics* (Basic Books, New York, 1965), p. 101.

16 Reeves, *Round About a Pound a Week*, p. 131.

17 H. Hunscher and M. Huyck, 'Nutrition', in *Consumer Problems in Wartime*, ed. K. Dameron (McGraw-Hill, New York, 1944), p. 414.

18 I. Fisher, "The influence of flesh-eating on endurance," *Yale Medical Journal*, 13 (1907), p. 207.

29

Women in Prison:
Surviving Holloway

Josie O'Dwyer and Pat Carlen

At the borstals she had been in previously Josie had viewed her own violent behaviour as being nothing more than part of the general prison game; a game whose rules had already been decided by others; a game which she had usually won. Holloway was to be different. Josie had only been there ten minutes when she battered down the door of her cell. The response was one which she will never forget.

I was seventeen years old and that was my first taste of brutality. First, there were women officers and then the men came along to take me off to the annexe. There were no women about after that. When the men got hold of me I was in agony. I went the whole way to the annexe – which is quite a distance – with my arms literally twisted up and my feet hardly touching the ground. They got my legs and then my arm so that it was behind the back of my knee with my foot pressed down on top of it, which was very painful. Somebody else got hold of my toes and were pulling them apart. When they do that it's like electricity and you can feel each toe separately. You have to separate your mind from your body all the time and in the dead centre of your head there is something saying, 'They're hurting me on purpose.' This was the horror. I was not even struggling any more, but they were still meaning to hurt me, like torture. They took me down the annexe stairs which are really, really steep and, instead of my feet touching the top bit of the stairs, I went actually touching the inside bits. At the bottom they let me go and I just skidded along on my chin and took all the skin off. I was dragged by my hair into a cell and then my clothes were literally ripped off me. When I was absolutely naked they just kicked me round and round that cell until I curled up and cried like a baby, absolutely naked, in the corner. That was the first real pasting I had.

It was not to be the last. As well as the male officers whose special duty it was to carry obstreperous prisoners off to the strips there were those female officers, the 'heavy mob', who also liked to specialize in violence.

You had the heavy mob, you always had the heavy mob and they were the most vicious and the most frightening of the lot. Some of them would be absolutely massive. When they came for you it was terrifying. Something would happen on the wing and while the officers there would be telling you, 'It's OK calm down etc.' they would be rounding up the heavy mob in the rest of the prison. They accumulated just off the wing, no one at first would actually see them waiting for each other to turn up, and then it would be, nudge, nudge, 'She's had her chance now, here comes the heavy mob'.

When they give you a fucking good hiding they do get their jollies out of it and you can feel that they do. As they are carrying you to the block they are all reaching out for their pound of flesh – pinching you under the arm or on the inside of the thigh. One particular officer always steamed in and started poking you in the chest because she wanted you to hit her – that's what she got off on, the struggling and the fighting. They carry you by the 'necklace', the key chains and you can have three chains round your neck at any one time. You get purple bruises round your neck, a necklace of purple . . . you begin to blackout and you think, 'This is it, I'm going to die now.' I myself 'died' many times in prison because many's the time I've actually passed out going to the block. OK, I was fighting but there were always enough of them to restrain me, for God's sake. There was no need for them to nearly choke me to death. You fall into that blackness at last, and think, 'That's it, I'm dying.' That's your last thought before you wake up and they are stripping you, or you're alone in the cell. Sometimes, if you are still fighting when they get you to the cell they will inject you. If you know that the last time they injected you it didn't work and that *they* know that, then you wonder, 'Are they going to double that fucking dose this time? Will I actually overdose and not wake up again?' After all, you hear about people dying in prison, and no one questioning it. So you say to yourself 'I've spent eight years in some institution or other, I could so easily be put down, and the whole thing could be covered up by them saying: "She was being restrained . . . she was institutionalized . . . it was inevitable" '.

Your life is in their hands, and I could have died. But I didn't and I was lucky. I was a survivor.

The ever-present threats to both physical and psychological survival are accompanied by omnipresent fears of death, physical injury, emotional and psychological damage and madness. At the end of the disciplinary road lies Broadmoor, final lock-up for those young women who dare to take on the system and lose. Yet even though the latter group are in a minority, the *threat* of Broadmoor is at the back of the minds of many prisoners, particularly of those prisoners who realize, at the same time as they are fighting back, that they are also concomitantly damaging themselves. For although officer violence poses one of the main threats to survival in the women's closed prisons, it is not the only one. Other threats to survival include psychiatry, drugs, isolation, provocation ('winding-up') by the prison officers, institutionalization and sheer boredom.... We wish now to describe and discuss the phenomenon of 'winding-up', the major way in which prison officers can manipulate either the younger or the less stable prisoners so that in becoming emotionally disturbed to the point of violence they are more than ever vulnerable to, and officially deserving of, the prison's more draconian disciplinary techniques. To understand *why* some prisoners can so easily be 'wound-up' by prison officers, it is necessary to remember, first, that many women in prison have no one on the outside to care or even wonder about their fate in prison and, second, that those women who *do* have families and friends outside are, through prison censorship of letters and prison officer control of visits, cut off from all direct contact with them. As a result, whereas some women are vulnerable to prison officer abuse *because* they have no family, other women's dearest and closest relationships are invoked by prison officers in the service of one of their more exquisite forms of torture – the engendering of fears about a husband's or lover's faithfulness or about a beloved child's safety.

'Winding-up' begins as soon as the prisoner arrives at reception and, if the prisoner flips at that stage, prison life from then on can be one big wind-up.

> Prisoners can arrive any time from midday right up until nine or ten at night. They have to sit in reception all day. There's three officers in the reception room which is a big glass office. You're told to stand on a towel while these officers go through and mark down each article of clothing. Then they say, 'Right, drop the dressing-gown' and you do a twirl. There's people walking in the corridors while you're doing this. Then they give you your clothes, you have a bath and you go to the Sister who checks for crabs and lice – the whole works. After that you go up and sit in the dining-room waiting to see the doctor for another three or four hours in your dressing-gown. Actually, he doesn't examine you at all so why you have to sit in your dressing-gown all that time is beyond me. He says, 'Are you fit?' You say, 'Yes', and that's it. Then you wait until you've been allocated to the B3s, and the officer comes along with your

reception letter and your sheets, and off you go to the B3s where you're put either in a twin-bedded cell or a dormitory.

Nobody tells you what to do, you just follow them. No statutory rule book is issued, nothing. When you're unlocked first thing in the morning you wander out and no one says to you 'You must go up to the dining room and ask them for a place and a knife and fork.' So for the first few days some people don't eat. You're never *told* anything. You have to find out your rights for yourself. For instance, I once had to tell a woman whose family lived in New York that because she couldn't have visits she could have a phone call in lieu.

The indignities of reception, the secrecy of the system, can of themselves wind-up many women. Others, for a variety of reasons, are selected for special treatment by the prison officers themselves.

If they don't like the look of either the prisoner or what she's been charged with, then it's a wind-up job. And prisoners aren't stupid, they know they're being wound-up. You think, 'It must be my turn next', and then the person who came in behind you is called up before you. You think, 'They're trying to wind me up, fucking starting on me already.' Then they'll start making comments about your clothes – your socks smell, didn't you get a wash in the police-cell, things like that, well below the belt. I myself hate coming through reception. I can understand people being wound-up.

One particular inmate I remember. She was only about eighteen, quite cute really, only four foot and a dog-end. She'd been sitting waiting and, because she'd got cold, had put her clothes back on. 'Right', they yelled, 'come on, get your clothes off.' 'You can fucking wait for me now', she said, 'I've been sitting waiting for hours,' and she started shouting. She was unlucky. There were some coffee cups there and she knocked into them and they went over some prison officers. That kid got a pasting. You could see them dragging her up the corridor, taking off their watches . . . of course, they know who to pick on, the kids who've got no one.

The most horrific case I saw when I was working in reception at Holloway was the deaf and dumb woman who came in. She made this noise that actually hit you right in the guts. She didn't understand what was happening and they never bothered booking anyone with sign language. She kept on making the noise and the next thing, she was being dragged up the corridor in a strip dress which rode way above her neck while they were dragging her by the ankles. It was this noise that got me. I actually lost my head, shut both the double doors and shouted, 'I'm fucking reporting you lot.' But there was nothing you could do.

Prisoners do not report officers for fear of being put on a charge of making false and malicious accusations against an officer. Prison officers, on the other hand, having almost complete control of the prisoners' living quarters and timetables, can wind-up prisoners at every moment of the day. Association, visits, letters, prisoners' personal appearances, cell searches – all are but a few of the many potential sites and occasions on which prison officers can wind-up prisoners.

> In the old Holloway it was extraordinary *not* to have association but nowadays, in the new Holloway, you can say to an officer at teatime, 'Is there association tonight?' and she'll say, 'Yes', implying that the sooner you get into your cell, the sooner you'll be out. You think, 'Great!' And you sit there waiting for association. I'd be sitting there in my dressing-gown, my stuff ready so that I could be the first in the queue for a bath. Then minutes would go by and I'd think, 'They'll be opening up soon.' Fifteen minutes – not a sound! Then I'd start to think, 'Oh no! . . .' and I'd ring the bell, 'Is there association tonight?' 'No, not tonight.' 'Well, what did you tell me there was association for?' They would just walk away and not answer. By then I'd be really wound-up.

30

The Military Academy and the Male Body

Klaus Theweleit

All the cadets have a place within a direct order of rank. Each knows exactly which cadets are "above" him and which "below." Each has the power to command and punish those below and the duty to obey those above. The occupant of the lowest position in the hierarchy must find another whom even he can dominate or he is finished.

If a cadet fails to exercise his rights over his inferiors, he is despised or demoted. Thus the situation never arises. Privilege is universally exercised. There are no gaps in the cadet's daily round of duties. Only those who have sufficiently mastered the art of demand fulfillment can squeeze a few seconds for other activities.

Everything is planned and everything is public. Withdrawal is impossible, since there is no place to retreat to. Toilet doors leave the head and feet of the seated occupant exposed. Trousers have no pockets.

When the cadet receives a letter, he has to open it and present the signature for inspection. Letters signed by women are read by the officer distributing the mail and (usually) torn up. Only letters from mothers are handed on.

None of the cadets lives in private. The dormitories have open doors. Talking from bed to bed is forbidden. The dormitory is kept under surveillance through a window in a wooden partition, behind which an officer sits and keeps watch.

The beds are narrow, hard, and damp. Any boy found hiding his head under the pillows is labeled a "sissy" (*Schlappschwanz*). "Sissies" are put on "report." There are reports for every infringement; but the only way a boy can carry out the extra duties they impose is by neglecting his existing duties. If his negligence is noticed, he is put on report again. One crime punishable by report is a failure to keep equipment in order – which is unavoidable, since the regulations are too numerous to follow them all to the letter. Therefore after first report, others are bound to follow.

Boys who want to go to the toilet at night have to wake the duty officer. In this case, too, punishment invariably follows. Unusual behavior of any kind is punished by forfeit: the boy is deprived of food, leave, or the opportunities for relaxation that are in any case minimal, no more than momentary easings of pressure.

In cadets who wish to remain such, all this very soon produces a "quite extraordinarily thick skin."[1] The "thick skin" should not be understood metaphorically.

On his second day in the academy, Salomon had already sensed "that here, for the first time in his life, he was not subject to arbitrary conditions, but to a single law."[2] He experiences this as good fortune. He resolves to bear every punishment meted out to him, gives himself the necessary "internal wrench," and stands stiffly erect. Everything up to now has been "arbitrary" – and school continues to be so. School is an activity performed by teachers, powerless wielders of power – ridiculous. The boy enters the institution at the age of 12. It is at the beginning of puberty and under the "pressure" of its "water" (Freud)[3] that he experiences the good fortune of subjection to a law. Freud saw puberty as a phase of transition to fully formed sexual organization, the completion of which manifests itself in the capacity for heterosexual object-choice.[4] But the military academy transforms this "unusually intense wave of the libido"[5] into something other than "object-relationships."

The cadet never receives instructions; he recognizes his mistakes only in the moment of transgression from the reactions of others who already know the score. With slight variations according to his cleverness, each newcomer thus necessarily repeats the mistakes of his predecessors, who in turn recognize and welcome the apparent opportunity to treat their successors as they themselves have previously been treated. Justice works on the principle of equal torment for all. The principle is strictly adhered to; there are no grounds on which a mistake might be considered excusable.

The punishments meted out to fellow cadets are oriented exclusively to the body. For a minor transgression on his very first day, Salomon is made to balance a tray of knick-knacks on his outstretched hands (and woe betide him should any of them fall). He is then made to crouch with an open pair of compasses wedged between his heels and buttocks. If he moves even infinitesimally upward or downward, the compasses will either stab him in the buttocks or drop on the floor. But if he succeeds in staying still, the reward, as always, will be immediate advancement. He will no longer be the lowest in the hierarchy of "sacks"

(*Säcke*) – "sack" being the name for all newcomers who are treated accordingly, emptied out, punched into shape, and refilled.

Younger boys courageous enough to defend themselves gain respect. But even if they win the occasional fist-fight with older boys, punishment always remains the prerogative of their elders.

A further first day experience reported by Salomon: he recalls a talk by an officer on the importance of learning how to die.

Night, cold bed, cold blankets, the morning wash in cold water. The boy who hesitates, even momentarily, is immersed and showered by others. Breakfast by hierarchy. The boy who grabs a roll before his turn gets nothing. For the last in the pecking order, there remains the smallest portion, a crumb. To be last is impermissible.

Physical exercise, even before breakfast:

> If I failed to pull myself up far enough for my nose to pass the bar, or to keep my knees straight while pulling my legs upward, the dormitory leader would give generous assistance by punching the tensed muscles of my upper arm with his clenched fist. This did indeed make it possible to identify the ultimate limits of my strength.[6]

Every exercise reaches the "ultimate limits," the point where pain shifts to pleasure:

> The climbing apparatus was ten meters high; it had a ladder, various perches, and smooth wooden walls. We climbed up and jumped down, hesitating for one tense moment at the top, leaping blind, tasting the full weight of the drop, slamming into the ground with a force that sent a terrible shock reverberating from the heels through the lower back, then into the rest of the body.[7]

If the cadet has any kind of choice, it is one between different punishments. He is offered the alternative of a caning on the behind, or forfeiting leave – he chooses the beating. The body swallows attack after attack until it becomes addicted. Every exertion becomes a "means of enhancing an already intoxicated consciousness, of adding strength to strength."

The boy who fails to transform rituals of bodily pain into "intoxicated consciousness"[8] (the mental intoxication of a head that crowns a powerful body) is cast out, as was the spy from the ritual speech or the unwilling participant from block parade-formations.

One passage in Salomon's book describes a certain cadet named Ulzig standing rigid with terror. He is the only nonswimmer to have failed to jump from a three-meter board. Many have already had to be pulled from the water to save them from drowning. But they continue to jump, half-blind, their limbs aching, until they can swim. Salomon learns to swim on the third day; but Ulzig leaves the institution – he is fetched away by his father, a "mountain of a father," a major. The cadets would have liked to give him a good beating, but were stopped by the officer in charge of swimming (a leper is not for beating).

> I had gradually adapted. The service no longer appeared to me as a machine racing along mysteriously, its actions unexpected and apparently unmotivated. Instead, the few figures with whom I had any kind of relationship were now clearly and concretely emerging from the confusion. I was as determined as ever to defend myself when necessary, but my resolve was now less often broken by perplexity. Slowly, I began to lift my head higher.[9]

As Salomon himself becomes a component in the machine, he no longer perceives it as racing on its way somewhere above him. Once the machine is no longer external to him and he himself no longer its victim, it begins to protect him:

> In the end, I found myself living a life of absolute solitude. At times, I surrendered with a zeal born of desperation and unhappiness to this most painful of feelings. The only common feature in all my unrelated perceptions was . . . the exceptional and universal ruthlessness that underlay them. This was the only indication of any purpose behind the whole machinery of the Academy. It was the basis on which it was constructed and imbued with life. My merciless subjection to the bitter reality of absolute isolation had originally seemed incongruous in a place where no one even momentarily escaped observation or control. But even the warmest comradeship remained far removed from simple friendship and from the brotherly stream that flows from hand to hand and heart to heart.[10]

At this point in the book, Salomon has been only partially assimilated. While he considers "exceptional ruthlessness" an acceptable goal for the workings of the machinery, he himself remains half outside it, a lonely young man in search of "the brotherly stream." He then gradually comes to realize that the stream can be found only on the outside as a stream of pain. At this point, he integrates himself entirely.

> It was, I believed, my own inadequacy that erected an iron barrier between myself and my comrades. I tried repeatedly to break it down; but even the most forceful expression of my lost yearning for human warmth and clumsy intimacy would have been useless. Even outside the academy, an air of sordidness surrounded such gestures; inside, they were still more

likely to offend sensibilities. My pitiful efforts to struggle free of my cocoon rebounded against rubber walls; yet I continued to search for some escape. The futility of my efforts was made bitterly clear to me; yet at the same time, doors were opened as wide, at least, as they were able.[11]

Notes and References

1   Ernst Salomon, *Die Kadetten* (Rowohlt, Hamburg, 1979), p. 44.
2   Ibid., p. 48.
3   S. Freud, "Analysis terminable and interminable," *Standard Edition*, vol. XXIII (Hogarth Press, London, 1953–74), p. 226.
4   S. Freud, "An outline of psycho-analysis," *Standard Edition*, vol. XXIII (Hogarth Press, London, 1953–74), p. 155.
5   S. Freud, "Psycho-analytic notes," *Standard Edition*, vol. XII (Hogarth Press, London, 1953–74), p. 155.
6   Salomon, *Die Kadetten*, p. 42.
7   Ibid., p. 68.
8   Ibid., p. 49.
9   Ibid., pp. 55–6.
10   Ibid., p. 56.
11   Ibid., p. 57.

Index